GOVERNING COMPLEX CITY-REGIONS IN THE TWENTY-FIRST CENTURY

BRAZIL, RUSSIA, INDIA, CHINA AND SOUTH AFRICA

Philip Harrison

WITS UNIVERSITY PRESS

Published in South Africa by:
Wits University Press
1 Jan Smuts Avenue
Johannesburg 2001

www.witspress.co.za

First published 2023

http://dx.doi.org.10.18772/12023118523

978-1-77614-852-3 (Paperback)
978-1-77614-853-0 (Hardback)
978-1-77614-854-7 (Web PDF)
978-1-77614-855-4 (EPUB)

This publication is peer reviewed following international best practice standards for
academic and scholarly books.

GCRO | Gauteng
City-Region
Observatory

Gauteng City-Region Observatory (GCRO), a partnership between the University
of Johannesburg, the University of the Witwatersrand, Johannesburg, the Gauteng
Provincial Government, and organised local government in Gauteng (SALGA-
Gauteng).

Project manager: Inga Norenius
Copyeditor: Inga Norenius
Proofreader: Lee Smith
Indexer: Margaret Ramsay
Cover design: Hothouse
Typeset in 11 point Arno Pro

Philip Harrison addresses one of the most difficult subjects in urban studies: governance of the global South's city-regions. His careful research shows us how to navigate a multi-layered reality. It considers diversity, specificity, national and local institutional history, articulated with theory and method. Harrison shows us that it is possible to go beyond case studies while at the same time respecting local contexts. Like the BRICS city-regions themselves, the book avoids simple explanations and binary thinking, embracing complexity and giving us important insights. *Governing Complex City-Regions in the Twenty-first Century* is a powerful example of how to build theory from the South.

Renato Cymbalista, Professor of Urban Politics,
University of São Paulo

Government of big cities is contested, constrained and a continually changing exercise. Philip Harrison explores an unusual and highly varied selection of cases, none of them in the most-studied areas of the global north-west. The result is a readable and provocative account that offers no simple solutions, but will inform debate and further research.

Alan Mabin, Emeritus Professor, School of Architecture and Planning,
University of the Witwatersrand, Johannesburg

This is an ambitious book that teases out the diverse paths that lead to similar-looking, yet incredibly different, hypercomplex emergent mega city-regions in four continents. Commonalities are highlighted, as well as the important roles of trust, informal networks, tacit knowledge and negotiation that continue to govern human interaction, albeit refracted by each region's specific political context.

Partha Mukhopadhyay, Senior Fellow,
Centre for Policy Research, Delhi

This major original contribution to twenty-first century urban studies responds to the governance challenges of contemporary sprawling and dispersed urbanisation. It offers a much-needed decentring and enlivening of the analysis of city-regions. Detailed accounts and comparative insights from across the diversity of emergent urban-region governance arrangements in BRICS countries rework grounded vocabularies to propose new theoretical insights. The book highlights the sharp institutional and territorial conflicts and top-down directives, as well as the emergent discourses, new collaborations and the often informal ingenuity of actors that are shaping the future of urban regions.

Jennifer Robinson, Professor of Human Geography,
University College London

With its broad geographical coverage across the BRICS countries, this remarkable monograph offers insightful observations and comparisons of governing city-regions. It is an unprecedented, indeed, landmark study based on Philip Harrison's extended fieldwork in five countries. Rich, detailed and solid, this excellent book reveals that these city-regions are governmentally constructed through planning and administrative practices beyond the material linkages and diverse discursive presentations. It is key reading for anyone interested in understanding how metropolitan spaces are constructed and governed.

Fulong Wu, Bartlett Professor of Planning,
University College London

Contents

List of maps

Section one: Locational maps

Section two: Urban footprints

Section three: Municipal boundaries

Section four: China's city clusters

Preface

The context from which I write and research is the Gauteng City-Region (or GCR) in South Africa. It comprises the cities of Johannesburg, Tshwane (Pretoria) and several other smaller urban areas. Gauteng is the economic and political heartland of South Africa. It is a place of huge complexity embedded in a history of mining, colonialism, apartheid, political struggle and imperfect attempts to construct a democratic order. Social divides and inequalities run deep, and fostering collective action by bringing together different interests and actors to address common concerns and threats presents daunting dilemmas.

I have spent nearly two and a half decades in the GCR, working as a government official, a planning commissioner and an academic, engaging with and observing a complexly evolving city-region. As an official, I worked between 2006 and 2010 for the City of Johannesburg Metropolitan Municipality, which, unusually in international terms, is a single-tier metropolitan authority governing a population that is now around six million. However, the urban territory flows across the boundaries of Johannesburg and through the region of 15 million or more people. The GCR is itself embedded in a wider urban system and interconnects with rural areas formed from South Africa's mining and apartheid past.

The GCR is a difficult place to govern, and increasingly so with political factions and declining levels of trust among social actors. Periodically, over its roughly 130-year urban history, there have been attempts to create collaborative structures across municipal authorities, although within the countervailing circumstance of colonial and apartheid divides. The end of apartheid and the creation of metropolitan authorities and a provincial government, with a jurisdiction more or less coinciding with the apparent edges of urban agglomeration, offered a fresh opportunity for collaborative governance to address collective action dilemmas.

Some progress in overcoming spatial inequality was made with these new structures, especially in distributing basic urban infrastructure and services. However, the fundamental dilemmas remain or have been amplified – unemployment is at record levels, education is vastly unequal, many poor people remain spatially marginalised from places of work, mobility across the GCR is a daily challenge, energy supply is shamefully inadequate, public health facilities are deteriorating, infrastructures are poorly maintained and environmental quality is poor, especially along the old mining belt.

While there are many reasons for persisting legacies and new problems, a lack of coherence across government and inability to utilise the will and resources of non-state actors have contributed. In 2004, the premier of Gauteng launched the GCR as a prototype of collaborative governance bringing provincial and municipal government and civil society together in pursuit of a shared vision.

By 2016, the idea of the GCR was well embedded within government circles, but progress was slow. Except for the Gauteng City-Region Observatory (GCRO), which was set up in 2008 as a partnership between government and academe, observers were hard-pressed to identify the institutional imprint of the GCR. The study on which this book is based emerged from discussions with senior provincial government officials and researchers in the GCRO on the difficulties of making the GCR an institutional reality. We agreed that I would assist by looking for inspiration from the experiences of the other BRICS countries (Brazil, Russia, India and China), together with South Africa's histories.

The Gauteng provincial government, through the GCRO, sponsored a sabbatical I took in 2017. I spent about eight months in China, hosted by the School of International Studies at *Beida* (Peking University) in Beijing, and from this base was also able to spend time in cities including Shanghai, Nanjing, Shenzhen and Hong Kong. In the remaining four months of my sabbatical, I spent time in São Paulo, Rio de Janeiro, Delhi and Moscow before returning home to Johannesburg. During my travels, I had wide-ranging discussions with academic colleagues and government officials, although some of the latter are off-the-record and used in this book only as background information, as formal interviews in some countries require impossibly long processes for securing formal permission. I was able to access official documents and scholarly works available locally, and I was grateful for the support I received from friends and colleagues with translations from Chinese, Russian and Portuguese. The sabbatical also gave me time to begin an exploration of the rich literature on city-regions and their governance, even if these are still largely oriented towards regions in the global North.

I began my research with enthusiasm, hoping to compile a compendium of useful practices from city-regions in the BRICS countries and perhaps even to find a model that might work for the GCR. My ambitions were soon corrected as I found from both the literature and my empirical work how deeply contextual governance practices really are. While there are valuable insights to be drawn from other experiences, practice cannot be transferred in any straightforward way. I discovered that even the term 'city-region', so frequently used in my context, was not used universally across the BRICS. Where possible, I have deployed the same terms or proximate translations of the terms that are used in each country.

I realised that my task would be far more complicated than I had originally anticipated. To properly understand the governance practice in each place, I would have to engage more deeply than expected with the contexts within which they were embedded: with institutional histories, capacities, cultures, politics and languages. There were, of course, limits to what I could do, as I had five national and ten regional contexts to explore and a busy post-sabbatical life awaiting. I had to change the approach to my research.

I returned from my sabbatical and presented my preliminary findings at a series of seminars hosted by the GCRO. If participants were expecting answers to the dilemmas of the GCR, they were disappointed. There was no silver bullet. While I could draw insights from across contexts, there was ultimately no option but to engage critically, constructively and collaboratively with our demanding context in an ongoing effort to incrementally improve governance processes and arrangements. I also learnt that the institutional fix was only a partial solution and that building collaborative governance requires a patient process of developing mutual trust across official and personal networks (see Healey 2005).

There were, at least, sufficient instances of partial success: improved relationships had been established through formal structures and informal networks within the BRICS countries to encourage continued effort at working together. While city-regions are hugely complicated spaces for governance, they offer *relative* flexibility, as city-region governance is usually not fixed in a legal sense. They are places of emergence where governance can be somewhat experimental in comparison to areas under the jurisdiction of a single juristic authority. This, at least, is my hope, based on some pointers from the literature and my observations in the BRICS countries.

The book-writing process took far longer than anticipated. I will put it down to a busy life and the need to reflect on a topic that was both more complicated and interesting than I first imagined. But I appreciate the patience of my sponsors in the Gauteng provincial government, the GCRO and the publishers.

The book is intended to have an audience across sectors, including the academe, government and civil society, but it is mainly written with the practitioners of governance in mind. The primary purpose is to place the evolving practices of city-region governance across the BRICS regions into historical perspective, showing the evolution of physical change, of discourse in the official and scholarly languages and of institutional formation, mainly through a case-based narrative. The Introduction does, however, set out a methodological and conceptual approach. It explains how I draw on historical, comparative and inductive research methods, as well as on historical and contemporary approaches and concepts. Chapter 1 is contextual, providing an international account of the ways in which the physical form of the city-region ('the material') has co-evolved with the theories and concepts used to explain the nature of the city-region ('the discursive'), and the ways in which the city-region is planned and managed ('the governmental'). From chapters two to six, I provide a case study of each country, drawing on the themes identified in chapter one. In chapter seven, I offer some comparative and concluding reflections. After all this, I cannot offer any quick fix or best-practice solution, but I nonetheless hope this book will contribute to a longer-term process of remaking governance in the GCR, elsewhere in the BRICS, and in city-regions globally.

Acknowledgements

Writing a book takes a community and I have many people to thank.

The research forms part of a broader initiative on city-region governance within the Gauteng City-Region Observatory (GCRO), an organisation which is a knowledge partnership between two leading universities in Gauteng, and provincial and municipal government. The Gauteng provincial government provided the financial support which enabled the research, while staff in the GCRO provided ongoing motivation, practical support and intellectual inspiration. As provincial officials, Rashid Seedat and Nalini Naicker assisted in the initiation of the project and provided patient encouragement throughout the protracted process. Rashid went on to head the GCRO and continued his support. Many of the GCRO staff took time to read and comment on chapters, and I am grateful to all, but I am especially indebted to Rob Moore, the GCRO's previous executive director, Graeme Götz and Richard Ballard.

Support came from beyond my home environment in Gauteng. I benefitted immensely from colleagues in the BRICS + City Lab, which is an unfunded and informal network of researchers across large cities in the BRICS. Between 2015 and 2019 we travelled collectively through the BRICS, participating in workshops and fieldtrips, thus jointly deepening our understanding of the various contexts. Among the individuals who contributed were Partha Mukhopadhyay, Fedor Kudryavtsev, Alexander Puzanov, Ivan Kuryachiy, Gleb Vitkov, Tu Qiyu, Renato Cymbalista, Kazuo Nakano, Eesha Kunduri, Patrick Heller, Rob Moore and Ivan Turok.

Much of the initial research was conducted during my sabbatical in 2017, and I am immensely grateful to individuals who aided me at that time. My research base was the Centre for International Studies at Peking University in Beijing, and my wonderfully supportive host was Liu Haifang, with ongoing practical assistance from Liu Jun. Colleagues at the University of the Witwatersrand (Wits) assisted me at the time by keeping the home fires burning and here I must mention Margot Rubin and Thammy Jezile who managed my office at Wits in my absence.

There were many other individuals who provided encouragement along the way. The research was framed as comparative urbanism, and I am grateful to a community of urbanists who provided continual inspiration. Jenny Robinson, a trailblazer in comparative study, has been tremendously supportive, and so have others. While assembling my material into this book, I have been involved in other international comparative studies involving cities and city-regions as diverse as Johannesburg, London, Shanghai, Lilongwe, Accra, Dar es Salaam, Toronto and Chicago, and insight from these comparisons has fed back into the BRICS study. At risk of excluding sources of knowledge and intellectual inspiration in comparative work, I wish to acknowledge Fulong Wu, Alison Todes, Romain Dittgen, Sylvia Croese, Wilbard Kombe, Evance Mwathunga, George Owusu, Roger Keil and Xuefei Ren. I must give special mention to Alan Mabin, who provided ongoing support to the BRICS project, assisting with interviews in São Paulo, Belo Horizonte and Delhi, and providing discerning comments on the draft manuscript. Our common interest in city-regions coalesced into a comparative study of national capital regions.

There are also individuals who assisted greatly in the production of the book, including the anonymous reviewers, Sarah Taylor, who provided painstaking editing, and Mncedisi Siteleki, who produced most of the maps.

I must mention the publisher and its editorial team. Wits University Press celebrated its centenary in 2022 and continues to receive awards for its contribution to academic publishing. I am grateful to Wits University Press for agreeing to produce this volume, and for the care it took in the publishing process. My thanks go to Veronica Klipp and Roshan Cader, and their production team including Kirsten Perkins, Andrew Joseph and Inga Norenius.

I prepared the book while employed as the South African Research Chair in Spatial Analysis and City Planning, a position funded by South Africa's National Research Foundation (NRF) and hosted by the School of Architecture and Planning at Wits. I acknowledge and appreciate the contribution of the NRF through the South African Research Chairs Initiative (NRF Grant No. 79114).

The list of people I interviewed or had informal discussions with is long and I will not provide it here, but I am immensely grateful for their time and contribution. I have thought hard about how to acknowledge individuals while protecting their identity, and I have decided to use interviews and discussions mainly as background material. The exceptions are academic colleagues whose job it is to express views through scholarly publication, and also colleagues employed within government structures in my own context where I can assess degrees of sensitivity. In these cases, I have acknowledged individuals as sources of information and ideas in the text and endnotes.

Finally, and most vitally, my thanks go to my wife, Yang Yan, and my son, Taishan. The production of this book made inroads into our family life and I am grateful for their forbearance. However, my gratitude extends beyond this. Yan has opened an extraordinary window into a new world for me, and I was hugely dependent on her for insight and practical support in navigating the complexities of China and its mega-sized city-regions. Taishan had the formative experience of travelling the BRICS countries as a young child, including Moscow in mid-winter, and this may have compensated for his father's distractions and occasional absence while the book was produced. While grateful to all who contributed, no one but I bear any responsibility for the limitations of the book and opinions expressed.

Acronyms

ANC	African National Congress
BJP	Bharatiya Janata Party
CPSU	Communist Party of the Soviet Union
DA	Democratic Alliance
DDA	Delhi Development Authority
DDM	District Development Model
DMA	Delhi Metropolitan Area
Emplasa	*Empresa Paulista de Planejamento Metropolitano* (Metropolitan Planning Corporation of São Paulo)
EPCIs	*Établissements public de coopération intercommunale* (Public Institution for Inter-municipal Co-operation)
Fundrem	*Fundação para o Desenvolvimento da Região Metropolitana do Estado do Rio de Janeiro* (Foundation for the Development of the Metropolitan Region of the State of Rio de Janeiro)
FYP	Five Year Plan
GBA	Greater Bay Area
GCR	Gauteng City-Region
GCRO	Gauteng City-Region Observatory
GNCT	Government of the National Capital Territory
GTA	Gauteng Transport Authority
MDA	metropolitan development authority
MR	Metropolitan Region (this refers to the formally designated Metropolitan Regions in Brazil only)
NCR	national capital region
NCRPB	National Capital Region Planning Board
NCT	national capital territory
NDRC	National Development and Reform Commission
NRDC	Natural Resources Development Council
OECD	Organisation for Economic Co-operation and Development
PDUI	*plano de desenvolvimento urbano integrado* (urban integrated development plan)
Plambel	*Superintendência de Desenvolvimento da Região Metropolitana de Belo Horizonte* (Agency for the Development of the Metropolitan Region of Belo Horizonte)

PRD	Pearl River Delta
PSDB	*Portuguese Partido de Social Democracia Brasileira* (Brazilian Social Democratic Party)
PT	*Partido dos Trabalhadores* (Workers' Party)
PWV	Pretoria-Witwatersrand-Vereeniging
RDAC	Regional Development Advisory Committee
RMBH	Planning Agency for Metropolitan Development
SEDRU	State Secretariat for Regional Development and Urban Policy
WJTPC	Witwatersrand Joint Town Planning Committee
YRD	Yangtze River Delta
ZAR	*Zuid Afrikaansche Republiek* (South African Republic [also known as the Transvaal])

CARTOGRAPHY

Section one: Locational maps

MAP 1 Location of Brazil's metropolitan regions

Brazil's three major metropolitan regions are in the south-east of the country.

Data source: DIVA-GIS. Cartography: Mncedisi Siteleki

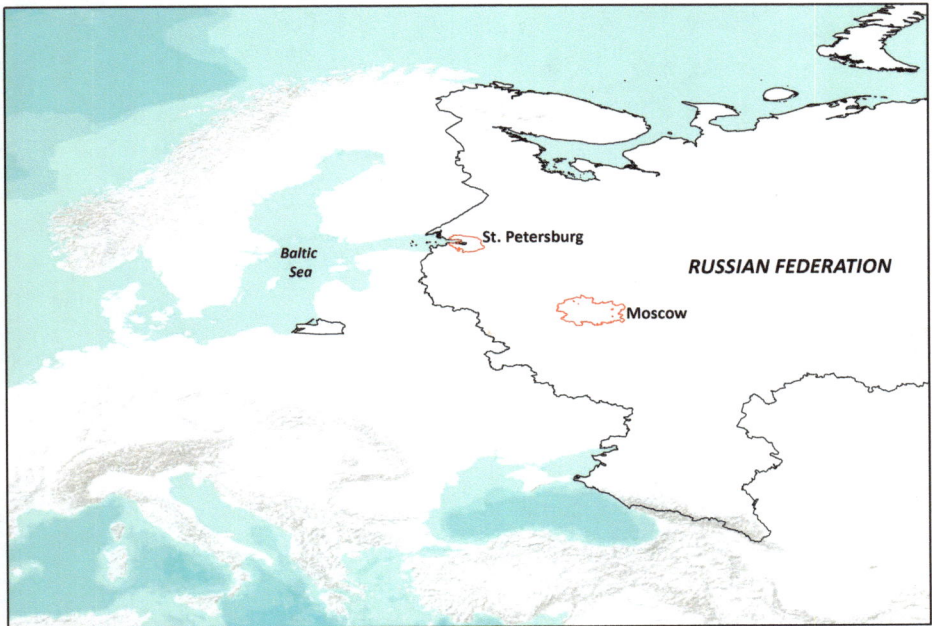

MAP 2 Location of Russia's major urban agglomerations

Russia has two major urban agglomerations in the west of the country.

Data source: DIVA-GIS. Cartography: Mncedisi Siteleki

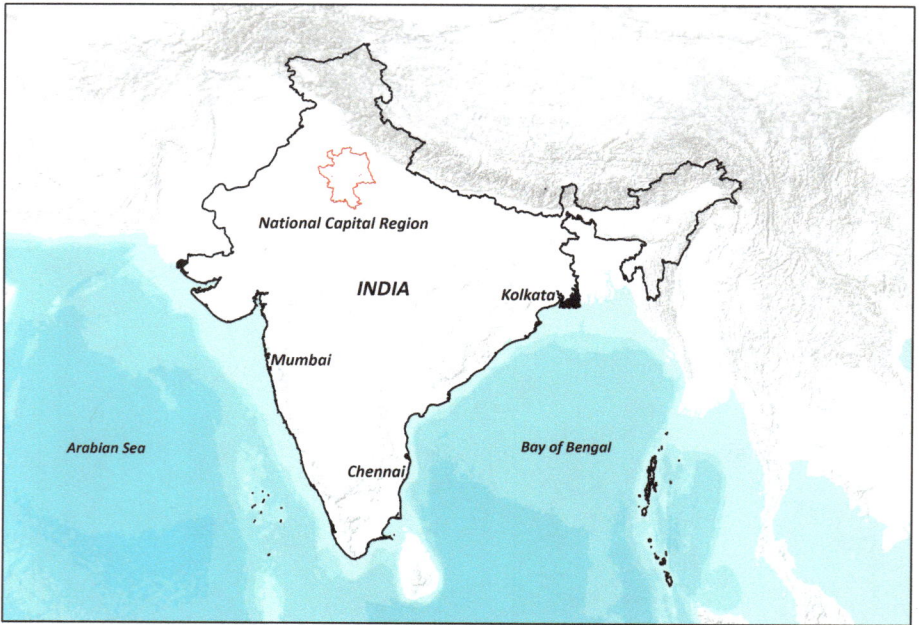

MAP 3 Location of the National Capital Region and major metropolitan cities in India

The National Capital Region is a large territory in the north of India, centred on Delhi, with the metropolitan cities of Mumbai, Kolkata and Chennai further south.

Data source: DIVA-GIS. Cartography: Mncedisi Siteleki

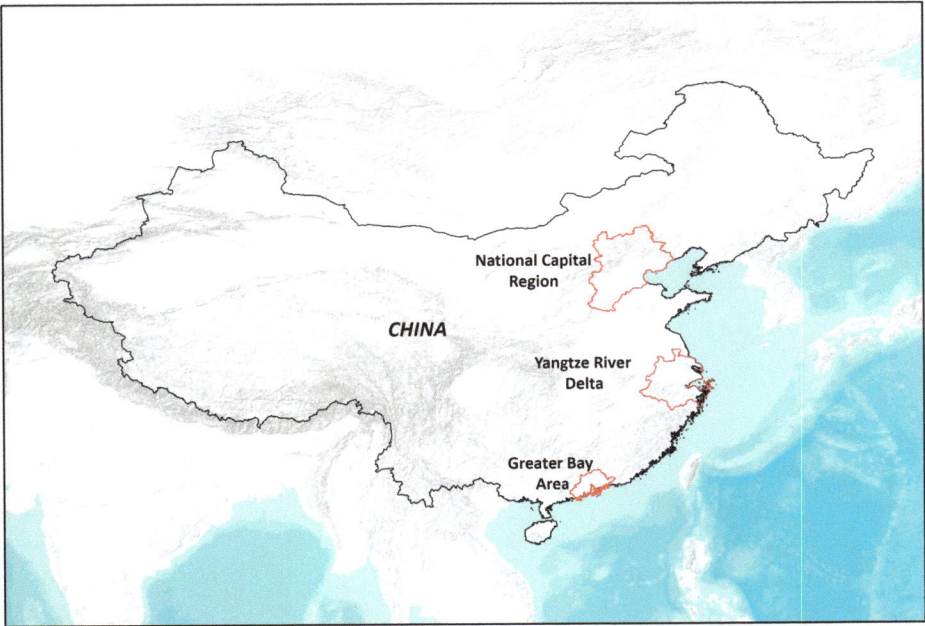

MAP 4 Location of China's three largest city clusters

China's three megacity clusters are located along the eastern seaboard of the country.

Data source: DIVA-GIS. Cartography: Mncedisi Siteleki

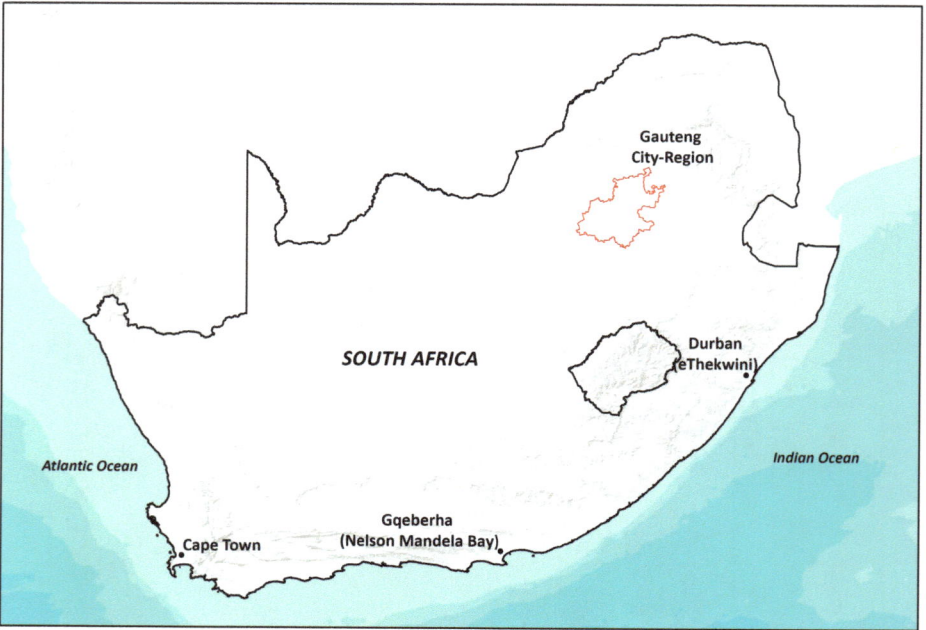

MAP 5 Location of the Gauteng City-Region and other major urban centres in South Africa

South Africa's largest city-region is located in the northern interior of the country with the other major metropolitan regions along the coast.

Data source: DIVA-GIS. Cartography: Mncedisi Siteleki

Section two: Urban footprints

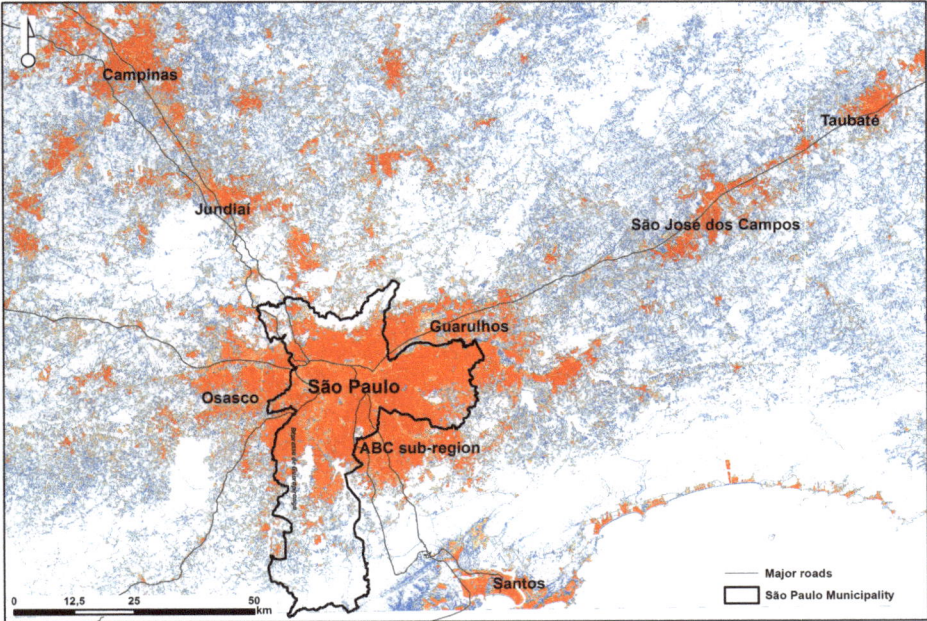

MAP 6 The urban footprint of São Paulo Metropolitan Region

The urban footprint of São Paulo has spilled over the boundaries of the core city into the surrounding region, with corridors of urban development extending further outwards along major transportation routes.

Data source: Global Human Settlement Layer (GHSL). Cartography: Mncedisi Siteleki

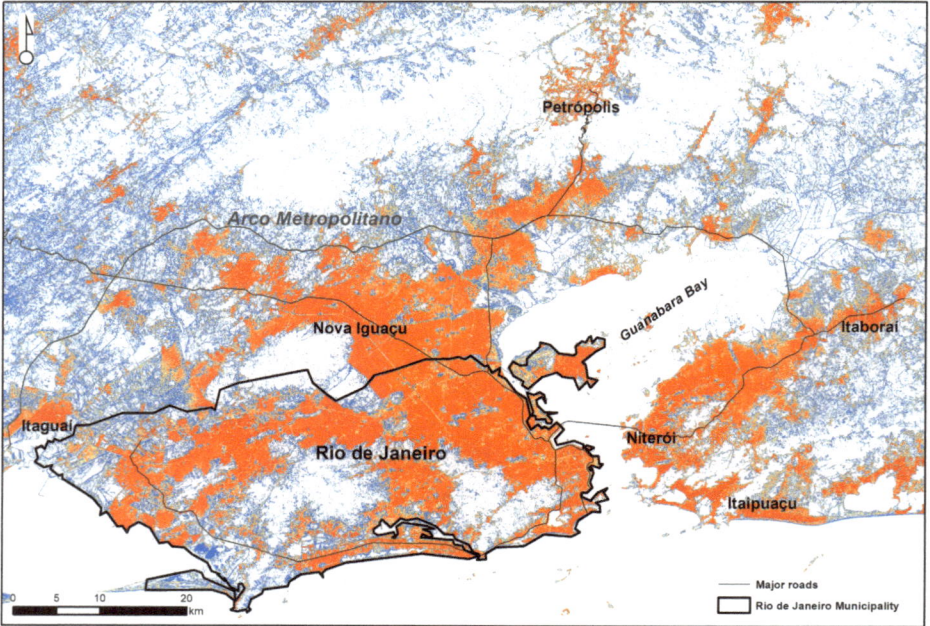

MAP 7 The urban footprint of Rio de Janeiro Metropolitan Region

The urban footprint of the Rio de Janeiro Metropolitan Region extends along the coastline and inland but is fragmented by a rugged topography.

Data source: Global Human Settlement Layer (GHSL). Cartography: Mncedisi Siteleki

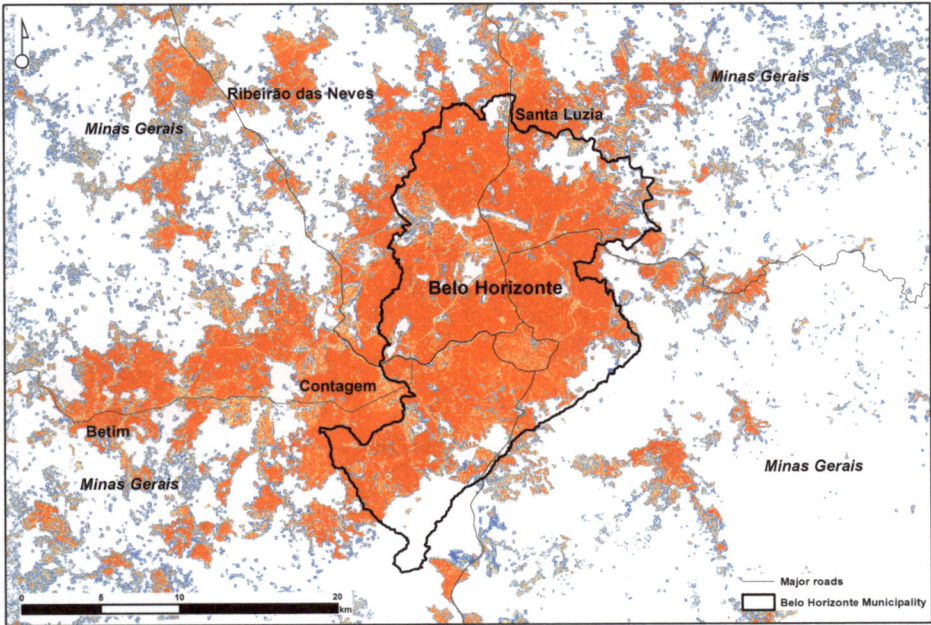

MAP 8 The urban footprint of Belo Horizonte Metropolitan Region

Belo Horizonte has a smaller metropolitan region than São Paulo and Rio de Janeiro but the urban footprint has spilled over the boundaries of the core city, mainly to the west, into the districts of the state of Minas Gerais.

Data source: Global Human Settlement Layer (GHSL). Cartography: Mncedisi Siteleki

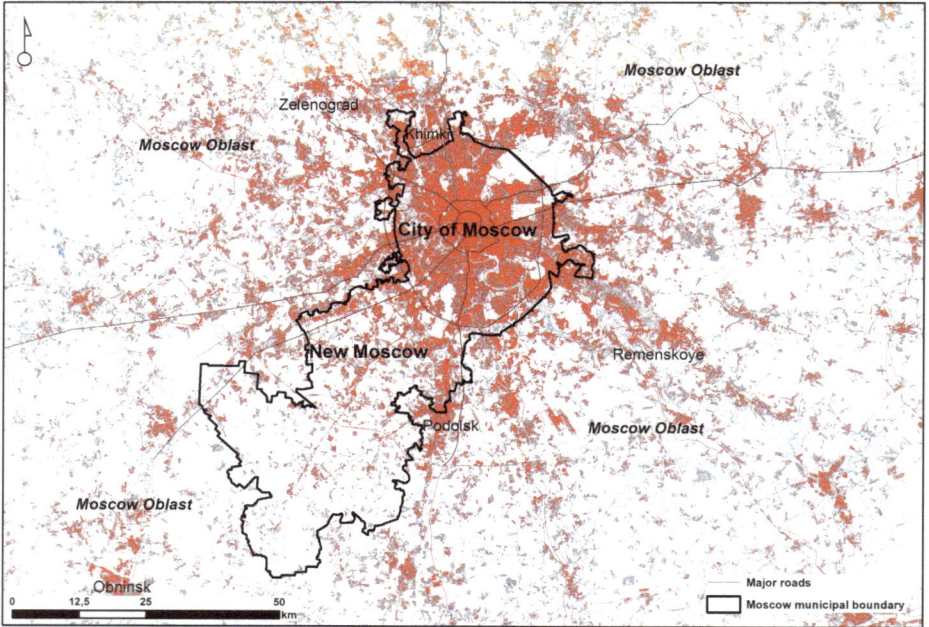

MAP 9 The urban footprint of Moscow urban agglomeration

The urban footprint of Moscow was quite compact during the Soviet era but has since spilled over into the territory governed by the Moscow *Oblast* and especially along the major transportation routes extending outwards from the core city.

Data source: Global Human Settlement Layer (GHSL). Cartography: Mncedisi Siteleki

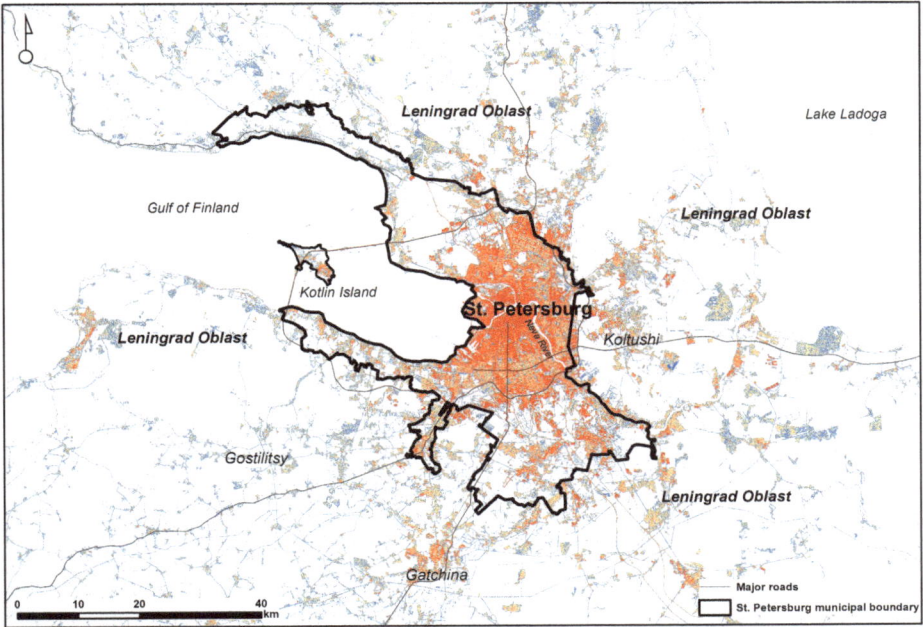

MAP 10 The urban footprint of Saint Petersburg urban agglomeration

The urban footprint is still largely contained within the boundaries of Saint Peterburg but with limited spillover into the territory administered by the Leningrad *Oblast*.

Data source: Global Human Settlement Layer (GHSL). Cartography: Mncedisi Siteleki

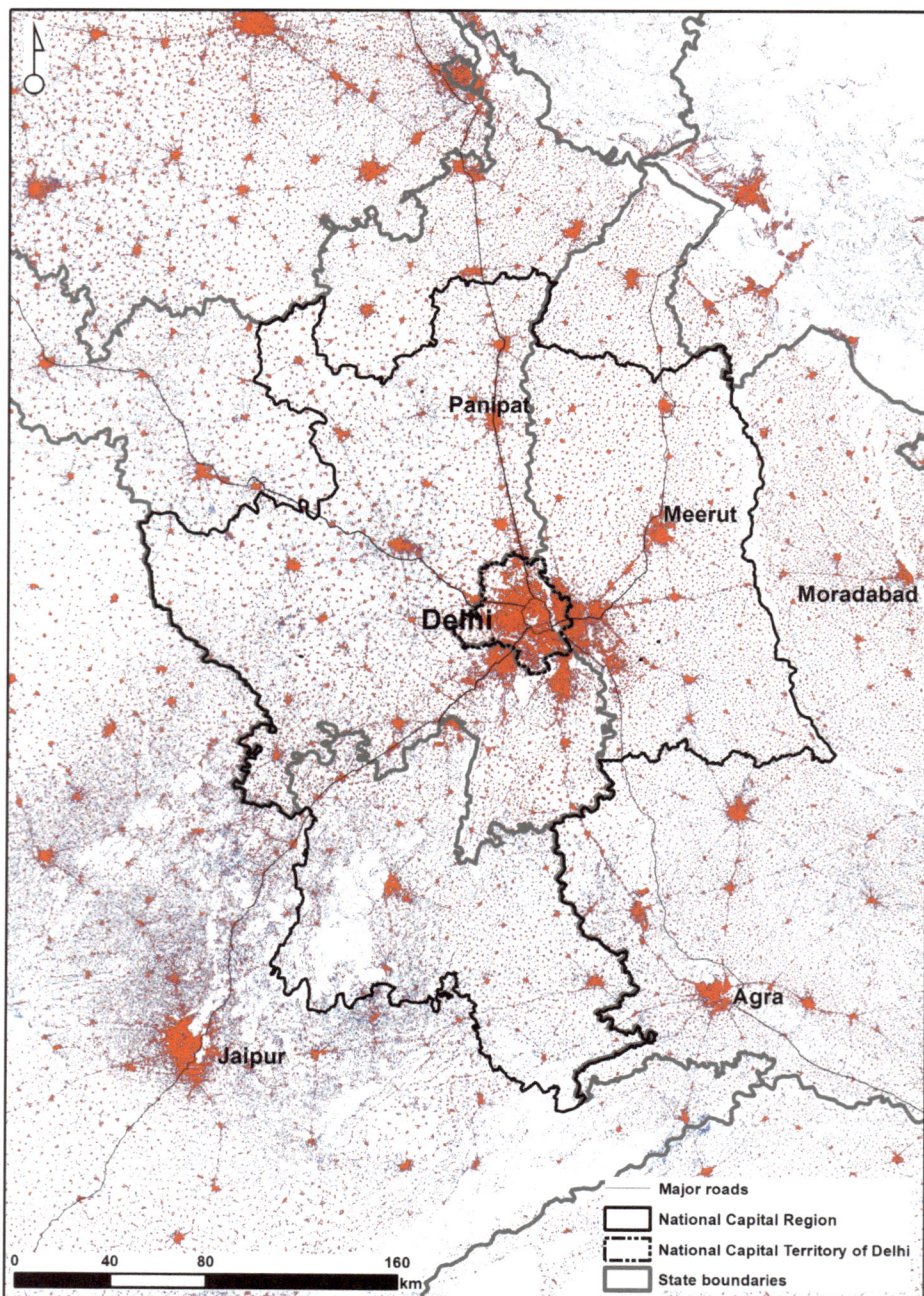

MAP 11 The urban footprint of India's National Capital Region

India's National Capital Region is centred on the mega urban agglomeration administered within the National Capital Territory of Delhi, with a diffuse network of smaller urban areas across the remaining part of the extensive region.

Data source: Global Human Settlement Layer (GHSL). Cartography: Mncedisi Siteleki

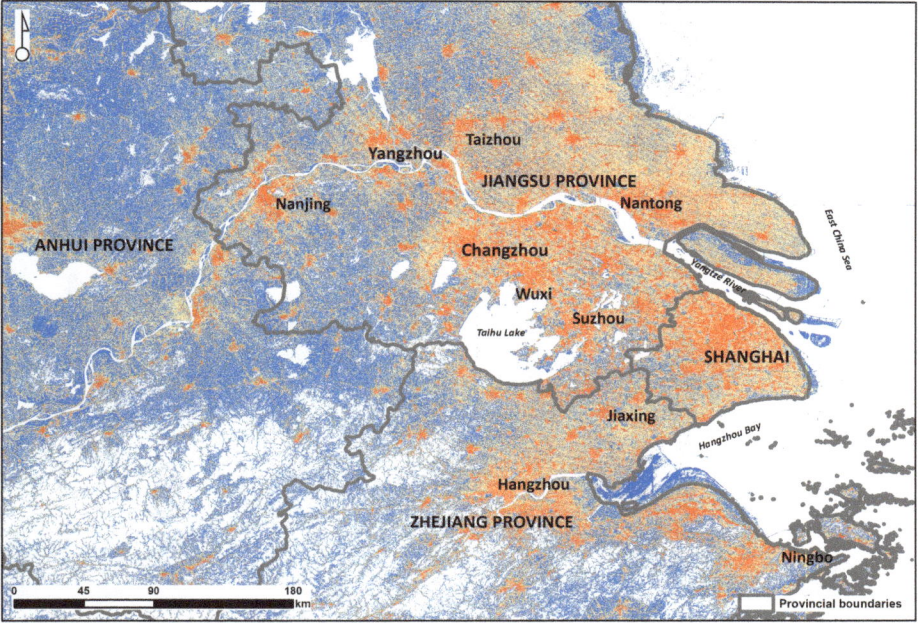

MAP 12 The urban footprint of the Yangtze River Delta city cluster

The Yangtze River Delta is a mega multi-nodal urban cluster. Shanghai is the largest urban hub but there are other major centres such as Nanjing, Hangzhou, Suzhou and Ningbo.

Data source: Global Human Settlement Layer (GHSL). Cartography: Mncedisi Siteleki

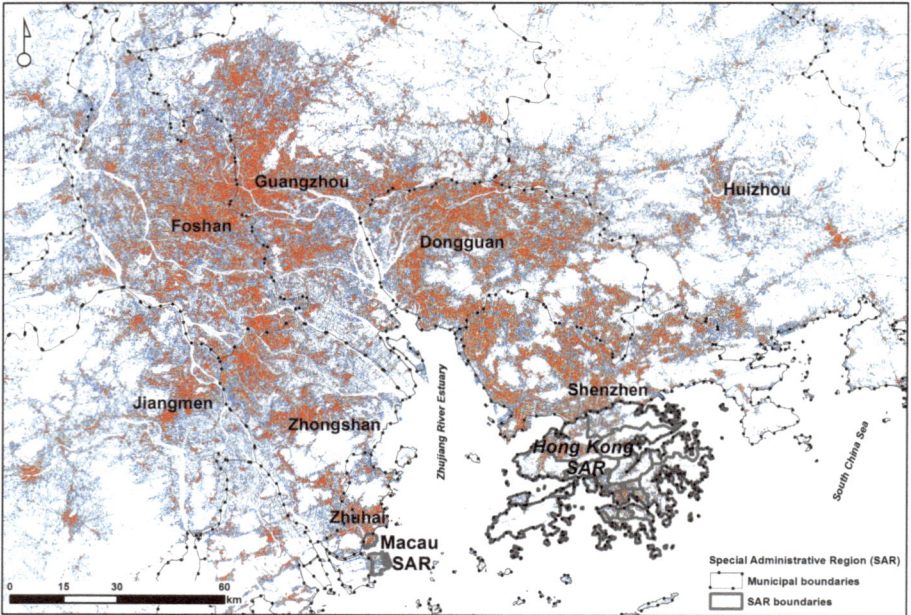

MAP 13 The urban footprint of the city cluster in the Greater Bay Area of China

The Greater Bay Area of China is one of the most recently evolved mega urban clusters globally. Its extensive urban footprint envelops the Zhujiang River Estuary and includes the large agglomerations centred on the cities of Hong Kong, Guangzhou, Shenzhen and Dongguan.

Data source: Global Human Settlement Layer (GHSL). Cartography: Mncedisi Siteleki

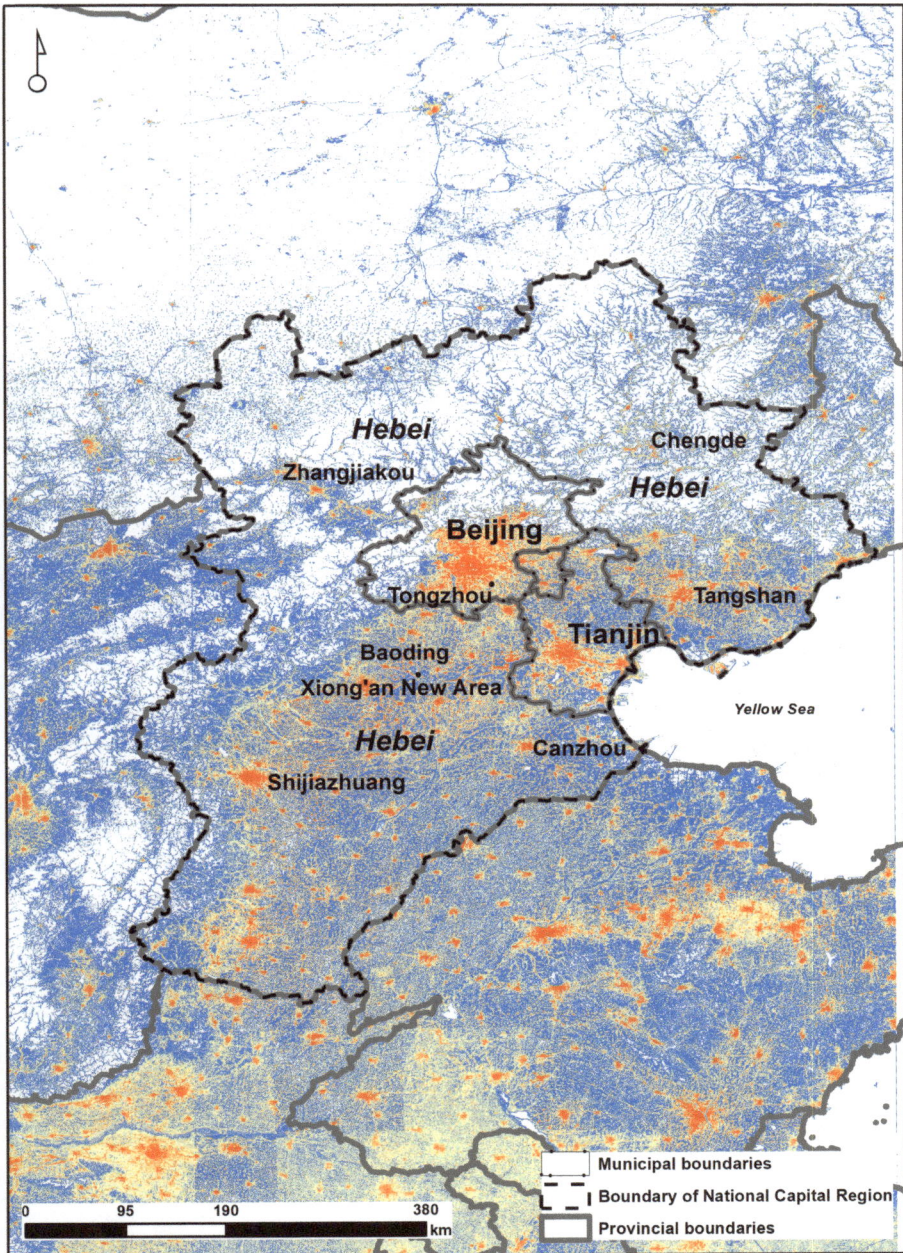

MAP 14 The urban footprint of the National Capital Region of China

The National Capital Region of China is a massive territory with the dual-centred agglomeration of Beijing-Tianjin as its core, and a network of smaller urban centres, including the Xiong'an New Area, across the extensive territory of Hebei province.

Data source: Global Human Settlement Layer (GHSL). Cartography: Mncedisi Siteleki

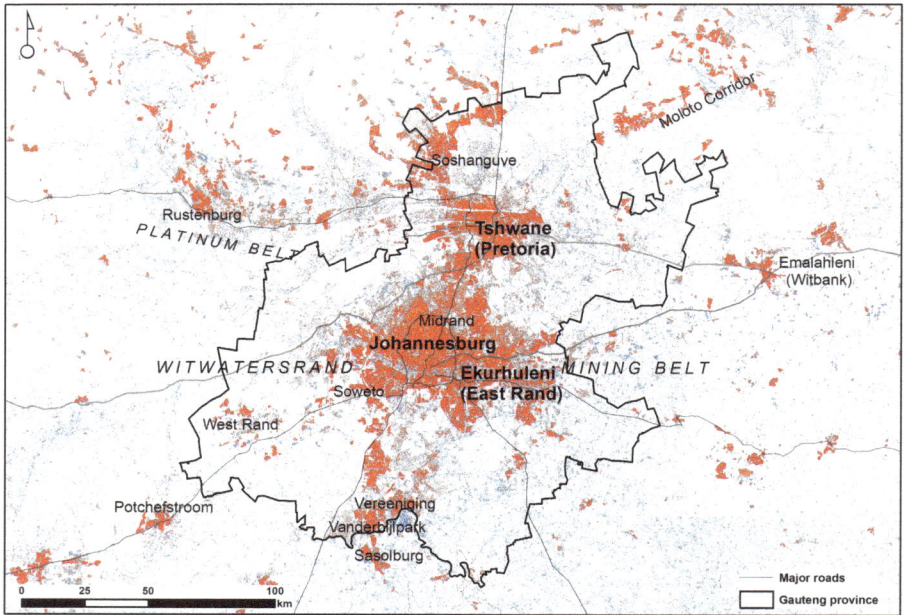

MAP 15 The urban footprint of the Gauteng City-Region

The Gauteng City-Region falls largely within the province of Gauteng but the urban footprint extends into neighbouring provinces, including, for example, the Platinum Belt around Rustenburg in North West province, and the Moloto Corridor and the coal-mining and industrial towns around Emalahleni in the province of Mpumalanga.

Data source: Global Human Settlement Layer (GHSL). Cartography: Mncedisi Siteleki

Section three: Municipal boundaries

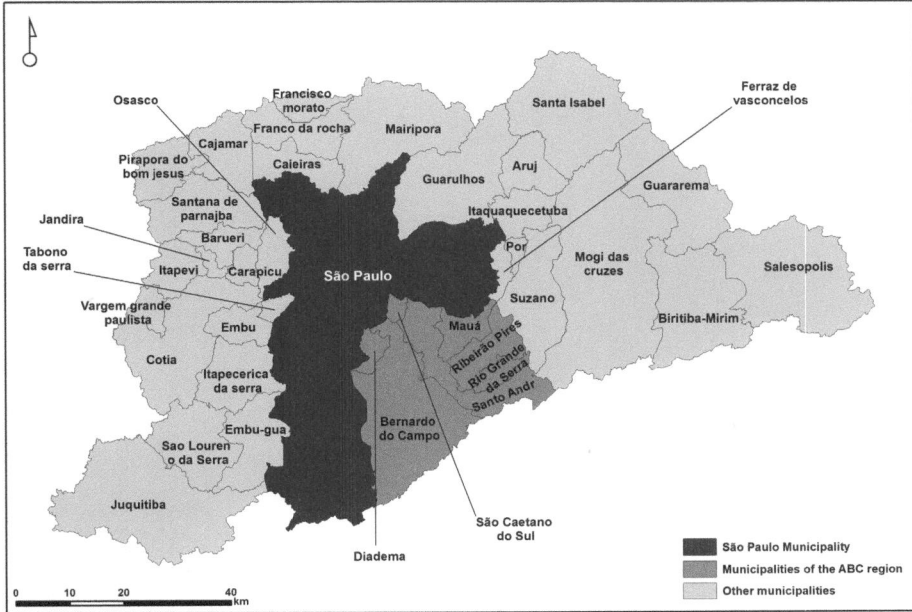

MAP 16 The municipal boundaries of São Paulo Metropolitan Region

Around one-half of the population of the approximately 22 million people in the metropolitan region live within the core municipality of São Paulo, with the other half living across 38 other municipalities. Six of these municipalities have come together in a collaborative arrangement to form the ABC sub-region of São Paulo.

Data source: DIVA-GIS. Cartography: Mncedisi Siteleki

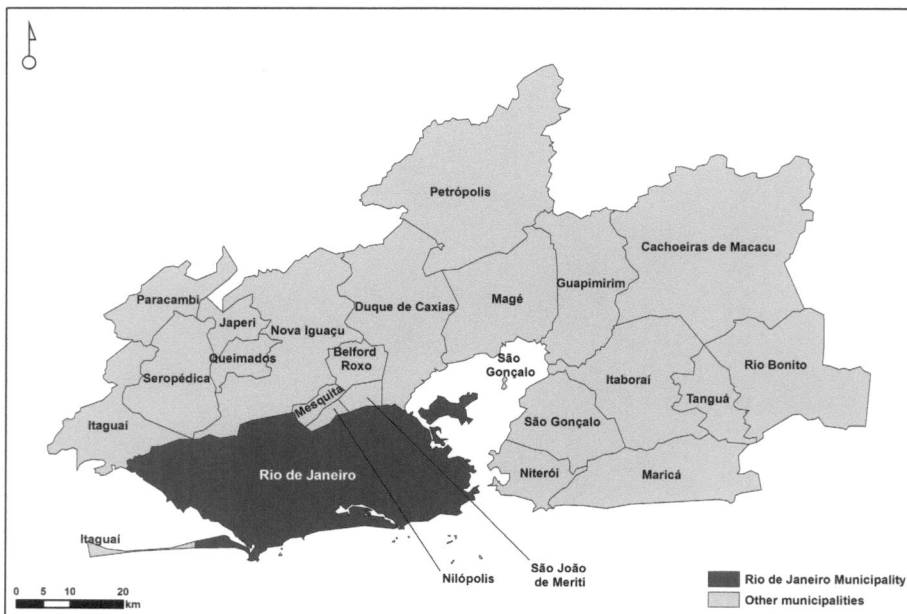

MAP 17 The municipal boundaries of Rio de Janeiro Metropolitan Region (Grande Rio)

The approximately 13.5 million people of the Rio de Janeiro Metropolitan Region live across 23 municipalities, with around one-half in the core municipality.

Data source: DIVA-GIS. Cartography: Mncedisi Siteleki

MAP 18 The municipal boundaries of Belo Horizonte Metropolitan Region

With a population of around six million people, Belo Horizonte comprises 34 municipalities, although the bulk of the population live within the core municipality.

Data source: DIVA-GIS. Cartography: Mncedisi Siteleki

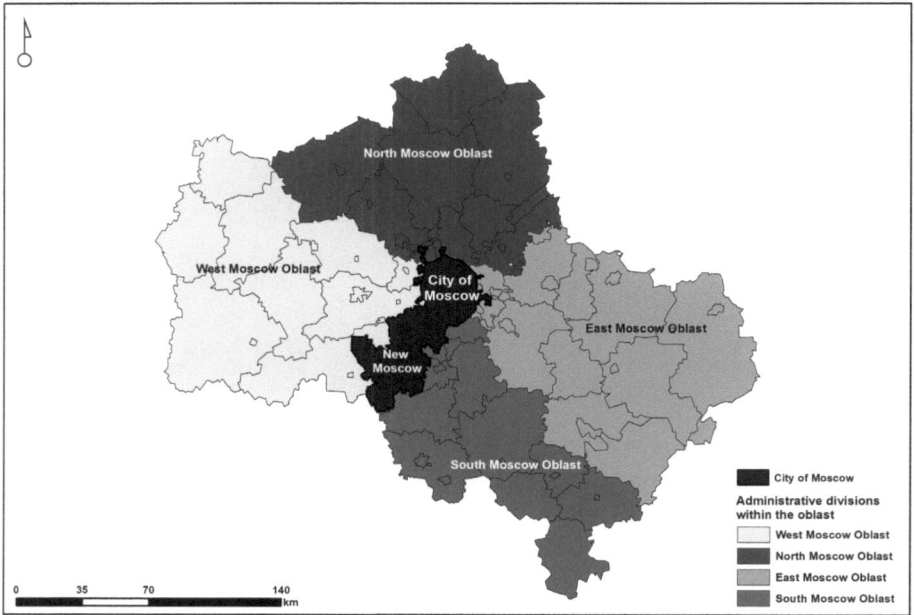

MAP 19 The administrative divisions of Moscow urban agglomeration

Moscow is a powerful core municipality that has annexed territory from the *oblast* (the regional administration) including an area known as New Moscow. The *oblast* is divided into administrative districts and into multiple local government jurisdictions.

Data source: DIVA-GIS. Cartography: Mncedisi Siteleki

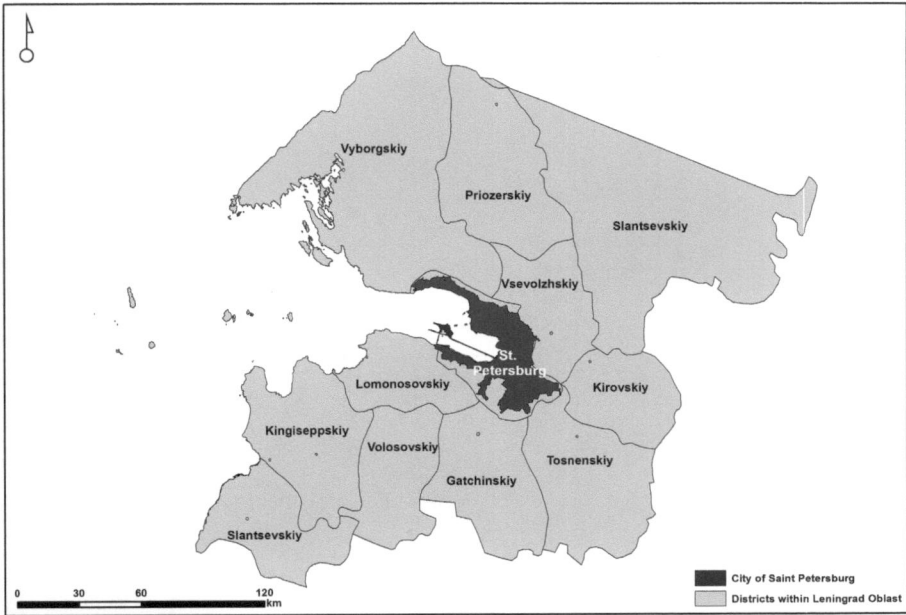

MAP 20 The municipal boundaries of Saint Petersburg urban agglomeration

Saint Petersburg is the dominant administrative jurisdiction but the administrative districts of the surrounding Leningrad *Oblast* contain the overspill of the agglomeration.

Data source: DIVA-GIS. Cartography: Mncedisi Siteleki

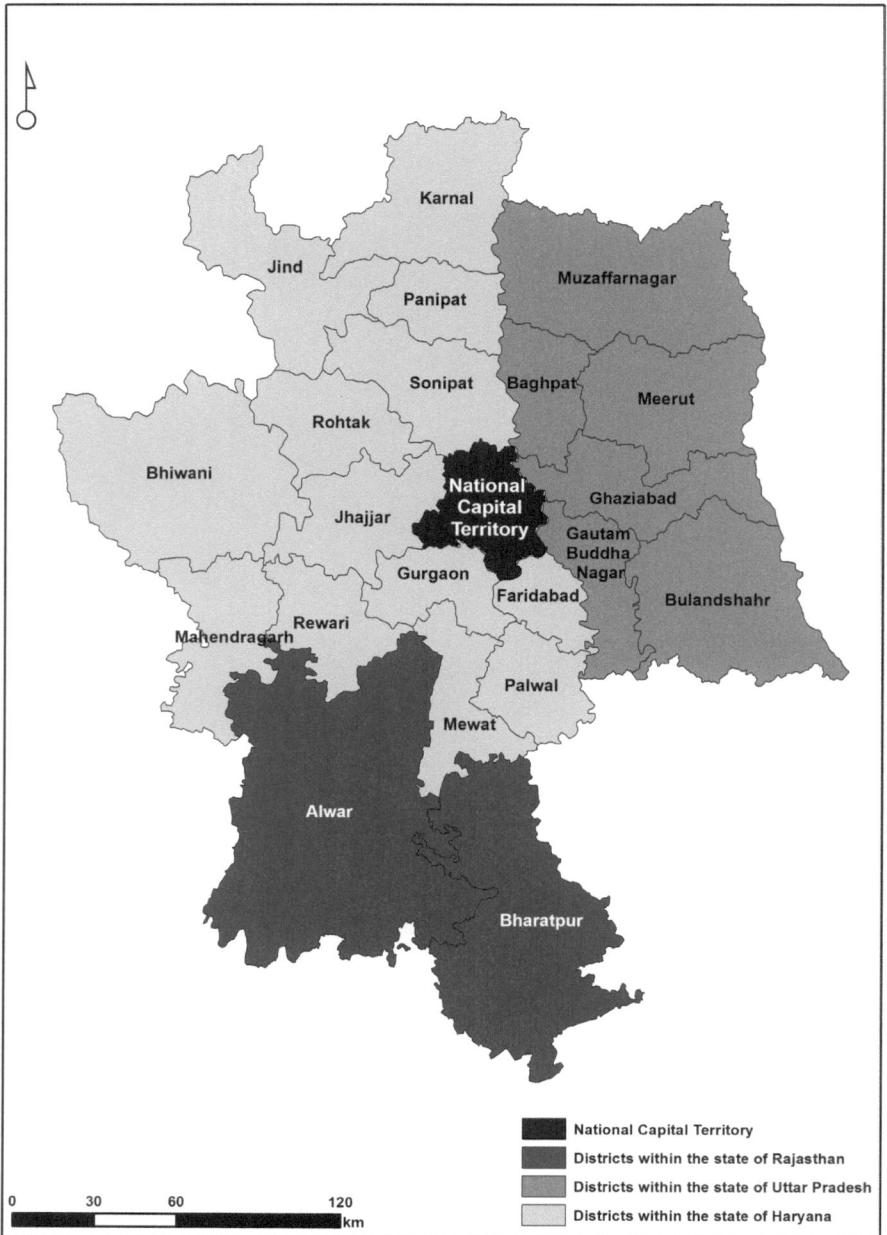

MAP 21 The administrative divisions of India's National Capital Region

India's National Capital Region includes the National Capital Territory of India, which is a quasi-state territory, and parts of the states of Haryana, Uttar Pradesh and Rajasthan, which are, in turn, divided into administrative districts (shown on the map) and a complex subdivision of multiple municipal jurisdictions (not shown on the map).

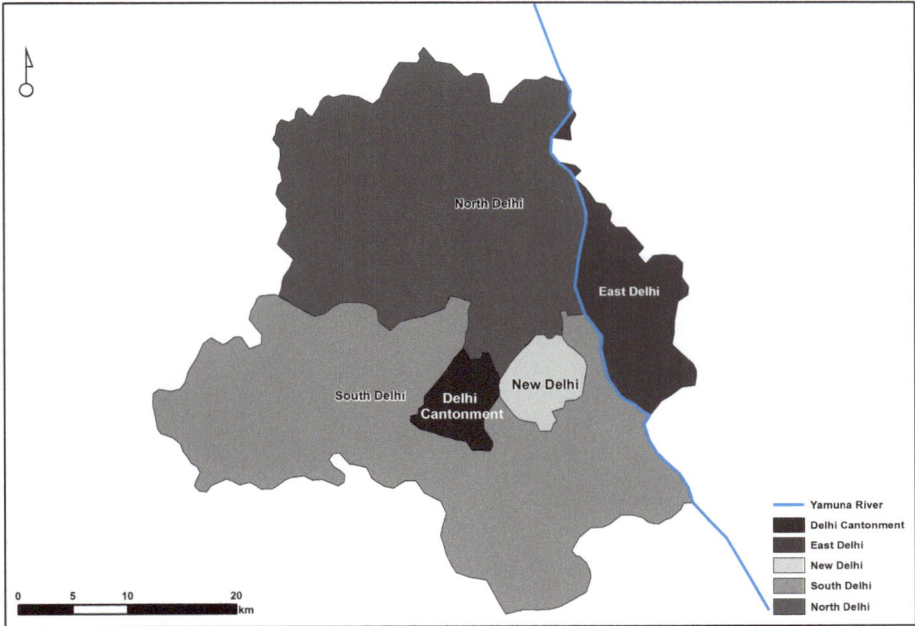

Data source: DIVA-GIS. Cartography: Mncedisi Siteleki

MAP 22 The municipal boundaries of Delhi's National Capital Territory

The National Capital Territory forms the core of the National Capital Region and comprises the three municipal corporations of North, South and East Delhi (previously a single corporation), New Delhi, which is the national capital precinct of India, and the Delhi Cantonment, which houses the headquarters of the Indian Army and other military facilities.

Data source: DIVA-GIS. Cartography: Mncedisi Siteleki

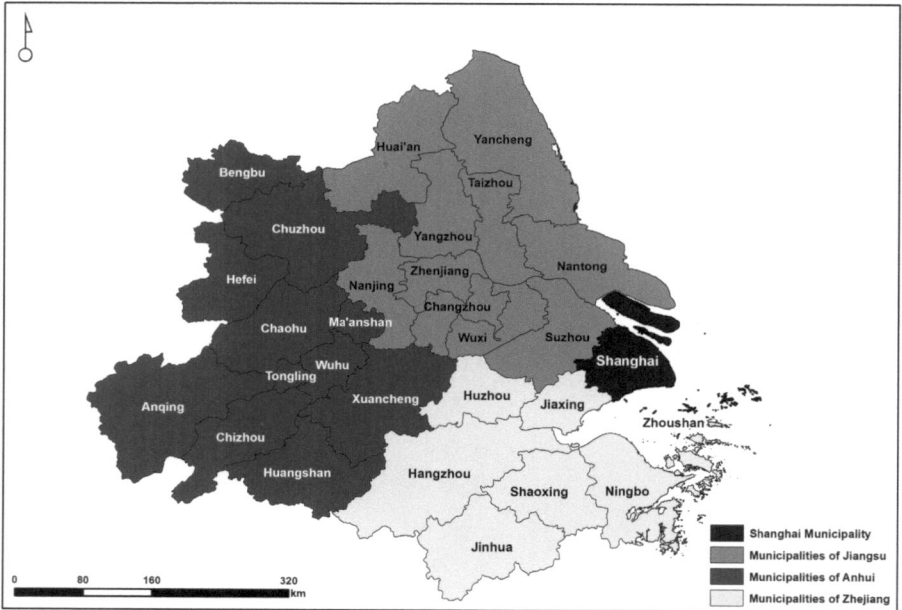

MAP 23 The municipal boundaries of the Yangtze River Delta

The Yangtze River Delta includes Shanghai, which has the status of both a municipal and provincial government, and municipalities across the provinces Jiangsu, Zhejiang and Anhui. As elsewhere, municipalities are large, often covering a large metropolitan area.

Data source: DIVA-GIS. Cartography: Mncedisi Siteleki

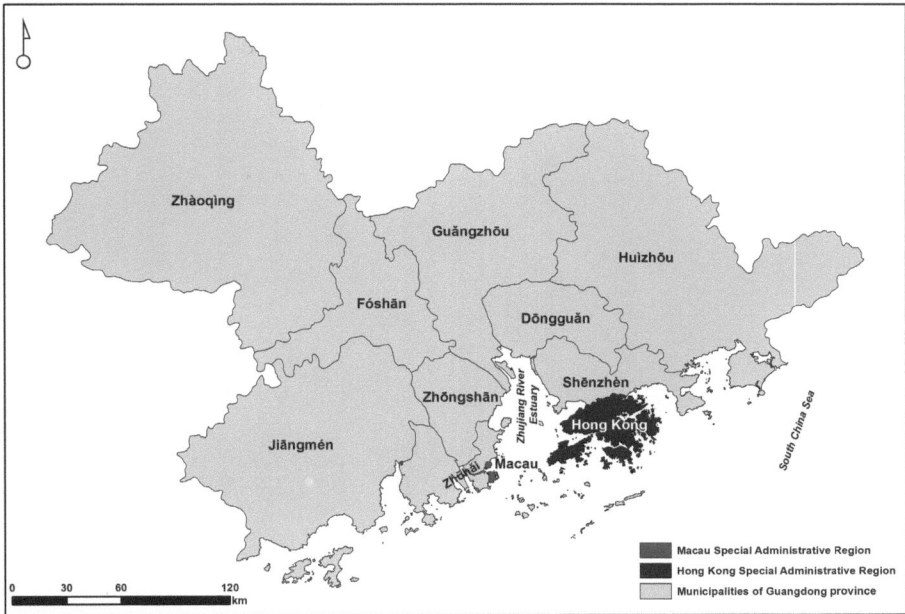

MAP 24 The administrative entities of the Greater Bay Area of China

The Greater Bay Area of China is administratively complex. It includes the two special administrative regions (SARs) of Hong Kong and Macau which were established under the Sino-British Joint Declaration of 1984 and the Sino-Portuguese Joint Declaration of 1987. These are semi-autonomous regions, although their laws may be overridden by China's National People's Congress. The remainder of the Greater Bay Area comprises municipalities within Guangdong province of mainland China.

Data source: DIVA-GIS. Cartography: Mncedisi Siteleki

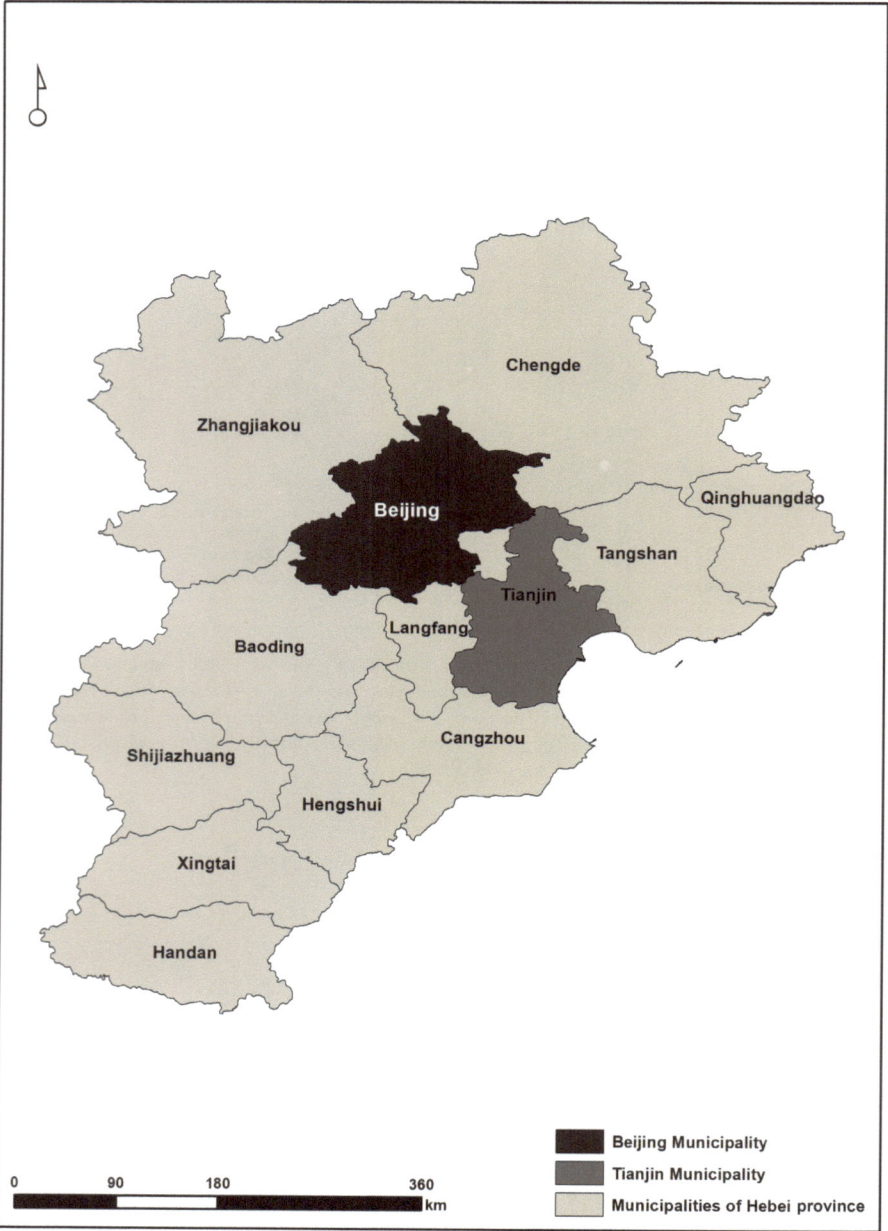

MAP 25 The municipal boundaries of the National Capital Region in China

The National Capital Region of China is a vast territory comprising the urban municipalities of Beijing and Tianjin, which hold provincial status within China's governmental hierarchy, and the municipalities across the entire Hebei province.

Data source: DIVA-GIS. Cartography: Mncedisi Siteleki

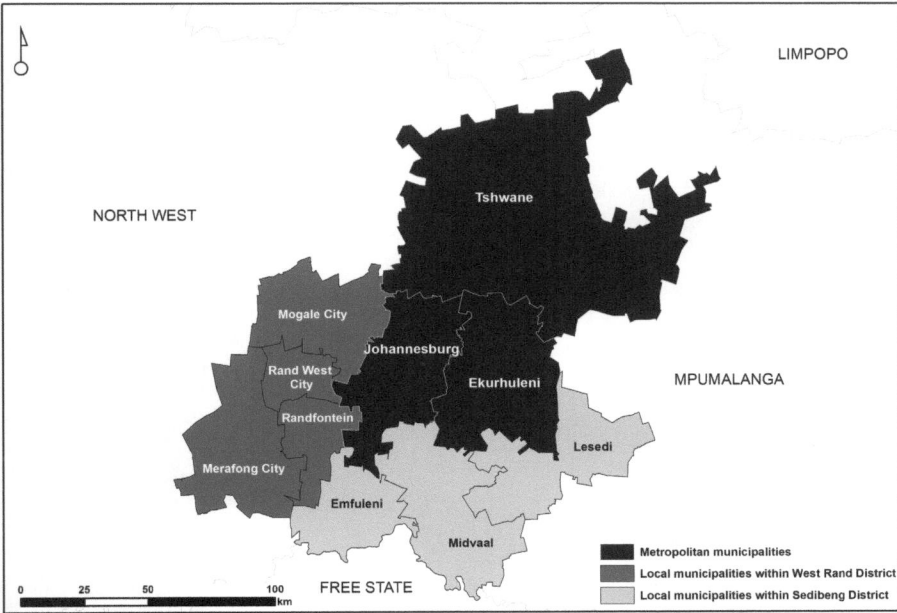

MAP 26 The municipal boundaries of Gauteng province in South Africa

The map indicates the municipalities that comprise Gauteng province in South Africa. These include three metropolitan municipalities –Johannesburg, Tshwane and Ekurhuleni – which govern as a single tier of administration, and the local and district municipalities that form part of a two-tier municipal administration. The Gauteng City-Region does, however, overlap partly into the Free State, Mpumalanga and North West provinces.

Data source: Gauteng City-Region Observatory (GCRO). Cartography: Mncedisi Siteleki

Section four: China's city clusters

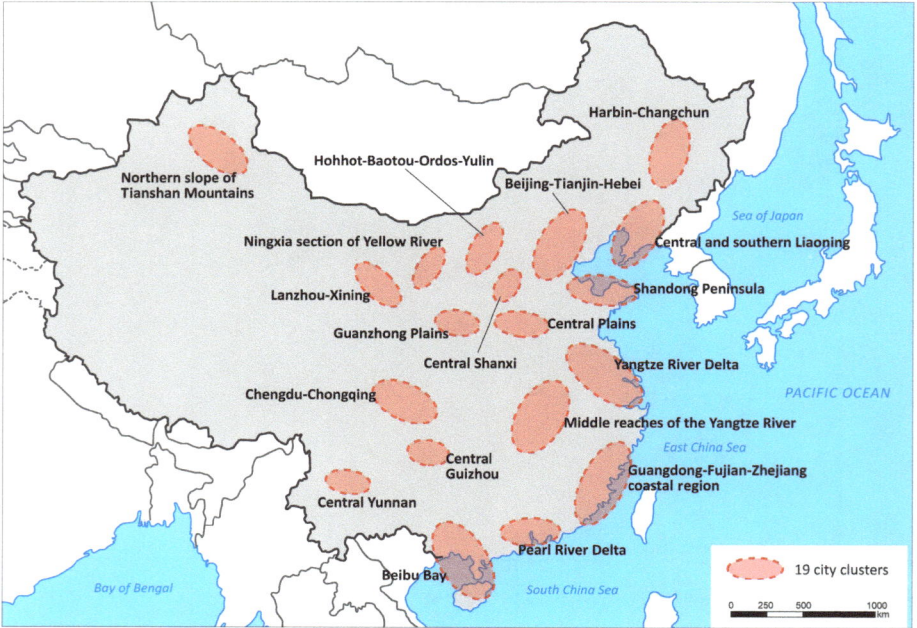

MAP 27 A schematic representation of China's city clusters

This map shows the city clusters that were indicated in schematic form in China's 11th Five Year Plan 2006–2010.

Data source: China's National Development Reform Commission, 2006.

Cartography: Original map redrawn by Janet Alexander

Introduction: Exploring hyper-complexity

The dilemma of collective action

Urban governance at any scale is complicated, but large city-regions are the 'talking pigs' – the cases *in extremis*.[1] Because of their size, dynamism and indefinite boundaries, they are a governmental context of hyper-complexity.

Modern forms of governance are constructed within demarcated territories, layered from the national to local, but this arrangement is increasingly tested by the ongoing expansion of urban footprints across jurisdictions. To address the overspill, the boundaries within which governments operate must be continually redrawn or other mechanisms of joint action created. This is not only a matter of horizontal coordination, as actors across all scales of government are engaged at the local and regional levels. Even within a single jurisdiction, there is a complex mix of governmental, private and civic actors with different interests and modes actively engaged in governance processes. Michael Neuman (2007, 319) describes the coalescence of government structures into 'multi-scalar large institutional networks'. Paul Aligica and Filippo Sabetti (2014, 9) refer similarly to 'a complex social reality of multiple decision centers and multi-layered, overlapping jurisdictions'.

While governing at the scale of a city-region is technically complicated, the biggest challenges are political and institutional, and personal motivations and relationships. Planning theorist Patsy Healey (2005, 147) calls the city-region a context of 'relational complexity', while Willem Salet et al. (2003, 377), in their comparative study of city-regions across Europe, define city-region governance as the task of 'organizing connectivity'.

Public choice theorists Elinor Ostromand and Richard Feiock have placed collective action dilemmas at the centre of their analysis, which I find to be a useful launching pad for my own enquiries (for example, Ostrom 1990, 2009; Feiock 2009, 2013).

They start with an analysis of how institutional fragmentation produces challenges in managing externalities, spillovers and common property resources. To provide public benefits and prevent environmental destruction, social actors must agree to collaborate, and this happens when the individually calculated benefits of working together are greater than the costs and risks of doing so. The city-region presents an acute dilemma of collective action, as the group size is large, societies are heterogeneous, and levels of trust and reciprocity in these competitively charged environments are often low. There are also many forms of territorial jealousy, with local actors adopting positions of self-protection and self-promotion. However, there is cautious optimism in the literature, acknowledging that conditions of trust may be gradually improved through repeated collaborative interactions. Also, where the costs and risks of more formal collaborations are high, collaboration may still occur within informal interpersonal networks (Leibovitz 2003; Feiock 2009, 2013; Ostrom 2009; Simmie 2012).

While drawing on the above, the book takes a different approach by focussing on the historically produced contexts that shape decision making. Public choice theory has been criticised for abstracting transactional calculations from the culture, discourse, politics and relational networks of individual contexts (Barnes and Sheppard 1992). Contemporary public choice theorists are mindful of this challenge, with Antonio Tavares and Richard Feiock (2018, 303) accepting, for example, that 'relationships are embedded in larger social, political, and economic structures'. But the orientation of the theory is still towards the logic of individual choice. It is also quiet on the institutional politics that continually intervene in choice-making.

This study focuses on the continuous struggle to govern large and dynamic agglomerations of urban settlements that cross multiple jurisdictional boundaries. I argue that the political necessity of delivering benefits to residents compels governmental actors to collaborate in order for city-region governance to happen in multiple ways across all regions. However, it often happens inadequately and partially, with poor outcomes for urban citizens and the environment on which citizens all depend. By understanding how contemporary forms of city-region governance, with their limitations and possibilities, were produced over time, my hope is that we may find pointers for future improvement.

While this hope is normative, I seek to offer a non-normative (and non-judgemental) account of city-region governance. There are forms of city-region governance in all the cases I study, and all are partial and imperfect, as elsewhere in the world. However, rather than trying to evaluate which are better or worse, I seek to explain why various forms have emerged in each context, and how they have evolved. Clearly, some are more effective than others, but they are all so contextually related that normative evaluation in one context may be misleading for another. However, improved understanding of each city-region and insights from elsewhere may improve contextual practice over time.

The question is how to research a field as diverse, complex and fluid as this. My answer, in this book, is to use the overlapping concepts of induction, emergence, (historical) process tracing and comparison. I will introduce each in turn below.

Induction

The methodological dispute between deductive and inductive reasoning goes back to the debates between Plato and Aristotle in ancient Greece. We now know that reasoning processes are a complex hybrid of both forms and that we continually work between deductive and inductive reasoning in real life. The methodological question is where to place the emphasis.

I began the research in a largely deductive mode. I had the concepts of city-region and city-region governance in mind, and I set out to explore their application across the BRICS (Brazil, Russia, India, China, South Africa) countries. However, I soon faced difficulties in what first appeared to be a straightforward research process. The five countries I was looking at had different linguistic, scholarly, political and institutional traditions, and my assumption of a universal concept, applicable with some variation, was flawed. Every country had large and complex agglomerations of urban activity, but they were not all called city-regions and, even when they were, meanings differed.

In my home context, we refer to the Gauteng City-Region (GCR), which includes Johannesburg, Tshwane (Pretoria) and a complex agglomeration of smaller urban centres. In Brazil, however, the Greater São Paulo agglomeration is not known as a *cidade-região* (city-region) but rather, variously, as a *região metropolitana* (metropolitan region), a *macrometrópole* (macro metropolis) or a *complexo metropolitano expandido* (expanded metropolitan complex). In Russia, the term городская агломерация (or *gorodskaya aglomeratsiya*) is translated as 'urban agglomeration'. However, the term had its origins in Soviet-era economic planning and using it as a direct equivalent of 'city-region' loses inflections that persist into the present.

In India, the term 'metropolitan area' is commonly used, with 'city-region' reserved for reference to the National Capital Region (NCR), which forms a vast swathe around Delhi. But, the GCR in South Africa and the NCR in India are two very different constructions. While the GCR is called a city-region because it is a large agglomeration of interconnected settlements, the NCR is a city-region because it is an expansive territory of relatively low density (in Indian terms at least) delineated to absorb population and activity from the congested national capital, Delhi.

China also has this conception of an NCR. However, it has other terms for its urban agglomerations. The economic circle (经济圈 or *jingjiquan*), drawn in the 1980s from usage in Japan, evolved into the idea of a city cluster (城市群 or *chengshiqun*), which gained official recognition in national planning. Other terms, more familiar in the Western context, such as 'city-region', are also used but they co-exist with East Asian etymology, and their meanings cannot be directly conflated.

For Yimin Zhao (2020, 528), a vernacular name for concepts or artefacts embodies 'historical-geographical conjuncture' and 'local-historical conditions' and so the attempt to reduce it to a universal designation is sterilising.[2] I learnt from my study, and from the provocation of Zhao (2020, 538), that we need to make the 'effort to attend to "words" and to language issues in general'. I, therefore, turned towards a more inductive approach that tried to begin with an understanding of the distinctiveness of each context, and how language and meaning are constructed within these contexts. It is an imperfect attempt at induction, as I found it very difficult to avoid 'linguistic assumptions [and] home country bias' (Cox and Evenhuis 2020, 428). In the end, I found it impossible to avoid the use of the generic term 'city-region' and related terms such as 'metropolitan region' and 'urban agglomeration', but I have tried to contextualise and historicise their use and acknowledge the entanglement of global language, and national and regional vernaculars.

Even if we set aside the question of language and adopt 'city-region' as the common term, there are challenges in its meaning (Rodríguez-Pose 2008). 'City-region' is used, for example, to refer to urban formations as small as Malmö in Sweden and as immense as the Yangtze River Delta (YRD) in China (Tosics 2007; Li and Wu 2018). More disparately, 'city-region' is used to refer variously to a physical space (for example, Weber et al. 2016), a geographic imaginary (for example, Huang 2006), a product of global economic change (most famously, Scott 2001), and the outcome of political interests and contests (Jonas and Ward 2007). In my use of the inductive method, I try to historicise and contextualise the terminology.

Inductive reasoning is not a simple matter of drawing data from below into theory-making. Kathleen Eisenhardt et al. (2016, 1114) write of it as 'an iterative process of gathering raw data, producing progressively better-defined and grounded higher-order concepts through constant comparison and mind-expanding techniques, and creating underlying theoretical arguments that connect constructs'. It is this iterative process that makes induction an appropriate choice for the messy world that urban studies engages with. Eisenhardt et al. (2016, 1113) write that inductive methods 'excel in situations for which there is limited theory and on problems without clear answers'. Christian Schmid et al. (2018) show how induction supports theory-building by moving beyond the constriction of existing vocabulary to the production of language that relates to actual observation and experience.

Emergence

The idea of emergence helps us recognise and explore governance processes that are not consciously designed but are produced through gradual interactive and adaptive processes.

The idea of emergent properties goes back to nineteenth-century theory on bio-logical evolution. It refers to complex, high-order characteristics that arise in the nat-ural world through a combination of lower-order parts – characteristics that cannot be reduced to the sum of their parts.[3] In the mid-twentieth century, there was some crossover between the biological concept and social theory. The Austrian economist and social philosopher Friedrich Hayek used 'emergence' to refer to 'features of the world that are indeed the result of human action but not the result of human design' (cited in Lewis 2012, 368). He used the term 'emergent properties' to refer to social structures that evolved over long periods from individual actions but could not be directly inferred from these actions.

Emergence annoyed the positivists as the causal links could not be proven and the term was suppressed for most of the twentieth century, gaining respectability again from the 1970s as positivism waned in influence. In the 1980s, there was a new cross-over into the social sciences. Henry Mintzberg and James Waters (1985) distinguished between deliberate practices that are designed or explicitly orchestrated to resolve governmental challenges and emergent practices that arise over time as actors learn through grappling iteratively with problem solving in complex environments. This provoked a long debate in management studies between the so-called design school and learning school. Mintzberg did acknowledge, however, that there is a continuum between design and emergence, and it is not always easy to distinguish between the two processes. Other writers used the term 'emergent properties' to refer to social attributes that are more than the sum of individual behaviours, including, for example, cultural identity (Lewis 2012), linguistic practice (Meara 2006), complex economic systems (Schenk 2006) and multi-actor networks (Stern 2015).

In urban scholarship, little has been written of emergence or emergent properties. Hye Lim and Jaan-Henrik Kain (2016) are a rare exception in their identification of the emergent properties of cities as complex, intense and diverse. There is some reference, however, to emergent properties in urban governance. In the *Handbook of Megacities and Megacity Regions*, editors Danielle Labbé and André Sorensen (2020, 47) make the suggestive argument that local governance is itself an emergent property of urban development and that 'urban transitions force the development of complex sets of urban institutions to regulate, build, and maintain urban space'.

Catherine Durose and Vivien Lowndes (2021) highlight the fuzzy boundary between emergence and design. Designed institutions may seem emergent, but this is because of their incompleteness. Durose and Lowndes (2021, 1773) write that urban governance is 'replete with examples of institutional blueprints that have gone awry, governance reforms that are never accomplished, and policy regimes that are inad-equately specified for implementation in diverse contexts'. At the same time, emer-gence may establish routines that evolve into enduring and coherent formations that may even seem designed. Margaret Shannon (2002, 10) explains that 'for emergent institutions to persist over time, however, they must institutionalize the creative, generative capacity of collaboration'.

The question, methodologically, is how to discern emergence (Vicente 2013, 137). For Keith Sawyer (2007, 317), emergence happens in 'complex configurations of many people engaged in overlapping and interlocking patterns of relationship with each other'. This suggests the need for micro-studies and even for a deep ethnography that can separate emergence – the 'signal of patterns' – from the noise of everyday micro-practice (Young 2010, 8). This is not possible for a wide-ranging comparative study such as the BRICS countries comparison, but historical tracing may assist in identifying the emergent or designed origins of governance arrangements.

There are other concepts, such as adaptive systems and self-organising systems, that emphasise the iterative and dynamic processes that gradually and cumulatively produce significant change (Martin and Sunley 2007, 575). For James Rosenau (2007, 88, 95), these processes engage complexity in a way that designed processes cannot, enabling 'governing the ungovernable'.

How these processes work in practice is difficult to trace. Richard Freeman (2007) refers to bricolage as the recombination of existing elements for new purposes, rather than an attempt to create something new, while Durose and Lowndes (2021, 1781) describe how governmental actors 'interpret institutional designs on an ongoing basis, using discretion and improvisation to fit cases to rules and resources, in changing environments'. Wolfgang Streeck and Kathleen Thelen (2005) explain different forms of incremental adjustment to governance: 1) displacement (the gradual rise and replacement of existing structures); 2) layering (the addition of new forms onto the existing); 3) drift (change through intentional neglect); 4) conversion (intentional redirection or influence); and 5) exhaustion (gradual depletion or breakdown). Others emphasise the gradual learning process that happens through the interactions within interpersonal networks (Freeman 2007; Martin and Simmie 2008).

Much of the existing literature on city-regions is concerned with the different modes of governance, ranging from ambitious, formalised structures of overarching coordination to informal, interpersonal networks, with much in-between.[4] There is less attention to the formation of these modes. Public choice theorists offer a perspective, explaining that informal collaborations, for example, have low transaction costs and emerge when formal institutions are not transactionally viable (Feiock 2009, 2013; Tavares and Feiock 2018). Concepts such as emergence, bricolage and adaptive governance emphasise the generative role of continual problem-solving interaction within interpersonal networks.

This book explores the full range of governance processes and institutions produced under different conditions. It avoids a normative positioning, accepting that different formations are produced through different histories, cultures and politics. While orchestrated and hierarchical arrangements, for example, may undermine local governance, some forms of service delivery may, in fact, require these approaches (Swyngedouw 2009). Similarly, while informal networks offer flexibility and have few of the costs of major institutional formations, their downsides include a lack of transparency and accountability (Simmie 2012).

Process tracing

A key premise underlying the BRICS study is that governance arrangements cannot be extracted from context, so a best-practice approach is fundamentally flawed. While we can learn from other places and be inspired to think more creatively about our setting in the process, we cannot transfer solutions coherently. Simply put, the context-producing history of places matters to what is possible in terms of institutional solutions.

To understand how institutional formations have evolved, it is necessary to trace their formation in relation to a shifting context. The phenomena we study are complex and invariably have a tangled relationship with context, leading Bonnie Nardi (1996, 69) to ask, 'How can we confront the blooming, buzzing confusion that is "context" and still produce generalizable research results?' This book does not attempt to generalise, but it does place the historical distinctiveness of different cases in a conversation that leads to a set of theoretical propositions. It is an inductive approach, with Pratima Bansal et al. (2018, 1192) explaining that 'whereas hypothetico-deductive logic seeks universal laws or mechanisms, historical analysis recognizes the temporal and spatial historical embeddedness of organizational phenomena'.

The research is broadly informed by historical institutionalism, which explains the norms, values, behaviours and patterns of social organisation in terms of an evolutionary pathway. Bansal et al. (2018, 1190–1191) describe a process approach that explores 'change, emergence, adaptation, and transformation' in a world that 'is in constant flux, where individuals and the environment are mutually constitutive'. This historical institutionalism is brought together with discursive institutionalism, which emphasises the role of ideas, meaning and narrative (the different ways of conceiving) in shaping governance (Krueger et al. 2018). Kalsa Granqvist et al. (2021, 845) combine these two threads of institutionalism when they write of how 'dynamically constructed ideas, such as the imaginary of the city-region, potentially reside in the very foundation of institutions'.

The research builds on prior studies of city-region governance that have used a historical approach. For Mike Hodson et al. (2020, 201) city-region governance 'takes place not on a blank canvas but rather layers over pre-existing arrangements'. Referring to the case of Manchester in the UK, they argue that the rescaling of governance to the city-region may only be understood as 'a long-term historical process'. Brita Hermelin and Bo Persson (2021) draw on historical institutionalism in their discussion on city-regions in Sweden. They emphasise the stability and persistence of governmental arrangements but also the gradual incremental changes through the layering of new forms onto what exists. André Sorensen (2020, 52) offers a further dimension when he argues that 'differences of timing relative to world events, differences in the sequence of transitions, of position in the global economy at the time of transition, and of the pacing of these sequences, has produced and is producing huge variation in outcomes among places'.

Understanding and representing historically produced context is critical to the analysis. Here there are two contending ideas to draw on. The idea of political culture implies that there are historically produced civic psychologies across countries, and even across regions within countries. Ronald Inglehart (1988, 1212) pointed to national variations in levels of political trust, for example, although arguing that 'trust is not a fixed genetic characteristic: it is cultural, shaped by the historical experiences of given peoples and subject to change'. Political cultures also affect levels of political participation, nationalism versus individualism, traditions of localism, tolerance of populism, use of violence, hierarchy, degrees of organisational discipline, attitudes to gender, and more. For some theorists, 'a political system is most stable, functional, and effective, when its political structure and political culture are congruent with each other' (Zhang 2015, 5).

For other theorists, however, the idea of a national culture can be conservative and typecasting. While history may produce shared orientations, culture is never fixed, and there is usually more variation within a country than between countries, with intersecting variables including race, gender, sexuality, class and age.

There is a vigorous debate over governance and political culture in East Asia, for example (see chapter five). Some have argued that the Confucian underpinning of political culture explains an apparent tolerance for hierarchical, even authoritarian, forms of governance. Michael Davis (1998) warns, however, of over-determining the role of Confucian culture, referring to pro-democracy protests and democratic transitions that have happened in East Asian countries. Nevertheless, in their study of New York, Paris and Tokyo, Peter Newman and Andy Thornley (2013) recognised the role of political culture in shaping different organisational and process outcomes. This suggests the dangers of either essentialising or ignoring the role of political culture.

Other writers prefer a focus on power relations and political interest, and orient toward the idea of political settlement in understanding historically produced contexts (Kelsall 2018). For Jonathan John and James Putzel (2009, 4), a political settlement is 'the bargaining outcomes among contending elites' or 'a pact of domination' that shapes the distribution of rights and entitlements across society and space.

For Mushtaq Khan (2011, 1), 'a political settlement emerges when the distribution of benefits supported by its institutions is consistent with the distribution of power in society'. In this way, 'the distribution of power becomes embedded in institutional arrangements that sustain it' (Khan 2011, 8). However, power configurations are fluid, so political settlements are not static. Khan explains that when there is an asymmetry between power and institutional organisation, 'organizations will mobilize, bargain and put pressure on other organizations and the state to change formal and informal arrangements to bring the distribution of benefits back into line with their actual relative power' (Khan 2011, 2). The other mechanism of equalisation, however, is the informal redistribution of resources through patronage, which brings resource distribution in line with the expectations created through the configuration of power (Khan 2011).

When a combination of formal and informal adaptation cannot resolve the divergence between power and institutional benefits, the political settlement may unravel and social stability will be restored with a new pact of domination (Khan 2011; Kelsall 2018). For John and Putzel (2009, 17), an analysis of governance must, therefore, be informed by an understanding of 'the elite bargain at the heart of a political settlement'.

Political culture and political settlement are different theoretical orientations, but I draw on both in explaining context. A bargaining process, for example, is not abstracted from historically produced political cultures which shape actors' norms, values and behaviours (Coakley 2009).

The methodological question is how do we undertake process tracing, relating context to change over time? Historical research involves the patient construction of a narrative using multiple sources, and the product is generally a rich description of sequential events. Process tracing is a subset of historical method. Process tracing cannot end with description as it is a tool of theory-building, so it must explore cause and effect over time. It is concerned with understanding how a particular practice, discourse or organisational arrangement (or set of any of these) originated and evolved (Bengtsson and Ruonavaara 2017).

Some writers are concerned with the open-ended nature of narrative construction and argue for more structured approaches to process tracing, using a set of recognised analytical techniques (Bengtsson and Ruonavaara 2017). Others, however, have welcomed the flexibility of process tracing, applying their judgement in relating history to context and using available concepts including, for example, path dependency and critical juncture (for example, Sorensen 2018). I take the latter approach in this book, as I bring process tracing together with a comparative approach.

Comparison

Colin McFarlane (2010, 725) asked, 'What might be the implications for urban studies if we take "comparison" not just as a method, but as a mode of thought that informs how urban theory is constituted?' If we do so, we align urban studies within development in the field of cognitive psychology, which recognises that 'the ability to make informative comparisons is central to human cognition' (Larkey and Love 2003, 781).

This understanding of the permeant nature of comparison is surfacing across many disciplines but urban studies are notable for their vigorous contribution. There is a collection of highly influential works on contemporary urban comparison, including Jan Nijman (2007), Kevin Ward (2008, 2010), Colin McFarlane (2010), Jennifer Robinson (2011, 2016a, 2016b, 2022) and Jennifer Robinson and Ananya Roy (2016) and Roger Keil and Jean-Paul Addie (2015). Also, a new generation of comparative scholarship with a creative and experimental bent is emerging – for example, Xuefei Ren (2020); Julie Ren (2022); Shaun Teo (2022); Frances Brill (2022); Astrid Wood (2022) and Miguel Kanai and Seth Schindler (2022).

The new comparative urbanism has a strong theory-building orientation. To McFarlane (2010, 739), it 'offers one possible route through which alternative theories of the urban might emerge' while Robinson argues that by bringing new cases and voices into the conversation, we produce 'a new geography of theorising' (Robinson 2016b, 196). The methodological hope is that, over time, cross-contextual insight may build into explanatory theory, which may at least offer a strong presumption for cases beyond the initial comparison.

Jamie Peck (2015, 160) cautions, however, that 'comparative theorization has been unevenly met and often more through difference-finding and deconstructive manoeuvres than through projects of urban-theoretical renewal and reconstruction'. The theory-building task of the new comparative urbanism is certainly more complex than theorising in the past, when generalising across global diversity – often from a handful of cities in the global North – was intellectually acceptable. There are also tetchy debates in the contemporary literature over the possibilities of abstracting insight from individual cases into a wider theory.

Nonetheless, I hope to make a modest contribution to what I expect will be a slow process of building and refining grounded theory as the repertoire of comparative cases gradually increases. Even if theory-building is a long and uncertain practice, the value of comparison is revealed in how 'reflecting on one case through the other [thickens] interpretations of each' (Robinson 2022, 1526).

This new comparative urbanism is a loose collective, but it is held together by a few common features. First, it departs from the structures of more traditional comparative study. Traditional approaches to comparison generally required similarity between cases, and the dimensions of comparison were decided through an a priori framing. The new approach is more permissive, accepting that *difference* is a valid basis for comparison and allowing the grounds for comparison to emerge through the research. This is a source of surprise. Joel Gehman et al. (2018, 287) explain that with this more experimental mode, 'researchers walk in the door and don't have a preconception of what relationships they're going to see'.

Second, there is methodological pluralism. For Robinson (2016a, 3), 'the challenge is to develop methods and theoretical practices which allow conceptual innovation to emerge from any urban situation or urbanization process'. There are multiple ways of doing this, with the appropriate method determined by context and purpose.

Third, the new comparative urbanism sets out to broaden the geographies of urban theory. McFarlane (2010, 726) called for attention to a 'multiplicity of cities', moving away from the dominance of the global North in providing 'objects of reference'. However, while challenging the bias towards the North, the new comparative urbanism did not respond with a 'southern urbanist' retort. Instead, Robinson (2016a, 4) called for 'more global urban studies', accepting that 'new concepts might then be initiated from anywhere' and that there are many creative combinations for comparative work (Robinson 2016b, 188). Following this line of thought, Teo (2022) brought Shenzhen and London together in a gradual process of theory-building through iterative conversation, while Robinson et al. (2022) explored large urban projects in Johannesburg, London and Shanghai. These combinations are experimental, with the nature of the comparison evolving through the research process. Brill (2022, 1757) observed how bringing 'new places into existing conversations irrevocably [alters] the conversations themselves' while Julie Ren (2022, 1741) argued for a 'more differentiated set of references and linguistic diversification . . . rather than reifying a shared grammar of urbanisation'.

The BRICS study is inspired by, and draws liberally on, the insights of the new comparative urbanism. It accepts comparison not just as a method but as a mode of thought. Within a framing of methodological pluralism, it is an approach of comparative historical process tracing that begins with the distinctiveness of individual cases but then tries to draw insights together in a simulated dialogue.[5] Insights from individual contexts may serve as propositions or provocations for others. This is a form of 'posteriori comparison', which allows the richness of the research to shape the dimensions of comparison (Montero and Baiocchi 2021, 1536).[6]

There is no prescription for comparative process tracing. As Gehman et al. (2018) have explained, there are so many levels of analysis that constant judgement and iteration are required. The one persisting methodological challenge is about 'negotiating generalization and particularity' (Cox and Evenhuis 2020, 425). Neil Brenner and Christian Schmid (2015, 164) write that 'the recognition of context dependency – the need to "provincialize" urban theory – stands in tension with an equally persistent need to understand the historically evolving totality of inter-contextual patterns, developmental pathways and systemic transformations in which such contexts are embedded, whether at national, supranational or worldwide scales'.

Comparative historical work may assist in the complex task of disentangling the distinctiveness of individual cases from the effects of global processes such as neoliberalisation or financialisation. But even so, it is not an easy task. The BRICS research confirmed for me the value of engaging first with the distinctiveness of individual cases, developing my understanding of the complexity of each, before engaging in cross-contextual comparison. This was modified only by the fact that I was developing this understanding in parallel across cases and so, subconsciously at least, the process of comparison may have started earlier.

However, in beginning with singularity – or singularities in parallel – I found it difficult to gauge the wider significance of what I was looking at. Were, for example, the governance practices in the cases I was looking at innovative or exceptional in global terms? Were they part of broader patternings? How could I begin with singularity and maintain a sense of the 'historically evolving totality' (Brenner and Schmid 2015, 164)? My partial answer to the dilemma came towards the end of the research when I produced a historically framed global overview of the co-evolving material, discursive and governmental constructs of the city-region (see chapter one). At that point, my individual case studies were placed in a global framing, and I could evaluate the significance and understand the interconnections in a way I could not do before. The move back and forth between the synoptic view and an understanding of locational specificity is a form of 'frame-switching' that offers an alternative to the current methodological disputes within urban studies (Van Meeteren et al. 2016, 296).

Choosing the BRICS

The preface to this book explains the background to the research project and alludes to the pragmatics and politics of selecting BRICS. In the choice of the case studies there was a dialogue with government officials in my home region. In my context, a study of the BRICS countries was politically agreeable in a way that comparison with countries in Europe and North America was not. At the time, South Africa had newly joined the BRIC (which then became the BRICS), and there was considerable official interest in interacting with and learning from this country cluster. It was not difficult to settle on the BRICS as a framing for the comparison, as I saw in the BRICS a productive analytical platform for generating comparative insights. Traditionally, perhaps, the BRICS countries would not have been considered as a framing, since it is a collection of very different contexts. When Jim O'Neill coined the term BRIC (Brazil, Russia, India and China) in 2001, he had identified a grouping of countries that had the potential, over time, to challenge the dominance of the global economic mainstream (O'Neill 2001). But it soon became obvious that the idea of the BRIC as a grouping of similar countries was an analytical fiction, more so when South Africa, a modestly sized country economy in global terms, joined the cluster in December 2010 to form the BRICS. BRICS is a hugely diverse collective in which the constituent countries are dissimilar across all dimensions, except for their position outside the mainstream of the global North (although even this is ambiguous, given Russia's position as a mature industrial economy and China's current position as the world's second largest economy). Economically, gross domestic product ranges from US$0.39 trillion for South Africa to US$15.54 trillion for China, and gross domestic product per capita from US$2 309 for India to US$12 026 for Russia (both at 2018 prices). In terms of demography, China's population is 24.5 times greater than South Africa's. In relation to the urban, India's level of urbanisation is around 34 per cent compared with Brazil's 84.4 per cent, with a total urban population ranging from around 38 million in South Africa to 840 million in China. Rates of annual urban population growth range from 0.18 per cent (or near static) in Russia to 2.42 per cent in China. Politically, BRICS range from the messy democracies of India, Brazil and South Africa to the authoritarian rule of China and Russia.

It was this diversity, however, that potentially offered a rich basis for a study emphasising the contextual embeddedness of city-region governance within distinctive historical, cultural, economic, political and other contexts. The recent work of Jennifer Robinson and others was important in assuring me that difference was valid grounds for comparative study.[7] My research also follows on from a significant earlier contribution. Klaus Segbers of the University of Free Berlin edited a book published in 2007 entitled *The Making of Global City Regions: Johannesburg, Mumbai/Bombay, São Paulo and Shanghai*. It was not framed in terms of the BRICS (South Africa only joined the grouping in 2010) but, significantly, the four city-regions selected to illustrate the emergence of global city-regions outside the global economic core are in the present-day BRICS (Segbers 2007).

I was also inspired by an urban scholarship that has emerged in the context of political transformations, comparing South Africa, India and Brazil using themes such as informality, urban social movements, race and space, mega events and more (for example, Huchzermeyer 2004; Heller 2012; Hofmeyr and Williams 2011). These were pioneering comparative studies across countries, previously referred to as IBSA (India, Brazil and South Africa), where there was an apparent shared sense of development challenges.

However, other comparisons in BRICS were less common. Ren (2020) pushed the boundaries in her work on governing the urban areas in India and China with a focus on land, slums and air pollution. Importantly, Ren showed how the very different approaches to dealing with these issues are conditioned by the distinctive histories of the two countries. Russia has remained out of the mix, an apparently very different country, although there are studies of urbanisation processes in BRICS that have included Russia (for example, Turok 2014; Baffi and Cottineau 2020).

Apart from the provocations of difference, there are other reasons why the BRICS was analytically appealing. First, the BRICS countries are still significantly underrepresented in city-region scholarship relative to their urban weight, despite the growing interest in China at least. Cumulatively, BRICS account for around 39 per cent of the world's urban population, including 41 per cent of the world population living in urban agglomerations of more than five million people (United Nations 2018), but city-region scholarship is still dominated by western Europe and North America despite a broadening in recent years. There is still potential to expand the geography of knowledge in ways that may have implications for the theorising of city-regions and their governance. The rapidly emerging work on China, for example, is already highlighting the significance of national state-guided city-regionalism in a literature still partly dominated by North American emphasis on private-sector and local state-led city growth coalitions.

Second, cities in the BRICS are an example of 'interstitial cities' that do not easily fit into bounded categories (Sayin et al. 2022, 265). Like other cities mentioned by Özgür Sayin et al. (2022), including Istanbul, Doha, Manila and Warsaw, the city-regions of the BRICS have elements associated with the global North and South (and East and West) and are neither dominant nor marginal in global terms. Research on these cities 'raises important questions about urban theory ... because they do not easily fit, or align with, one of the dominant theoretical perspectives in global urban studies' (Sayin et al. 2022, 276). There is of course the danger of the interstitial city becoming a new category in itself, but for the moment, it is an idea that adds conceptual flexibility to urban studies, and to this book, allowing the experience of the various case studies to talk into debates that have been geographically pigeon-holed (for example, informality in the global South and financialised capitalism in the global North).

As I progressed with the research, I became increasingly aware of the new scholarship on planetary urbanisation (for example, Merrifield 2013; Brenner 2014, 2018; Brenner and Schmid 2013, 2015; Keil 2017, 2018; Schmid 2018). This literature was a provocation, challenging both my conception of city-regions and the territorial basis I selected for comparison. Building on Henri Lefebvre's notion of the complete urbanisation of society, the idea of planetary urbanisation unsettled an urban scholarship still reliant on bounded categories such as the city (or indeed, the city-region). It became increasingly clear to me that each of the city-regions I had selected was part of a wider and more complex territorial formation from which it could not be separated. This is most extreme for Greater Delhi, which forms part of a great swathe of urban settlement extending along the Ganges and Indus river valleys, but the point applies in all cases. Ideas of planetary urbanisation also create a dilemma in relation to the governance requirements for delineating territory. Michael Leaf (2020, 33) writes that the urban is impossible to delimit but accepts that 'jurisdictional clarity is a necessary condition for the efficient functioning of government'. I have not resolved these dilemmas but have tried to highlight them through the study.

Synthesising purpose

Sorensen and Labbé (2020, 11–12) observe that 'human scale experiences' within the context of 'mega urbanization processes' are mediated by the quality of urban governance. This is true for all forms and scales of urban settlement, but the challenges of urban governance are underscored with greatest intensity within the largest and most complex urban configurations, which are referred to as city-regions, amongst other names.

In the book I have tried to work iteratively across a broader understanding of urbanisation processes, discursive flows and the travelling practices of government (see chapter one), and the peculiarity of the individual contexts within the BRICS (chapters two to six). In chapter seven I try to address the difficult question of what remains distinctive to the cases, and what can be generalised across them in a gradual process of theory-building.

As the narrative unfolds, I draw on the ideas and proposed methods in this introductory chapter to show that:

- an inductive approach, drawing from contextual meaning, understanding and language, can blend with a careful use of abstracted concepts such as the city-region and city-region governance;
- city-region governance is often an emergent outcome resulting from the accumulation and sedimentation of disparate intentions, actions, practices and chance outcomes, rather than a result of intentional design;
- the best-practice approach fails to acknowledge this emergence and how embedded individual models of city-region governance are in locationally specific historical processes; and
- comparative method, which values difference as much as similarity, enriches an understanding of each individual context and may, over time, produce theory (or propositions) with more general application.

Finally, the book fills in some of the empirical gaps in the understanding of city-regions in parts of the world that are still under-researched relative to their urban weight and which, as interstitial spaces in a global sense, relate diversely to other places.

Notes

1   For a discussion on the value of using 'talking pigs' as case studies, see Kathleen Eisenhardt et al. (2016).

2   Yimin Zhao (2020) explored the rich and contextualised meanings of the Chinese word 结合部 *jiehebu* in relation to the universalised English word 'suburban' in her article '*Jiehebu* or suburb? Towards a translational turn in urban studies'.

3   Examples are cognition and consciousness that are produced through the physical arrangement of things like lobes, cords and neurons.

4   The in-between forms include inter-municipal consortia, special servicing districts, collaborative councils of municipalities and third-party coordinating bodies such as regional economic agencies.

5   This process was supported by real dialogue that happened over time within an informal network of researchers across cities in the BRICS countries, called the BRICS + City Lab.

6   Sergio Montero and Gianpaolo Baiocchi (2021) go further in arguing that case study selection could happen posteriori.

7   One commonality across BRICS is that each country has experienced dramatic shifts ('critical junctures') in the recent past – the return to democracy in Brazil after military rule; the collapse of state socialism in Russia; far-reaching economic liberalisation in India; the ending of Maoist rule in China; and the ending of apartheid in South Africa. A BRICS study thus allows us to investigate both incremental and rapid processes of institutional change.

1 The global view: The city-region as material form, discourse and governmental practice

Introduction

This chapter explores the 'inter-contextual patterns' within which the case studies are embedded (Brenner and Schmid 2015, 164). It deploys both a soft realism and the idea of co-evolutionary adaptation.

For the soft realist, the discursive can never capture the totality of what is there, but it does not float free of reality because of the ongoing iterative process of observation, imagination, description and redescription. In the co-evolutionary process, actors continually interact with a changing material world and are learning, responding and adapting (Van Assche et al. 2021). Mutual adaptation processes are invariably partial and imperfect, but over the longer term, it is possible to discern the relationships.

To André Sorensen (2020, 50), for example, governance is a necessary and emergent response to the materiality of the urban:

> The growth of cities demands the establishment of institutions of city governance, city planning, infrastructure provision, land development control, public health, education, transport, waste management, and many, many others, as contemporary cities cannot exist without such institutions and the systems they support. Urbanization processes in this way force an extraordinary series of contingent institutional choices about everything from municipal boundaries to legal powers, taxation capacity, local services, property regulation regimes, infrastructure systems, and other.

Simin Davoudi and Elizabeth Brooks (2021, 56) reveal the emergent nature of discursive practices, showing how they are normalised as they 'gain traction through deliberation, repetition, and circulation'. For Willem Salet et al. (2015), these discursive practices interpret material change and inform governmental responses.

In this chapter, I provide a global scan, structured historically, of the city-region's interacting material, discursive and governmental dimensions. It shows how these dimensions are mutually constituted, with considerable variation across time and space.

Getting physical

While cities have an ancient lineage, complex, sprawling agglomerations are historically recent. In pre-industrial times, the physical spread of cities was restricted by transport technologies and defence requirements. There were, however, urban networks structured along trade routes and some of these, such as the Hanseatic League in northern Europe and the silk routes across Asia, had incipient forms of networked urban governance (Dash 2010; Fink 2012).

The sprawl started in Great Britain during the First Industrial Revolution and extended into continental Europe. Initially, there was a form of proto-industrialisation, with cottage industries producing an intricate spatial patterning of village growth and interconnection. From the Second Industrial Revolution in around the late eighteenth century, large factories replaced local artisans, and industrial towns and cities were superimposed over the earlier landscape. In Great Britain, Lancashire (Liverpool-Manchester) was the classic industrial landscape, with other agglomerations emerging in the West Midlands, Yorkshire and Clydeside (Antunes 2003). London took a different trajectory, emerging as the world's premier urban hub by the nineteenth century – a result of its primacy within the expanding British Empire.

These changes spread to continental Europe in the nineteenth century, facilitated by changes in transport technology. The Ruhr Valley in Germany developed as a complex agglomeration of mining and industrial settlements without a dominating city, and there were similar developments along the Meuse Valley in Belgium and in the north of France (Jackson 1977). In the Netherlands, the *Randstad* – the ring of cities including Amsterdam, Rotterdam, The Hague and Utrecht – evolved as the rail network expanded, while Greater Paris retained its monocentric focus as it extended outwards along rail routes (Gallois 1923; Kasraian et al. 2016).

The Po Valley in North Italy had a different history, with villages coalescing over time as agriculture mixed with industry. Eventually, a polynucleated urban region developed with hubs including Milan, Turin, Verona and Venice (Del Fabbro 2020). Elsewhere along the Mediterranean, industrialisation was slower, and cities remained compact until the second half of the twentieth century when weak planning controls and irregular development led to urban areas spreading out along the coastline (Salvati et al. 2013). Combined, a broadly semi-circular, mass-scale agglomeration of interconnected city-regions formed in western Europe, which was given the curious name, the 'Blue Banana' (Faludi 2015, 26). Industrialisation came later in Eastern Europe, but state-led growth in the Soviet Union from the 1930s produced large agglomerations, including Greater Moscow and Saint Petersburg. However, until the end of the Soviet era, these were compact urban areas; their rapid spatial expansion happened under post-Soviet liberalisation (United Nations 2018).

Urban expansion in the United States of America (USA) took off in the mid-nineteenth century, facilitated by industrialisation, the railway network and a steady flow of immigrants. New York emerged as the organising core of the USA, eclipsing London by the 1920s as the world's largest urban agglomeration. Rapid urban growth along the East Coast of the USA, from Boston, through New York, to Washington D.C., created a mega agglomeration of a similar scale to the urban network in western Europe (Gottman 1961; Dickinson 1964).

By the 1950s, the USA was 64 per cent urbanised, with major urban agglomerations having also developed around the Great Lakes (centred on Chicago) and southern California (Los Angeles-Long Beach-Santa Ana). Through the second part of the twentieth century, overall urban growth slowed, but there was continued dynamism in the Sun Belt; agglomerations evolving in the American south included Dallas-Fort Worth and Miami-Atlanta (United Nations 2018). In Canada, Greater Toronto emerged as the most prominent agglomeration, connecting to the Great Lakes in the USA (Hagler 2009). Compared with Europe, these North American agglomerations are low density and spatially extensive.

Japan was the next site of major growth, with the rise of Tokyo-Osaka as Asia's first major urban agglomeration (United Nations 2018). Although a large city for centuries, Tokyo experienced a massive growth spurt after World War II, doubling in size in only two decades and emerging as a global command-and-control centre. A greater urban region evolved, extending westwards from Tokyo to Kobe, producing the world's third mega agglomeration after western Europe and the north-east coast of the USA. However, growth slowed considerably by the 1980s as urban levels reached over 75 per cent. Currently, Japan's level of urbanisation was projected to be 92 per cent in 2021, leaving little further opportunity for urbanisation (United Nations 2018).

The emergence of China as East Asia's next major hub of agglomeration happened decades later. China was still only 19 per cent urbanised in 1980 but increased rapidly to 64 per cent in 2020. The catalyst for rapid urbanisation was economic reform in the post-Maoist era associated with rapid export-led industrialisation. However, the physical expansion of city-regions was also driven by the commodification of land and housing, large-scale investment in infrastructure, changing lifestyle preferences and the creation of new satellite cities and industrial zones. Shanghai was already a large city in 1980, but its subsequent explosive growth happened within a tightly clustered agglomeration of cities, producing a mega city-region with a population approaching 200 million people. A new mega city-region evolved in the south of China, catalysed by massive industrial growth and connecting cities including Guangzhou, Shenzhen and Hong Kong, while Beijing-Tianjin emerged as the core of the third mega city-region. Initially, the growth was along the eastern seaboard, but secondary agglomerations emerged in the interior around cities including Wuhan, Chengdu and Chongqing, although without the same spatial complexity (United Nations 2018).

After Japan, the next wave of development was in Latin America. In 1950, the only globally significant city in Latin America was Buenos Aires, with Argentina already highly urbanised. However, Latin America was in the process of a dramatic shift from an agrarian base to a manufacturing economy, using a model of import-substituting industrialisation. The mass movement of rural migrants into cities, providing labour for the new economy, led to a 'historically unprecedented' increase in urbanisation levels (Leaf 2020, 34). São Paulo and Mexico City emerged as mega agglomerations of world scale, followed by Rio de Janeiro, Lima and Bogotá. Urban growth rates reduced from the 1970s, and with Latin America now the most urbanised continent in the world, additional urbanisation is likely to be limited. However, urban form will continue to change. From the 1980s, for example, the spatial structure of city-regions became more complex as industry responded to the economic crisis by relocating to the urban edge.

Africa's rapid urban growth took off in the post-colonial era. By the 1950s, the only large urban agglomerations were Cairo and Greater Johannesburg (or the Witwatersrand), which had developed from the late nineteenth century as a network of mining settlements. From the 1950s, many African cities grew rapidly as colonial-era controls on population movement were removed, and rural economies suffered growing levels of stress. However, unlike in Latin America, this growth was not driven by industrialisation, with most urban dwellers surviving on a low wage and mainly in the informal service sector.

At least three mega agglomerations have emerged in Africa, with the Gauteng City-Region (GCR) in South Africa (a wider region than the Witwatersrand) as a possible fourth. Cairo remains the largest, followed by Lagos and Kinshasa. There are, however, emerging mega-sized city-regions, including Luanda in Angola and Dar es Salaam in Tanzania, with others potentially following. In West Africa, a mass-scale urban corridor with interconnected city-regions is developing along the coastline from Lagos to Abidjan (Choplin and Hertzog 2020). Unlike Latin America, Africa's level of urbanisation is still relatively low at 43.5 per cent (having increased from 14 per cent in 1950), and there is still considerable opportunity for further urbanisation, especially in East Africa and West Africa (United Nations 2018). The expansion of urban regions in Africa is taking hybridised forms, with both formal investment in large-scale infrastructure and new city development, and incremental self-build – often in areas under traditional authority.

South and South-East Asia also had very low levels of urbanisation at the end of the colonial era (approximate 15 per cent). Urbanisation levels have increased to around 37 per cent for South Asia and 50 per cent for South-East Asia, which is still low in global terms. However, recent literature suggests that these statistics must be viewed cautiously, as industrialisation and urbanisation in the region has a close relationship with the agrarian economy, with no clear distinction between rural and urban (Ghosh and Meer 2021). Glover (2021, 35) writes of 'urbanisation in the village', referring to in-situ urbanisation, with the emergence of small-scale, agrarian-related industry.

Nonetheless, mega-sized agglomerations have emerged in South Asia. In 1950, Calcutta (now Kolkata) were already large cities in global terms, but other large agglomerations have emerged, including Delhi, Dhaka, Karachi, Lahore, Hyderabad and Chennai. The urban expansion is hybrid, with a gradually industrialising country-side and modern investments in new satellite cities, large transport infrastructures and satellite industrial zones. The world's most populous urban corridor has developed along the Ganges and Indus river valleys, linking Bangladesh, India and Pakistan. In South-East Asia, mega-sized agglomerations have emerged around Jakarta-Bandung in Indonesia and Manila in the Philippines, but Bangkok, Kuala Lumpur and Ho Chi Minh City are also at the core of large city-regions.

What drives the emergence and growth of these city-regions and wider configurations? There are contextually specific answers, but the catalysing force in all cases is agglomeration economies. In Europe and North America, and in East Asia and Latin America, industrialisation induced large-scale urbanisation concentrated around the major manufacturing hubs. For South Asia, South-East Asia and Africa, however, industrialisation was closely linked to agrarian transformation, or urbanisation happened without industrialisation, with service-related activities providing the economic base.

While economic agglomeration is necessary for the emergence of a city-region, there are many physical forms it can take. Transportation networks and liberal land regimes are catalysts for spatial stretching. Alasdair Rae and Garrett Nelson (2020, 188) write, for example, of 'everyday mobility – commuting patterns – as the empirical foundation on which to base a megaregional geography of the United States'. Other writers relate recent scholarship on urban de-densification and urban sprawl to debates on the making of complex urban agglomerations, or city-regions (Hwang and Woo 2020; Mabin 2021).

Much of the literature on city-region formation orients to a focus on either the economic or the political logics of city-region formation. Allen Scott (2001, 2019) prioritises the economic underpinnings, arguing that the growth sectors of the new economy, including digital, knowledge-based and cultural-cognitive industries, are shaping globally competitive city-regions. Writing from a vantage point in the USA, Scott focuses largely on the role of private actors and multi-actor growth coalitions.

Andrew Jonas and Kevin Ward (2007, 173), on the other hand, write that 'city-regions ought to be conceptualized as contingent products of practical acts of political construction'. While they emphasise the politics at play (the agendas) in the discursive and governmental construction of the city-region, Gavin Shatkin (2020) draws on case studies in South-East Asia to highlight the role of the state, across levels, in producing the urban infrastructures – new container ports and airports, highway expansion, high-speed rail, new city development and special industrial zones – that are stretching and complexifying the city-region.

Recent literature with case studies from Africa offers a further perspective, point-ing to the self-built city-region. Armelle Choplin and Alice Hertzog (2020), for exam-ple, write of the sprawling urban corridor along the West African coast. Here there are glitzy projects of global capitalism synergising with the interests of the political-commercial elites of West Africa. But, between these modern hubs is the incrementally built, makeshift city 'produced by urban dwellers pouring bag after bag of cement into their production sites' (Choplin and Hertzog 2020, 218). For Choplin and Hertzog (2020, 208), 'the urban space is a place of circulation – of commodities, goods and people – rather than a space of production'. They write that 'the megaregion in West Africa invites us to rethink contemporary urban forms and how they are currently unfolding' (Choplin and Hertzog 2020, 218).

The literature on the production of city-regions is diverse, geographically informed, and reminiscent of the classical parable of the blind men and an elephant. Collectively it offers an abundant perspective on the materiality of the historical and contem-porary city-region. The city-region has a compelling physical presence in the urban landscape, and this is not incidental to the rise of the city-region as a concept and a practice.

What the city-region will be in the future is a matter of informed speculation. The literature, however, touches only briefly on the future of city-regions. Sorensen and Labbé (2020, 3) provocatively suggest that the mega city-regions that have developed in the recent past are part of the 'endgame of urbanization'. With levels of urbanisation rising in many global regions to near saturation level and overall population growth rates declining, city-region growth is tapering off. However, there are still global regions, notably South Asia and Africa, where there are opportunities for considera-ble growth over the next three to five decades at least, while city-region growth over the past century or so across the world will leave a complicated legacy for centuries to come. Key concerns are the resource constraints and the effects of climate changes on urban agglomerations, including on Africa's west coast where rising sea levels are threatening major cities.

Struggling for words

The scale and speed of urban growth and change has been disorienting, and scholars have battled to find adequate vocabularies to describe its outcomes. Neil Brenner and Christian Schmid (2015, 155) ask, 'Through what categories, methods and cartographies should urban life be understood?' – a question that scholars have grappled with for over a century.

In the early twentieth century, the Scottish biologist Patrick Geddes searched for ways to represent the expansion of Greater London and reached out to a set of vivid metaphors:

> Greater London – with its vast population streaming out in all directions – east, west, north, and south – flooding all the levels, flowing up the main Thames Valley, and all the minor ones, filling them up, crowded and dark, and leaving only the intervening patches of high ground pale . . . This octopus of London, polypus rather, is something curious exceedingly, a vast irregular growth without previous parallel in the world of life. Perhaps likest to the spreadings of a great coral reef. (Geddes 1915, 26)

But if London was a great octopus, what were the emerging agglomerations of industrial England where towns and cities were coalescing into an apparent amorphous urban mass? Geddes (1915, 34) mulled over the matter, and then offered a linguistic invention linking the terms 'con' (together), 'urbs' (city) and 'ation' (a process): 'Some name, then, for these city-regions, these town aggregates, is wanted. Constellations, we cannot call them; conglomerations is, alas! nearer the mark at present but it may sound unappreciative; what of "Conurbations?"'

Charles Fawcett (1922, 111) translated Geddes' flair into a down-to-earth definition, writing that a conurbation emerged as 'a practical coalescence into one continuous urban area [although] each such conurbation still has within it many nuclei of denser town growth'. The conurbation was mainstreamed in 1951 when it was incorporated into the 1951 British census as a category (Freeman 1959).

Geddes' intellectual successor, Lewis Mumford, did not like the term but thought it appropriate for the object it referred to: 'the coalescing of urban communities into one vast man-hive, a tendency to which Patrick Geddes gave the deservedly ugly name of conurbation, cannot be treated as a permanent urban phenomenon' (Mumford 1946, 161).

Writing in the 1940s, Mumford was certain that mechanisation and the urban expansion it had produced had reached their limits and that a period of demographic, economic and territorial stability lay ahead (Mumford 1946). He had, however, confused his normative dislike of the conurbation with analysis and so failed to anticipate the rapid post-war expansion (Mumford 1946). Urban areas continued to expand and the term 'conurbation' spread through the British Commonwealth, where it was used to describe agglomerations, including the mining belt along the Witwatersrand in South Africa (Cole 1957), Greater Calcutta in India (Dutt and Chakraborty 1963) and Greater Toronto in Canada (Spelt 1963).

However, there was another term evolving. 'Metropolis' had its etymology in ancient Greece, meaning 'mother city' (Rodger 2012, 85). In the nineteenth century, London was referred to as 'the metropolis of the British Empire' (Elmes 1828, 1) and the 'great metropolis' (Grant 1837, 1). In the second half of the century, New York was also referred to as the 'great metropolis' (Browne 1869), and then as 'the metropolis of the Western hemisphere' (Youngman 1939, 19). Bombay was later described as the 'metropolis of the East' (Smith 1931).

The US census, searching for a way to describe populations spread across local jurisdictions, adopted the term 'metropolitan district' in 1910 to refer to the sphere of influence around a metropolis (Lepawsky 1936, 417). But it gave a quite mechanical definition for the district, referring to minimum population size and density (Lepawsky 1936; Blumenfeld 1965).[1] The International Statistical Institute in Europe offered a more dynamic definition, describing a metropolitan district as a place of daily activity that could be measured by the reach of daily intra-urban movement, and recognised some of Europe's major metropolitan areas, including London County, Gross Berlin and Le Plus Grand Paris (Lepawsky 1936).

The term 'urban agglomeration', used frequently in the English language from the 1930s, originated from the French *agglomeration urbaine* (International Statistical Institute 1911; Meuriot 1914, 418). The term is still widely used, including within national census agencies (for example, India). It has, however, meshed with the idea of agglomeration in economic sciences and was taken up in the Soviet Union from the 1950s, for example, to refer to the urban concentrations produced through industrial clustering (see chapter three).

The term 'city-region' was initially used rather generically. Geddes (1915, 26) had asked, for example, 'What shall we call a city region?' As the regionalist movement gained momentum in the 1930s, there was reference to city-regions, but this was to distinguish urban-centred regions from regions defined in terms of natural patterning, such as river basins (as in the Tennessee Valley in the USA, for example). There was resistance to the idea of the city-region, with the influential Natural Resources Committee in the USA insisting in 1935 that regions should be defined in terms of natural resources or regional interests rather than in relation to urban spread (Friedmann 1956). This changed in the 1940s, however. Sociologist Louis Wirth, for example, argued that metropolitan areas should be constituted as planning regions (Friedmann 1956), while Robert Dickinson wrote a book on city-regions, drawing on the work of regionalists such as Geddes (Dickinson 1947). In the 1950s, John Friedmann (1956, 13) argued for city-regions as the territorial basis for planning, pointing out that 'city regions are the nerve centers of economic life in an area. They are the seats of economic power where most of the population is concentrated, where most of the vital decisions affecting larger areas are made, and where the financial means are present for carrying these decisions into action. Any planning which ignores this primary fact about the spatial structure of an economy must be judged unrealistic'.

The term 'city-region' was, in fact, not used widely in the 1960s, becoming more popular in usage from the 1970s onwards, with the rise of a discourse around economic agglomeration.

The next set of linguistic innovations related to the emergence of urban landscapes of a mega size. In 1957, Jean Gottman produced a short paper, expanded into a book in 1961, which used the classical Greek term *megalopolis* to describe the massive urban agglomeration that had evolved along the eastern seaboard of the USA.[2] The megalopolis was a mega conurbation of multiple interlinked towns and cities with overlapping hinterlands and was later used to describe other urban formations in the USA, such as the Great Lakes Crescent (Lang and Knox 2009).

'Megalopolis' was soon deployed to refer to the massive urban agglomeration that had emerged along the south-east coast of Japan (Tokyo-Osaka-Nagoya-Kobe-Yokohama). The term captured the attention of urban sociologist Isomura Eiichi, and of Japan's celebrity planner Kenzo Tange, who translated it as *megaroporisu* in the 1961 Tokyo Master Plan (Ito and Nagashima 1980). However, in the subsequent conceptual evolution, *megaroporisu* was used together with earlier Japanese terms such as *obijotoshi* (belt-like city) and *kyotai-toshi* (huge belt city), with the written form of the Tokaido Megaroporisu including the characters for 'east', 'sea' and 'belt' (or 'road'). The ideas have further hybridised into the concept of the *Taiheiyō beruto* (太平洋ベル), or Pacific belt, referring to a string of cities stretching for nearly 1 200 kilometres along the southern coast following the spine of Japan's high-speed rail network (Urushima 2015).

The Europeans were cautious in applying the term 'megalopolis' to their mega-urban network, although the Greek planner Constantinos Doxiadis referred to the megalopolis as a stage in the transition to the ecumenopolis, or universal city, a quirky forerunner to contemporary notions of planetary urbanisation (Doxiadis 1962, 1975). Jacques Robert (1976, 331) eventually wrote of 'megalopolis formation in north-west Europe' connecting multiple conurbations, and Gottman (1981, 85) wrote of 'managing the megalopolis in Europe'. Klaus Kunzmann (1996, 143) was later to refer to a 'Euro-megalopolis'.

In the 1960s, the three megalopolises were in the USA, Japan and western Europe, but the world was on the cusp of a dramatic wave of urbanisation crossing the global South, which was to produce new mega formations. Some writers applied the term 'megalopolis' to the new formations (for example, Li and Phelps 2018), but others hyperbolised and hybridised other terms, with reference, for example, to 'mega-city regions' (Xu and Yeh 2011, 17; Yeh et al. 2015, 2458), 'polycentric mega-city regions'

(Zhao et al. 2017, 147), 'emerging mega conurbations' (Friedmann and Sorensen 2019, 1), 'hyper-complex urban regions' (Friedmann 2020, 21) and 'super mega-city regions' (Yeh and Chen 2020, 636). This language was an application of terms in the Anglo literature of the global North. However, less attention has been paid to the use of terms in the vernacular, as indicated in relation to Japan, and as used in China (for example, *chengshiqun,* roughly translatable as city cluster) (see chapter five).

While scholars were battling to find the terminology to capture the scale and intensity of the new waves, another thread of description was evolving. The 'world city' or 'global city' referred to a handful of places – New York, London and Tokyo most commonly – that played command-and-control functions in the global economy (for example, Hall 1966; Friedmann and Wolff 1982; Sassen 1991). These concepts came together with the idea of the city-region in 1999 when Allen Scott of the School of Public Policy and Social Research at the University of California, Los Angeles, organised a conference on global city-regions. The key papers at the conference were reproduced in the 2001 edited volume *Global City-Regions: Trends, Theory, Policy* (Scott 2001).

Scott was responding in part to arguments that information technology was undoing spatial agglomeration, with location no longer mattering. He argued that 'rather than being dissolved away as social and geographic objects by processes of globalization, city-regions are becoming increasingly central to modern life' (Scott 2001, 11). In the edited volume, Saskia Sassen (2001, 79) wrote that global city-regions have become 'the core elements of the organizational structure of the global economy'. Scott and colleagues explained the rise of the city-region in terms of the competitive logic of global capitalism, and this, as previously indicated, provoked a vigorous debate.

At around the same time, Neil Brenner published his influential piece 'Globalisation as Reterritorialisation'. Like Scott, he rejected the idea of *de*spatialisation, arguing instead that there was a *re*territorialisation of social and economic organisation. Drawing on European experience, he identified a diffusion of power from national governments upwards to the European Union and downwards to city-regions. However, unlike Scott, he accepted that these processes were contested, incremental and indeterminate, and were not fixed by an economic logic (Brenner 1999).

This provided the cue for others, with Ward and Jonas (2004, 2134) arguing that contemporary city-regionalism is 'best understood as an ongoing struggle for control of space rather than a new emergent form of capitalist territorial competition and development'. Pauline McGuirk (2007, 184) drew from the experience of Sydney, Australia, to argue that city-regionalism is a 'territorialisation of politics' emerging mainly through contests over the distribution of social products rather than through the functional demands of capitalist production. Jonas and Ward (2007) went on to identify diverse regionalist agendas, apart from competitiveness, which included spatial integration, the redistribution of public benefits and environmental sustainability.

The debate soon heated, but recent contributions suggest a cooling down, with more focus on the empirics of what is really happening. John Harrison (2010, 17, emphasis in the original) called for less haste in reaching conclusions, suggesting that 'the processes by which city-regions are constructed politically are the mediated outcome of trans-regional economic flows *and* political claims to territory', while Jean-Paul Addie and Roger Keil (2015, 407) call for attention to 'real existing regionalism'.

Another controversy was, however, in the wings. In *La Révolution Urbaine* (1970), the French philosopher Henri Lefebvre had written of the 'complete urbanisation of society' (cited in Merrifield 2013, 910). The argument was that, with urban society everywhere, the city as a discrete object has become a 'historical entity' (cited in Merrifield 2013, 910). With delays in translation, Lefebvre's work took time to percolate into Anglo literature.

However, over the past decade or so, the concept of planetary urbanisation, with different shades of interpretation, has burst into the literature (for example, Merrifield 2013; Brenner 2014, 2018; Brenner and Schmid 2013, 2015), with Keil (2017, 2018) exploring the theme of extended urbanisation through the theme of global suburbanism. For these theorists, pervasive urban processes are producing an urban landscape that is dynamic, extensive, multi-scalar and interconnected, and cannot be contained within bounded categories. The main target of critique is the idea of 'the city', which Brenner and Schmid (2015, 152) say 'now appears as no more than a quaint remnant of a widely superseded formation of capitalist spatial development'.

However, Brenner and Schmid (2015) also express discomfort with a concept such as the city-region, which implies a degree of bounding, although at a broader scale. They were nevertheless careful to acknowledge that agglomeration remains *one* of the processes shaping 'the uneven thickening and stretching of an urban fabric' (Brenner and Schmid 2015, 167). As a response to a furious critique of planetary urbanisation, Brenner (2018, 574) reiterates that 'concentrated urbanization (the process of agglomeration and its wide-ranging consequences) remains a constitutive dimension of urbanization'.

Planetary urbanisation does, however, present a challenge to the discursive tradition we have followed above from Patrick Geddes in the early twentieth century, which has focussed mainly on the primary nodes of urban agglomeration. How this tradition may reconcile with a new perspective that recognises the more extensive and diffused patterning of urbanisation remains to be seen. There are clear lines of tension in the current literature but also indications of an emergent synthesis. John Harrison and Jesse Heley (2015, 1116) write, for example, 'of a multifunctioning globalising countryside' and emphasise the increasing economic significance of the 'interstitial spaces' between city-regions.

There are also practical tensions to resolve. The material realities of more diffuse, extensive and variegated patterns of urbanisation are now reflecting within a scholarly discourse through the idea of planetary urbanisation, but it is not yet clear what this implies for governance. Whereas the language of planetary urbanisation avoids bounded categories, governance has practical requirements for bounding (for example, for the purposes of statistics, planning, revenue-raising, resource allocation, infrastructure networks, service catchments and land management).

Struggling for practice

In the co-evolutionary perspective, governance actors grapple daily with the complexities, fragmentation, fluidity, demands and unruliness of large urban agglomerations (see, for example, Healey 2005; Friedmann 2020; Sorensen and Labbé 2020). Over time, repetitive practices emerge that may institutionalise into a better response to the challenges than previously, although continual change will always require further adaptations.

This perspective challenges the idea of large urban agglomerations descending into ungovernability. For Patrick Le Galès and Tommaso Vitale (2013), governance of large city-regions more or less happens. This is because, for a governing elite, the political consequence of a breakdown of collective service would be devastating, and so practical solutions to governance, even if makeshift, must be found.

The challenge is producing the will, capacities and mechanisms for collective action across multi-jurisdictional city-regions (Salet et al. 2003; Healey 2009). Evidence suggests that some form of city-region governance emerges in response to these challenges, although it may lag behind material reality and be incomplete or even misplaced (Hodson et al. 2020; Granqvist et al. 2021).

What emerges is highly variable. At the one extreme are new, formally constructed governance arrangements such as a metropolitan- or city-region authority that either replaces or is hierarchically placed over local government. This is the institutional fix (Healey 2009). At the other extreme are the informal networks of collaboration, but there are multiple arrangements and processes in-between, including voluntary associations of local authorities, joint ventures, collaborative councils, special-purpose districts, ad hoc committees, growth coalitions, jointly produced plans, and data-sharing and other knowledge infrastructures. There is also a mix of actors involved in these structures. There is variable participation of local, other subnational and national governments but also, in places, the involvement of private business and civil society.

The form of governance, including the mix of participation, is shaped by context. The following sections provide a brief scan of context and variation across global regions, beginning with the regions where rapid urban expansion first began and ending with the regions where the locus of dynamism now rests. One of the difficulties in organising the overview is the uneven geography of knowledge on metropolitan- and city-region governance. However, the balance is shifting, with a vibrant literature emerging on parts of East Asia, for example, and important new work on Latin America.

Europe

The richness of Europe for this study rests in both the extensive existing literature and the cultural and governmental diversity across the continent, which has informed a tradition of comparative study (Salet et al. 2003; Tavares and Feiock 2018).

One of the dimensions of difference is the form of local government. Great Britain, for example, has a quite archaic form of local government, with counties (or shires) that were formed around tribal groupings a thousand years or so ago bearing little relationship to settlement patterns that emerged with industrialisation (Dickinson 1964), although there has been partial reform in recent decades. In central Europe, Napoleonic-era reforms rationalised local government but produced hierarchical government structures. By contrast, in Scandinavia, there is a tradition of decentralised local governance despite a post-war legacy of social democracy, which gave the national state a role in ensuring equitable socio-spatial arrangements. There are often strong localist cultures embedded in tight local ties in the Mediterranean regions, while Eastern Europe bears the legacy of state socialism.

For Antonio Tavares and Richard Feiock (2018), these differences are central to the possibilities for different forms of metropolitan governance, explaining the heterogeneity across the continent. Where governmental arrangements are more legalistic and hierarchical, formal metropolitan governance structures are more likely to develop. However, where there is a long tradition of decentralised government, voluntary mechanisms generally work best, although these may institutionalise over time into formal structures. Where there are strong local ties, broader territorial arrangements are non-existent or weak, and where there is a recent history of authoritarian governance, local actors may zealously protect their autonomy (Tavares and Feiock 2018).

Within Europe, national-level reforms in Great Britain, France and Italy have produced a new wave of institutional change, while in federal Germany, where city-region governance is regulated by the *Länder* (federated states), there is more intranational variation. The European Union, unique globally as a strong supranational authority, incentivises metropolitan governance through mechanisms such as the integrated territorial investments funding facility, introduced in 2014 (Lackowska and Norris 2017). Unusually, this also supports metropolitan- and city-region governance across national boundaries, including, for example, the Greater Region (Luxembourg, Saarbrucken, Metz, Trier), the Vienna-Bratislava Metropolitan Region and the Øresund Metropolitan Region (Copenhagen, Malmö) (Van Hamme et al. 2021; Nelles and Durand 2014).

Beyond the formal structures of metropolitan governance in Europe, there are many soft spaces that rely on norms of trust, reciprocity and informal interactions (Jacuniak-Suda et al. 2015; Tavares and Feiock 2018). The European literature draws attention to the civic basis for metropolitan governance, including the possibilities for creating joint learning processes between government, civil society and the market, institutionalising democracy at the metropolitan level and nurturing a sense of citizenship at this level (Lidström and Schaap 2018).

Historically, the first forms of metropolitan governance may have emerged for Greater London. Initially, the coordination across parish and county governments was sector-specific, as in the London Police Board established in 1829, but in 1889 these were consolidated in the London County Council (Dickinson 1964). However, even as the county council was established, London continued to grow, making its boundaries obsolete. In other city-regions such as Lancashire, it was even more difficult to achieve consolidated governance, as there was no equivalent to London's county council.

By the early twentieth century, reformers were calling for a more rational organisation of local government in England, following the settlement patterns produced by industrialisation, but the historically entrenched interests of the counties and the large landowning class meant that little progress was made (Gomme 1914). By the mid-twentieth century, practical considerations prompted the national government to reorganise services and utilities, such as electricity boards, gas supply, postal services and hospital boards, regionally. In 1951, the census authority defined conurbations as 'aggregates of local authority areas' and defined six of these across England and Wales. However, local government was unreformed (Dickinson 1964).

Various commissions were established to investigate the problem through the 1940s and 50s until, in 1961, a royal commission proposed that the old London County Council be replaced with a Greater London Council and that the number of boroughs within the region be reduced from 94 to 32. The proposals were implemented in 1965, and the jurisdiction of the Greater London Council broadly matched the extent of contiguous urban development at the time (Goldsmith 2004).

Again, other metropolitan areas proved more complicated. In Lancashire, for example, there was a messy agglomeration of at least 76 local authorities with essential coordination happening through ad hoc structures only. In the 1970s, however, metropolitan structures were set up for Manchester, Newcastle and Leeds, but the timing was poor as sentiment was shifting away from big government, and there were bitter struggles between the mainly Labour-dominated metropolitan authorities and the old county governments controlled by the Conservative Party establishment. Margaret Thatcher abolished the metropolitan structures for Greater London and the other areas in 1986, with little opposition as they had failed to establish much popular legitimacy (Goldsmith 2004).

New Labour pursued a regionalist position after being elected to power in 1997, establishing the Greater London Authority in 2000, and dividing England into eight regions, each of which had a regional assembly advised by a regional development agency. However, while the Greater London Authority and its mayor were directly elected, the regional assemblies were indirectly elected through constituent local authorities. New Labour eventually dissolved the regional assemblies when it failed to achieve direct elections, but towards the end of its term, it did introduce combined authorities for metropolitan areas, which enabled local authorities to combine resources and provide joint services. However, the Greater London Authority achieved a surprising level of popular legitimacy with widespread support for its initiatives, including congestion charges and community policing (Harrison 2017; Hodson et al. 2020).

In June 2010, the Conservative–Liberal Democrats coalition government came to power with a strong localist agenda and a determination to dismantle New Labour's regionalism. However, its goal to significantly devolve powers to the local level could not be achieved in the context of weak and fragmented local governance. Thus, ironically, the devolution agenda was associated with the return of a city-region agenda. The coalition retained the combined authority, introducing the 'city deal' as a devolution mechanism. A combined authority could negotiate a city deal with the national government, which would include devolution. The Greater Manchester Combined Authority led the way with a city deal in 2014, followed by Liverpool City-Region, West Midlands (Greater Birmingham) and North of Tyne (Greater Newcastle) (Hodson et al. 2020).

The extensive literature on Great Britain's experience points to the highly politicised nature of city-regionalism, the dominance of national government in orchestrating the city-region agenda, the shift from redistribution to economic competitiveness as the driving motivation and the ongoing, experimental nature of the process, with a complex layering and relayering of governance arrangements (see, for example, Harrison and Heley 2015; Beel et al. 2018; Harrison 2017; Hodson et al. 2020). Although there is a sharp critique of elements of the city-region agenda, especially the apparent absence of a discourse on redistributive justice, there is acknowledgement that the reforms open the way for regional experimentation with inclusive forms of city-regionalism (Harrison 2017; Beel et al. 2018).

Local government in France has been historically weak and fragmented, within a hierarchical system in which powers are concentrated in national government, although there were degrees of decentralisation from the 1980s. However, the governance requirement has encouraged local authorities – the *departements* and *communes* – to enter various forms of inter-municipal collaboration. Voluntary associations called *communautés urbaines* were formed by the 1960s and, in 1999, the Chevènement Act enabled the establishment of *établissements public de coopération intercommunale* – EPCI (public intercommunal cooperation institutions) – to provide services on behalf of municipal groupings (Zimmermann and Feiertag 2018; Demazière and Sykes 2021). The informal norms of cooperation that have developed over decades now underpin these more formal cooperation mechanisms (Tavares and Feiock 2018).

In 2010, the Sarkozy administration made inter-municipal collaboration compulsory by creating the EPCI. It also established the *métropole* as a particular form of EPCI for regions with more than 500 000 people. In 2014, the national government responded to slow progress by designating eight *métropoles* for the major urban regions. Each *métropole* has an assembly comprising representatives of the constituent local government, and the mayor of the largest municipality is the mayor of the *métropole*. By law, a *métropole* may perform public functions, and municipalities may voluntarily cede functions to the structure (Zimmermann and Feiertag 2018; Demazière and Sykes 2021). The literature points to uneven success and to challenges such as local resistance to transferring powers to the *métropoles*, but also to instances such as the Grand Lyon *Métropole*, where the new arrangements are innovative and have been carefully negotiated to ensure legitimacy (Zimmermann and Feiertag 2018; Demazière and Sykes 2021).

Greater Paris has a distinctiveness because of its size and complexity, and coordination mechanisms have evolved. There is now a layering of metropolitan and city-region scale governance arrangements including the *Arrondissements of Paris* or City of Paris (with around two million people), the *Métropole du Grand Paris* or Greater Paris Metropolis (with seven million), the *Région Île-de-France* (with 12 million) and the *Aire Urbaine de Paris* or Paris Metropolitan Area (with around 15 million), although this last form of territorialisation is for census purposes only (Mabin and Harrison 2022).

Until the 2000s, these structures were dominated by the national government. The City of Paris was governed directly from the centre until 1975, and, while the *District de la Région de Paris* (District of the Paris Region), the forerunner to the *Région Île-de-France*, was created by President de Gaulle in 1959, it was given powers over planning and urban development only in the 2000s. President Nicolas Sarkozy (2007 to 2012) pursued a grand regionalist project for Greater Paris, which included the Grand Paris Act, the construction of the Grand Paris Express and the drive towards the *Métropole du Grand Paris*, which was formed in 2016, bringing together 130 municipalities in a collaborative structure (Mabin 2021). Within the French system, tensions remain, with the persisting reluctance to prioritise territory such as Greater Paris embedded in the constitutional guarantee of equality, playing out against a discourse on urban competitiveness that privileges the leading urban centres (Newman and Thornley 2013).

The Italian national government passed a law enabling voluntary cooperation of municipalities across city-regions in 1990, but take-up was limited. In 2001, the national Constitution was changed to state that the Republic of Italy consisted of the national state, the provinces, municipalities, regions *and metropolitan cities*, but again with limited response. The financial crisis of 2008, however, drew attention to the inefficiencies of fragmented governance, restoring the initiative. Finally, in 2014, the national Parliament passed the Delrio law to create *città metropolitana* (or metropolitan cities), each of which was to have a metropolitan mayor (the mayor of the core municipality), a metropolitan assembly (indirectly elected with councillors drawn from the respective municipalities) and a metropolitical conference (consisting of all mayors of the municipalities). The implementation of the law is complicated by resistance from existing structures such as the provinces but, as in the case of Great Britain and France, the academic response both acknowledges the limitations of the reform and indicates the space it opens for regional experimentation and innovation (Zimmermann and Feiertag 2018).

Germany is a federation, with city-region governance a matter for the 16 *Länder* (federated states) to decide on. There is an early history, with the formation of the Ruhr Regional Planning Federation during the time of the Weimar Republic in the 1920s (Schmidt 1928), but commitment to metropolitan governance has vacillated over the decades, although with a current revival.

There are well-established metropolitan structures in the Frankfurt Rhein-Main, Stuttgart and Hanover regions, but more partial structures, or no structure, in other regions. In all cases, there are complex relationships between the *Länder* and the metropolitan authorities, with the *Länder* often simultaneously supporting the establishment of metropolitan structures and resisting their strengthening as they are potentially competing structures (Zimmerman 2017; Gualini and Fricke 2019).

In the case of Frankfurt, there has been a long jostling with the state of Hesse from the first attempts to set up a Frankfurt-dominated metropolitan association in the 1920s. In 1975, the *Umlandverband Frankfurt* (Greater Frankfurt Association) was set up by state law with 43 member municipalities, but its coordination powers were very limited, and in the 2000s the state and city governments set up rival initiatives. In the 2000s, the state of Hesse finally approved the Frankfurt Rhein-Main Metropolitan Region Act, formally constituting the Regional Authority of Frankfurt Rhein-Main as the body responsible for joint planning and service delivery across 75 municipalities (Zimmerman 2017).

In the case of Stuttgart, recent developments towards governance structures across the city-region build on an embedded regional consciousness and a long history of collaborative networks. An informal association of municipalities provided a platform for the institutionalisation of the *Verband Region Stuttgart* (or Regional Association of Stuttgart) in 1994 by the state of Baden-Württemberg. The *Verband Region Stuttgart* has a directly elected regional assembly with functions including regional planning, transport, tourism and economic promotion (Basten 2011). The fortunes of the

Verband Großraum Hannover (Greater Hanover Association) track the ideological positions of the ruling party in the Lower Saxony state governments. The association goes back to 1962, but in the 1980s it was dissolved by a conservative government and replaced by an agency dedicated only to transport management. In 1992 it was re-established, but with limited authority, and in 2001 it was constituted under state law with a directly elected regional assembly and a regional president, with functions including public transport, waste disposal, local social welfare, planning, hospitals, and economic promotion.[3]

Elsewhere in Germany, metropolitan governance is less ambitious. Attempts to merge the city-state of Berlin and the state of Brandenburg in the 1990s failed due to adverse public opinion but a Berlin-Brandenburg Joint Planning Department was set up (Gualini and Fricke 2019). The Hamburg Metropolitan Region cuts across the jurisdictions of three federated states, and this has complicated attempts to set up a formal structure, but it provides a soft space for inter-jurisdictional relationships that build on long traditions of regional collaboration rather than legislative change (Jacuniak-Suda et al. 2015). Munich has no formal regional administration, but there is a strong regional identity and a tradition of inter-municipal collaboration and negotiation (Zimmerman 2017).

Elsewhere in Europe, there are a few other cases of formally constituted metropolitan structures. The Brussels Capital Region forms one of the three states in the Federal State of Belgium and has its own parliament with a high level of autonomy. However, the Brussels Capital Region does not include all settlements on the edge of the metropolitan city, and wider coordination is weak (Van Hamme et al. 2021). Budapest and Prague have elected metropolitan governments that were established with the ending of communist rule, but the autonomy of the Budapest Assembly has been reduced under the current conservative national government. Elsewhere in Eastern Europe, metropolitan governance is weak, although the European Union's funding facility has encouraged some collaborative initiatives (Lackowska and Norris 2017). For a discussion on the Russian Federation, and the challenges of coordination between city and regional (*oblast*) government in the Soviet and post-Soviet eras, see chapter three.

Within the Mediterranean, there are few cases of metropolitan governance. A structure for the Lisbon Metropolitan Area is effectively a branch of the national Ministry of Territorial Cohesion (Van Hamme et al. 2021). Athens forms part of the Attica Region, which has a metropolitan-scale structure established in 1986, but the structure works through four sectoral committees that meet on an ad hoc basis and have no decision-making powers (OECD 2015). An important exception is the *Àrea Metropolitana de Barcelona* (the Barcelona Metropolitan Authority), which has considerable autonomy and a wide range of competencies. It coordinates across 36 municipalities and was constituted by a law of the Catalan Parliament in 2010. In terms of structure, it includes an elected metropolitan council, a governing board and a council of mayors (Van Hamme et al. 2021).

The *Randstad* in the Netherlands has a near iconic status as a city-region, but Bart Lambregts et al. (2008, 46) lament that its governance arrangements are 'far from "best"'. A collaborative body, *Regio Randstad* (Randstad Region), was set up in 1991, and there were proposals to establish a metropolitan authority for the region. However, the initiative lost momentum with national political change and spatial jealousies over privileging of the *Randstad* over other regions. In the absence of a formal governance arrangement, cooperation agreements between local authorities have emerged in parts of the city-region (Lambregts et al. 2008; Spaans and Zonneveld 2016).

In Switzerland, power rests in the cantons, but small metropolitan areas have evolved around Zurich, Basel and Lake Geneva, where inter-municipal associations have emerged, with some, such as the Zurich Metropolitan Conference, formalised through legal agreements (Schenkel and Plüss 2021). In the case of Vienna, there is an emergent cross-border region with Bratislava in Slovakia with embryonic forms of city-region governance, including a joint planning concept, cross-membership on planning boards and the designation of cross-cutting bio corridors (Patti 2017).

Scandinavia has had a very different history and there are far greater levels of embedded trust. Greater Oslo has a collaboration between 78 municipalities, established in 2005, called *Osloregionen* (Oslo Regional Alliance). It has a small secretariat supporting collaborative action and relies mainly on informal networks for success (Tolkki and Haveri 2020). Greater Stockholm has a county council, but it is weak relative to the municipalities, and most of the inter-municipal collaboration happens within voluntary associations of municipalities (such as the Association of Stockholm County Municipalities). The Øresund Region is a cross-border region, linking Copenhagen in Denmark with Malmö in Sweden. Again, there is no formal metropolitan structure but a series of cooperation agreements (Barres 2021). In the Helsinki Metropolitan Area, municipalities came together to prepare the Greater Helsinki Vision 2050. Informal cooperation has, however, been gradually institutionalised with the recent launch of the Helsinki Region Cooperation Assembly, which is currently considering inter-municipal agreements around land use, transport and climate-change response. Helsinki also actively participates in urban networks around the Baltic Sea.

North America

The political culture in the USA has not supported the development of formal structures of metropolitan (or city-region) governance. There is a strong localist orientation and an embedded suspicion of large government, although Katherine Johnson (2006) has argued that the lack of metropolitan authorities also reflects the resistance of state governments to the creation of competing centres of authority. However, the practicalities of governance have produced multiple forms of local collaboration, with varying levels of formality, including special-purpose agencies and districts for the joint delivery of services such as public transport, water, waste disposal, policing and education (Lackowska and Norris 2017). With the focus on a heterogeneous collection of institutional relationships and agencies, none of which replace traditional local government or produce overarching governmental structure, North America offers a model that is now known as the 'new regionalism' (Kübler 2017).

In the early twentieth century, however, the progressive reform movement argued for a large-scale reorganisation of local government in response to new industrial and urban realities. In the 1920s, there was some progress with the establishment of planning commissions for metropolitan areas and the preparation of metropolitan-wide master plans. In 1922, the Regional Plan Association was set up as an independent, not-for-profit agency in New York State, which went on to prepare a succession of plans for the region that have long since guided the actions of local actors (Haveman et al. 2007).

There was less success with institutional change, with strong political resistance locally to any metropolitan authority, or attempts to consolidate local government. There were initiatives to consolidate adjoining city and county governments, and there were a few successes, although always after intense politicking. The City of Pittsburgh and Allegheny County in Pennsylvania state were joined, for example, although in a federal compromise arrangement (Reed 1929). In most cases, however, amalgamation was never achieved. Since 1904, for example, there have been multiple attempts to join St. Louis City and St. Louis County, with the most recent attempt failing in 2019 (Hunn 2019).

The system of special districts emerged by the 1930s to resolve the immediate practical dilemmas in local governance. William Fox and Annette Fox (1940, 176) referred to this approach as 'piecemeal adaptations' and expressed the hope that it would evolve over time into more comprehensive forms of collaboration. Ralph Fuchs (1936) conceded that the institutional rationalism of the progressive movement was not attuned to the embedded impulses of American localism and that a more patient, incremental approach was the most practical way forward.

Further progress was interrupted by World War II, and then by the radical McCarthyism of the 1950s. There was, however, restored interest in metropolitan governance in the 1960s and 70s, but this was reversed under neoliberal governance in the 1980s. In the 1990s, metropolitan regionalism mainly took the form of growth coalitions to achieve metropolitan competitiveness. A range of new instruments was introduced, including joint ventures, public-private partnerships and councils of local governments. They reflect competition and entrepreneurialism within urban governance, but also the common mode of deal-making between the public and private sectors (Newman and Thornley 2013). By the 1990s, the traditional form of the metropolitan city with a core surrounded by suburbs had shifted to more complex, polycentric territorial forms, with much of the new development in suburban and edge-city locations, and so more complex territorial alliances evolved, reflecting the reduced dominance of core cities (Brenner 2002). There were exceptions within these broad patterns; for example, in Minnesota, a twin-city federation evolved across the cities of Minneapolis and St. Paul, while Portland, Oregon, has a metropolitan agency that has focussed on an environmental regionalism, which includes strong compact city approaches (Brenner 2002).

Canada took a partially different path. After World War II, it held a position between the USA's libertarianism and Europe's social democracy, although there was considerable variation across the provinces that were responsible for local government structures. The province of Ontario created a two-tier metropolitan structure for Greater Toronto in 1954, achieving recognition internationally as a successful example of the metropolitan model. In 1971, 13 municipalities in Greater Winnipeg in Manitoba were amalgamated into a single authority and in 1998, after intense debate, a single-tier authority was created for Greater Toronto. It is, however, a modest-sized area in global terms, with around 2.5 million residents and with residents in outer-lying areas resisting incorporation. The wider city-region, colloquially called the Extended Golden Horseshoe, has no formal mechanism of collaboration, leaving the provincial government as the major player in coordinating governmental activity (Collin and Tomàs 2004).

The most recent wave of new metropolitan structures is led by the province of Quebec, resonant with developments in France. From about 2000, the province encouraged the development of *communautés métropolitaines* (metropolitan communities). Local authorities within Greater Ottawa were merged into two *communautés métropolitaines*, creating a twin-structured region. In the case of Montréal, the *Communauté Métropolitaine de Montréal* (Montréal Metropolitan Community) was established across 63 municipalities with joint planning as its main function. In 2006, the municipalities within the core zone were amalgamated to form a single local authority, but there was intense local resistance, and the municipalities were reinstated in 2006. However, the *Agglomération de Montréal* (the Agglomeration of Montréal) was established as an upper-level authority for the region. It consists of the mayors of the 15 constituent municipalities and has powers over transport, housing, public safety and economic development (Tomàs 2012).

British Columbia has developed a different model of metropolitan-scale partnership. Vancouver Regional District was established in 1967, consolidating special-purpose districts into a single agency. However, rather than developing along technocratic lines as most structures of this kind did, it emphasised participatory service delivery and the continued role of local government. Metro Vancouver, as its successor, is a federation of 21 municipalities, rather than a metropolitan authority, focussing on strengthening regional partnerships (Tomàs 2012).

Australasia

In Australia's federation, local government has limited power. It is created and closely supervised by state governments but is also highly fragmented. Like the USA, there was a reform movement in the early twentieth century with unsuccessful attempts to create metropolitan governments in Melbourne and Sydney. In recent decades, Labour governments especially have supported collaborative arrangements such as the regional organisations of councils. However, state governments are reluctant to support potentially competing structures, so metropolitan governance remains nascent (Tomlinson 2017). Beyond government, growth coalitions involving business, civil society and academic institutions have been established in the larger cities, in the form of committees for cities and regions (Waite 2021).

New Zealand has more centralised authority than is the case in federal Australia, and so national government has been able to take the initiative. Committees for cities and regions were also set up in New Zealand's cities, but the national government decided on the institutional fix for the capital, Auckland. In 2010, the eight municipalities in the metropolitan region were amalgamated to form the Auckland Council (McArthur 2017).

East Asia

There is a deficit of study on this global region, even though it has long-established metropolitan authorities. A partial exception may be mainland China (discussed in chapter five), which is attracting a growing literature, but English-language literature on other East Asian countries remains limited. A key question in respect of East Asia is why large-scale metropolitan structures were created and sustained while similar efforts in other global regions have faltered. The extent to which the political culture in the region has underpinned this process is a matter for debate.

In 1943, during the height of World War II, the imperial government of Japan consolidated more than 80 municipalities into the Tokyo metropolitan government (東京都庁, *Tōkyōto-chō*) headed by an appointed governor. This was done to ensure rapid response to wartime demands but also to respond to calls, from the time of the Great Kanto Earthquake in 1923, for unified governance within the 'metropolitan circle' (Zhang and Deng 2017, 36). After the war, the Tokyo metropolitan government was retained, but the structures were democratised with the election of the Tokyo metropolitan government assembly and governor.

Over time, the Tokyo metropolitan government became increasingly centralised and bureaucratised, prompting political demands for more decentralised and responsive governance. Twenty-three wards with elected mayors were established in 1975, with significant decentralisation of functions to the wards in 2001 (Godo 2020). Unlike other prefecture-level structures in Japan, the Tokyo metropolitan government raised most of its revenue internally and so maintained a degree of autonomy from the national government. In recent decades, the Tokyo metropolitan government has resisted national policies detrimental to its interests and has strengthened its position by developing relationships with municipalities within a wider city-region. In the 2000s, the Tokyo metropolitan government mayor promoted the concept of the Tokyo circular megalopolis, convening the Capital City Forum in 2006 with mayors across an extended region, and in 2009, the forum collaborated with national government in the preparation of the Tokyo Capital Region Plan (Newman and Thornley 2013).

In Korea, the Seoul metropolitan government was established in 1949. It is a centralised administration with an elected mayor, although it has 107 divisions for administrative purposes. Over time, the jurisdiction of the metropolitan government has expanded to incorporate new urban growth. With the advantage of coordinated administration, Seoul has implemented large-scale metropolitan projects with a current focus on digital infrastructures (Moon 2017).

In Taiwan, Taipei is a special municipality, equivalent to a province. It was tightly controlled by the central government until 1994 when local elections were introduced, and since then there have been intense contests between central and local governments (Li et al. 2016). The municipality is only part of the wider city-region, and in 2010, New Taipei was formed as a special municipality incorporating a network of smaller cities around the core. New Taipei envelops Taipei but close collaboration has evolved between the two administrations, with the establishment of the Taipei-New Taipei Collaboration and Exchanges Platform in 2015 (Taipei City Government 2022).

Latin America

After Japan, it was Latin America that experienced the next wave of urbanisation. Chapter two gives an account of evolving metropolitan governance in Brazil, a country that has a vibrant urban scholarship and has attracted some attention in international scholarship. However, Latin America is underrepresented in the literature, although an important recent contribution is the edited book *Metropolitan Governance in Latin America* (Trejo Nieto and Amézquita 2021).

Broadly, emerging literature reveals that Latin America has struggled with metropolitan-scale coordination in the face of local interests and sentiments that resist wider governmental formations. A legacy of centralising authoritarian rule across much of Latin America is zealous efforts to protect local autonomy. With few mechanisms to deal with the large-scale effects produced by Latin America's historically unprecedented rates of urbanisation from the 1950s through to about the early 1980s, serious problems emerged in terms of infrastructure, mobility and housing. Although urbanisation rates have slowed significantly, institutional catch-up has been slow, and governance failures remain. There has been a gradual improvement, however, through voluntary local collaborations, sector-based agencies and, most recently, inter-sectoral structures set up in terms of new national laws (Trejo Nieto 2021a).

The Mexico City Metropolitan Area, the largest agglomeration in Latin America after São Paulo, remains an immense challenge. It is notorious for its fragmented and contested governance (Trejo Nieto 2021b). It has around 75 local authorities across two states and the previous Federal District of Mexico, with no formal mechanisms to integrate planning and address critical metropolitan-wide problems such as water, waste, housing and transport. Even the less formal mechanisms such as inter-municipal collaborations are weak and limited. The Metropolitan Development Law of 2021 may support better coordination, but the problem of implementation within the immense political complexities of the region is considerable. Alejandra Trejo Nieto (2021b, 116) simply concludes that 'the metropolitan governance of Mexico City currently offers a bad scenario for development and wellbeing'.

Bogotá in Colombia is another context where metropolitan-scale collaboration has been elusive. This is despite internationally recognised success with innovative governance in the *Distrito Capital*, the core urban area, including the now-famous *Transmilenio* (a bus rapid transport system). Historically, metropolitan growth was managed by annexing peripheral municipalities to the *Distrito Capital*, but this did not keep pace as urban growth accelerated and a multi-jurisdictional metropolitan region emerged. Over time, various attempts to strengthen metropolitan collaborations failed because of resistance from local interest, with current inter-municipal collaborations 'scarce and fragile' (Amézquita 2021, 62). Luis Guzman et al. (2017, 202) write of 'The Bogotá Metropolitan Area that never was'. Metropolitan Lima in Peru also has a highly complex and fragmented system of service provision, with multiple agencies existing for service provision managed across the levels of government (Stiglich and Vásquez 2021).

Elsewhere, there are some signs of progress. In Argentina, the military dictatorship (1975 to 1984) dissolved local government and coordinated across Greater Buenos Aires with technocratic efficiency. As with Brazil, the association of metropolitan coordination with dictatorship provoked a strong localist response. However, the practical requirements of governance produced sector-specific agencies for metropolitan governance, including for food-supply logistics, waste disposal, water and catchment management (Rojas 2017; Lanfranchi 2021).

In 2016, federal government set up the Buenos Aires Metropolitan Area Consultative Commission with federal, provincial and municipal representatives to explore the possibilities for metropolitan governance, and the provincial government set up the metropolitan Cabinet to coordinate between the province and core urban municipalities. For Francisca Rojas (2017, 285), these were 'promising first steps'. The need for joint action to tackle the Covid-19 pandemic brought federal, provincial and local representatives together in coordinating forums, and this assisted in nurturing proposals for metropolitan governance, including a metropolitan institute to provide a knowledge infrastructure for the region, a metropolitan corporation to unify the different service-delivery agencies, a metropolitan agency for integrated planning and an elected metropolitan parliament (Lanfranchi 2021).

In the case of the *Región Metropolitana de Santiago* (Santiago Metropolitan Region) in Chile, discussions on metropolitan development have continued for over 40 years, with approaches shifting in line with political developments. Attempts at regionalisation of governance in the 1970s faltered in the 1980s when Augusto Pinochet centralised governance in his office. With democratisation in 1990, there was a new initiative to set up a regional coordinating council for municipal action, but inter-local disputes scuppered the initiative. In 2018, however, Chile introduced a law on regional government and administration, and, at the time of writing, a metropolitan structure is due to be established, headed by an elected governor and supported by an advisory committee of mayors and a metropolitan development fund. Its success depends on overcoming continued resistance from local interests (Van Treek et al. 2021).

South and South-East Asia

These regions are also significantly underrepresented in international literature, with the partial exception of India (see chapter four), where there has been a quite vibrant internal debate on the shortcomings of metropolitan- and city-region governance. There have been multiple attempts to promote metropolitan governance across these regions, but metropolitan governance remains weak, with rapid urban growth plagued by multiple governmental failures. A feature of governance across these regions is patronage politics, with formal systems limited in the face of the personalised informal networks of governance.

There are many similarities across South Asia, due mainly to the legacy of the British governmental system. Local governments were historically weak, with the political settlement handing power to national and state or provincial governments, and recent attempts at decentralisation have been resisted by elites at these levels. As in the case of Delhi (see chapter four), local democracy in the large cities of Pakistan and Bangladesh is undermined by parallel governance systems. While there are elected city governments, urban planning and profitable land development functions are controlled by unelected development authorities reporting to higher levels of government. In the case of Dhaka, the elected Dhaka City Corporation exists together with the Capital Development Authority (*Rajdhani Unnayan Kotripokho*), which reports to the national government and is insulated from local accountability. In Pakistan, the elected Lahore Metropolitan Corporation is shadowed by the powerful Lahore Development Authority, an instrument of the Punjab provincial government. Also, like cities in India, the delivery of water, electricity, waste management and other services is structured through a plethora of bureaucratic bodies that operate outside the jurisdiction of the elected local corporations (Etzold and Keck 2009).

Beyond this dual-structured formal system, informal networks are pervasive. In Bangladesh, for example, the *mastaan* serve as intermediaries between the local population and rent-seeking officials. They effectively control access to services in exchange for loyalty and personal favours, forcing citizens to navigate their networks and renegotiate the rules of governance daily. So, while the urban agglomerations in South Asia do have local governments with a wide territorial jurisdiction – the Lahore Metropolitan Corporation, for example, governing a population of 11 million people – the powers of the authorities are severely circumscribed by the presence of non-elected bodies, and of informal, personalised networks of authority (Etzold and Keck 2009).

In South-East Asia, there is more diversity in colonial legacy and thus more variation in governmental systems, but informal networks are a pervasive presence. With few exceptions, consolidating metropolitan governance has been immensely difficult. The two largest agglomerations, centred on Jakarta and Manila, are in countries that experienced authoritarian governance followed by a transition to democracy, and so there are some similarities. The idea of a Greater Jakarta goes back to the 1950s with the concept of the Jabotabek region (Jakarta, Bogor, Tangerang, Bekas) introduced in the 1960s.[4] In 1975, President Suharto created BSKP Jabodetabek by decree as the coordinating structure for the expanding region, with representation from the provinces and municipalities, but with supervision from the national government (Firman 2014).

However, BSKP Jabodetabek evolved as a weak coordinating structure, with a poorly capacitated secretariat and limited cooperation from its constituent municipalities. Tommy Firman (2014, 225) called it a 'powerless coordinating forum'. Local and provincial interests have resisted attempts to strengthen the structure, with common suspicion of the intent. Instead of coordination, the city-region has fragmented institutionally as it has grown physically. In 2000, a new province was created, and new municipalities and governmental agencies were formed (Rustiadi et al. 2015). Cooperation between local authorities happens, but is limited and fractious (Firman 2014; Rustiadi et al. 2015). While the management of *Jabodetabek* falters, an even greater urban agglomeration is in the making as the structure interlinks with the Bandung City-Region along an urban belt of more than 300 kilometres across (Rustiadi et al. 2015). National government seems to have given up on the attempt to resolve the chaotic governance of this national capital region (NCR), identifying a site for a new national capital on the island of Borneo.

In the Philippines, the Metro Manila Commission was established as a coordinating body in 1975 by decree of President Marcos. However, while its Indonesian counterpart battled to gain traction, Metro Manila evolved as a commanding structure, albeit representing national rather than regional interests. The governor of Metro Manila was the formidable First Lady, Imelda Marcos, who simultaneously held the position of head of the powerful national Ministry of Human Settlements (Manasan and Mercado 1999).

The People's Power Revolution, which ousted the Marcos regime in 1986, brought the commission to an end. In 1990, however, President Aquino responded to the hiatus in governance by establishing the Metro Manila Authority to perform services requiring metropolitan-scale coordination. This happened together with a devolution of powers to local government, and the Metro Manila Authority was governed by the Metro Manila Council, which comprised the mayors of the member municipalities. The Metro Manila Authority was embedded within the region, but it relied on the 17 independent-minded municipalities for cooperation and funding. This remained the case even after 1995, when the Metro Manila Authority was reconstituted as the Metropolitan Manila Development Authority. The Metropolitan Manila Development Authority is weak, allowing governance to be manipulated by the interests, networks and coalitions constituted by Manila's historical political families. Du Huynh (2020, 33) was blunt in assessment: 'Opposite to Seoul, Manila is a failure.'

In Thailand, the Bangkok Metropolitan Area is governed by the Bangkok Metropolitan Council with representatives elected from its constituent districts. It is, however, also a weak structure with a limited financial base that struggles to steer the Bangkok Metropolitan Area against the powers of both national and local (district) governments. National government maintains a strong interest in the capital region, with Douglas Webster and Chuthatip Maneepong (2009) indicating that only around 10 per cent of capital expenditure in the Bangkok Metropolitan Area was channelled through the metropolitan structure.

In the case of Kuala Lumpur in Malaysia, the core city is governed through the federal territory, but there is a far larger metropolitan region known as *Lembah Klang* (Klang Valley). While local governance is fragmented across multiple districts and municipalities, the central government plays a key role in coordinating activities within this capital region. The federal territory is managed directly by the prime minister's office, with the prime minister's Economic Planning Unit coordinating many of the activities across the wider region, including through megaproject development, such as the Multi-media Super Corridor (Bunnell and Nah 2004).

Ho Chi Minh City in Vietnam is also embedded within a strong governmental hierarchy. Like cities in China, a large single municipality was set up for Ho Chi Minh City after the communist victory in 1976 and was granted provincial-level status. Urban expansion did eventually supersede the municipal boundaries, and wider regional coordination is now facilitated through regional plans prepared by the central government (like China) (Nguyen et al. 2016).

Africa and the Middle East

Africa and the Middle East are severely underrepresented in the international literature, especially given the current weight of urban growth. A common theme across the regions is the role of national governments in controlling city-region governance, although with some exceptions. Informal networks are pervasive, and, in sub-Saharan Africa, these include networks of traditional authority with a rural origin, which tie rural and urban governance together in intimate relationships (Beall et al. 2015; De Boeck 2020). Given these contextual realities, Vanessa Watson (2021) argues that city-region governance is an unfitting concept for Africa, imposed from the global North, although Jo Beall et al. (2015) argue that the idea of city-region governance should be expanded to incorporate these contextual patterns.

In much of North Africa and the Middle East, governance is centralised and hierarchical. This is the case in Egypt, where the country is divided into governorates, each headed by a governor appointed by the national president. Greater Cairo spreads across three governorates and includes seven satellite cities developed and administered by the Ministry of Housing's powerful New Urban Communities Authority. There are no formal coordination mechanisms across these authorities, except, still indecisively, in the transport sector (Sims 2017). Failed attempts to achieve this have included a Capital City Law, which was dropped after the revolution of 2011, and a 2012 proposal for a Greater Cairo supreme council. For David Sims (2017), there is no obvious political will for metropolitan governance in Egypt, and nothing will happen unless the relationship between central and local administrations is fundamentally altered.

Iran's governmental system is also hierarchical, cascading down from the supreme leader, but is complicated by a dual system of authority that combines theocracy and presidential democracy. The governance of the Tehran Metropolitan Region is structured within vertically aligned authorities (the parallel Islamic councils and municipalities, with their different upward-reporting structures). Horizontal integration is weak and there are significant conflicts of interest between municipalities in the core of the Tehran Metropolitan Region and those on the periphery. However, there are special, nationally managed programmes for the Tehran Metropolitan Region, with national ministries involved in sector-based coordination (Lalehpour 2016).

Unlike Cairo and Tehran, Istanbul has evolved a specific form of city-region governance, although also structured within a strong governmental hierarchy. The province of Istanbul governs a population of around 13.5 million people and has a governor appointed by the president. Its primary function is to coordinate the activities of national government departments within the city-region. The Istanbul Metropolitan

Municipality, established in 1984, covers the full jurisdiction of the province. It has an elected mayor and a municipal council consisting of representatives of its constituent districts. The Istanbul Metropolitan Municipality holds considerable powers, including those delegated from the province. Institutionally, this is an unusual arrangement. However, the structure of these formal institutions obscures the complex nature of networked governance within the city-region. Fatma Ekdi and Mahyar Arefi (2019, 182) refer to 'palimpsests of multiple layers of historic, geo-political, and socio-economic complexity'.

The largest agglomeration in sub-Saharan Africa is Greater Lagos, and this is an exception to the hierarchical governance structures in Africa and the Middle East. Nigeria was set up as a federation, and Lagos State, set up in 1967, serves as a city-region authority of sorts. The civil war and military dictatorship forestalled any form of democratised city-region governance, but this changed when military rule ended in 1999. Lagos State emerged as one of Africa's acknowledged success stories in city-region governance. The governor of Lagos and the State House of Assembly are directly elected, with the first governors of Lagos post-1999 credited with improving the finances of the state and directing funding into infrastructure improvement (Olukesusi and Wapwera 2017).

The second agglomeration in sub-Saharan Africa is Kinshasa, the capital of the Democratic Republic of the Congo. Like Lagos, the province of Kinshasa has both an elected assembly and a governor. However, Kinshasa is marked by weak administrative structures, discretionary rules and informal administrative processes, with the state governor under severe duress to align with the national president. Filip de Boeck's work shows how post-colonial Kinshasa exists as a complex urban agglomeration without a functioning modern state (De Boeck and Plissart 2014). Instead, Kinshasa is 'rooted in the kinds of rural and pre-colonial worlds that the colonizer tried so hard to eradicate and the city itself has wanted to expel from its surface for a long time now' (De Boeck 2020, 7).

The third agglomeration is the GCR in South Africa, discussed in chapter six. It is an example of a city-region within a complicated framework of cooperative governance, rather than a mandated governmental hierarchy. However, the institutionalisation of city-region governance has been slow.

Beyond the GCR, the next layer of large urban agglomerations in sub-Saharan Africa includes Luanda (Angola), Dar es Salaam (Tanzania) and Nairobi (Kenya). Angola is highly centralised with its personalised politics cascading from the top. The province of Luanda encompasses much of the urban region and oversees the nine municipalities, but it functions largely as an implementing structure of national government, with the governor and vice-governors appointed directly by the national president. Even so, the national presidency plays a direct role in urban planning and urban projects, often bypassing the province (Croese 2018; Gastrow 2020).

Tanzania does not have provinces. Instead, municipal governments report directly to the central government. Dar es Salaam is governed separately across four municipal areas, although there was an attempt in 2000 to establish a form of metropolitan governance with the creation of the Dar es Salaam City Council to coordinate administration across the municipalities. The Dar es Salaam City Council was composed of the municipal mayors, nominated councillors and the members of parliaments representing local constituencies. However, the Dar es Salaam City Council lacked the authority to coordinate much across municipalities, although it did manage individual projects, and facilitated informal cooperation. However, even this meek structure was a threat to an autocratic leader, and President John Magufuli disbanded the Dar es Salaam City Council in January 2021 (Mtengwa 2021).

There is a far more empowered regional authority in the case of Nairobi, Kenya. An initial move towards regionalisation happened in 2008, when the Ministry of Nairobi Metropolitan Development was set up to coordinate across the 15 separate municipal authorities. The ministry achieved recognition for its participatory processes in metropolitan planning (Myers 2015). In 2010, a new national Constitution devolved powers from the ministry to the Nairobi County Council, which has a combination of elected and appointed members. The Nairobi County Council is an important instance of metropolitan governance in Africa but its jurisdiction does not encompass the full extent of the city-region. It governs around five million of the ten million people in the greater region.

There are many other under-researched examples of city-region governance across Africa's diversity. In Ghana, for example, a metropolitan assembly was established in 1991 for the Greater Accra Metropolitan Area. Development has, however, spilled over the boundaries of this area, resulting in the emergence of a new concept, the Accra City-Region. There is an outline plan for the city-region, but no formal institutional mechanisms have been established to date (Musah 2022). In Abidjan, Côte d'Ivoire, a single-tier metropolitan authority was established in 1991, a decade before the creation of single-tier authorities in South Africa's metropolitan cities. In Dakar, Senegal, where there is a long tradition of decentralised governance, the *Communauté Urbaine de Dakar* (Dakar Urban Community) is a voluntary association of municipalities (Resnick 2021).

Conclusion

Somewhat ambitiously, this chapter has explored the material, discursive and governmental dimensions of city-region (also metropolitan) governance across the globe. This scan sets up the context for the more detailed case studies to follow. Without the scan, the significance of the case studies would be difficult to assess.

In addition to providing the wider milieu, this chapter has made two essential points. The first is that the three dimensions of the city-region – material, discursive and political-administrative – are co-evolving, although often in an indirect and meandering way. Urban actors of different kinds grapple with changing material conditions, producing the connections across the three dimensions, as uneven as they are.

The second is that the geography of knowledge matters. The geographies within which knowledge is produced, or which inform knowledge, are germane to the content of the knowledge. Some of the tense debate across the North Atlantic, for example, relates to the contextual foundations of description and theory. More significant is the unevenness in knowledge production between regions in the global North and those elsewhere. Although there is an improvement in the global spread of study, our understanding of city-regions remains only partially informed. The case studies that follow are an attempt to further balance knowledge production in the field without negating the richness of insight that has come from Europe and North American scholarship.

Notes

1   For the US census, a metropolitan district has a core city of at least 50 000 inhabitants surrounded by a sphere of influence with a population of at least 100 000, and a contiguity of spatial formation.
2   Jean Gottman was a Ukraine-born, French geographer who escaped the Nazis to work in the USA.
3   See the Region Hannover website at https://www.hannover.de/Leben-in-der-Region-Hannover/Verwaltungen-Kommunen/Die-Verwaltung-der-Region-Hannover.
4   It was later renamed Jabodetabek with the inclusion of the Depok district.

2 The governance of Brazil's metropolitan regions

Introduction

The possibilities for collective action across Brazil's mega agglomerations rest in the political cultures produced through Brazil's 500 years of colonisation and decolonisation and, more immediately, in the political settlement reached in Brazil's transition from military rule to democracy. Political cultures were initially forged within the context of absolutist state structures, mercantilism, the Catholic Church and a slave-based plantation economy and, later, within the context of post-colonial struggles to establish a modern democracy. A complex and hybrid political culture emerged, with many regional inflections.

This chapter begins with a brief account of the history in which contemporary initiatives are embedded, followed by a contextual overview of urban Brazil. It then provides a more detailed account of the evolving discourse and practice of metropolitan governance, focussing on Brazil's three largest metropolitan regions – São Paulo, Rio de Janeiro and Belo Horizonte (Map 1). The main argument in the chapter is that Brazil's political cultures and political settlement privilege a localist ideology that militates against metropolitan governance. However, the pragmatics of governance require forms of collaboration that have gradually evolved, although unevenly and with periodic setbacks. Some forms have been enabled by federal or state legislation, while others have emerged more organically from collaborative initiatives at the metropolitan or sub-metropolitan scales.

The historical embedding

By the end of the nineteenth century, Brazil's large, plantation-based economy had produced a patchwork of regional oligarchies centred on powerful landowning families. These dynasties gave rise to regionally based political parties with networks of clientelism, allowing citizens to access the protection and services of government in exchange for their loyal support of the oligarchs. This practice of clientelism shaped a political system in which government officials were connected to regional and local bosses (*coronéis*) through a complex system involving a network of mutual obligations and traded favours (*coronelismo*) (Selcher 1989). However, there were counter trends, with modernising elites assembling around São Paulo from the late nineteenth century. A political settlement was reached in 1898 between the elites of São Paulo and the oligarchs in semi-peripheral states such as Minas Gerais and Rio Grande do Sul, with the far-flung regions held in check by this arrangement (Hagopian 1996). The monarchy had ended, and an oligarchical republic was in place, which returned some stability.

The political settlement held together until the Great Depression and the collapse of Brazil's coffee-based economy, but was reconstituted under the populist and near-authoritarian rule of President Getúlio Vargas, who held office from 1930 to 1945, and then again from 1951 until his suicide in 1954. The economic base of the political settlement changed as Vargas built an industrial economy through state ownership of key industries and domestic market protection. Vargas projected himself as 'the father of the poor' (Wolfe 1994, 80), personalising governance and shaping a paternalistic state that mediated between employers and labour unions in a government-led corporatist arrangement. Authoritarian populism had largely replaced oligarchical federalism, but the oligarchy persisted in the outer regions and was replicated in the local governance arrangements emerging in Brazil's growing cities (Williams 2001).

After Vargas, a modern, democratic Constitution was adopted in 1946, although governance remained centralising. President Kubitschek de Oliveira (1956–1961) emphasised the goal of national modernisation, famously declaring that there should be 'fifty years' progress in five' (Maram 1990, 38). While promoting a national project, he also accommodated regional interests, most notably by planning for a new capital, Brasilia, in the country's interior (Maram 1990).

The country was changing rapidly, with millions of people moving from the neglected countryside into burgeoning cities, providing low-cost labour for the expanding industrial sector. Many migrants found a precarious urban foothold in scantily serviced *favelas* (informal settlements). Kubitschek's successor, President João Goulart (1961–1964), responded by introducing more socially oriented policies, including the empowerment of local councils. These measures were, however, resisted by the elites, and growing tensions were poorly managed, providing the pretext for a military coup in 1964 (Marques 2016).

The military established a regime of 'authoritarian modernisation' with strong technocratic and centralising tendencies (Marques 2016, 38). However, even with considerable capacity for force and repression, the military was unable to manage the territorial vastness of Brazil without accommodating regional oligarchs, and so forms of traditional clientelism persisted (Skidmore 1988). The military regime was also concerned with keeping up political appearances and so did not destroy the political class – as happened in Argentina and Chile, for example – keeping some of the trappings of democracy, including a two-party political system (Skidmore 1988).

The regime's technocratic reforms led to early improvements in system efficiency, with the accelerated growth between 1967 and 1973 known for a time as the 'Brazilian miracle' (Skidmore 1988). Further, there were developmental interventions, such as creating the *Banco Nacional de Habitação* (National Housing Bank) to channel federal funds into urban housing and urban infrastructure. The National Housing Bank was to control vast resources and serve as the kingpin of the real estate market in Brazil (Rolnik 2011).

However, this technocratic authoritarianism reduced capabilities for adaptation, and when the world economy changed course following the oil crisis of 1973, the Brazilian miracle ended abruptly. The military regime failed to stabilise the economy and entered the 1980s with a deepening economic crisis and growing opposition from civil society, including mass demonstrations on the streets of the major cities (Skidmore 1988).

The military leadership was divided between hardliners determined to hang onto power and reformists hoping to manage a gradual transition to civilian rule. Vacillating between reform and repression, with no success at either, the military lost its will to govern, finally agreeing to relinquish the executive to civilian leadership. There was a messy beginning to restored democracy, with a succession of compromised post-military leaders, but a progressive new national Constitution for the federal democracy was finalised in 1988 (Hagopian 1996).

An important feature in the transition to democracy was the activation of civil society and the rise of a localist ideology in reaction to the centralisation under military autocracy. In this context, ideas of localism and democracy were entwined. In the political settlement of 1988, more than 5 500 *municípios* (municipalities) were recognised as units of the federation with powers to pass their own laws in fields including education, health, transport, social welfare and land administration (Selcher 1998; Rolnik 2011).

While civil society was influential in the transition, the Constitution was, ultimately, an elite pact. It adopted a rights-based approach to government, offering many democratic openings, and dispersed power down the levels of the federation, especially to local government. While the new legal framing could not remove all vestiges of the old orders – oligarchies, corporatist arrangements and authoritarianism – there was sufficient flexibility in Brazil's constitutional arrangement to allow for evolution towards a more inclusive democracy (Hagopian 1996).

Brazil's post-military government and economy were stabilised in the 1990s under President Fernando Cardoso (1995–2002) of the *Partido de Social Democracia*

Brasileira, PSDB (Brazilian Social Democratic Party). The stabilisation measures introduced through the *Plano Real* in 1994 when Cardoso was Minister of Finance, ended an era of hyper-inflation and restored economic growth, but elements of austerity caused considerable hardship for many Brazilians. There is continued debate as to whether the Cardoso era was a necessary foundation for future progressive policies or an injurious period in Brazil's history during which the remnants of the developmental state apparatus were dismantled (Hagopian 1996; Rolnik 2011).

The *Partido dos Trabalhadores* (PT), or Workers' Party, emerged in the late 1970s on the industrial outskirts of São Paulo but evolved into a broader-based political movement in the political transition of the 1980s, linking with the progressive wing of the Catholic Church, urban social movements, rural land movements, radical intellectuals and civil rights activists. As a political movement, it emphasised local activism and decentralism – unlike the traditional left, including the Brazilian Communist Party, which held onto bureaucratic centralism (Abers 1996; Baiocchi 2003).

As a radical movement in the 1990s, the PT took control of various municipalities where it experimented with progressive policies such as people's budget processes (most famously in Porto Alegre) and special zones of social interest (the ZEIS) for the upgrading and mainstreaming of informal settlements. In 2002, the PT came to power nationally when Lula da Silva was elected as national president. Although the PT moderated its earlier radicalism once in power, it implemented several progressive programmes through the federal government, including the *Bolsa Família* with its direct cash transfers to poor families; the *Programa de Aceleração do Crescimento* (Growth Acceleration Programme), which funded large-scale job-creating infrastructural developments; and the *Minha Casa Minha Vida* – MCMV ('My House, My Life') programme providing three million new houses. The PT benefitted from a strong economy in the early 2000s, with data indicating that levels of inequality, poverty and household vulnerability declined during the first decade of PT rule. However, some Brazilian scholars have criticised the PT administration for its model of administrative social redistribution, which did not engage with the structures of power and interest that sustained social inequality (Rolnik 2011; Marques 2016).

The PT was not immune to the persisting logics of clientelism and patronage, and networks of influence connected business to political leaders (Rolnik 2011). It became embroiled in a series of corruption scandals, and Lula's successor, Dilma Rousseff, was impeached in 2016, with allegations of budgetary mismanagement. Civil society remobilised, taking to the streets to protest against corruption and the failures of the public transport system. The PT lost massively in the 2016 local government elections, with the number of municipalities under its control dropping substantially from 638 to 254.

Politics took a conservative turn in the late 2010s, spurred on by disillusionment with formal institutions and political structures, and the turn to populism internationally (as in Donald Trump's election victory in the USA). In the 2018 elections, the right-wing populist, Jair Bolsonaro, was elected national president, and there were parallel shifts in state governments, including in São Paulo and Rio de Janeiro where Bolsonaro's allies were elected as governors. In turn, however, public opinion turned against Bolsonaro and his allies, who were accused of mishandling the Covid-19 pandemic.

Brazil's history has produced a complex mix of political cultures including the personalisation of power, patrimonialism, corporatism, populism, activist civil society and legalism. Some of the contradictions this creates are apparent in Brazil's legal system. There is a strong formalistic element in Brazilian political culture with a lot of bureaucratic red tape, and many laws, decrees, directives, codes and other administrative regulations. But the application of Brazil's legal system is described by the term *jeito*, which means to manoeuvre around an obstacle. It refers to a flexible practice, including circumvention or avoidance of the law, as well as creative interpretation and selective application. This arguably opens the system to corruption that is endemic but also provides a safety valve for a governmental apparatus which may otherwise seize up under its regulatory weight (Rosenn 1984).

Debates around the extent and consequence of Brazil's clientelist cultures continue. Clientelism, with its 'personalised reciprocities', is stronger in the outer-lying regions, but it permeates urban governance in many ways (Ansell 2014, 2). With the expansion of universal social programmes such as *Bolsa Família*, the personalised ties that individual politicians have with voters have weakened (Ansell 2014), but populism threatens to re-establish traditional patterns.

In the major cities, there is a complex mix, with clientelism and ideals of democratic urban citizenship co-existing. Rebecca Abers and Margaret Keck (2006, 604) write: 'In Brazil's hybrid political culture, formalism co-exists with informality and patronage-based standards of authority with meritocratic ones.'

The urban context

Brazil's cities expanded massively from the 1930s in response to national policies of import-substituting industrialisation, with urbanisation levels rising from 36 per cent in 1950 to the current 87 per cent. It is now one of the most urbanised countries in the world, with only a few countries, including Japan, Israel and Argentina, exceeding this level. In the process, the urban population in Brazil increased from around 19.5 million in 1950 to 186 million in 2020. Annual rates of urban growth peaked at around 2.54 per cent in the 1950s, dropping to just under one per cent in the 1990s, and around 0.87 per cent is projected for the period from 2020 to 2025 (with Brazil now having among the slowest-growing urban populations in the global South) (United Nations 2018).

In terms of individual concentration of urban population, the changes between 1950 and 2020 in the three largest agglomerations were:

- São Paulo, from 2.3 million to 22 million (with around 34 million people living in an expanded metropolitan area) (Map 6);
- Rio de Janeiro, from 3 million to 13.5 million (Map 7); and
- Belo Horizonte, from 0.4 million to 6.1 million (Map 8).

São Paulo is ranked by the United Nations as the fourth largest agglomeration in the world, after Tokyo, Delhi and Shanghai, while Rio de Janeiro is ranked sixteenth. Beyond the big three, Brazil has medium-sized metropolitan areas with 2020 population estimates for areas such as Brasilia at 4.6 million; for Fortaleza, Pôrto Alegre and Recife at 4.1 million; Salvador at 3.8 million and Curitiba at 3.7 million.

In the 1950s and 60s, economic activity was concentrated within the core cities of these agglomerations, but the economic crisis from the mid-1970s led to spatial restructuring and the emergence of more complex metropolitan regions. This happened as some manufacturing firms in the core relocated to smaller cities along the metropolitan edge, in search of cheaper land and labour. Migrants diverted into these cities in response to the employment shift but also because housing and living costs were lower.

In the academic literature, the processes at play were referred to variously as 'polarization reversal' (Townroe and Keen 1984, 45), 'concentrated deconcentration' (Lobo et al. 2015, 219) and 'polygonised development' (Diniz 1994, 293). Scholars have recognised, however, that processes were incomplete and that the core cities remained important, even as other cities have grown, although their functions have shifted from manufacturing into post-industrial sectors (Diniz 1994).

These processes were clear in the designated São Paulo Metropolitan Region (MR), which developed as a highly complex spatial formation (Map 6). In the case of the Rio de Janeiro MR, these processes were accelerated, from the 1970s on, by the creation of large state-owned industries on the metropolitan edge (the *Baixada Fluminense*), offshore gas and oil discoveries and the construction in the 1980s of the deep-water port at Itaguaí (Map 7). In 2007, a semi-circular beltway called the *Arco Metropolitano* was built along the inland edge of the MR, connecting areas that had previously related functionally only to the inner core. Rio de Janeiro's metropolitan space had been re-territorialised, strengthening its functioning as a complex city-region (Klink 2014).

Similar processes were observed in the Belo Horizonte MR (Map 8). At the end of the 1970s, the region was still overwhelmingly dominated by a single core. This changed and Heloisa Costa et al. (2014) refer to a complex spatial structure with five meso-regions and five micro-regions, and Carlos Lobo et al. (2015, 219) talk of 'reverse commuting' in the region with workers commuting outwards from the core to employment nodes on the periphery.

As these and other MRs in Brazil became more complex and dispersed, their outer edges intersected, creating an extended landscape of urbanisation, especially across the country's south-east, from Belo Horizonte in the north to Pôrto Alegre in the south.

The politics of the MRs also shifted as they transformed spatially. Political fragmentation was overlaid on the institutional fragmentation produced under the 1988 national Constitution. Most political parties were small and regionally based, and political control was often divided between levels of government and across the MRs (although, for short periods, one or other party, including the PT and PSDB, gained a national profile).

The complexities of metropolitan-wide politics cannot be explained here, but I refer briefly to the changes in the core cities. There was a political pendulum in São Paulo as right-leaning mayors, concerned with social and spatial order in the city, were followed by left-leaning mayors oriented toward social access and inclusion, before the shift back to the right and then to the left. Since the return of democracy in the 1980s, PT mayors have held office in São Paulo on three occasions but were never elected to a second term. This lack of political continuity partly has to do with the fine balance of interests within a megacity that includes a strong share of Brazil's economic and political elites and a large working class.

Rio de Janeiro has a history of traditional left-wing politics, characterised by bureaucratic centralism rather than civic activism. From the 1990s, however, Rio had a succession of idiosyncratic mayors who ran the city as their domain. In the lead-up to the Summer Olympic Games of 2016, Mayor Eduardo da Costa Paes provided technocratic leadership, although there were allegations of fraud. He was followed in 2016 by an evangelical pastor and right-wing populist, Marcelo Crivella, although Paes returned in 2021. Pervading Rio's politics is the presence of large *favelas*, many of which are controlled by drug lords, with local government approaches towards this informality vacillating between accommodation and confrontation.

Belo Horizonte has a different political culture from the other two MRs. In the late nineteenth century, it was built as the new capital of the state of Minas Gerais, dominated by a rural oligarchy. Over time, tensions between the clientelist politics of the region and the modernising inclination of the capital have played out. However, the pragmatics of governance has forced the different actors into mutual accommodation, and coalition politics have successfully evolved as a dominant mode of governance. When the PT took power in Belo Horizonte, it did not attempt to rule alone as it did in São Paulo, for example. Whereas its programmes were less radical than those of PT governments elsewhere, it remained in office for an extended period and was able to achieve sustained implementation (Wampler 2007).

While Brazil's municipalities were empowered through the political settlement, governance still happens within an inter-federative framework. There are competing relationships between the large municipalities and state governments, with the federal government also playing an important role in framing what happens locally. In the early post-democracy era, the federal government withdrew from the urban terrain. Under Cardoso's austerity regime in the 1990s, levels of urban socio-spatial inequality increased, as famously described by Teresa Caldeira in *Cities of Walls* (Caldeira 2001). It was a time of expanded *favelas*, the retreat of the wealthy into gated estates and growing territorial control by drug lords (Caldeira 2001; Arias 2006). In the 2000s, the federal government re-engaged with urban policy, creating both a National Council of Cities to support ongoing participation in the urban terrain by civil society, and a Ministry of Cities to coordinate national support for local government (Avritzer 2006; Rolnik 2011). In 2001, the National Congress of Brazil approved the groundbreaking *Estatuto da Cidade* (Statute of the Cities), which formally incorporated the right to the city into Brazil's legal system and provided a range of administrative instruments for achieving this right.

The governance problematic

The *Estatuto da Cidade* did not address the metropolitan dimensions, and the governance of Brazil's large and complex urban agglomerations remains a real predicament for its decentralised federalism. Much of Brazil's economic strength rests within its large urban agglomerations but so do its most obdurate problems, including mobility, housing, resource vulnerability and crime. However, because of institutional and political fragmentation and an entrenched localist ideology, it is difficult to forge the required forms of collaborative action.

Brazilian scholars have engaged with this concern. Celina Souza (2003, 149) asks, 'How can we make a common territorial space in a political system where power is simultaneously divided and shared?' (translated). Luiz Ribeiro and Orlando dos Santos Junior (2010, 56) argue that the inequities and dysfunctionalities of Brazil's metropolitan cities have much to do with the 'incompleteness' of the federal project: 'the political elites appear incapable of mobilizing themselves around an institution-building project that takes advantage of the productive forces and the potential concentrated in the Brazilian complex, rich and diversified metropolitan system, a project that could avoid the environmental and social disasters seen today in most of Brazil's MRs'. Finally, Jeroen Klink (2017, 323) speaks of a 'metropolitan paradox': 'while most city-regions and metropolitan areas usually see the bulk of countrywide social deficits and economic potential and, as such, should figure high on the national development agenda, they have notoriously deficient institutional, organizational, and financial frameworks to guide their planning and management'.

This paradox is apparent across all of Brazil's MRs, but in this chapter, I focus on the three largest. In the São Paulo MR with approximately 22 million people (in its narrow definition), around one-half of the population is governed within the core municipality. The other half live within a further 38 municipalities (Map 16). In the case of the Rio de Janeiro MR (also known as Grande Rio), 13.5 million people live across 23 municipalities, also with around one-half in the core municipality (Map 17). With a population of around six million people, Belo Horizonte comprises 34 municipalities (Map 18). Across all three MRs, dominant features include the fragmentation of local government, especially on the urban peripheries, the vertical divisions of political control and frequent interruptions in political authority.

With this paradox in mind, I move into a historical account of the evolving mechanism for joint action across Brazil's three largest urban agglomerations. I first consider the period of authoritarian centralism and continue through the democratic era where local autonomy was zealously protected.

Discourse and practice
Under military rule

Brazil's largest cities were growing rapidly in the 1950s and 60s as migrants poured in from rural areas. With migrants self-housed in *favelas*, Brazil adopted a low-cost model of urbanisation, but this negligent approach had its contradictions, including the risk to the elites of social disorder (Turok 2014). Under military rule, metropolitan governance emerged as a technocratic response to the urban challenge.

In the early 1950s, a Brazilian writer, Lucas Lopes, explored the San Francisco Valley as a metropolitan region for planning purposes, and drew parallels with Rio de Janeiro and Belo Horizonte in Brazil (Lopes 1952). By the 1960s, there was increased reference in the international literature to Brazil's cities as metropolitan regions, and the celebrated North American planner John Friedmann, who had written extensively about metropolitan regions, was a consultant in Brazil (Friedmann 1956, 1964; Perloff 1968).

There was thus a discourse for Brazil's junta to draw on. In 1969, a constitutional amendment made provision for the designation of *região metropolitanas* (MRs), which would receive special funding allocations from central government, and where coordinated planning was required. The amendment was given effect in the Complementary Law No. 14 of 1973, which designated eight MRs – São Paulo, Belo Horizonte, Pôrto Alegre, Curitiba, Salvador, Recife, Fortaleza and Belém. Rio de Janeiro was designated the ninth in 1974 (Spink 2005; Barreto 2012).

MRs were ultimately controlled from the top. The military government appointed state governors, who appointed the members of the governance structures for the MRs. Each MR had a deliberative board (the decision-making structure), a consultative board and a planning agency (effectively a sub-structure of the State Planning Office). There was nominal involvement from municipalities, which provided a list of potential members of the deliberative board, from which the governor would select two members. The other five were appointed directly by the governor. The decisions of the deliberative board were binding on municipalities in the region, allowing the military regime, through the state governor, to encroach on local planning powers. However, local government was incentivised to accept this metropolitan set-up as municipalities within MRs qualified for national fiscal transfers channelled through the National Housing Bank (Spink 2005; Barreto 2012).

The effect of the MR structures is debated. By the time the structures were in place in the late 1970s, the military regime was already under severe pressure, with a troubled economy and reduced resources for supporting MRs. The death knell came in 1985 when the National Housing Bank collapsed (Ribeiro and dos Santos Junior 2010). For Klink (2014), the MRs did little, if anything, to change the dysfunctional patterns of urban growth. As agents of the military region, with a largely top-down structure, MR governance lacked the relational capacity to draw in the support of key regional actors in urban processes. There were regional variations, however, with Costa et al. (2014) observing that the MR structures in Belo Horizonte were embedded in a more collaborative planning culture than elsewhere.

The system did bring some technical capacity to MRs – for data collection and analysis, and planning. For my case studies, the planning agencies were, respectively, the *Empresa Paulista de Planejamento Metropolitano* (Emplasa [Metropolitan Planning Corporation of São Paulo]), *Fundação para o Desenvolvimento da Região Metropolitana do Estado do Rio de Janeiro* (Fundrem [Foundation for the Development of the Metropolitan Region of the State of Rio de Janeiro]) and *Superintendência de Desenvolvimento da Região Metropolitana de Belo Horizonte* (Plambel [Agency for the Development of the Metropolitan Region of Belo Horizonte]).

Into the democratic era: autonomous localism and its limits

In the 1980s, civil society mobilised around a decentralising agenda, metropolitan governance being associated with the top-down rule of the military regime. During the Constitution-making process, parliamentarians received over 35 000 submissions, with only 14 dealing with MRs (Souza 2003). Nevertheless, MRs were not entirely forgotten in the Constitution, with Article 25 empowering state governments to designate MRs (previously a national responsibility). However, Peter Spink (2005) argues that this reference to MRs was a case of a mechanical path dependency rather than of any specific interest on the part of the Constitution-makers.

Curiously, given the overall neglect of metropolitan governance under democratic government, more than 80 MRs have been designated by state governments (Costa et al. 2018). For Antonio Fernandes (2013, 13), these designations were 'dead letters', as very few of these MRs have metropolitan characteristics. There is no scale threshold for MRs, the only requirement being that urban development crosses jurisdictional boundaries, and so some MRs have as few as 20 000 people. For Ilson Barreto (2012), municipalities jointly applied to be MRs for status recognition in the vague hope that the funding flows through MR structures, which applied under the military regime, would eventually be restored.

In Klink's view (2017, 324), the creation of MRs was of little consequence and 'effectively not much happened'. The far more consequential process in the 1990s and into the 2000s was the further fragmentation of municipal government, with more than 1 000 new municipalities created through a process known as emancipation (Spink 2005; Lima and Neto 2018). In the 1990s especially, Brazil's newly empowered municipalities were in frantic competition for inward investment and other available resources, with little collaboration to address common concerns. For Fernandes (2013, 13), this pointed to the limits of 'autonomous localism'.

Klink (2014, 629) refers to the 'hollowing out' of MR structures from the 1980s. In the São Paulo MR, Emplasa survived as a residue of the past, but it lacked the powers – or even the will – to plan, functioning largely as a metropolitan information agency.[1] Nevertheless, the pragmatics of government compelled governance actors to coordinate in specific areas. The most pressing areas for collaboration were managing transport systems and ensuring the sustained provision of water. For coordination in transport, the state government set up the Metropolitan Enterprise for Urban Transportation (*Empresa Metropolitana de Transportes Urbanos de São Paulo*) and the São Paulo Company for Metropolitan Trains (*Companhia Paulista de Trens Metropolitanos*).

Water governance was an area of considerable complexity. Water security was threatened by the large informal settlements expanding in the water catchment zones, and there was growing tension over land management. In 1991, the state government introduced a Water Act, which created a framework for negotiating disputes that included water basin management committees with representation from state government, municipalities and civil society (World Bank 2015). This was to inform later federal legislation and was an early example of region-wide associational governance in Brazil. However, in a compelling paper on water governance, Abers and Keck (2006) explained the immense complexities of making this work in the context of diverse interests and Brazil's personalised and clientelist political cultures. They wrote that 'the attempt to create the new system ran head on into some of the most embedded characteristics of Brazilian politics' (Abers and Keck 2006, 617).

Grande Rio had a different history, related to the core city's previous role as the national capital. Between 1960 and 1975, there was a form of MR governance within the (national capital) state of Guanabara. However, in 1975, Guanabara was disbanded, and its territory was included within the far larger state of Rio de Janeiro. Rio de Janeiro was designated as an MR, but this hardly compensated for the dismantling of Guanabara. In the democratic era, the MR structures, including Fundrem, the planning agency, were disassembled (Klink 2014). After this, there was no metropolitan planning capacity, although there was ad hoc collaboration between municipalities, including for water management.

The metropolitan structures in the Belo Horizonte MR were less tarnished by military rule than elsewhere, and, in 1988, the state of Minas Gerais set out a revised governance structure for the MR. Plambel was kept on as the planning agency, and a metropolitan assembly called Ambel was set up, comprising the mayors of all municipalities and one representative each of the state executive and the state legislature. It was supported by a metropolitan development fund. However, even in Belo Horizonte, these were difficult times for metropolitan governance, with municipalities remaining suspicious of the intentions of the revised system. Plambel functioned more as a research body than a planning agency until it was finally shut down in 1995. However, as elsewhere, the practicalities of governance required some form of sectoral coordination, and, for example, a joint agency of municipalities was set up to manage the transport sector (Costa et al. 2014).

By the beginning of the 2000s, metropolitan governance in Brazil hardly existed, although as São Paulo academic Renato Cymbalista explained to me, 'Metropolitan coordination happened out of necessity and mainly within individual sectors.'

In the gap: the rise of voluntary inter-municipal cooperation

From the 1960s there were sporadic cases of inter-municipal agreements for sector-specific collaboration. The national Constitution of 1988 recognised inter-municipal sharing as a service delivery option for municipalities, but it left the mechanisms for achieving this to future legislation. By 2001 almost one-half of Brazil's 5 500 plus municipalities were involved in some form of inter-municipal collaboration, mainly in areas such as sanitation, housing and primary education (Spink 2005).

The first significant case of inter-sectoral collaboration emerged from the ABC sub-region of Greater São Paulo in 1990 (Klink 2017). The sub-region, south-east of the core city, has a population of under three million and comprises seven municipalities (Santo André, São Bernardo do Campo, São Caetano do Sul, Diadema, Mauá, Ribeião Pires and Rio Grande da Serra, with the sub-region getting its name from the first three). Its identity as an industrial and working-class sub-region developed from the 1930s as car manufacturers, including Ford, Volkswagen, General Motors, Mercedes and Scania, set up production plants in the area. As Brazil's economy sagged in the late 1970s, the workers mobilised in the newly formed National Federation of Trade Unions and in the PT as a new political party. A leading union organiser in the ABC was Lula da Silva (Rodríguez-Pose et al. 2001).

Economic conditions deteriorated again from the late 1980s, with around 60 000 manufacturing jobs lost in the sub-region between 1989 and 1995 (Rodríguez-Pose et al. 2001). However, instead of engaging in a fiscal war, as elsewhere in Brazil, the municipalities of the ABC sub-region came together voluntarily in December 1990 to establish the Inter-Municipal Consortium of the ABC sub-region (Rodríguez-Pose et al. 2001). Academic informants in São Paulo suggested that the German *Landkreise* (or regional circles) may have been an influencing model.

The consortium was established with a fragile legal basis as a private association of public bodies. The founding contract established a senate-type arrangement, with all seven municipalities having equal voting rights but with financial contributions proportional to the tax income of the municipalities. The arrangement proved enduring as the broad structure continues to the present day, although most decision making happens through consensual rather than voting processes.[2]

The initial focus of the consortium was the economic crisis, reflecting a deep concern among local actors that 'the ABC sub-region would become like Detroit' (a city in the USA that had suffered severe decline following the departure of the auto industry).[3] The consortium brought the municipalities, unions and private business together in an economic visioning process despite historically antagonistic relations. Over time, the consortium moved into other areas of collaboration, including solid waste, transport, risk management, social support, urban security and education.

Political champions play a critical role in initiating and sustaining the collaborative arrangements. In the beginning, the champion was Celso Daniel, the PT mayor of Santo André and a close confidante of Lula da Silva. However, after he lost an election in 1993, municipal support for the consortium declined, although civil society maintained some momentum with the establishment of the Citizens Forum of the ABC. The local government elections of 1997 returned Daniel to office, and he persuaded fellow mayors to renew support for the consortium while the Citizens Forum evolved into a Consultative Council for the Consortium.

Daniel also secured the support of state governor Mário Covas, despite his belonging to a different political party. Covas assisted the consortium in formalising some of its collaborative relationships by establishing a regional chamber with municipal, business, civic and academic representation. It structured its work through a series of regional agreements.

The ABC model garnered wider influence when Lula da Silva was elected national president in 2002. In 2005, the National Congress passed the Public Consortium Law that institutionalised inter-municipal consortia in Brazil. After the law took effect in 2007, many new inter-municipal consortia were established across Brazil.

While its influence was spreading, the ABC Consortium experienced troubled times in the 2000s. Governor Covas died unexpectedly in 2001, and Mayor Daniel was murdered in 2002. Momentum was restored in 2008 when Luiz Marinho, a charismatic union leader and a previous federal minister in Da Silva's cabinet, was elected as PT mayor of São Bernardo do Campo. Marinho was a political broker who drew effectively on his relationships with the federal government to benefit the region, including through the establishment of *Universidade Federal do ABC* (ABC Federal University) and the development of a regional logistics hub, airport and aerospace industrial cluster. In an interview with *The Guardian* on 18 May 2015, Marinho emphasised the value of personal relationships and trust in regional development, referring to his roles over the years as a union leader, local government official and national minister.

After 2008, the staff complement, budget and programmes of the ABC Consortium expanded significantly. The success of the consortium was reflected in the attention it received in national and international literature (Rodríguez-Pose et al. 2001; De Souza Briggs 2008; De Lima Caldas and Moreira 2013; Klink 2017). There have also been attempts to replicate the consortium in other parts of the São Paulo MR and beyond. By 2017, a further four inter-municipal consortia had been registered within the São Paulo MR in terms of the enabling federal legislation of 2005.

There were limitations, however. The first is the historically weak relationship between the core municipalities within the MRs and these consortia. The mayor of São Bernardo, for example, expressed his concern that 'São Paulo municipality is absent in all inter-municipal processes', indicating that this was even the case when the PT ruled in the municipality of São Paulo and across the ABC.[4] Secondly, there is the challenge of replicability. The ABC Consortium is rooted in a sub-region with a shared working-class history and culture, and a sense of shared identity clearly assisted in sustaining the collaborations. There are few sub-regions which are similar. Further, new challenges emerged with political change, including the October 2016 local government elections, which were devastating for the PT, wiping out the so-called Red Belt across the ABC sub-region and producing a new context of uncertainty for the consortium. However, by then, the consortium was deeply embedded in local politics, institutions and social networks, and it has continued to expand its role in the sub-region, including through knowledge exchange partnerships with local universities.[5]

The 2000s and gradual turn to metropolitan governance

The failure to address the metropolitan scale in the *Estatuto da Cidade* of 2001 may have been a turning point, with the concern for MRs gradually reappearing on the agenda from that point on (Souza 2003).

In 2004, Walter Feldman, a member of the Chamber of Deputies (the lower house of the National Congress), representing São Paulo for the PSDB, introduced a draft bill in support of metropolitan governance and planning. The bill was withdrawn after three years in committee because of uncertainty over the constitutionality of metropolitan planning, after parties in Rio de Janeiro and Salvador da Bahia had approached the courts to declare metropolitan governance an intrusion into the autonomy of municipalities (IPEA 2019).

With federal legislation on hold, the initiative rested with the state governments. In 2006, the governor of São Paulo signed an agreement with the municipalities in the São Paulo MR to establish an Integrated Transport Executive Committee to oversee a more comprehensively integrated metropolitan system (World Bank 2015). In 2011, the state legislature passed Complementary Law No. 1139/2011, making provision for a metropolitan development council (consisting of state and municipal representatives), an advisory council (civil society), a regional enterprise agency and a regional development fund. Emplasa, which had survived from the military era, was given an expanded role in support of these institutions. These structures were not very different from those in the late military era, and there was still no direct participation of civil society in decision making, although its voices were present in the advisory council (Klink 2017). There was no urgency in implementing the legislation, and little progress was made in setting up the new structures. Emplasa was, however, comprehensively restructured, becoming the executive arm of the State Secretariat for Metropolitan Affairs (Klink 2017).

Even as metropolitan governance for São Paulo was battling to gain traction, scholars and some government agencies acknowledged the mega scale of the agglomeration around the city, which superseded the descriptor *região metropolitana*. Terms that emerged to differentiate the mega agglomeration of São Paulo from Brazil's 80 MRs included *Macrometrópole Paulista* (Macrometropolis of São Paulo), *Complexo Metropolitano Expandido* (Expanded Metropolitan Complex) and *Região Metropolitana Extensa de São Paulo* (Extended Metropolitan Region of São Paulo). Brazil's *Observatório das Metrópoles* (Observatory of the Metropolis) even claimed the emergence of a *megarregião* (megaregion) as the urban agglomerations around Rio de Janeiro and São Paulo gradually coalesced along a long connecting corridor (Observatory of the Metropolis 2017). The governance implications of these larger territorialisations were, however, never explained.

In the case of Rio de Janeiro, there was no coordination mechanism at the scale of the MR except for the state government, although it was in a competitive relationship with the core city. This lack of coordination created practical problems with the large-scale investments following the oil and gas discoveries (Klink 2013).

The construction of the *Arco Metropolitano*, the beltway along the outer edge of the MR, highlighted the multiple challenges of inter-jurisdictional coordination and, in 2007, the Comperj Forum was set up by decree of the state governor to facilitate the logistics of this ambitious development. Chaired by the governor, the forum included municipalities that belonged to the Inter-municipal Consortium for the Development of the Eastern Region of Fluminense (Conleste). It excluded the municipality of Rio de Janeiro, however, indicating a rift in spatial interests between the municipalities along the periphery that were coming together through the *Arco Metropolitano* and the core municipality, which was effectively marginalised by the initiative (Klink 2013, 2014).

There were some attempts in the 2000s to improve MR-wide coordination in individual sectors. For example, the *Agência Metropolitana de Transporte Urbano do Estado do Rio de Janeiro* was established as the metropolitan transport authority for the region, linking state transport agencies and municipalities, but it has low institutional capacity and plays a mainly advisory role. In the lead-up to the 2016 Summer Olympic Games, there was growing concern about the inability of the state government and municipalities to coordinate the delivery of infrastructure. Faced with the possibility of a failed global event, the Organising Committee for the Olympic Games was set up as a special-purpose body with representation from all levels of government. However, the coordination requirements for infrastructure went beyond what the committee could deal with (Klink 2014).

When the state government negotiated a US$485 million loan for Olympic-related infrastructure, the World Bank used the opportunity to leverage a metropolitan agenda. It brought in global experts, funded study trips from Rio de Janeiro to countries such as Canada, France, Germany and Singapore, and hosted seminars, lectures and workshops on metropolitan governance (Loureiro and Leite 2018). The immediate catalyst for a shift towards metropolitan governance was a 2013 judgment in the Federal Supreme Court in Rio de Janeiro that ownership of common services should vest in a joint structure of municipalities, and that the creation of such a structure was not inconsistent with the principle of municipal autonomy. In 2014, the *Câmara Metropolitana de Integração Governamental* (Metropolitan Chamber for Government Integration) was established by agreement between the governor of the state of Rio de Janeiro, the mayor of Rio de Janeiro and the mayors of 20 other municipalities in the MR. It had the task of negotiating a solution for metropolitan governance and proposing to the *Alerj* (state legislature) draft legislation for this purpose within 120 days.[6] It took much longer than anticipated as there was resistance from municipalities to the process, with the ongoing fear that metropolitan governance would erode local autonomy. The legislation was submitted to the *Alerj* only after the passage of the *Estatuto da Metrópole* (to be discussed below) in 2015, creating the problem of inconsistency between federal and proposed state legislation and causing further delays.

While initiatives in the São Paulo and Rio de Janeiro MRs had not gone beyond the approaches inherited from the military era and were not supported by the capacities needed for implementation (Klink 2013, 2014), a more interesting initiative emerged from the Belo Horizonte MR, where collaborative cultures were more embedded (Ribeiro and dos Santos Junior 2010).

In 2003, Aécio Neves took office as the governor of Minas Gerais and set up a State Secretariat for Regional Development and Urban Policy (SEDRU). Although Neves was from the (centrist) PSDB, he found an ally in the PT mayor of Belo Horizonte, Fernando Pimentel. In 2004, on the advice of SEDRU, the state Constitution was amended to allow for representation of municipal government and civil society in metropolitan structures.[7]

In 2006, laws were passed in the state legislature making provision for a metropolitan assembly, a Deliberative Council for Metropolitan Development and a Planning Agency for Metropolitan Development (RMBH), which was a successor to the disestablished planning agency, Plambel.[8] The intended key instruments of governance were a Metropolitan Plan for Integrated Development and a Fund for Metropolitan

Development, supporting projects in line with metropolitan objectives. Fifty per cent of the core funding was to come from the state government and the other half from the municipalities, proportional to their current net revenues.

On paper, the structures did not seem to deviate much from the previous techno-cratic model. However, there was a major difference in substance, with municipalities brought in as full partners and space given to civil society. The decision-making rule in the metropolitan assembly is that the state government and (the combined) munici-pal representatives have an equal share in decision making. In the deliberative council, which recommends decisions to the metropolitan assembly, neither the state nor the municipality has a majority control, with representatives from civil society holding the balance of power (Aragão 2018).

In 2009, the RMBH initiated a participatory process of plan-making with around 3 000 registered participants in the process, representing 600 institutions, of which around 300 were from civil society (Aragão 2018). The participatory process was extensive, involving multiple workshops with participants mobilising in different ways to secure a voice, including, for example, through the *Frente pela Cidadania Metropolitana* (Metropolitan Citizen Front). A feature of the process was the role of a consortium of local universities in drafting the plan, drawing on the inputs of technical and participatory processes. Among the innovations in the process was the concept of *cidadão metropolitano* (metropolitan citizens), with technical innovations including the introduction of the *zona de interesse metropolitana* (zone of metropolitan interest), which is layered on the traditional land-use zoning (Aragão 2018).[9]

Despite clear successes in the Belo Horizonte MR, there were persisting tensions, reflecting the broader environment of Brazil's metropolitan governance and planning. The role of the state of Minas Gerais and the municipality of Belo Horizonte in the process remains ambiguous, with continued uncertainty over which agency is leading the process. Although municipal mayors participate openly in the process, there is continuing concern among some that metropolitan-wide processes compromise local autonomy.

The Statute of the Metropolis of 2015 and beyond

In 2013, the Federal Supreme Court opened the way for federal legislation on metro-politan governance when it confirmed that metropolitan governance was compatible with the principles of local democracy and municipal autonomy (Costa et al. 2018). This enabled the National Congress to reopen discussion on the previously shelved bill, and to rewrite the bill through a more participatory process. The lower house gave its unanimous approval to the bill in March 2014, with the Senate following in December 2014. President Dilma Rousseff signed the *Estatuto da Metrópole* (Statute of the Metropolis) into law on 12 January 2015 (Costa et al. 2018; Government of Brazil 2018).

Several factors finally brought the law into being, including the demonstration effect of metropolitan governance in places such as the Belo Horizonte MR; the ongoing lobbying of influential agencies such as the Brasilia-headquartered Institute for Applied Economic Research (IPEA); the role of individual members of Congress; and the practical experience of governmental fragmentation, including in the run-up to the 2014 FIFA World Cup and the 2016 Summer Olympic Games (Costa et al. 2018). The Act represented a further evolution in Brazil's decentralised federalism (Selcher 1989) and modified the dominant approach of autonomous localism. While it was the outcome of inching change in attitudes, the law nevertheless surprised many urban actors (Klink 2017).

In terms of content, the Act proposes bringing state and municipal governments together in inter-federative relationships. It leaves the exact form of these arrangements to the discretion of state governments, but it sets in place some common requirements. Underlying principles include the participation rights that municipalities and civil society have. Every MR is to have an executive authority that will include all federative units within the territory, a deliberative body where civil society will be represented, a technical agency for planning and a system of allocating resources. The governance instruments include a *plano de desenvolvimento urbano integrado* – PDUI (urban integrated development plan) – for each MR, together with inter-municipal sectoral plans, public consortia, management agreements and cooperation agreements (with the Act acknowledging the 2005 legislation on inter-municipal consortia). The PDUI must be prepared within three years from the promulgation of the Act, with severe penalties for politicians, including loss of eligibility for office, if the plan is not prepared within the given time. The Act also made provision for a National Integrated Urban Development Fund, which would have restored a flow of federal resources to MRs. However, this provision was vetoed by President Rousseff because of depleted federal resources, leaving uncertainty over the financing arrangements for metropolitan governance (Government of Brazil 2018).

Although the Act may not have gone much further than the legislation already in place in Minas Gerais, and even São Paulo, it made clear that metropolitan governance was a requirement rather than an option and that a fully participatory approach was required. While some municipalities remained wary, the law was generally well received in the professional domain, where there were hopes that it would bring significant change. However, there were also sceptical voices pointing to the implementational difficulties ahead (Santos and Vasques 2016).

The immediate challenge was the preparation of the PDUI, which created tension. In the case of São Paulo, the municipality was completing its master plan, and the ABC Consortium was already producing a participatory sub-regional plan. The commencement of an Emplasa-led planning process in 2016 was unsettling for these processes.[10] The consortium saw itself as taking the 'slower process of getting things right' through collaborative visioning, building partnerships and engaging seriously with civil society, and was now faced with a rushed process that could take planning, once again, in a technocratic direction.[11]

The process revealed different approaches to planning, but it went ahead in terms of the timeframes. The São Paulo MR's structures were set up at the beginning of 2017 to supervise the plan-making process and finally approve the plan. One of the by-products of the process was the closer relationship established between the ABC Consortium and the municipality of São Paulo, then under the leadership of the PT mayor, Fernando Haddad, as they jointly engaged Emplasa in the PDUI process. While some of the actors had concerns about Emplasa as a technocratic agency, the agency's capacity was upgraded with the hiring of new officials and better financial resourcing, and the PDUI was formally approved on 2 May 2019.[12]

In Rio de Janeiro, the *Estatuto das Metrópole* was inserted into the drawn-out process of negotiating an arrangement for metropolitan governance. In September 2015, the *Câmara Metropolitana* finally submitted draft legislation for metropolitan governance to the state assembly. The chamber had attempted to build partnerships and broaden the debate, but it was a difficult environment and the outcome was limited, reflecting the attempts by municipal representatives to preserve their autonomy. The bill dealt with specific areas of common interest (transport, solid waste and basic sanitation, and spatial planning). The legislation included the establishment of a deliberative council that would be chaired by the governor, with the 21 mayors of the MR having voting powers proportional to the number of inhabitants in each municipality. Even so, there was unease as the voting formula seemingly concentrated power within the hands of the state government and the core municipality. There was also criticism over the neglect of civil society in these arrangements (Loureiro and Leite 2018).

This draft state legislation coincided with the new federal legislation and fell short of its standards. It also came at a time of 'political atrophy' in the state of Rio de Janeiro (Ribeiro and Britto 2018). Therefore, the state legislation did not proceed until 2018, with the passing of Complementary Law 184/2018. Nevertheless, faced with sanctions for not approving the PDUI on time, the state government entered a contractual arrangement with the municipality of Rio de Janeiro to produce the plan, drawing on World Bank financing and expertise. Rushing the process, it commissioned a private consortium to prepare the plan. Despite disagreements between the state government and the consultants, the PDUI was completed and then approved on 18 December 2018, under the title *Modelar Metrópole*.[13] The final product was technocratic in orientation, but it did deal with some of the critical regional-level conflicts within the MR, including the construction of a large dam that faced popular opposition, the separation of drainage and sanitation systems, environmental problems at the port and disputes around social services.

In Belo Horizonte, a plan-making process was concluded before the arrival of the *Estatuto das Metrópole*. The process was nonetheless consistent with the participatory requirement of the federal legislation and there was therefore no difficulty in complying with the PDUI provision. The disappointment in Belo Horizonte was that implementation was slower than hoped, as the economic crisis in Brazil had left the state's Fund for Metropolitan Development severely depleted (IPEA 2019).

In each of the three MRs, a PDUI was concluded and approved on time, although with varying degrees of quality in terms of process and substance. Elsewhere in Brazil, however, there were major challenges in meeting the time requirement. The Act was amended to extend the completion deadline by three years, to December 2021, and to drop the legal sanction against governors and mayors for non-compliance. For some, this removed the teeth the Act had, effectively making compliance voluntary (IPEA 2019).

More seriously, Brazil took a conservative turn under right-wing populism, and many of Brazil's new leaders across the federation levels had little interest in metropolitan governance or planning. In some cases, they were antagonistic. One of my Brazilian colleagues lamented the changes, including the amendment to the Act, referring to a 'deep and hard attack on all kinds of regulation in Brazil including planning'. *The Guardian* reported on 18 July 2019 that, on his first day in office, President Bolsonaro closed the Ministry of Cities, ending Brazil's 'great urban experiment' (although the ministry was, in fact, far past its prime in the early years of Lula da Silva's first presidency) (Scruggs 2019).

These changes translated unevenly across the federation. In the state of São Paulo, João Doria, the right-wing mayor who replaced the PT's Fernando Haddad, became governor in January 2019. As a businessman, the governor viewed himself as a manager rather than a politician, campaigning for privatisation and the downsizing of government. In May 2019, under his advice, the state legislature resolved to close the recently rejuvenated Emplasa, with its functions absorbed into the state secretariat. Some media commentary indicated that the closure of Emplasa was a major setback for metropolitan governance, involving the destruction of planning capacity when it was sorely needed (Maglio 2019).

In the state of Rio de Janeiro, Governor Eduardo da Costa Paes, the previous city mayor with a reputation for technocratic efficiency and an interest in regional governance, unexpectedly lost the election to Wilson Witzel, a supporter of Jair Bolsonaro. Even in Belo Horizonte, with its history of collaborative politics and coalition governments, there had been a rightwards turn. Overall, the metropolitan governance agenda in Brazil had fallen on evil days.

However, Brazilian politics is fluid. Nationally, Bolsonaro lost support for his handling of the Covid-19 pandemic and his undermining of democratic institutions, and he was defeated by Lula da Silva in the national elections of October 2022. However, the federal nature of Brazil and the splintering of party politics constrain presidential powers, and the election of Bolsonaro allies as governors of the states of São Paulo, Rio de Janeiro and Minas Gerais (where Belo Horizonte is located) is a major kerb on potential presidential initiatives to restore momentum to the metropolitan governance agenda.

Conclusions

The prospects for metropolitan- or city-region-scale governance in Brazil are shaped by the path dependencies of a historically shaped political culture and constitutional set-up, but also by the adaptive capacity of the governmental system.

In particular, the strong commitment to local autonomy in Brazil's re-established democracy – an understandable response to a history of heavy-handed centralist rule – complicated efforts to address matters of collective concern across large urban agglomerations. Brazil may be in 'a classical scalar trap' where circumstances at a particular time resulted in a governmental arrangement that proved inadequate later (Klink 2014, 640).

Nevertheless, there is capacity for adaptation in the governmental system, and there was a slow and fitful evolution from a simplistic interpretation of local autonomy to a more complex federalism, better positioned to respond to collective challenges (Selcher 1989). This culminated in the *Estatuto das Metrópole* of 2015. Also, in the absence of adequate metropolitan-scale arrangements, emergent responses, including inter-municipal consortia, were eventually institutionalised in federal legislation. Changes within Brazil's politics, however, continually intervene in the processes of governmental reform, and the turn to right-wing populism has meant that the *Estatuto das Metrópole* has been less transformative than hoped for.

These difficulties have prompted various rounds of reflection on what is possible within Brazil's political cultures and settlement constraints. There is broad consensus that Brazil's metropolitan regions could be governed far better, even though, as Cymbalista put it to me, Brazil's cities 'manage somehow.' For Cymbalista, a major institutional restructuring for metropolitan governance would require a massive exertion of bureaucratic and political energy for uncertain results. The more practical solution, he suggests, is to find the solutions that are already there and progressively improve and extend those. This supports an earlier reflection by Xavier de Souza Briggs (2008, 198) that Brazil's alternative to large-scale institutional change is to pursue 'a slower and more strategic learning-oriented path', and Jeroen Klink's wide-ranging analysis of metropolitan governance in his various contributions. More recently, Eduardo Marques has shown in his edited book, *The Politics of Progressive Incrementalism*, how there has been a gradual accumulation of positive change in São Paulo, despite failures and frequent setbacks (Marques 2021).

Finally, the institutional analysis provided in this chapter and various other contributions must be read together with ethnographic or other, more detailed local studies such as Aaron Ansell (2014), revealing how governance really works in practice as Brazil's complex mix of political cultures plays out in governance networks and processes.

Notes

1   This was explained to me by my academic colleagues Renato Cymbalista and Kazau Nakano in São Paulo.
2   As explained to me by officials of the ABC Consortium.
3   As commented to me by academic Jeroen Klink.
4   As explained to me by University of São Paulo academic Renato Cymbalista.
5   For updates on the continued work of the consortium, see https://consorcioabc.sp.gov.br.
6   See the Camara website: http://www.camarametropolitana.rj.gov.br/.
7   State of Minas Gerais Amendment to the Constitution No. 65, of 25/11/2004.
8   See the website of Plambel: http://www.rmbh.org.br.
9   See also the website of the RMBH: www.agenciarmbh.mg.gov.br/.
10 This was explained to me by participants in these existing planning processes.
11 As explained to me by the Federal University of ABC academic, Jeroen Klink, in 2017.
12 As explained by Jeroen Klink in 2019.
13 See the PDUI: https://www.modelarametropole.com.br/wp-content/uploads/2018/09/Resumo-executivo-Plano-Metropolitano-versão-digital-EN-2-compressed.pdf.

3 The governance of Russia's urban agglomerations

Introduction

Current debates on Russia's political culture focus on the characteristics of authoritarianism, centralism and conformity, questioning the possibilities for building a sustainable democracy (Pipes 2004). However, as Adrian Campbell (2016) explained, the current phase of centralising authority under President Putin is part of a long trajectory of history with an established pattern of devolution followed by periods of reinstated central control.

While Russia's current politics are hardly amenable to collaborative forms of governance, support for authoritarianism has varied over time and may be the outcome of historically embedded social contracts in which the population concede personal rights in return for security, rather than a fixed political culture (Feldmann and Mazepus 2018). Also, focussing only on the mechanisms of vertical integration from the Kremlin downwards (the authoritarianism) obscures forms of horizontal collaboration that have evolved in the post-Soviet era.

This chapter begins with a reach back into history, exploring how contemporary processes may be shaped by long histories and more recent political settlements. It further provides a brief context to urban Russia. The focus then shifts to the fitful evolution of collaborative governance in the post-Soviet era in relation to Russia's two largest urban agglomerations centred on Moscow and Saint Petersburg.

Shaping the political cultures and settlement

Russia emerged as a nation state through a long process of empire building that began in the eighth century CE, leaving the challenge of how to sustain territorial integration for future generations. To maintain territorial coherence, Russia has vacillated between extremes. At times the empire was held together through autocratic – even tyrannical – rule but at other times the bond was negotiated through allegiances and tributes to a common ruler by partly autonomous vassal states.

By the nineteenth century, the patrimonial rule of Russia's tsars had evolved, partly, into a bureaucratic state with a form of modern governmental hierarchy. From 1860 on the rudiments of local self-government emerged as peasant communes, and evolved into structures known as the *zemstvos*, which experimented with electoral processes (McKenzie 1982). While the tsar was no democrat, in 1864 he accepted legislation that recognised the *zemstvos* as representative structures, autonomous of the formal government hierarchy. By the 1880s, the Russian elite was divided between the liberals who supported local self-governing structures and the conservatives who insisted that local bodies had to be subordinated to the higher levels of the state. The conservatives prevailed, and the counter reforms of 1890 brought the *zemstvos* into the state hierarchy (McKenzie 1982; Campbell 2016).

This was a pattern that was to repeat through Russia's history. The October Revolution of 1917 brought the hope that Vladimir Lenin's ideas of self-determination would translate into some form of devolved democracy. Instead, governance evolved into the hierarchical and bureaucratic Soviet Union, of which the Stalinist dictatorship was its most extreme form. In 1956, after the terrors of Stalinism, Nikita Khrushchev called for a revitalisation of local *soviets* (local councils), suggesting a tentative shift towards a restoration of some local autonomy (Hahn 1988). However, Khrushchev was removed, and the Brezhnev era from 1964 was a period of protracted institutional stagnation, with minimal progress in governmental reforms. In this phase, change happened through neglect: Timothy Colton (1995, 565) referred to this as 'the slackening over time of the thumbs of the state'. As centralised authority decayed, rent-seeking local and regional elites established their own domains for autonomous action and patronage.

Gorbachev's perestroika (restructuring) in the late 1980s was an attempt to revitalise the Russian polity. However, the reforming elite split into the factions led respectively by Mikhail Gorbachev and Boris Yeltsin, and both the Soviet Union and the Communist Party had collapsed by the end of 1991. Gordon Hahn (2002) argues that the troubled development of democracy in post-Soviet Russia has to do with the nature of this transition and the political settlement. The political transformation was engineered by a faction of the elite rather than in response to mass mobilisation as in some contexts in Eastern Europe, which left civil society stunted and unable to contain the ambitions of the post-Soviet elite.

For decentralists, the post-Soviet era began promisingly in 1995, when a federal law established local government as an autonomous sphere. However, the law's implementation coincided with a period of deep economic crisis, and the prospects for effective local action were dim. For the national elites in the mid-1990s, empowering local government was a useful offset to the threats posed by regional barons, but as this threat was neutralised, the national government closed the space for autonomous local action (Gel'man 2015).

Vladimir Putin took office as president in 2000, determined to re-centralise control and restore structure to a country that had experienced a chaotic transition. The Putin era has been characterised by an authoritarian conservatism with a pendulum swing away from the liberal reformism of the Gorbachev and Yeltsin eras. Characteristics of this conservatism include the emphasis on patriotism, traditional Russian values, the Orthodox Church, moral restoration and the strong leader (Jonson 2018). The state is weakly institutionalised, with authority resting in a super-presidential system and individualised leadership. Where local autonomy is strong, such as in the case of Moscow, the national elite has loyalists in power locally (Gel'man 2015).

However, in the large cities at least, this authoritarian conservatism may imply a social contract of sorts rather than a deeply grained culture of subservience to authority, and the ground may shift as conditions change (Bernsand and Törnquist-Plewa 2018).

Urban context

As a brief context, the Russian Federation is highly urbanised (75 per cent, with around 105 million people in urban areas), yet there are only two urban agglomerations that are significant in global terms (Map 2). The City of Moscow has a population of around 12.4 million within a wider urban agglomeration of around 18 to 20 million (depending on how it is defined), while Saint Petersburg has around five million people, with six million in the wider agglomeration. The next largest agglomeration is Novosibirsk, which has around 1.5 million people (United Nations 2018).

Institutionally, Russia is a federation of 88 entities, ranging from *oblasts* (regional or provincial government) to autonomous republics for linguistic or ethnic minorities. There are also around 12 000 municipalities, of which about 600 are recognised as cities. Three of these municipalities – Moscow, Saint Petersburg and Sevastopol (in the annexed region of the Crimea) – have federal status.

To provide a brief context of the two major agglomerations: Москва (Moskva or Moscow) is in Central Russia and evolved from a small river port in the thirteenth century CE to become the capital of the Grand Duchy of Russia. It evolved through the centuries into a large city as the Grand Duchy expanded into the Russian Empire. In the seventeenth century, however, it experienced a series of disasters, including fires that ravaged most of the city and a plague that destroyed around 80 per cent of the population. Tsar Peter the Great decided to start anew and build a new capital, Saint Petersburg, formally established in 1703. Peter the Great was a Westerniser, and it was no coincidence that the Russian capital was built facing Europe and part of the trading network along the Baltic Sea. Saint Petersburg was the larger and more important city through the nineteenth century, but the October Revolution changed this. In

1918, the Bolsheviks transferred the capital back to Moscow, and it was Moscow that expanded rapidly into the leading city of Russia and the Soviet Union.

There are enduring differences in governmental approaches between the two cities. As the national capital, Moscow has tended toward a more bureaucratic and centralised governance model, while Saint Petersburg has historically been more strongly influenced by European approaches to local democracy, with their greater emphasis on decentralised arrangements.

Both Moscow and Saint Petersburg are encircled by territory administered by an *oblast* (or region). This is different from the other BRICS (Brazil, Russia, India, China and South Africa) countries, where the city falls within the provincial- or state-level administration and where there is a sharing of power across the levels. In Russia, Moscow and the Moscow *Oblast*, and Saint Petersburg and the Leningrad *Oblast*, are institutionally separated federative subjects without a formal requirement to establish any inter-federative structure. There is a doughnut-shaped institutional arrangement with the *oblast* encircling, but not encompassing, the core municipality.

However, the urban footprint of Moscow now extends far into the *oblast*, which is now over 80 per cent urbanised, with a series of interconnected settlements including four small cities of between 200 000 and 300 000 each and 17 large towns with populations of between 100 000 and 200 000 (Map 9). The settlement pattern is not amorphous, though. Beyond the expanding concentric structure of Moscow, settlement forms a mainly linear pattern extending along the major transportation routes that radiate outwards from the core (Akishin and Akishin 2017). Functionally, there is also a close relationship between Saint Petersburg and the Leningrad *Oblast*, with at least 400 000 residents of Leningrad moving daily to work in Saint Petersburg and about 700 000 residents of Saint Petersburg spending their summers in Leningrad (Vaitans et al. 2020) (Map 10).

While city and *oblast* are constitutionally equal in status, the two cities in this study carry far greater influence in the system than their *oblast* neighbours because of the unequal democratic and economic weight (see Table 3.1) and, less visibly, because of upward political connections.

Territorial administration	Population size (in millions)	Size of economy (in million US$, 2013)[1]	Gross domestic product per capita (in US$, 2013)
City of Moscow	12.4	364 655	30 277
Moscow *Oblast*	7.2	79 977	11 279
City of Saint Petersburg	5.0	78 262	15 406
Leningrad *Oblast*	1.8	21 717	12 357

TABLE 3.1: Comparing city and *oblast*

Source: Europa 2016

Having provided the necessary context of Russia's long history, political cultures, political settlement and the development of the urban, I turn now to the governance forms within Russia's major urban agglomerations as they evolved from the time of Soviet rule, through the transition period and into the post-Soviet era.

City and *oblast* under Soviet rule (see Maps 19 and 20)

Under Soviet rule, achieving vertical integration down the party hierarchy was the dominant imperative and essential for maintaining authoritarian rule against potential sub-national challenges. Nevertheless, some form of horizontal or territorial integration was required to ensure the spatial functioning of the planned economic production and integration system. The dominant mechanism of territorial integration was the Communist Party of the Soviet Union (CPSU), which brought together cadres from the cities and the regions in interlinked structures (Golubchikov 2004).

Moscow and Saint Petersburg (city and *oblast*) under the Soviets

In July 1918, the Moscow City Council was created at a provincial Congress of Soviets of Workers', Soldiers' and Peasants' Deputies. The supreme body was the Plenum, which elected the executive committee, with departments established for the necessary administrative actions. At this stage, the Moscow City Council operated as part of the Moscow province (later *oblast*). There was a joint political structure – the Council of People's Commissars of Moscow and Moscow Province – while the 1921 Regulations on Councils in Moscow and the Moscow Province required operational unity between the activities of the city and the province. In fact, the Moscow City Council was simply known as the Moscow Provincial Council of Workers, Peasants and Red Army Deputies (Bruz et al. 2019, 146).

Moscow was, however, separated from the *oblast* for administrative reasons in 1931 as industrialisation led to the expanded growth of the city, creating the dual system of governance that persists to the present. For a time, however, there was cross-cutting membership of the city and *oblast* structures, allowing for some level of coordination, but this was discontinued in 1955. From then, coordination, to the extent that it happened, was achieved at a higher level in the party hierarchy. Power and focus also shifted over time from the *oblast* to the city.

The 1935 General Plan for the Reconstruction of Moscow was Stalin's vision for the world's premier socialist city. It was ambitious, with monumental elements such as the underground rail system and grand boulevards lined with apartment blocks, but it also tried to contain the city's growth in terms of population and physical size. Moscow had grown rapidly from 1.8 million at the time of the October Revolution in 1917 to 3.7 million by 1935, and the plan proposed to cap the population at five million by 1960, with physical expansion contained by a ten-kilometre-wide swathe of open space around the city, separating it from the region (Colton 1995).

However, Moscow's agglomeration effect was powerful, and the city's population continued to rise, although the greenbelt did help contain the physical spread, producing a city that was compact in global terms. Nevertheless, there were periodic extensions to the city at the region's expense to accommodate new development. Under Khrushchev's premiership, the city expanded as the great belt of concrete-panelled apartment blocks built up public housing around the outskirts of Moscow. In 1971, Moscow's Third General Plan proposed a Greater Moscow with the excess population to be housed in eight new towns beyond the outer edge of the greenbelt. However, this was the beginning of a prolonged period of institutional decay in the Soviet Union under Leonid Brezhnev's premiership, and the capabilities needed for implementation were progressively reduced. Only one satellite city was built, and the vision of a Greater Moscow gradually dissipated (Colton 1995). During the Brezhnev era, the controls on migration into Moscow caused many people working in the city's jurisdiction to settle in the *oblast*, while the housing estates on the edge of Moscow gradually pushed out into the region (Colton 1995).

Settlement in the *oblast* was institutionally neglected. Colton (1995, 475) explained that 'Moscow's rulers were not keen to take on the problems of the larger city region'. Donald Filtzer (2006) pointed to the adverse environmental effects of this neglect. For example, the rivers serving the *oblast* were polluted daily by around 500 000 cubic metres of waste from Moscow, with serious impacts on human health.

Nevertheless, concerns with regional-scale coordination were not entirely removed from the agenda, resurfacing during the perestroika era under Gorbachev's leadership in the mid to late 1980s. Colton (1995, 692) reported that the issues of Moscow's relationship to its hinterland 'personally concerned Yeltsin and Zaikov, the third- and second-last leaders of the Moscow CPSU'. Zaikov requested Premier Gorbachev to establish a unified party structure (*obkom*) for the city and *oblast*, but the party leaders in the *oblast* objected, resentful of the continued annexation of territory for the city. The draft 1989 General Plan for Moscow offered a regional framework with a strong environmental consciousness, but with the Soviet Union on the brink of collapse, this was not an opportune moment for regional coordination (Colton 1995).

Saint Petersburg was a quite different case. Leonid Limonov (2013, 3) argues that 'from the beginning of the 18th century, and until 1991, the City and Region represented a single, integral, socio-economic organism'. He suggests a cultural basis for integration between the two entities as 'residents consider St. Petersburg and the adjacent parts of the Leningrad region as a single area of life' (Limonov 2013, 14). The other difference is that, while Moscow was in the geographical core of Russia and had a powerful national orientation, Saint Petersburg looked both outwards and inwards, forming a critical hub in both the Baltic-European and Russian transportation systems (Limonov 2013).

After Saint Petersburg's founding, it was incorporated within the province of Ingria and, despite being the capital of Russia at the time, was administered as part of the province. In 1927, a decade after the Russian Revolution, the Leningrad region was established as an amalgamation of four provinces with a population then of 6.5 million people, of which 1.7 million lived in Leningrad City (now Saint Petersburg).

In 1931, Leningrad City became a separate administrative entity, but party authorities continued to accept the city and *oblast* as a common territory. The Leningrad Regional Communist Party Committee was politically responsible for both jurisdictions, with the first secretary to the Leningrad *Oblast* also serving as the first secretary to Leningrad City. This arrangement persisted through the Soviet era. This joint committee presided over joint strategy and plan-making into the late Soviet era. This included 'Intensification-90', a regional economic programme for developing the city and *oblast* prepared in 1985, and the Joint Master Plan for the Development of Leningrad and Leningrad Region, approved by the USSR (Soviet Union) Council of Ministers in 1987. The plan may, in fact, have been envisaged as a step toward the administrative reunification of the city and the region. However, political change meant that its implementation was dramatically cut short, with the significant exception of the construction of the Ring Road (Limonov 2013). Limonov (2013, 3) explains:

> In the Soviet era, the City and Region were complementary to each other. For the City, the Region served as a reserve for expansion, an important source of food supply and replenishment of human resources, a recreational area, and a site for placing branches of a few large municipal enterprises. For the Region, the City performed educational, cultural, medical, commercial, and transport functions, was an important supplier of various industrial and consumer goods, and a place of employment for some of the residents.

The rise of the urban agglomeration

Using the veneer of science, the planner had to determine the spatial forms that would best support state-led industrialisation. It was in this context that the idea of the urban agglomeration (городская агломерация pronounced as *gorodskaya aglomeratsiya*) gained traction, explaining in part why the term 'city-region' (город-регион) is not commonly used in Russia.

Urban agglomerations were understood to be economically functional units and the term was used to describe the growing urban-industrial nodes of the Soviet Union. The earliest use of the term occurred in studies conducted during the 1950s, but there was a spate of research on the topic in scientific institutes in the 1970s and 80s, with an academic field called 'agglomeration studies' emerging within the economics departments of universities. For histories and interpretations of the Russian concept of urban agglomeration, see G.M. Lappo and V. Ya. Lyubovnyi (2011) and N. Musinova (2019).

Recent definitions of 'urban agglomeration' do, in fact, resonate with ideas of the city-region in Western scholarship:

> A compact and relatively developed set of mutually complementary urban and rural settlements, grouped around one or several powerful cities-nuclei and united by diverse and intensive connections into a complex and dynamic unity [translated]. (Geography n.d., para. 1)
>
> 'Large urban agglomeration' – a set of compactly located settlements and territories with a population of over 500 000 people associated with the joint use of infrastructure facilities and intensive economic, labor, and social connections. (Government of the Russian Federation 2019, 2)

However, despite the apparent similarity in meaning, the discursive origin of the Russian urban agglomeration is different to that of the Western city-region.

Although the term 'urban agglomeration' became increasingly common, its translation into governance arrangements was never clear. Governance happened through the party hierarchy and *Gosudarstvennyy Planovyy Komitet* (State Planning Committee), the complex mechanism of national economic planning disaggregated into smaller scales. Integrated settlement or spatial planning was never the driver, so it was not easy to translate an economic concept such as the urban agglomeration into a governance mechanism. Also, with the institutional decay in the 1970s and early 80s, there was little interest in reorganising governance (Lappo and Lyubovnyi 2011).

The lost opportunities of the transition

The dramatic collapse of the Soviet Union and the dissolution of the CPSU in 1991 marked the sudden end of the only mechanism that existed for coordination between the city and the *oblast*. Without institutional mechanisms for coordination, the connection was entirely through party structures – tenuously so in the case of Moscow and more intimately so in the case of Leningrad. Oleg Golubchikov (2010) argues that under communist rule, there was an ostensible commitment to spatial equality, with large cities such as Moscow and Saint Petersburg having some responsibility for their backyards. However, with the ending of communist rule, they were released from this responsibility and could focus on positioning themselves within global corporate networks and in relation to the powers of the central government.

There were nevertheless attempts, in the early 1990s, to create integrated structures for the governance of the wider Moscow and Leningrad regions. Gavriil Popov, the first democratically elected head of the Moscow city government, strongly supported a 'Unified Capital Region of Moscow', winning Yeltsin over to the idea, and even persuaded the outgoing president of the disintegrating Soviet Union, Mikhail Gorbachev, to appoint a commission to investigate its practicality (Colton 1995).

In April 1991, Russia's Supreme Soviet instructed the City and *Oblast* of Moscow to poll their respective residents on creating an amalgamated territory. In the city, residents voted 61 per cent in favour. The *oblast*, however, would not even conduct the poll, resentful of Moscow's territorial annexation and aware that the region would be dominated by the numerically and economically dominant city. The federal government at the time did not have the strength or willingness to overcome this resistance.

The opportunity was lost, and, by the mid-1990s, the leaders in the city were opposed to amalgamation, having calculated the cost of bringing the level of services in the *oblast* to the same standard as that of the city. By that time also, the national leadership had lost interest in the idea of amalgamation, fearing that more power for sub-national governments would pose an active threat to the centre, including, potentially, from the politically ambitious mayor of Moscow, Yury Luzhkov.[2]

Nevertheless, in 1996, the legislative assemblies of the city and *oblast*, the respective dumas, set up The United Commission of the Moscow City Duma and the Moscow Region Duma to coordinate legislative activities. This proved, however, to be a low-key structure as power shifted decisively in the 1990s from the legislatures to the executive.

There was also a lost opportunity in Saint Petersburg. Like Moscow, the collapse of the CPSU led to the immediate disintegration of all mechanisms of institutional coordination between the city and the *oblast*. Here too, there were calls for an amalgamated territory, but political interests and ambitions blocked the move. The divide between the city and the region widened when Leningrad was renamed the City of Saint Petersburg, distinguishing the city from both its communist past and from the region, which retained the name Leningrad *Oblast* (Limonov 2013).

Both Moscow and Saint Petersburg entered the 2000s with the city and the *oblast* as close neighbours, but without any formal institutional coordination mechanism. Their only option in resolving disputes and concerns about coordination was ad hoc negotiation, which was persistently complicated by institutional and political rivalries, and often had unsatisfactory outcomes (Limonov 2013). Before turning to the Putin era after 2000, it is necessary to indicate what was happening politically and institutionally in the two core cities during the 1990s.

President Yeltsin appointed Luzhkov as mayor of Moscow in 1992 and assisted him in installing a super-mayoralty. Personal relations were a pivotal factor in sustaining the vertical connection between the federal government and the City of Moscow. Under the protection of the president, Luzhkov set up a formidable patrimonial regime in Moscow, notoriously using city ownership of land and financial institutions to channel resources to business cronies (Jensen 2000).

While Luzhkov ran a kleptocracy that massively enriched his cronies, he also understood the need for social legitimation: 'He would make sure the lives of average Muscovites improved, whilst the latter would not take issue with the way business was done in Moscow' (Büdenbender and Zupen 2016, 302). However, the governance pact unravelled with the financial crisis of 2008 as credit lines dried up for city government and Luzhkov was unable to maintain the networks of patronage within his fiefdom.

While Luzhkov's personal power eventually waned, he had set up a highly centralised structure. The city administration was divided into ten prefectures (*okrugs*) and 125 sub-prefectures (*upravi*), but the real power was vested within the central administration, especially within the mayor's office. The heads of the lower divisions are appointed from above, and the elected councils for sub-prefectures are purely advisory. The mayor handles city finances directly and appoints seven vice-mayors for portfolios, including utilities, social development, economic development, transport, housing and planning. The mayor's strength also comes from the relative financial autonomy of the city, with around 95 per cent of the city revenue raised internally, compared with an average of 56 per cent for other cities in Russia, excluding Saint Petersburg. At the same time, however, the mayor has a direct line to the national president through the status Moscow has as a federal city, and all links between the city and federal administrations go through the mayor's office.[3]

In Saint Petersburg, the post-Soviet story also begins with the personalised rule of a charismatic mayor (later governor), Anatoly Sobchak. The mayor, however, had an uneasy relationship with President Yeltsin and fled into exile in Paris in 1996 to avoid a corruption probe. His replacement, Vladimir Yakovlev, was a safe option for Yeltsin.

With its different political culture, Saint Petersburg developed a more decentralised governance structure than Moscow. Saint Petersburg transitioned from a municipal authority under a mayor to a regional authority headed by a governor, comprising 111 municipal formations with their charters. A bottom-up form of coordination has emerged in Saint Petersburg through associations of municipal entities. The Municipal Chamber of Saint Petersburg, for example, brings together 34 municipal entities, while the Union of Municipal Formations brings together nine entities in a collaborative formation.

The struggle to collaborate in the post-Soviet era

The return of vertical integration

Vladimir Putin came to power in 2000 and worked systematically to ensure restored vertical integration. The challenge he faced was the power and autonomy of sub-national authorities, which had consolidated during the chaotic transition of the 1990s (Gel'man and Ryzhenkov 2011; Büdenbender and Zupen 2016).

In the case of Moscow, Putin faced a political rival, Luzhkov, who had his eye on the presidency and relationships were immediately strained. However, Luzhkov had been weakened by the 2008 crisis, and he was finally removed as mayor in 2010. He was replaced by a previous chief of staff in Putin's office, Sergey Sobyanin.

Sobyanin was a skilled technocrat. When he came into office, he faced mass protests on the streets of Moscow that threatened both local and national stability. However, he soon deployed his managerial skills to placate the restless middle class. He brought young, well-educated staff to replace older bureaucrats and used technology to transform governance systems. The changes in Moscow attracted international attention, with even *The Economist* observing that 'Moscow has become a laboratory for a different kind of governing model: rather than repress or alienate, the Moscow authorities look to placate those sympathetic to the opposition by offering a softer, more agreeable, altogether less risible place to live' (*The Economist*, 20 December 2012).[4]

Sobyanin was able to reinstate the tacit pact with citizens who were impressed by his managerial competency and the changes in the city. However, national and local politics are entwined, and Sobyanin's relationship with Putin concerned the liberal middle class (Shestopal and Yakovleva 2016). In the 2013 local elections, Sobyanin was nearly unseated by the Putin critic, Alexei Navalny. In 2018, he was rewarded for his work with a comfortable win, but the 2019 Moscow Duma elections were more complicated, with mass street protests in reaction to the disqualification of various opposition candidates and a sharp decline in support for Putin's United Russia, which managed only 32 per cent of the votes in Moscow.

The bond between Putin and Sobyanin was sustained despite the difference in temperament and approach between the two leaders. This bond ensured Moscow's continued autonomy as a sub-national government despite the erosion of sub-national powers elsewhere; Putin had little need to intervene with his trusted acolyte, Sobyanin, in office, who provided both competency and loyalty.[5]

The story in Saint Petersburg was different. Yeltsin's man, Vladimir Yakovlev, was redeployed to a region in the far south of Russia, and replaced by a firm Putin ally, Valentina Matviyenko, who was largely unable to placate the liberal-leaning citizens of the city. She was replaced in 2011 by a previous *Komitet Gosudarstvennoy Bezopasnosti* (Committee for State Security) member, Georgy Poltavchenko, but his deep conservatism further alienated the citizenry. Poltavchenko was removed as governor in 2019, as there were fears of heavy losses for United Russia in the 2019 regional elections. He was replaced by Alexander Beglov, but, at the time of writing, Beglov was battling to retain the support of the political elite in the city, and there were rumours of Putin's dissatisfaction with his performance (Pertsev 2022).

The battle for horizontal integration

Whereas vertical integration was more or less secured in Putin's Russia (the legitimacy problems in Saint Petersburg notwithstanding), horizontal integration remained a governance challenge. A top-level official in the City of Moscow, for example, acknowledged to me that 'coordination between the City and the Region is very weak; nearly non-existent'. According to this official, areas where coordination is required include 'transport infrastructure, ecological maintenance, location of new housing, waste management, economic development and coordination of bulk infrastructure at the interface of the city and the region'. Various informal and ad hoc attempts to coordinate 'simply have not worked as a direct result of the different priorities, politics, issues and interests between the city and the region', and 'the only area in which coordination is actively happening is transport infrastructure, and this is because of an intervention by the federal government'.

This need for coordination was a consequence of private-sector-driven sprawl into the region. The compaction of the Soviet era had given way to rapid urban expansion driven by the private motor vehicle, privatisation of housing and the disintegration of formal planning controls. A specifically Russian phenomenon was the development of *dachas* (or second homes) in the region for summer residence (Golubchikov and Phelps 2011).

Development in the region placed a huge strain on the *oblast*, which had to provide the infrastructure for this growth. Points of tension emerged along the boundary with the city over the coordination of bulk infrastructure, transport linkages and (the lack of) environmental protection. In 2007, the Moscow *Oblast* introduced a general development plan to improve the coordination of development within its jurisdiction, but this did not resolve the poorly managed interface with the City of Moscow. Oleg Golubchikov and Nicholas Phelps (2011) provide the example of Khimki, an amorphously shaped satellite city just over the border from Moscow that had been developing since the 1990s. Some of the interface problems were resolved when the City of Moscow adjusted its boundaries to incorporate new developments or engaged in ad hoc or informal coordination modes, but the broad problem remained.

Similar problems emerged at the interface between the City of Saint Petersburg and the Leningrad *Oblast*, although at a significantly smaller scale. For example, at least 700 000 residents of Saint Petersburg live in their *dachas* between May and September each year, massively increasing the burden on the *oblast*. Needing a tax income, the *oblast* encouraged development along its border with Saint Petersburg, but this included hazardous activities such as aluminium smelting, sewage processing and waste landfill sites, with environmental consequences for the city (Limonov 2013). In 2007, lobbying from Saint Petersburg prompted the federal government to propose a law to the national Parliament for special controls on any new development within 50 kilometres of the city boundary, but the legislation was withdrawn after an angry response from the Leningrad *Oblast*, rejecting it as an intrusion into its powers (Limonov 2013).

The city and the *oblast* were drawn into growing competition for resources and investment as the Saint Petersburg-Leningrad urban agglomeration emerged as a major hub of the oil and gas industry in Russia. There have been significant investments, including a new port, a large new dam, a motorway and a new airport, requiring logistical coordination. However, the major mode of engagement between the two regional authorities is competition, with each administration deploying generous incentives to lure investors (Limonov 2013).

For both Moscow and Saint Petersburg, the federal government's taxation system is a source of grievance for the *oblasts*, presenting an ongoing obstacle to collaboration and exacerbating the problem of the *dachas*. Russia's tax system is complex, with the federal government dependent for its revenue largely on VAT and a tax on oil production, while regional governments are funded mainly through corporate and personal income tax. The payment of personal income tax is made to the employer's registered region of employment and not to the region in which the employee resides. This presents a major challenge for the Moscow and Leningrad *oblasts* as they govern the commuting belt around the core cities, losing tax income from their residents to the cities where employment is concentrated (Borchert 2000). The *oblasts* have objected to the funding system, arguing it is severely weighted against them. In 2008, the Moscow *Oblast* initiated a federal bill to reform the system but made no progress against the enormous lobbying power of the City of Moscow (Limonov 2013). One of my informants in Moscow referred to the competition between authorities over taxation as 'a matter of struggle and envy'.

A federal response (beyond the Moscow and Saint Petersburg urban agglomerations)

As Nadir Kinossian (2016) explains, spatial policy in post-Soviet Russia has vacillated between an active attempt to achieve spatial balance across the Russian Federation through decentralisation, and a modernising agenda that accepts the role of concentrated growth in large cities as an engine of national economic growth.

A Ministry of Regional Policy was created in 1998 to ensure territorial coherence across Russia, becoming the Ministry of Regional Development in 2004, but the tension between decentralisation and agglomeration remained. Over time, however, a mediated position emerged within the ministry that aimed to develop secondary agglomerations as a counterweight to Moscow and Saint Petersburg, building on the established concept of urban agglomerations (Lappo and Lyubovnyi 2011).

From around 2006, the ministry explored the possibility of some form of metropolitan governance for urban agglomerations. In 2010, during Dmitry Medvedev's modernising tenure as national president, the Office of the President proposed up to 20 metropolitan regions for special budgetary attention in order to catalyse economic growth and innovation. In 2013, the ministry set up a working group for the socio-economic development of metropolitan regions and, through a bidding process, 16 pilot regions were selected for programmatic attention (Kinossian 2016).

This process gave de facto recognition by the federal government to the idea of metropolitan governance, although there was still no formal legislative provision. Municipalities were incentivised to participate in the programme through federal funding streams, with funding provided once constitutive municipalities' mayors had signed an inter-municipal cooperation agreement and a metropolitan regional development plan had been produced.

The process was experimental, and there is no guarantee of success, with a 2016 review indicating that good progress had been made in only five of the 16 pilots. Many municipalities were uncertain about participation; while it brought federal resources to their localities, and there were practical benefits to be had in collaborating with neighbours, there were also fears that the process would strengthen the positions of regional administrations (and ultimately of federal government) over municipalities, as the *oblasts* were playing a coordinating role in the process. Kinossian (2016) was cautiously optimistic that these experiments might gradually evolve into meaningful processes of metropolitan governance.

There has been an incremental process to give official or legal status to these initial experiments, despite the abolition of the Ministry of Regional Development in 2014, ostensibly because of duplication with other ministries. In May 2014, the Basic Federal Law on Local Government was amended to allow for the amalgamation of municipalities into an urban district. By 2017 there were ten instances where this had happened, although there were local protests out of concern that these amalgamations represented a further centralisation of government and undermined local authority (Musinova 2019).

By 2014, the first draft of the Spatial Development Strategy for the Russian Federation up to 2025 was released. It proposed a polycentric spatial structure for Russia, with development focussed on urban agglomerations connected by high-speed transport networks. The Ministry for Economic Development took over responsibility for the strategy, and when its final version was released in February 2019, the idea of urban agglomerations within a polycentric network was strongly embedded within an economic logic (Government of the Russian Federation 2019).

There was, however, continued uncertainty as to what urban agglomerations meant in governance terms (Association of Siberian and Far Eastern Cities 2018). In November 2018, Russia's Federal Council (the parliamentary body representing sub-national governments) launched a participatory process for considering the forms and methods of managing urban agglomerations.

Moscow and Saint Petersburg were not participants in the experimental programme, as the programme was intended to create counterweights to these cities, but also because of the limited available federal resources, which were weak incentives for cities that were already well resourced financially (Kinossian 2016).

Moscow: stumbling towards sector-based coordination

There are strong centralising mechanisms of coordination within the City of Moscow. A senior official explained to me how the city implements large inter-sectoral programmes. The typical approach is for the mayor to designate one of his vice-mayors as the responsible person for the project, who then convenes an inter-sectoral working group. The mayor holds the purse strings and releases the budget as required.

Coordination between the city and the *oblast* remains weak. Except for the cooperation in the legislative sphere, formal engagement between the two administrations is mainly limited to technical collaboration between service utilities, and ad hoc joint committees for individual sectors, although I was advised that these committees are 'super weak'.[6] Practical considerations do, however, require informal problem solving on an ongoing basis. At the 2017 Moscow Urban Forum, for example, Mayor Sobyanin shared a stage with the governor of the Moscow *Oblast* but when asked about coordination between the city and the *oblast*, Sobyanin answered that he has an excellent personal rapport with the governor and that there was little need to create formal structures.[7]

The interests of the city and the *oblast* diverge in many respects, and notwithstanding personal relationships, there are ongoing institutional challenges. The City of Moscow, for example, has an interest in using land beyond its boundaries for cemeteries and landfill sites, but these are hardly income-spinners for the *oblast*. It is, however, in the interests of the *oblast* to promote industrial and other economic development in its territory, supported by large-scale family housing, which counters the city's attempt to regulate sprawl.

More seriously, the city's continued annexation of land in the *oblast* exacerbates tension. Most recently, land annexation to Moscow has come at the federal government's initiative. In 2012, Prime Minister Medvedev sponsored one of the most ambitious annexations. Concerned with growing congestion in the City of Moscow, which was negatively affecting the functioning of the federal government, he announced that federal government offices would relocate to a New Moscow beyond the current urban edge. In August 2012, he proclaimed the annexation of a large swathe of land within the *oblast* to Moscow, nearly doubling the jurisdiction of the territory held by the City of Moscow. A six-month international design competition was held, with an international consortium proposing a new zero-carbon federal district (Holloway 2012). However, this extraordinary venture has lost impetus, with President Putin reportedly showing little real appetite for the development. While a large-scale move of federal government departments to New Moscow is increasingly unlikely, there is new residential development in the territory, spurred by relatively low land costs (Argenbright et al. 2020).

Transport is the one area where there has been significant progress with coordination, although this was initiated by the federal government. Moscow was a notoriously congested city, with its concentric formations exacerbating the effects of morning and afternoon rush hours. This directly affected the federal government's functioning, which had offices in the Kremlin in the central city.

Federal government intervened and, in November 2010, then President Dmitry Medvedev demanded coordinated action between the city and the *oblast*, warning that a lack of action was impacting national economic prospects.[8] In February 2011, then Prime Minister Vladimir Putin issued an order for the establishment of a Coordination Council for Transport for the City of Moscow and the Moscow *Oblast* (Government of the Russian Federation 2011a).

The federal government set up the joint council with the federal Minister of Transport as chairperson. It included the mayor of Moscow and the governor of the Moscow *Oblast*, as well as senior officials from the Federal Finance and Economic Development ministries. Federal government remained actively involved in transport affairs in the region, with the president, for example, putting Mayor Sobyanin and Governor Vorobyov on the spot at a public meeting in August 2013, insisting that they explain how they were prioritising and coordinating joint action in the sector.[9]

With this being a federal initiative and a possible embarrassment to the two regional administrations, it did provide the necessary structure for collaborations between the city and the *oblast* to emerge. Among the significant initiatives of the coordination council was the construction of the Moscow Central Circle belt railway, which linked a new transportation network to the regeneration of a derelict industrial belt.[10] The work of the Coordination Council for Transport also meshed with the activities of the Coordination Council for the Preparation of the 2018 FIFA World Cup, as the development of regional transport infrastructure was a priority for the games.

There was one area in which the City of Moscow took a strong initiative. In the period after the Russian occupation of Crimea in 2014, Moscow was experiencing degrees of international isolation. A group of young professionals persuaded the City of Moscow to adopt the theme 'Age of Agglomerations: Rethinking the World Map' for the 2017 meeting of its flagship Moscow Urban Forum.[11] The idea was taken up enthusiastically by a mayor eager to reassert his city within global networks and to emphasise Moscow's role in national development, which was challenged by Russia's new national spatial policy. The event was underpinned by a major commissioned report positioning Moscow in relation to other major agglomerations including Paris, London, New York, Buenos Aires, Beijing, Shanghai, Seoul, Tokyo and Sydney (PwC 2017).

While the mayor's interest in urban agglomerations had to do with reasserting Moscow's image and position, local professionals indicated that this new (officially appropriated) discourse opened the space to discuss matters of agglomeration-wide governance. There was a growing understanding among professionals, in and outside the city administration, that Moscow would not function optimally as a globally competitive urban agglomeration unless it resolved matters of coordination with the *oblast*.[12] The mayor's vision has, however, been dealt a devastating blow by the international response to the Russian invasion of Ukraine. Resources are likely to be more limited than before, while Russia's international isolation seriously diminishes attempts to project Moscow as a global city-region.

Saint Petersburg: innovating for cooperation

Although cooperation mechanisms collapsed with the ending of Soviet rule and the relationship between the City of Saint Petersburg and the Leningrad *Oblast* had become competitive, there were still memories of collaboration. This, together with practical considerations, led to joint initiatives by the 2000s.[13] The concept of an integrated region was increasingly accepted. The Fifth General Plan for Saint Petersburg, 2005 to 2025, identified a Zone of Active Influence for Saint Petersburg extending into the *oblast*, defined as a one-and-a-half-hour commute into the city centre (Vaitans et al. 2020).

In 2005, the governors of Saint Petersburg and Leningrad signed the Agreement on Co-operation and Mutual Assistance in Commercial, Economic, Scientific, Technical, Cultural and Social Areas of Life. A major area of concern was waste disposal and unauthorised dumping along the border of the city and the region, and a decision was taken to establish a coordinating council to address these problems, although Limonov (2013) observes that this venture failed to make a positive impact. Other agreements on clarifying borders, coordinating passenger transport and collecting statistics were signed in 2009/10.

As it did with Moscow, the federal government took the initiative in relation to transport. In 2008, the Ministry of Transport created a joint working group involving the federal government, Saint Petersburg and Leningrad to develop the Saint Petersburg-Leningrad transport hub. In 2011, the federal government established the Coordinating Council for the Development of the Transportation System in Saint Petersburg and Leningrad (Government of the Russian Federation 2011b). Like Moscow, the council is chaired by the Minister of Transport but includes high-level officials from Saint Petersburg and Leningrad.

The governments of Saint Petersburg and Leningrad took their initiative in December 2013, establishing a Coordination Council for Socio-Economic Development. Chairpersons of the council are the vice-governors of Saint Petersburg and Leningrad, with council members including the heads or deputy heads of the various departments of the administrations. The council meets at least every three months to achieve effective interaction at the executive level in areas including economic development, land-use planning, transport and engineering networks, waste disposal and environment protection (Vaitans et al. 2020).

The gradually expanding collaboration between the two regional administrations was consolidated in the preparation of 'The Concept of Urban Co-development of

Saint Petersburg and the Territories of the Leningrad Region for the Period up to 2030 and Perspective for 2050'. In 2014, the Institute for Territorial Planning, also known as Urbanica, together with the Centre for Strategic Research for the North-West, proposed a territory for integrated development for Saint Petersburg and Leningrad. This evolved into the zone of mutual influence, a framework for territorial-based cooperation that was approved by the governors of Saint Petersburg and Leningrad in 2018 and incorporated into the revised General Plan for Saint Petersburg.

There is another significant dimension to Saint Petersburg's positioning within broader urban networks, with the city forming part of the Nordic-Baltic network of cities. A representative of Saint Petersburg participated in the first Conference of Foreign Ministers of the Baltic Sea Region, held in Copenhagen in March 1992, and Saint Petersburg became one of the founders of the Union of the Baltic Cities.

In June 2002, when Russia held the presidency of the Council of the Baltic Sea States, an inter-governmental political forum for regional cooperation, Saint Petersburg hosted the Fourth Summit of the Heads of States. In the 2000s, there was a rapid increase in Saint Petersburg's networking with Baltic states and cities: Konstantin Khudolei and Dmitry Lanko (2009, 54) write about 'an unflagging interest of Saint Petersburg to everything "Baltic"'. One of the areas of cooperation was environmental, with joint initiatives significantly reducing pollution in the marine environment.

The Nordic-Baltic Space Transnational Development Plan was released in 2019 under the auspices of Metrex, the Network of European Metropolitan Regions and Areas. Although this is an EU-linked initiative, and Saint Petersburg was not a formal member of the network, the plan was clear that Saint Petersburg was part of the polycentric network of city-regions. Saint Petersburg was a core city within the Gulf of Finland Macro-Region, comprising Helsinki (Finland) and Tallinn (Estonia), and important within the wider Nordic-Baltic Loop. Proposals to realise the Gulf of Finland Macro-Region included a high-speed *Train à grande vitesse* along the coast of Finland to Saint Petersburg (Gordon 2019).

These are concepts and proposals that draw Saint Petersburg toward Europe and into a relationship with the West, but this sat uncomfortably with the nationalist impulse and the official orientation towards Moscow. The Saint Petersburg General Plan 2005 tried to balance the imperatives through both strengthening the position of the city with the Baltic Sea region and in the north-west of Russia, but the contradictions widened over time (Government of Saint Petersburg 2005). The Russian invasion of Ukraine in 2022 was a deadly blow: Saint Petersburg was suspended from membership of the Union of the Baltic Cities just as Russia was suspended from its membership of the Council of the Baltic Sea States.

Conclusion

The Russian case brings into sharp relief questions of both vertical and horizontal integration. Across history, approaches to sustaining coherence across the vast territory of the Russian Federation have vacillated from negotiated deals between the centre and sub-national units, to centralised power with directives from the top. Concerns with vertical integration preoccupy the elites in contemporary Russia.

However, in Russia's major agglomerations, the practicalities of governance have required the development of forms of horizontal coordination, some imposed from above and some emergent from within the region. Historically, city governments expanded their boundaries to incorporate new developments, but post-Soviet urban expansion into the regions was so great that new solutions were required. The solutions to date have been mainly limited, ad hoc and sectoral. However, the crisis in urban mobility prompted the federal government to compel city and *oblast* authorities to come together in a formally structured joint arrangement.

There are regional variations in political culture, and the differences between Moscow and Saint Petersburg may have played a role in the capacity to collaborate. Over the past decade there are indications of innovative approaches to collaboration emerging from the Saint Petersburg-Leningrad urban agglomeration. Within Moscow, the idea of the city-region has been deployed as a concept to position the core city within global urban networks, and not primarily as a means of coordination, but its use may evolve and open opportunities. Beyond Moscow and Saint Petersburg, the federal government has experimented with approaches to incentivise collaboration across urban agglomerations, but the outcomes remain uncertain.

Finally, Russia's deteriorating geopolitical and economic position may have significant impacts, reducing the ability of the state and private actors to engage in joint programmes such as the development of major infrastructure. An immediate consequence of the conflict in Ukraine was Saint Petersburg's exclusion from urban networks in the Baltic region.

Notes

1   I converted to US$ using an average exchange rate for 2013 of 31.9 rubles to the dollar.

2   Luzhkov worked hard to cultivate good relations with regions across Russia to further his presidential ambitions. He signed cooperation agreements with no fewer than 70 of Russia's 88 regions, often providing generous loans. His Fatherland Party, which was to be the platform for his presidential bid, was an alliance of regional leaders.

3   The powers of the mayor and the functioning of the administration were explained to me by high-ranking officials in the City of Moscow.

4   These changes were apparent during my visit to Moscow in 2016, and through discussions with city officials, including in the mayor's office.

5   As confirmed in discussions with senior officials in the Moscow administration during 2016.

6   Explained to me by a senior official in the City of Moscow in 2017.

7   I was in attendance.

8   See the 'Introductory Remarks' by Deputy Prime Minister Sergei Ivanov at a meeting in Moscow of the Government Commission on Transport and Communications in the online government archives: http://archive.government.ru/eng/docs/13631/.

9   See the transcript of a meeting on developing transport infrastructure in Moscow and Moscow Region in the government archives: http://en.special.kremlin.ru/events/president/transcripts/19023.

10 For updates on this major development, see the official website of the Moscow mayor: https://www.mos.ru/en/city/projects/development/.

11 See the 2017 archive of the Moscow Urban Forum: https://mosurbanforum.com/archive/2017/.

12 Interviews with officials and professionals in Moscow in 2016 and 2017.

13 It may have helped also that the offices of both the Saint Petersburg and the Leningrad administration were in Saint Petersburg.

4 Metropolitan and city-region governance in India

Introduction

'Like some ancient palimpsest'

There is nothing simple about India; we could get lost in debates over India's political culture. As James Chiriyankandath (1996, 46) put it: 'It is unlikely that we could refer to a peculiarly Indian political culture in any more-or-less meaningful sense than we could to an all-European political culture, embracing the post-Communist east as well as the member states of the European Union.' The secular rationalism of Jawaharlal Nehru's modernising project is there together with Gandhian spirituality, religious mythology, linguistic identities, regional vernaculars, caste, charismatic traditions, dominant masculinity, family dynasties, market rationalities, socialist orientations, personal rent-seeking, bureaucratic elitism and much more. The founding prime minister, Nehru, described India as being 'like some ancient palimpsest on which layer upon layer of thought and reverie had been inscribed, and yet no succeeding layer had completely hidden or erased what had been written previously' (Nehru cited in Khilnani 2003, xv).[1] For Chiriyankandath (1996, 46), India has a 'plural heritage' but also 'the capacity to accommodate rival cognitive systems'. Nevertheless, aspects of Indian political culture do surface more forcefully at times although always in a complex intersection with others. In contemporary India, for example, *Hindutva* (Hindu national consciousness) as a cultural ideology has become politically significant, although it has not fully eclipsed secular traditions of governance.

This is the broad context for India's metropolitan and city-region governance experiments. The chapter continues with a historical account that further explores India's many political cultures and its evolving political settlement, which has given significant powers to state governments at the expense of local authorities. It then provides a brief introduction to urban India before exploring the discourse and practice of metropolitan and city-region government with a particular focus on Delhi and the surrounding national capital region (NCR).

Historical embedding

The impossible question is where to begin and how much detail to provide as India's contemporary diversity and complexity have deep roots in the multiple histories of the Indian sub-continent. Rather than a single state, historical India was a patchwork of interrelated polities, although there were periods in which individual states came to dominate large parts of this territory, such as the overlapping (Hindu) Maratha Confederacy (1674 to 1818) and the (Muslim) Mughal Empire (1526 to 1857). The British Raj adopted a model of political centralism, but it was forced into a messy accommodation with indigenous rulers to sustain some measure of consent for its rule (Corbridge and Harriss 2000). On the eve of India's independence in 1947, there were 565 princely states over which the British exercised varying degrees of influence.[2]

Colonial rule did not erase diversity, but it did produce the *idea of* India as a singular construct, which was taken up by the post-colonial elite. Sunil Khilnani (2003, 5) writes, 'the possibility that India could be united into a single political community was the wager of India's modern, educated urban elite . . . It was a wager on an idea: the Idea of India'. There were, however, competing visions of what characteristics this India should have. There was, for example, the spirituality and rural romanticism of Mahatma Gandhi, contending with the modernising secular modernity of Nehru and his followers (Khilnani 2003).

Nehru played a major role in shaping the image of India in its national Constitution as 'a sovereign, socialist, secular, democratic republic'.[3] However, the gap between the modernising elite and the mass of the people was vast, and vernacularisms, such as religion, language, caste and kinship, were only temporarily silenced (Corbridge and Harriss 2000). The secularism of Nehru's Indian National Congress (generally known as the Congress Party) was progressively moderated from the 1970s onwards to accommodate these identities. Despite the founding ideals of the post-colonial elite, politics in India was 'never simply a commitment to abstract values and ideas – of pluralism and democracy – but was rooted in a practical understanding of the compulsions and constraints of Indian politics' (Khilnani 2003, xiii).

After Nehru, the Congress Party gradually lost its overall dominance, and the Bharatiya Janata Party (BJP), established in 1980, took India a further step away from the secular impulse of the first generation of post-colonial leaders by drawing together rural and urban movements around an ideology of Hindutva, which promoted the association of India with Hinduism (Sharma 2003). However, Hindutva has also had to accommodate other strands of consciousness and does not represent a wholesale return to pre-modern identity politics. Lucia Michelutti (2007, 639) wrote that India is a modern political democracy that has been 'vernacularised'.

Intensely political processes mediate the tensions in contemporary India. For Khilnani (2003, 9), 'politics is at the heart of India's passage to and experience of modernity . . . India does not merely "have" politics but is constituted by politics'. Khilnani (2003, 9) further writes that 'politics at once divides the country and constitutes it as a single, shared, crowded space, proliferating voices and claims, and forcing negotiation and accommodation'.

With this as a broad and invariably simplified account of political culture in India, I go on to introduce four critical, historically produced elements of context in contemporary India: 1) the weakness of local democracy and local government in the political settlement (and inadequacies of attempts to decentralise); 2) economic liberalisation; 3) the pervasiveness of informality; and 4) the immense regional variation.

The weakness of local democracy in India stems from the sentiments of the founding post-colonial elite, with the triumph of Nehru's world view over that of Mahatma Gandhi. While Gandhi wrote that 'for me, India begins and ends in the villages' (cited in Jodkha 2002, 3343), Nehru insisted that the villages embodied an India that was 'naked, starving, crushed and utterly miserable' (cited in Jodkha 2002, 3348). As a result, India's federation was left incomplete, with very few powers allocated to local government and almost no constitutional protection for local government. A vibrant democracy emerged, but largely at national and state levels (Ren and Weinstein 2013). The lack of meaningful local participation may partly explain a dilemma in India's governance: 'What begs explanation,' writes Akhil Gupta (2012, 18), 'is the widespread acceptance of the violence being done to the poor at the same time that popular sovereignty is constituted through them.'

In the 1980s, the democratic left and the neoliberal right took up a decentralisation agenda. For the right, decentralisation or devolution was part of the process of liberalising India's overcentralised and overregulated economy, and for the left, it meant giving the poor a voice in policy making and resource allocation (Ren and Weinstein 2013). In 1992, the 73rd and 74th constitutional amendments made provision for a significant devolution of powers to rural and urban local governments, respectively, with requirements for tax sharing with local government, holding regular local elections, setting up ward committees for direct local representation, preparing local plans through participatory local processes and reserving council seats for marginalised segments of the population.[4] The decentralisation outcomes have, however, been limited, with the overall distribution of power between union (meaning central), state and local governments remaining largely unaltered (with some important exceptions), mainly due to the reluctance of state government to surrender power to local government (Kennedy 2009; Ren and Weinstein 2013; Sivaramakrishnan 2013).

The second element of context is the far-reaching effect of economic liberalisation. Unlike the other BRICS (Brazil, Russia, India, China and South Africa) countries, India has not had a major political rupture in the recent past, not since its break with colonialism during the 1940s. However, the deregulation of the economy in the early 1990s was a major shock wave with far-reaching implications, and coincided more or less with the collapse of communism in Russia, the acceleration of economic reform in China, and the transition to democracy in Brazil and in South Africa.

Independent India was established as a democratic *socialist* state although its form of socialism was more akin to the Fabian socialism of the British Labour Party than the state socialism of the Soviet Union. While there was no attempt to secure state ownership of land, for example, there was state-led industrialisation and centralised planning through a National Planning Commission, which formulated five-year plans as the Soviet Union and China did. There was also the so-called Licence Raj, a complex permissions system for setting up a private business.

There was tentative liberalisation in the 1980s under Rajiv Gandhi's leadership, but there was shock treatment in 1991 when Prime Minister P.V. Narasimha Rao moved rapidly to reduce import tariffs, privatise industries, liberalise financial markets, open the economy to international investors and dismantle the Licence Raj. Subsequent governments, Congress Party- and BJP-led, have continued this agenda (with Modi, for example, combining religious nationalism with a pro-business orientation).

The consequence of neoliberalism is widely debated. On the positive side, economic growth rates surged from less than three per cent per annum to a range of between six and eight per cent, and there is now a highly visible Indian middle class. As Fernandes (2004, 2428) puts it: 'The new Indian middle class represents a visible embodiment of the potential benefits of globalisation, a visibility that disrupts the possibility that late industrialising nations such as India might be forgotten in contemporary processes of globalisation.' The critique of liberalisation rests in its distributive consequences. Leela Fernandes (2004, 2416) argues that the post-liberalisation focus on the wealth and consumption practices of the middle class is associated with a 'growing amnesia towards poverty and the poor'.

The third aspect of context is the prevalence of informality. For Ananya Roy (2009a, 84), 'informality exists at the very heart of the state and is an integral part of the territorial practices of state power'. What informality means for governance is a complex matter. Some writers emphasise the corrosive effects of informal governance or shadow governance. Barbara Harriss-White (1997, 12) called it 'the basis for a regime of private extortion', with state authority increasingly residing 'in the private social status of state agents: in their class origins, caste, gender, age and in the private social relations of their locality' (1997, 19). Others explain the personalised and arbitrary rule that low-level bureaucrats exercise over a poor, still largely illiterate population through processes of personalisation, clientelism, reciprocity and dependence (Roy 2009a; Gupta 2012).

However, as Stuart Corbridge et al. (2005) point out, informality in governance is often a critical source of adaptive and operational capacity in a system where formal processes are slow, encumbered and bureaucratic. Other work points to the complex intersections between formality and informality, which produce continually shifting modes of governance. Roy (2009b, 8) writes of the 'ever-shifting relationship between what is legal and illegal, legitimate and illegitimate, authorized and unauthorized'. To Seth Schindler (2014a, 2596), 'preconceived notions of "formality" and "informality" are of little value in understanding urban processes, and instead it is necessary to understand how the boundary between formal/informal is produced and contested both juridically and through everyday practices of enforcement and evasion/subversion'. For Schindler (2014b, 402), there are 'a multiplicity of governance regimes' – 'a new Delhi everyday'.

The fourth aspect of context is the immense regional variation in India. The country is a federation of 29 states and seven union territories, each having their legislative powers but, more significantly, each having different political cultures shaped through different histories.

Mumbai (previously Bombay) in the state of Maharashtra, for example, has had a long mercantilist tradition, being the headquarters of the British East India Company from 1687 and one of the largest trading ports on the Arabian Sea after the opening of the Suez Canal in 1869. More recently, it has developed into India's financial capital. Mumbai's contemporary vision to develop into a world-class city, 'India's Shanghai', is driven by a growth coalition comprising industrialists, the state government and urban professionals (Weinstein 2014). Significantly, Mumbai and Maharashtra have a far stronger tradition of local government than elsewhere in India.

In Kolkata (previously Calcutta) and across West Bengal, a strong working-class tradition emerged from late nineteenth-century industrialisation. It was also the historical hub of India's anti-colonial struggle, although the nationalist movement emerged from upper-class Hindu society. Kolkata is distinct in having had the world's longest-serving democratically elected communist government (1977–2011) when West Bengal was ruled by the Left Front, which was dominated by the Communist Party of India. Politics is fluid, and after 2011, West Bengal was ruled by the All India Trinamool Congress, which has its roots in peasant struggles against land grabbing and evictions, partly displacing the influence of the urban working-class movement (Roy 2011).

The state of Kerala in the south-west of India also has a strong leftist tradition, but Kerala has a strong tradition of civil society and democratic local governments, whereas West Bengal has been conventionally centralist (Williams 2017). In the national capital, Delhi, political cultures have been partly shaped by the strong presence of politicians and bureaucrats. Bangalore is a relatively new city, with growth that has been driven by liberalising world-city agendas and global outsourcing of information technology services. There is a strong focus on business interests and a governance model that involves a close intersection between private corporations and an entrepreneurial state government. Chennai, for example, has a curious combination of communitarian (Tamil-based) regionalist politics and technocratic governance, while Hyderabad's de-politicised governance with weak local structures may reflect, in part, the legacy of centuries of aristocratic rule by the ancient Nizam dynasty. There are, of course, many other examples of regionally situated political cultures across the vastness of India (Kennedy 2020).

Urban context

For Gandhi, the future of India lay in its villages. In 1950, two years after Gandhi's assassination, India was overwhelmingly rural, with an urbanisation rate of only 17 per cent. The urbanisation level has gradually trended upwards to the current 35 per cent, but because of India's mega population, it meant an increase in the urban population from 64 million to 483 million by 2020 (United Nations 2018).

Thus, while India's urbanisation is still modest in global terms, there are very large cities and city-regions. The (estimated) growth of India's megacity populations between 1950 and 2020 was:

- 1.4 million to 30.3 million for Delhi;
- 3.1 million to 20.4 million for Mumbai;
- 4.6 million to 14.8 million for Kolkata;
- 0.7 million to 12.3 million for Bangalore;
- 1.5 million to 11 million for Chennai; and
- 1.1 million to 10 million for Hyderabad (United Nations 2018).

These are the populations of the metropolitan cities and not the wider city-regions, which are significantly larger in some cases. Despite the relatively low urbanisation rate, India has three of the world's 20 largest urban agglomerations – Delhi, Mumbai and Kolkata, with Delhi ranked second after Tokyo, Japan (Map 3).

It was only from the 1990s that cities in India commanded significant political attention. Prior to this, rural interests were overwhelmingly dominant, and the legacies of anti-urban ideology were strong (Kennedy 2020). By the 1990s, around 30 per cent of India's population was urbanised, including in the mega-sized concentrations that were increasingly difficult to ignore. With economic liberalisation, attention shifted to urban-based sectors, while state authorities in the more competitive economic environment increasingly viewed cities as 'strategic assets to be leveraged' (Kennedy 2020, 103). Importantly also, the progressively influential middle class was increasingly concentrated in cities.

The decentralisation drive associated with the 73rd and 74th constitutional amendments was 'hi-jacked by state governments unwilling to empower urban local bodies', but impacted places like Mumbai with 'long and rich municipal traditions' (Kennedy 2020, 105).

While the antipathy to large cities has shifted over time to a pragmatic acceptance of urbanisation, degrees of ambivalence remain. K.C. Sivaramakrishnan (2014, xxiv) observed that 'the big city is a theme that continues to be shrouded by doubt and bewilderment'. Urban reforms began cautiously in the 1980s but took shape in the 1990s when the union government introduced its first city-specific development interventions, including megacity grant schemes linked to the preparation of metropolitan development programmes. This culminated in the hugely ambitious Jawaharlal Nehru National Urban Renewal Mission launched in 2005 to unleash the creative vitality of large cities (Kennedy 2020). With the new funding, large-scale infrastructural projects were built across India, including mass transit, expressways and an airport, which transformed and metropolitanised the urban landscape.

While infrastructural development in India was historically government-led, the cost and scale of these initiatives required private partnerships, which have become influential in governance processes. Given India's labyrinthine institutional environment, however, the rules and plans of existing authorities were often bypassed in order to deliver the projects (Kennedy 2020). In addition, with weak local government in many places, there was little local democratic pressure to distribute the benefits of these megaprojects equitably; development thus often failed to translate into sustained social improvement for the poor urban majority. Loraine Kennedy (2020, 112) writes, 'The urban middle classes, the primary beneficiaries of growth, are directly and indirectly shaping city development to reflect their vision of the desirable city and their identity therein.' With an overwhelming focus on producing the residential, consumption and mobility spaces of the rising middle class, there is an active dislocation of the urban poor through both forced resettlement and market-based displacement to make way for these spaces, as described in various critical commentaries (Fernandes 2004; Banerjee-Guha 2009; Kennedy 2009).

The growth of metropolitan-scale cities accelerated with the rapid development of special economic zones in the 2000s and 2010s, designated according to terms of legislation passed in 2005. The special economic zones were concentrated around India's six largest metropolitan regions, with investment focussed on information technology and information technology-enabled services. Bangalore is most famous for its new economy-driven urban growth, but this form of development along the metropolitan edge has happened in other places, including Chennai's information technology corridor, the inner ring of satellite cities around Delhi (especially Gurgaon) and Navi Mumbai, across the bay from Mumbai.

This growth pattern has created new governance challenges. Although they are functionally linked to their wider regions, special economic zones are zones of exception with their own special rules. They are governed mainly by unelected and technocratic corporations, reporting to state government, and outside the jurisdiction of local government (Kennedy 2020).

Solomon Benjamin's writing on occupancy urbanism reminds us, however, that within this context of mega-scale development, there are other processes at work. Benjamin (2008, 724) reminds us that 'megaprojects intending to globalize Indian metros like Bangalore confront a subversive politics on the ground. Master plans designate large territories for development in higher-level policy documents, but in reality these territories remain "occupied" by pre-existing settlements and see newer ones developing'. Thus, while mega-scale investments driven by coalitions of state governments and large corporate interests are shaping urban space, there is 'an economy of interconnected small firm production and retail, closely connected to land issues and local government' (Benjamin 2008, 720).

Marie-Hélène Zérah's (2020) work on Mumbai makes a related point, drawing from a different context. Mumbai is a city known for its municipal traditions, megaprojects, new public management reforms and metropolitan-wide growth coalition. It is a city that is characterised in terms of neoliberal government, but Zérah (2020, 119) explains that *even* in Mumbai, the neoliberal turn is 'incomplete and paradoxical'; financialisation, megaprojects, rule-based governance and the urban growth regime hybridise with bottom-up capitalism, the use of intermediaries, predatory practices and many flexible forms of adaptation.

Rather than being an ungovernable city, Mumbai is governed through a complex hybrid of well-capacitated formal structures and 'localized, informal and contingent sites of knowledge and power' (Zérah 2020, 130).

With this understanding of the complexity and hybridity of governance in practice in urban India, I turn to an account of the co-evolution of discourse and practice around metropolitan and city-region governance in India.

Discourse and practice
Early post-independence – 1950s to 1970s

Lalit Batra (2009, 1) points out that the urban question was 'curiously absent' from the imagination of post-independence India. As explained, the idea of an urban India contradicted Gandhian thought but was also surprisingly absent in Nehru's vision of a modern industrialised nation. Much of his mega infrastructural investment was regional rather than urban, and he remained uneasy about the growth of large cities. Despite his concerns, however, cities were growing and, with official neglect, were poorly provided for in terms of services and infrastructure.

India's intellectual elite, mainly British trained, were aware of ideas of metropolitan areas circulating in the first half of the twentieth century, but the catalysts appear to have been a World Health Organization study of sanitation in crisis-ridden

Calcutta in 1959 and a World Bank Mission in 1960 to the same city that recommended the establishment of a metropolitan planning agency (Mukharji 1962; Bhattacharya 1965).

In 1961, the state of West Bengal established a Council of Coordination for Development of the Calcutta Metropolitan Area and a metropolitan planning organisation. These institutions and their planning exercises were funded and guided by the Ford Foundation and the Institute for Public Administration, both headquartered in New York. The Ford Foundation was also a prime mover in preparing the Delhi Master Plan, which also emphasised a metropolitan scale of planning and development (Bhattacharya 1965).

In a parallel development, the national statistical agency, Census India, grappled with the challenge of enumerating the population of urban areas that were spreading across jurisdictional boundaries. In 1961 it introduced the designation 'town groups', which eventually evolved into the idea of an urban agglomeration, defined as 'a continuous urban spread constituting a town and its adjoining outgrowths, or two or more physically contiguous towns together with or without outgrowths of such towns' (Office of the Registrar General 2018, para. 2).

At this point in the discursive evolution, it is worth noting that, while English is used for official purposes by the union government, state governments may specify their official languages through legislation. Less than a third of the states use English as an official language, and there are 22 scheduled official languages across India. So, while terms such as 'city-region', 'metropolitan area' and 'urban agglomeration' are used in India, there is immense linguistic complexity, with meanings differing in their nuance and subtle shifts in translation.

The left-wing administrations in West Bengal (Kolkata) have been more inclined toward metropolitan planning than the mercantilist administrations of Maharashtra (Mumbai) or even the left-wing administrations of Kerala, which have emphasised decentralised governance (rather than democratic centralism). Nevertheless, the idea of metropolitan governance diffused across the large cities of India. During the 1960s, the state of Maharashtra set up a metropolitan planning organisation for Greater Bombay, and the state of Tamil Nadu did so for Greater Madras (Chennai). The next phase began in the 1970s, with the establishment of the metropolitan development authorities (MDAs). Again, West Bengal took the lead in establishing the Calcutta MDA in 1970, chaired by the chief minister of West Bengal, and its day-to-day operations fell under the supervision of the West Bengal Planning Department, although some board members were selected from local corporations (meaning municipalities). The move was, in fact, bitterly opposed by the mayor of Calcutta, who understood how much MDAs would erode the already reduced powers of local corporations. However, the opposition was overridden by the state government with the active support of India's centralising prime minister, Indira Gandhi (Sivaramakrishnan 2014).

MDAs were subsequently set up for Madras (1972), Bombay (1974), Hyderabad (1975) and Bangalore (1975), all under their respective state authorities, with varying degrees of carefully selected local representation. Bombay had, for historical reasons, the strongest local corporation in India, and it was able to negotiate a better deal than the other cities, with the mayor of Bombay serving as one of the two vice-presidents of the MDA. Nevertheless, even in this case, the balance of power was oriented toward the state government (Sivaramakrishnan 2014).

In most metropolitan cities, there was little that the local corporations could do as the political settlement at the time of India's independence had left them weak and unprotected. K.C. Sivaramakrishnan (2013, 86) offered a scathing assessment of the MDAs, charging that 'they have become mere creatures of state governments with neither the necessary strategic flexibility nor political legitimacy'. Sivaramakrishnan has also argued that MDAs failed comprehensively in their task of simplifying institutional arrangements across metropolitan regions. Instead, the decades since the 1970s have 'witnessed a remarkable increase in the range of multiple actors for performing multiple tasks in the MRs [metropolitan regions]' (Sivaramakrishnan 2014, xxxv).

Within the overall narrative on metropolitan India, my primary case study in this chapter, Delhi, was distinctive because of its capital city status. Kennedy (2009, 62) explains that 'Delhi's unique position as the nation's capital city naturally influences its governance structure, and limits in many ways its scope for autonomous decision-making'. A senior official in Delhi explained to me: 'Delhi was a pet child of Prime Minister Nehru, who did not want it to be governed as a separate state. He wanted to keep it under central control.'

Prime Minister Nehru wanted an ordered capital, a showcase of India's modernity, and was not satisfied with the ad hoc responses to growth pressures in Delhi. He feared that the chaotic growth of capital with the influx of refugees after the partition of India in 1947 would disturb his vision of a modern India. He set up the Birla Commission in 1950, which recommended a single planning and land development authority for Delhi, set up in 1957 as the Delhi Development Authority (DDA), reporting directly to the union government. Although initially envisaged as a temporary body to address the post-partition crisis, the DDA was soon embedded within the governance structure, and it remains a powerful body to the present day, still reporting directly to the union (central) government (Mehra 2013). There are periodic calls for the DDA to change its reporting lines to make it more regionally or locally accountable, but the institutional position of the DDA is deeply embedded, and it is hardly in the interest of the union government to make the change.[5]

The DDA was effectively the MDA for Delhi but, with its union government backing, was more powerful than the MDA. Importantly, it gained a near monopoly position over land development in Delhi. It acquired 240.8 square kilometres of land in the city and launched an ambitious housing programme, creating residential colonies (as housing estates are known in India) from the 1960s onwards, and making full use of rising land values to expand its revenue base.

Institutionally, the DDA existed in parallel with the regional government for Delhi. Greater Delhi was initially set up as a union territory under the direct administration of a chief commissioner appointed by the president of India, but, gradually, political pressures compelled the union government to give Delhi greater status and power (although never power over spatial planning and land development).

The post-independence concern with the growth of Delhi instigated the idea of an NCR. The envisaged NCR was of a scale much greater than that of metropolitan Delhi. Instead of being a more or less contiguous urban agglomeration like the metropolitan city, it was a conceptually defined territory, consisting of settlements of varying scales and intervening rural areas that often had only weak linkages with one another. The underlying idea was to eliminate the chaos and congestion of the national capital by dispersing its population and activities into the expansive region surrounding the city. The idea had partial origins in British planning thought – in the garden city and new town movements – but was also informed by the plans for new national capital cities such as Washington, Ottawa and Canberra. These were plans for small, orderly cities focussed on the symbolism and practicalities of their national capital functions (Mabin and Harrison 2022).

In 1955, the national Ministry of Health set up a Town and Country Planning Organisation which produced the Interim Master Plan for Greater Delhi of 1956, formally introducing the idea of an NCR. The most compelling part of the plan was the foreword, signed by India's first Minister of Health, Rajkumar Amrit Kaur. It was direct in its analysis of the problems:

> As Minister for Health, I have been greatly worried over happenings in regard to promiscuous buildings and lay-outs in Delhi and New Delhi over the last nine years and the seeming inability of anyone to 'hold the line'.
>
> Those of us who know Delhi, and even those who come here for the first time, cannot but be struck by the fact that all is not well with the Capital City.
>
> Matters have really come to a head. There is all round discomfort and discontent. Traffic jams and accidents, sprawling colonies without the vital conveniences of life in the matter of sanitation, overcrowding everywhere and particularly in miserable slum areas, miles of ribbon developed hut shops, chronic water shortage, all add to the distress which is bad at any time but is well nigh intolerable during the rainy season. (Ministry of Health, Government of India 1956)

The foreword also pointed towards a solution: 'The ultimate grand objective is a Regional Plan, not just or even necessarily a larger Delhi, but in social, functional and economic fact a three dimensional plan for a really *greater* Delhi' (Ministry of Health, Government of India 1956, ii, emphasis in the original).

In the pages of the plan, the 'really *greater* Delhi' was called the 'National Capital Region' (Chapter VIII), and there was also a recommendation for a 'National Capital Area Planning Commission' (Chapter IX).

However, not much happened in the construction of the NCR over the next three decades. In 1961, an advisory board was set up by the national Ministry of Urban Development to oversee the planning and development of cities within 250 kilometres of the capital, but it soon floundered in the face of the planning powers possessed by the states (Nath 2007). In 1962 the Delhi Master Plan was completed by the DDA. It was an ambitious plan to create a world-class capital, and its focus was on Delhi itself, but it restated the 1956 recommendations for an NCR and a planning structure for the wider region (DDA 1962).

The next move came in 1973, when an advisory board for the region was reconstituted under the Minister of Works, Housing and Supplies, with the members including the chief ministers of Haryana, Uttar Pradesh and Rajasthan, together with the lieutenant-governor of Delhi. But, in India's federal system, where the planning powers rested with the states (except in the case of the National Capital Territory [NCT] of Delhi), a national initiative of this sort depended on the cooperation of the states. Uttar Pradesh and Haryana were benefitting from urban growth in the near vicinity of Delhi and had no reason to support the diversion of growth to far-flung corners of the region, so they gave little support to the idea of an NCR (Nath 1988).

A draft regional plan was prepared in 1973 by the Town and Country Planning Organisation, with the ambitious goal of zero migration to Delhi by 2000. The plan proposed to divert growth to a series of ring towns. However, there was no statutory backing for the plan, and there was no funding for the infrastructure suggested. Amar Singh (1989, 182) put it mildly when he stated that 'as a result it was found that Delhi and its population continued to grow unabated and the ring towns did not develop in accordance with the plan'.

The national capital region takes shape in the 1980s

In 1981, the national Minister of Works and Housing addressed a letter to the chief ministers of Uttar Pradesh, Haryana and Rajasthan and the lieutenant-governor of Delhi, urging the creation of a statutory board for the NCR. The parties agreed to consider the matter, although the state governments insisted that the proposal would first have to be debated within their legislatures. This happened, and the National Capital Region Planning Act of 1985 was passed by the national Parliament nearly three decades after the NCR had first been proposed.[6] The Act set up the National Capital Region Planning Board (NCRPB) that had the power to prepare a regional plan and to direct the states in the preparation of sub-regional plans (Map 11). The plans were intended to be prescriptive. As Section 29 of the Act stated, 'On and from the coming into operation of the finally published Regional Plan, no development shall be made in the region which is inconsistent with the Regional Plan as finally published.'[7]

The NCRPB was, by necessity, a form of associational governance as planning powers rested constitutionally with the states. It was chaired by the union Minister for Urban Development and included other union ministers, as well as the chief minister and lieutenant-governor of Delhi, the chief ministers of Haryana, Uttar Pradesh and Rajasthan, and their chief secretaries and state ministers. The board was supported by a planning committee comprising senior officials (including the chief planners) of the Ministry of Urban Development and the various state governments.[8]

When first delineated in 1985, the NCR covered 34 144 square kilometres, including the NCT of Delhi, nine districts in Haryana, six districts in Uttar Pradesh and a single district in Rajasthan. The Act also empowered the NCRPB to identify places outside the NCR to act as counter magnets, which would then receive prioritised access to government resources. The counter magnets included cities in the states of Madhya Pradesh, Uttarakhand and Punjab, including, for example, the city of Gwalior in Madhya Pradesh, 320 kilometres from Delhi. The underlying principle was that population and economic activity would be diverted from Delhi as far as these counter magnets.[9]

The NCRPB was a compromise structure that depended for its functionality on the ongoing acquiescence of state governments, which remained wary that it would intrude into their domains. Once inaugurated by Prime Minister Rajiv Gandhi, the NCRPB began work with some enthusiasm. By 1987 it had completed a draft regional plan, which was put out for comment, with the final document, known as Regional Plan – 2001, released in December 1988. The plan was doctrinaire in its commitment to containing the growth of Delhi and developing the counter magnets. The limit for Delhi's population was put at 11 million people which, in 1988, stood at about 8 million.

However, even as the plan was released, diverse interests were playing out, which undermined the possibilities for implementation. All parties involved formally accepted the plan, but there were already tensions. Haryana and Uttar Pradesh supported inner-ring development while only far-flung Rajasthan enthusiastically supported counter magnets. The DDA proposed high-density development *within* Delhi, which the NCRPB objected to.

The plan was broad, with the real teeth resting in the sub-regional plans to be prepared by the state governments. Except for Rajasthan, the states dragged their feet. They also ensured that the implementational capacity of the NCRPB was limited, to prevent effective enforcement. The staff structure provides only one professional planner; all other posts are technical or administrative – a tiny structure for a board responsible for planning a region with 40 million-plus people (Maps 21 and 22).[10]

The age of economic liberalisation from the 1990s

India's economic liberalisation in the 1990s was a massive boost to real estate development across metropolitan areas. While official policy remained one of containing metropolitan growth, in actuality, large-scale investments were directed into metropolitan regions. In this context, the MDAs shifted from the troublesome task of metropolitan planning and coordination to the acquisition, parcelling and selling of land for industrial, commercial and residential real estate. In the process, the Mumbai MDA, for example, emerged as one of the wealthiest state-owned agencies in India. To facilitate land acquisition and development (rather than to enable better territorial coordination), the territorial jurisdiction of MDAs was progressively extended (Sivaramakrishnan 2014).

There was one further attempt at creating a meaningful structure for metropolitan governance. India's celebrated but poorly implemented 74th Constitutional Amendment of 1992 included a formal definition of a metropolitan region as 'an area having a population of ten lakhs or more [meaning more than one million], comprised in one or more districts and consisting of two or more Municipalities or Panchayats or other contiguous areas, specified by the Governor by public notification to be a Metropolitan area' (Government of India 1992).

In terms of this definition, there are now 11 recognised metropolitan areas across India.[11] The Amendment also included a requirement that state governments set up metropolitan planning committees for each metropolitan area and that at least two-thirds of the membership of each metropolitan planning committee should be drawn from local corporations. This was a significant and promising departure from the MDA model and offered the possibility of a deliberative and associational form of metropolitan planning. However, there was a fatal flaw: the creation of the metropolitan planning committees was left in the hands of state governments, and it was clearly not in the interests of states to set up these structures in any meaningful sense. As Sivaramakrishnan (2013, 92) put it, the metropolitan planning committee 'has had no takers'.

West Bengal did set up a metropolitan planning committee for the Kolkata Metropolitan Region in 1996, but it was disbanded when the left-wing coalition was voted out in the 2011 state elections. A metropolitan planning committee was also established for Mumbai, but the state of Maharashtra tasked it with a complex set of minor responsibilities and the committee was soon bogged down in local details and conflicts (Nath 2007).

While the metropolitan planning committees have made little impact, there has been some attempt to achieve better local spatial integration by expanding the boundaries of municipal corporations; Hyderabad, for example, was amalgamated with an adjoining city to create a Greater Municipal Corporation. However, with the proliferating institutions of governance – including new territorial entities such as development corporations and special economic zones – most metropolitan areas are more institutionally fragmented than ever before, with local corporations still marginalised from metropolitan development processes.

Again Delhi, my primary case study, has had an altered trajectory, but one that is illustrative of the immense governance complexities of India's metropolitan areas. The Government of the National Capital Territory of Delhi Act of 1991 reconstituted Delhi as a quasi-state (Map 22). The Government of the NCT (GNCT) of Delhi has an elected legislative assembly headed by a chief minister, drawn from the majority party or coalition, but it is a double-headed beast. In addition to the chief minister, there is a lieutenant-governor appointed by India's president as the constitutional head of the authority. The relationship between the elected chief minister and the appointed lieutenant-governor is poorly defined, which sets the scene for debilitating power struggles (Heller and Mukhopadhyay 2016).

Bureaucratically, the Delhi government is also a massively complex entity. It operates within 11 districts and 33 subdivisions within these districts, delivering services provided by entities such as the Delhi Jal Board for water and sanitation. Electricity generation is the function of six state government-owned companies, and distribution is the responsibility of three companies (discoms) with 50/50 equity splits between state government and the private sector (Heller and Mukhopadhyay 2016).

When the mainstream parties – Congress Party and the BJP – were in power in the GNCT of Delhi, the institutional relationship between the union and the quasi state was more or less managed. However, in 2012 a civic movement coalesced into the Aam Admi Party (or Common Man's Party), which swept to power in the 2015 state elections, capturing 67 of the 70 seats in the Delhi Legislative Assembly. It was a staggering victory, wiping out the traditional Congress Party support in the slums and winning handsomely in most previously BJP-supporting, middle-class constituencies on the back of its popular anti-corruption message. A party with its origins in social activism now had to govern a complex city where institutional power was highly fragmented. It had to deliver on its generous promises to the electorate with a traditional bureaucracy while facing a politically hostile national government.

The tensions between the union government and the GNCT of Delhi were replicated in the relationships between the GNCT of Delhi and the local corporation, which remained under the control of the BJP. Over time, the powers of the local corporation had lessened (despite the promise of the 74th Amendment), with functions diverted into special entities or the GNCT of Delhi. In 2011, the GNCT of Delhi, then controlled by the Congress Party, moved to weaken the BJP-controlled Municipal Corporation of Delhi by dividing it into three (the East, North and South Delhi municipal corporations) (Map 22). A technical rationale was given for the move, with the Municipal Corporation of Delhi criticised for being too large and unwieldy, but this division was disastrous in terms of administration and equity as it left the poorest parts of Delhi under the weakest administration. Despite this, the local corporations still held significant job-related patronage, performing functions such as garbage collection with a large workforce. In retaliation for the BJP-controlled union government's refusal to include the Aam Admi Party-controlled GNCT of Delhi in its division of revenue for state governments, the GNCT of Delhi refused to transfer revenues downwards to BJP-controlled corporations.[12]

However, the relationship between the lieutenant-governor and the chief minister became the major flashpoint, with governance in the territory reaching a near stand-still. Communication was fraught, and tensions reached breaking point at times (*The Economic Times* 2018). In one instance, the chief minister claimed that he was unable to deal with the city's water crisis as the Delhi Jal Board's chief executive officer would not take his call, and air pollution could not be addressed as the union government's environmental secretary would not meet him (Mishra 2018).

The courts had to act as a deadlock-breaking mechanism. On 4 July 2018, the Supreme Court of India ruled that the primary power in Delhi rested with the elected chief minister, with the lieutenant-governor bound by the advice of the Council of Ministers (except in relation to planning, land and policing, which are functions remaining under national control). However, only one day after the judgment, a further conflict erupted over whether the chief minister or lieutenant-governor had the power to appoint and transfer officials (Rautray 2018).

The conflict between the chief minister and the lieutenant-governor spilled over into a conflict between the chief minister and the prime minister. Chief Minister Arvind Kejriwal declared that 'PM [Prime Minister] Modi neither talks to me nor looks at me nor allows me to talk' (Mishra 2018). The conflict became so severe it was featured in the international news magazine *The Economist* on 21 June 2018, in an article entitled 'India's national government and the city of Delhi are feuding'. The subheading was 'No grievance is too petty, no tactic too underhanded'.

On 27 April 2021, the union gained the upper hand in the conflicts when the GNCT of Delhi (Amendment) Act 2021 came into effect, putting the lieutenant-governor into a superior position relative to the chief minister. It requires the GNCT of Delhi to seek the opinion of the lieutenant-governor before taking executive action, and for all executive action to be taken in the name of the lieutenant-governor. For Chief Minister Kejriwal it 'was a sad day for Indian democracy' (Jain 2021).

While the GNCT of Delhi's governance is clearly massively difficult and contested, there are other scales of complication. The NCT of Delhi has a population of around 17 million and an area of about 1 483 square kilometres. As indicated, its governance in formal terms is divided between the DDA (dealing with planning, land and housing) and the double-headed GNCT of Delhi.

However, the NCT of Delhi is part of a larger metropolitan area including the inner-ring satellite cities Gurgaon, Greater Noida, Faridabad, Ghaziabad and Sonipat.

This is variously called the Delhi Metropolitan Area (DMA), the Delhi Urban Agglomeration and the Central NCR. It has a population approaching 30 million people over 2 000 square kilometres. Although the DMA is recognised as a metropolitan region in terms of the 74th Constitutional Amendment, there is no formal governance structure encompassing this territory, which therefore requires complex informal governance processes and ad hoc formal coordination structures.[13]

There were early proposals to amalgamate Delhi's satellite cities into the NCT but, in the 1980s under Rajiv Gandhi, state governments became more assertive, resisting this proposal and removing the possibility of an expanded NCT. Also, party politics has become more complex and fragmented over time, with vertically and horizontally divided political control now the norm.[14]

There are massive challenges in achieving meaningful collaboration. The state of Haryana wraps around three sides of the NCT of Delhi (Map 21). It is the largest recipient of investment per capita in India and has a state government with a pragmatic orientation. Kennedy (2014, 102) explains that 'in Haryana, political pragmatism means attending to the needs of the landowning groups, which are demographically and economically powerful'. In the water-scarce districts close to Delhi, landowners struggled to make a living from agriculture and so turned to real estate development (Kennedy 2014).

This was an enabling environment for a clique of real estate entrepreneurs, most famously K.P. Singh, who purchased large tracts of land to the south of Delhi, developing the new city of Gurgaon through his company DLF Limited (Singh 2015). Private-sector wheeling and dealing brought energy and speed to the development process, but the lack of planning and inter-jurisdictional coordination resulted in extreme challenges with infrastructure, especially in terms of road maintenance, sewer lines and water supply.

Uttar Pradesh is a different case. It is a vast, populous, mainly rural territory, with only the far western edges abutting the DMA. Uttar Pradesh's political elite tends mainly to its rural constituency and is often oriented towards a dogmatic Hindu nationalism. There is far less acceptance of private urban land dealing here than in Haryana, and where urban development is promoted, it is mainly government-led. The development of the industrial satellite of Noida, for example, was an initiative of the union government in the 1970s to decentralise industry from Delhi and divert rural migrants from Uttar Pradesh away from the national capital. In the 1980s, responsibility for the further development of Noida was given to a state-level development agency, the New Okhla Industrial Development Authority, while its twin city, Greater Noida, was later developed by the state-owned Greater Noida Industrial Development Authority (Potter and Kumar 2004).

There are thus very different planning and development cultures across the DMA, as well as diverse interests in an intensely occupied area, which are the source of many existing and potential conflicts. An example is the conflicts in the water sector. Nearly 70 per cent of Delhi's water comes from the Yamuna River, flowing in from the state of Haryana. But, as both Haryana and Delhi are water-scarce with high demand, there are ongoing disputes. In the 1990s, an agreement was reached to construct the 102-kilometre Munak Canal to direct water from the higher reaches of the Yamuna in Haryana into Delhi, but implementation of the agreement has been riven with tension. Haryana has periodically cut water supply to Delhi over disputes around payment and because of its own water shortages. On one occasion, when a local uprising in Haryana led to the blocking of the canal, the Indian army was called in to keep water flowing to Delhi (*The Times of India* 2016). In 2018, the High Court intervened to broker a series of interim agreements to keep the water flowing (*The Times of India* 2018).

Deteriorating water quality also presents a major crisis and requires coordinated action for implementation. The pollution of the Yamuna River has reached hazardous levels, with experts indicating that sections of the river serve only as 'a drain carrying sewage, domestic waste as well as industrial and trade effluents'.[15] Joint action in response has been sporadic and ineffective, despite the intervention of the courts – in this case, the National Green Tribunal – in demanding expeditious action.[16]

In the context of ongoing disputes and the lack of sustained institutional mechanisms for collaborative action, various mechanisms have evolved out of practical necessity. The first is the creation of special-purpose vehicles that operate outside the norms of existing authorities, bypassing the complexity of existing arrangements. In 1996, for example, a special-purpose vehicle was set up to deliver the Delhi metro rail system. The project was preceded by an extended period of political wrangling between union and state governments, with little prospect of actual implementation (Bon 2016). In 1996 there was eventual agreement that a special-purpose vehicle would be set up to make the metro happen. The Delhi Metro Rail Corporation was established as a joint venture between the union and state governments and was placed operationally under the direct supervision of the national Ministry of Urban Affairs. Funding and technical expertise came from the Japan International Cooperation Agency. These structures operated under a special regime with its own procedures, rules and norms. Nevertheless, as one of my informants in the Delhi bureaucracy explained, 'The union and state government stood absolutely behind the project, and the courts also intervened in support of the project when required.' Other examples of special regimes to deliver projects of national importance included those set up for the Asian Games of 1982 and the 2010 Commonwealth Games. One of the officials I spoke to lamented that the capacity and drive characteristic of these special regimes is not translated into day-to-day governance processes.

A second approach is more adaptive and limited, and involves the creation of technical instruments within the bureaucracy, often outside the public purview. For example, difficulties in bringing multiple actors together to support transit-oriented development along the metro lines caused the DDA to set up an internal unit, the Unified Traffic and Transportation Planning and Engineering Centre, to promote coordination. Since all government projects relating to transportation and traffic needed clearance through this centre, the unit had the leverage to bring the actors together around a common table.[17]

The third mechanism is the High Court of India, and there are many instances where the courts have intervened to resolve a seemingly intractable institutional dispute. Lavanya Rajamani (2007, 293) writes: 'In a system in which policy-makers and law-enforcers are perceived as apathetic, if not corrupt, and politicians are perceived as opportunistic demagogues rather than as visionary leaders, the Supreme Court of India has assumed the mantle of a "Supreme Court for Indians" and a "last resort for the oppressed and bewildered".' However, the courts have been criticised for overstepping their role by dabbling in processes that should be the domain of a democratically constituted legislature, and the High Court of Delhi is known for both its environmental commitment and activism, and judgments that have been detrimental to the urban poor (Rajamani 2007; Rubin 2013).

Finally, there are many instances where problem resolution coordination happens through informal networks operating within government structures. Officials and ex-officials in Delhi recalled many anecdotes of how relational networks sustain governance in the context of an unwieldy bureaucracy and a fraught political set-up. A current official spoke of 'the workings of an invisible hand' while an ex-official explained that his primary job was getting around the numerous *formal* obstacles to progress.

One of the examples provided by an official was in the transport sector. Taxis and motorised rickshaws (autos) were not permitted to cross from Delhi into neighbouring states, creating everyday difficulties for commuters, but an interim solution was found through an informal, practical engagement between officials in the GNCT of Delhi and neighbouring states. This informal resolution was eventually codified through the licensing of operators for travel across the DMA. In July 2017, Delhi's Supreme Court declared that commercial licences were not required for paratransit (two-wheelers and three-wheelers), which further assisted in smoothing transport processes across the DMA.

Officials indicated, however, that even informal networks are battling in the face of the political antagonism that surrounds Delhi's governance. While it was previously possible for a senior official to pick up a phone and call a contact in the national ministry or neighbouring state government, these simple acts are far less common and much more difficult now.

The National Capital Region

The NCR is much greater in size than the DMA, especially in terms of area. It has progressively expanded in size and now incorporates 58 332 square kilometres, nearly

30 times larger than the DMA. However, the population of 46 million people in the NCR is only about 1.5 times greater than that of the DMA. This is because, apart from the DMA at its core, the NCR consists largely of low-density rural settlements with very scattered urban settlements. The NCR is not a functionally integrated city-region but was instead designated *because of* its low density. It was intended as the container into which the excess population and activity of the NCT of Delhi and the DMA could be decanted (see Maps 11, 21 and 22).

The coordination requirement for the NCR is thus very different from that of the DMA. Coordination across the NCR is needed to reshuffle population and economic activities rather than making urban critical infrastructure services work. The challenge here is that many authorities within the NCR give only lip service to this intention, contradicting their real interests.

In the early 1990s, Prime Minister V.N. Rao (1991 to 1996) periodically chaired meetings of the NCRPB, helping to maintain its status. However, Rao was also the prime minister who had turbocharged economic liberalisation. During his tenure, state governments became increasingly competitive, making collaboration more difficult than before. In the 1990s, the courts and media gave the NCRPB some leeway, but, by the 2000s, it was apparent that there was no evidence of trends shifting in the direction of Regional Plan – 2001. The reality was that Delhi was growing rapidly in terms of population and jobs, as was the inner ring of settlements such as Gurgaon and Noida, with very little growth in the counter magnets. The credibility of the NCRPB and the idea of the NCR were waning.

The NCRPB was harshly criticised in the Indian media for its failures (for example, *NCR Tribune* 2002; Sachdeva 2004). A level of frustration is evident also in the minutes of the NCRPB, with the state governments still not having submitted their sub-regional plans and the GNCT of Delhi going counter to the intentions of the regional plan by releasing even more land for industry (NCRPB 2000).

The NCRPB set up a standing committee to explore ways to achieve the dispersal of industry into the region, but the Supreme Court of India decided to act, issuing directives in 1995 and 2000 for Delhi to close industries within its area of jurisdiction. Eventually, however, the courts had to back down as street riots broke out in response to impending job losses (NCRPB 1995, 2000).

The second iteration of the planning scheme, Regional Plan – 2021, was approved by the board in 2005. It slightly moderated the initial plan, giving retrospective approval for some of the deviations by the state governments, but the broad outlines of the decentralisation programme remained intact. Again, implementation did not go well. Uttar Pradesh and Haryana wanted the growth of the inner ring of satellite cities that fell within their territories to be counted as decentralisation. But the plan was clear; decentralisation meant the diversion of activity to the far-flung counter magnets (NCRPB 2005).

In 2009, Uttar Pradesh's government submitted plans to the NCRPB to approve the development of Greater Noida as a new satellite city and the development of the Yamuna Expressway, which would connect the inner ring of satellites. When the NCRPB had still not approved these plans by 2011, Uttar Pradesh decided to go it alone, granting approvals to real estate developers. The Allahabad High Court in Uttar Pradesh intervened in October 2011, halting the developments and insisting that NCRPB approval was required (Bisht 2011). Uttar Pradesh got its way in 2012 when the NCRPB finally approved the Greater Noida Master Plan. At the time, the NCRPB was chaired by a pro-development union minister who overrode objections from the board's planning committee (Sharma 2012).

The dispute between the NCRPB and the Haryana state government was more protracted and remains largely unresolved. The NCRPB rejected a demand by the state government that its entire territory be designated as falling within a decentralisation zone (NCRPB 2004). The ongoing conflict, however, is over the development of protected areas. The Aravallis is a scenic and forested area between Delhi and Gurgaon coveted by real estate developers for the mansions of the rich, but also prized for its rich environmental assets and recreational opportunities. It was delineated in Regional Plan – 2001 as an environmental conservation zone where construction was to be restricted to 0.5 per cent of the total area. The developer-aligned chief minister of Haryana, B.S. Hooda, demanded a revision of the plan, and when the NCRPB refused, he unilaterally issued planning permission to real estate developers. This set Haryana against the NCRPB but also caused conflict with the NCT of Delhi, as the Aravallis was a water catchment zone for the national capital (Dogra 2013; Sinha 2017). The NCRPB eventually conceded, granting state governments the right to determine the boundaries of their own environmental conservation zones (NCRPB 2015). Again, the Supreme Court of India intervened, instructing the NCRPB to enforce the full extent of the environmental conservation zone as indicated in Regional Plan – 2021 (Government of India 2017).

The NCRPB was under growing pressure from the courts across a range of issues. In 2013, a public interest petition had gone to the High Court in Delhi claiming that the state governments were ignoring the provisions of Regional Plan – 2021. They were 'going ahead and allowing development contrary to the Regional Plan, thereby defeating the very purpose of harmonious development of the NCR to save Delhi from population explosion and to avoid haphazard development'.[18] The states, in turn, insisted that Regional Plan – 2021 provided broad guidelines only and so did not bind them to specific land-use arrangements. The High Court was not impressed, delivering a judgment in September 2014, directing the NCRPB to be vigilant in guarding against violations of Regional Plan – 2021 and even advising the union government to dissolve the board if it was unable to enforce Regional Plan – 2021.[19] The media backed the courts, blaming the NCRPB for Delhi's many woes (Rajput 2013).

Faced with the extreme difficulties of imposing its will over the state governments, the NCRPB focussed increasingly on project financing rather than the coordination of regional development and the enforcement of plans. It raised funds from the World Bank, the Asian Development Bank and the German Development Bank and offered state governments loans at preferential interest rates (NCRPB 2014). This sustained the interest of the state governments in the NCRPB, even as they resisted the NCRPB's planning efforts. The state governments lobbied for as much of their territories as possible to be incorporated within the NCR to qualify for funding, and in 2013, the board responded by enlarging the NCR's area by 34 per cent, despite its patent failure to decentralise jobs into the existing region (Dogra 2013).

The BJP's national victory in the April 2014 general elections may, ironically, have rescued the NCRPB, allowing the board to focus on its evolving role in development financing rather than undertaking the seemingly impossible task of planning, coordinating and enforcing. Prime Minister Modi had little apparent interest in planning, even replacing the National Planning Commission of India in 2015 with a think tank called *NITI Aayog* (Hindi for 'policy commission').

With his neoliberal orientation on development, Modi was unlikely to pursue policies which would patently contradict market pressures. Rather than openly push for extended decentralisation, Modi's response to decongest Delhi was to support the ten mega freeway developments in the inner ring around the national capital. In April 2018, for example, the prime minister formally inaugurated the Eastern Peripheral Freeway around Delhi (*The Hindu* 2018).

However, even the most neoliberal government could not ignore the air pollution crisis threatening Delhi's future. In 2016, the NCRPB responded to the growing crisis by calling a special meeting to discuss air pollution and ordering state governments to present action plans for resolving the problem (NCRPB 2016). It may have been the first time that the NCRPB had responded with such determination.

However, a major challenge for the NCRPB in addressing an issue such as air pollution (and, indeed, water pollution) was how the NCR was delineated. The NCR was the empty container and did not correspond with the mega transnational urban (and dense rural) region stretching along the reaches of the Ganges River and Indus River basins from Bangladesh in the east to Pakistan in the west. Urecognised in official policy, this region, and not the NCR, was the primary source of Delhi's pollution. There was no perspective on the material realities of extended urbanisation.

Assessments of the performance of the NCRPB remained largely negative. When I visited Delhi in 2017, academics and professionals commented on the NCRPB: 'it has no teeth'; 'it is dead wood'; 'it is dysfunctional'. More recently, however, the NCRPB has revealed a degree of adaptive capacity. The opportunity for change came with the preparation of the NCR's third regional plan, Regional Plan – 2041, following the expiry of Regional Plan – 2021. The new plan indicates a pragmatic shift away from earlier anti-urban sentiment and the impossible dream of decanting Delhi into the counter magnets (Mabin and Harrison 2022). Notably, the plan calls the Central National Capital Region a 'Golden Ring of Opportunity' and acknowledges that the 'NCT Delhi shall continue to be the economic hub' (NCRPB 2021a, 4 and 16).

A further recent achievement of the NCRPB was signing the Combined Reciprocal Common Transport Agreement between the NCT of Delhi and the states of Haryana, Uttar Pradesh and Rajasthan for seamless movement of transport across the NCR. This extended the agreement within the DMA, which, as previously indicated, originated with informal problem-solving networks (NCRPB 2021b).

As sensible as the shift may be in terms of real trends and possibilities, the de facto abandonment of an ideal pursued since the 1950s raises the question of the continuing rationale for the existing NCR, and whether the NCR should not be reconfigured to represent the actual footprint along the Ganges Valley (and eventually, as geopolitics allow, within the wider transnational territory). The story of the NCR and the NCRPB may be one of the rise-and-fall of a particular discourse on city-regions, informed by a now archaic international discourse on decentralisation, and sustained in India by the legacy concerns of a post-colonial elite.

Before concluding, however, I must note the influence in India of the more recent international discourse on globally competitive city-regions. This has to do with Mumbai rather than Delhi, a city with a higher ranking internationally in terms of economic competitiveness. In Klaus Segbers et al. (2007), for example, Mumbai was positioned, together with Shanghai, São Paulo and Johannesburg, as a global city-region in the making. In the same year, Richard Florida et al. (2008) identified Mumbai-Pune as one of Asia's mega urban regions. In the policy domain, the chief minister of Maharashtra drew on the idea of this mega region in his concept of the Golden Triangle of Maharashtra, drawing together the metropolitan cities of Mumbai, Pune and Nashik.

Conclusion

In this chapter, the discussion has ranged from political cultures shaped through millennia-long histories to the institutional details of a contemporary planning board. It is difficult to thread together all the links, but this is the challenge of India's ancient palimpsest.

Underlying the undoubted complexities of India's formal institutional set-ups is so much more. There is, for example, the informal and the relational, which, while present in every context across the globe, have a particular intensity in India. To some degree, this chapter explored the working of relational networks within the bureaucracy, using the personal reports of officials and ex-officials in Delhi. As committed public servants, their narratives were, understandably, of how professional networks have worked to sustain governance processes during political stalemate or when formal systems have gridlocked. But there is another side to informality – shadow governance with its clientelism, extortion and corruption practices. Also, beyond my purview as a visitor to India was how relational networks intersect with vernaculars such as religion, caste, language and regional identity.

India – Delhi specifically – seemed like an iceberg to me with only the tip examinable in the time I had. There is, fortunately, literature that helps us understand some of the obscurity, including, for example, Schindler (2014b), who projects Delhi as a metropolitan area where the rules of governance are fluid and constantly negotiated in practice.

However, even the tip of the iceberg offers a profusion of insights into the governance of large and complex urban agglomerations. We can, for example, observe how a political settlement, which largely ignored the local sphere of government, has shaped and severely limited metropolitan governance over the decades. We can see through the historical narrative how spatial interests – often those of state governments but also of union and municipal governments – have played out in an institutional landscape that seems to multiply in complexity across each decade. Within India's intensely politicised environment, divergent interests are expressed in protracted wrangling, frequently impinging on the ability to govern.

Yet, in all of this, the governance imperative remains. Governing elites at all levels cannot risk a collapse in governmental arrangement, and so even Delhi, a complicated metropolitan city of around 30 million people with a confusing array of institutional arrangements and bitterly contested politics, continues to function. Arguably, it continues to thrive, although air pollution represents a major threat to its future prosperity.

India reveals the mechanisms that evolve within this complexity to sustain urban governance. Informal communications and actions are clearly part of the mix. But there are also more formal mechanisms involved, including the high courts of India, which provide deadlock-breaking mechanisms and create a special regime of governance to get around the existing system's obstacles. In this way, for example, a state-of-the-art metro system was implemented within the institutional clutter of Greater Delhi.

These mechanisms exist because the formal structures, specifically set up to achieve coordination across metropolitan areas and city-regions, have largely failed. For example, some of the MDAs are successful instruments of land development but are income-generating instruments of state governments and do not play a broader coordinating or collaborative role. The NCRPB has been hamstrung for decades by an impossible vision for the region's future and continuing resistance to this vision by state governments. Despite its high-level composition, it has been a very limited instrument of city-region governance.

Overall, the case of India reveals the deficiencies of metropolitan and city-region governance but also reveals that governance, albeit deeply flawed, continues with structures and processes – formal and informal – emerging to ensure that this happens. We may call this the pragmatics of governance.

Notes

1 Nehru was a leader of the nationalist movement in India in the 1930s and 40s and was prime minister of India from 1950 to 1964.

2 In Hyderabad, for example, the Islamic rulers, known successively as the Qutb Shahi and the Nizams, had ruled their city-state almost autonomously since 1591, and it took occupation by the Indian army in September 1948 to bring this domain into the union.

3 Preamble to the Constitution of India, 1950: https://www.constitutionofindia.net/constitution_of_india/preamble.

4 For the details of the 74th Constitutional Amendment, see https://legislative.gov.in/constitution-seventy-fourth-amendment-act-1992.

5 I was told by a previous senior official in India of a politician who, as a minister in the state government, was insistent in his call for the DDA to be transferred to the jurisdiction of the state, but when he became a minister in the union government was equally insistent that the DDA remained under national authority.

6 See http://www.janaagraha.org/asics/report/Delhi-Planning-Board-(NCRPB).pdf.

7 See http://www.janaagraha.org/asics/report/Delhi-Planning-Board-(NCRPB).pdf.

8 For the full membership, see the NCRPB website: http://ncrpb.nic.in/.

9 See the website of the NCRPB: http://ncrpb.nic.in/.

10 For the ongoing deliberations over these processes, see the minutes of the 37 board meetings between 1985 and 2017: http://ncrpb.nic.in/archive.html.

11 These are the Central National Capital Region, Mumbai, Kolkata, Chennai, Bangalore, Hyderabad, Pune, Kanpur, Visakhapatnam, Nagpur and Patna.

12 As explained to me by a senior official in the GNCT of Delhi.

13 The DMA/Delhi Urban Agglomeration/Central NCR emerged as Delhi and the historical cities of Ghaziabad and Faridabad gradually grew together, and as the new cities of Noida, Greater Noida and Gurgaon were established in the 1970s and expanded rapidly after economic liberalisation in the early 1990s.

14 This was explained to me by Professor N. Sridharan, Department of Regional Planning, Delhi.

15 *Manoj Misra vs Union of India and Others*. Before the National Green Tribunal, New Delhi. Original Application No. 6 of 2012 and M.A. Nos. 967/2013 & 275/2014. See http://admin.indiaenvironmentportal.org.in/files/Yamuna%20NGT%2013%20Jan%202015.pdf.

16 *Manoj Misra vs Union of India and Others*.

17 As explained to me by a planning professional in Delhi. See also the Unified Traffic and Transportation Planning and Engineering Centre website: http://www.uttipec.nic.in.

18 *Raghuraj Singh vs Union of India & Ors.* 2014. W.P.(C) 5559/2013 & CM No. 15049/2013. 30 September 2014, para. 1. See https://indiankanoon.org/doc/173248094/.

19 *Raghuraj Singh vs Union of India & Ors.* 2014, para. 18.

5 Governing the city clusters of China

Introduction

A case in extremis

Of all cases in the BRICS (Brazil, Russia, India, China and South Africa) countries, China has attracted the most attention in the governance of its large urban agglomerations, and there is a good reason for this. China's cities carry immense weight globally. The United Nations World Urbanization Prospects recognised 425 cities in mainland China with a combined population of 594 million (United Nations 2018). This is 23 per cent, nearly one-quarter, of the world total on both counts. Despite the increasing attention, urban scholarship on China is still underrepresented, relatively speaking. If we combine these cities into city clusters as China has done in its official policy, then we have three of the world's largest agglomerations (the others being the megalopolis along the north-east coast of the USA, the 'Blue Banana' in western Europe, and the *megaroporisu* along the south coast of Japan).

A focus on China's large urban agglomerations is important for other reasons. To begin, with its immense scale and rapid rate of development, China offers a case *in extremis*. Kathleen Eisenhardt et al. (2016, 1118) write that 'it is hard to argue that studying a "talking pig" – an extreme case – is not valuable. Extreme cases are particularly relevant to Grand Challenges [highly complex problems] because studying these cases can create broad awareness of the focal challenge'.

Secondly, China's city clusters provide a window into the governance dilemmas and contradictions faced by an authoritarian regime:

- the challenge of horizontal coordination within a vertically aligned political system;
- the economic benefits of agglomeration versus the political threats of large concentrations of people;

- the need to unleash local energies while maintaining control from above; and
- the practical requirements of managing the environmental spillovers and infra-structure requirements of mega-scale development.

In navigating the tensions, China has adopted a form of 'state orchestrated rescaling' although with varying degrees of managed, bottom-up initiatives and regionally based associational relationships (Wu 2016, 1134).

This chapter continues by locating the current dilemmas and practices within China's political cultures and histories and in the materiality of contemporary urban development. It then turns to the development of the discourse on city clusters, reflecting both vernacular and international influences. The main part of the chapter, however, is the account of evolving forms of governance across the three mega clus-ters – the national capital region (NCR) centred on Beijing, the Yangtze River Delta (YRD) extending inland from Shanghai, and the Greater Bay Area (GBA), including Shenzhen, Guangzhou and Hong Kong (Map 4).

Histories and cultures

There is an ongoing debate around the political cultures that shape contemporary China. On the one hand are writers who point to the long history of governmental hierarchy in China – going back to the formation of the Empire around 221 BCE – and argue that its persistence has cultural underpinnings. They argue that Confucian thought, emphasising deference to authority, societal harmony and communality, played a foundational role in supporting the longevity of state hierarchy in China (Pines 2012). With this legacy, China, in recent decades, has sustained authoritarian governance despite rapid economic growth and the emergence of a large, consumerist middle class after decades of rapid economic growth (Liu 2015).

Other writers are more sceptical, pointing out periodic challenges to governing authority, from the collapse of various imperial orders to the early twentieth-century communist insurgence and the pro-democracy uprising of 1989 (Davis 1998). For Zheng Yongnian (2009), the key point is not the shaping power of Confucian cul-ture but, rather, how the governing elites periodically recycled Confucian thought to legitimise authoritarian rule. For Wei-Wei Zhang (1996), current tendencies toward centralising authority have more origins in the territorial chaos after the collapse of imperial rule in the early twentieth century. When Mao Zedong established the People's Republic of China in 1949, national unity and the dominance of the national state were central elements of his modernisation programme.

It is impossible to conclude here on the ongoing debates around political culture except perhaps to follow Zhang (2015) in accepting the presence of historically pro-duced cultures, including Confucian culture, but also emphasising the fluidity and political use of culture.

Whatever the influence of an underpinning culture, history has bequeathed an enduring institutional form. During the Han Dynasty (202 BCE to 220 CE), nine large, specialised government ministries were formed and a governmental hierarchy was established, descending from the imperial centre through province, commandery, county and district (Pines 2012). While there have been adaptations through the centuries, the overall structure of the bureaucracy has been surprisingly resilient.

From political culture, I turn to political settlement. Here, too, the story is complicated, but at the risk of oversimplifying, the establishment of the People's Republic of China followed a military victory in a civil war and was not a bargained settlement. It was cast instead as the military triumph of rural peasants over feudal landlords. However, the rise of a bureaucratic bourgeoisie from the 1950s created a new power base, which Mao tried unsuccessfully to eliminate through the Cultural Revolution in the 1960s and early 1970s.

Deng Xiaoping's genius from the late 1970s was to reformulate a political settlement through subtle bargaining without formally doing so. He maintained a discursive continuity with Maoism while engineering far-reaching transformations in practice (Zhang 1996; Vogel 2013). Zhang (1996, 4) explains how Deng's creed of 'socialism with Chinese characteristics' gradually emerged as 'initially partial, unsystematic ideas [were] gradually elaborated, modified, and codified, into a more formalized doctrine'.

It is impossible to deal here with the complex evolution of China through the post-Maoist era, but there are points of necessary context for the narrative on the governance of city clusters. The first is to note some of the changing emphases under different national leaders. Consistent with his pragmatism, Deng experimented with market-based economies and global opening, most importantly in creating the Shenzhen Special Economic Zone, before extending reforms nationally (Vogel 2013). He famously reasserted his economic reform agenda after the setback of the 1989 crackdown by coming out of retirement to visit Shenzhen, securing the socialist market economy as the economic pathway (Zhang 1996; Vogel 2013).

Jiang Zemin, China's president between 1993 and 2003 and a previous mayor and party secretary of Shanghai, was a neo-conservative concerned with stability and preserving party control. However, he pursued an apparent policy of economic growth at all costs, with export orientation as a dominant approach. When growth slowed in the late 1990s, his influential premier, Zhu Rongji, engineered a new phase of economic liberalisation marked by China's membership of the World Trade Organization in 2001. Under Jiang's leadership, growth was sustained at over eight per cent per annum, although with negative environmental consequences and growing social inequalities. A landmark feature of Jiang's leadership was the re-emergence of Shanghai as a global city, with the development of the Pudong New Area as a centre of national and global finance.

Under President Hu Jintao, China's president between 2003 and 2013, there was a rebalancing of development in the interests of a harmonious socialist society, with more attention given to social equity and environmental considerations. Hu was, however, a low-key leader who struggled to manage the contending tendencies in the party and, under his leadership, the governmental hierarchy weakened.

Xi Jinping, president since 2013, has accumulated considerable personal power, strengthening the party and governmental hierarchies. He has been assertive globally, including through his Belt and Road Initiative, while domestically, he has pursued conservative policies, increasing state controls over society and business and emphasising national pride and the revival of Chinese culture. He has also strengthened China's focus on environmental protection.

Consistent with Deng's concern with balancing interests and preserving collective rule to contain individual ambition, there has been a tacit agreement to rotate leadership among party factions – Jiang Zemin as leader of the Shanghai faction, Hu Jintao as leader of a populist faction, and Xi Jinping as leader of the princeling faction (referring to its association with the revolutionary elite of the Maoist era). This may, however, be disrupted by Xi's consolidated power (Shukla 2021).

The second point of context is the real functioning of China's formidable party and bureaucratic hierarchy. Counterintuitively, the hierarchy includes high levels of functional decentralisation. The Chinese reforms accommodated local interest and released local initiative and energy through decentralisation down the hierarchy. There have been fluctuations in the national–local relationship, with fiscal decentralisation in the 1980s partially reversed in the 1990s, but sub-national governments in China still retain significant bureaucratic powers.

Furthermore, as the Chinese state has become more complex and functionally dispersed, government processes have required more internal deliberation and negotiation. Baogang He and Mark Warren (2011, 269) refer to 'authoritarian deliberation', while Ching Lee and Yonghong Zhang (2014, 1475) talk of 'bargained authoritarianism', describing how the authoritarian state maintains its stability through mechanisms of 'patron-clientelism', 'instrumental bargaining' and 'bureaucratic absorption'.

This draws on earlier work by David Lampton (1992), which pointed to the persistent presence of informality within the Chinese system through personal ties, reciprocity, patron-client relationships, bargaining and individual rent-seeking. The Chinese bureaucracy clearly has formal structures of meritocracy, but bargaining and informality – a 'process of reciprocal accommodation among leaders' (Lampton 1992, 37) – remain an important part of the governmental mix.

Li Zhang et al. (2016, 88) write that 'higher levels of government often establish ambiguous policies that lower levels interpret in different ways', while Fulong Wu et al. (2006, 138) cite a Chinese saying that 'for every measure from the top, there will be a countermeasure at the bottom'. This allows for adaptation and variation processes in practice, despite the hierarchy, although it is not clear what the longer-term effect of President Xi's tightening of national government control will be.

Urban context

In only three and a half decades between 1980 and 2015, China's urban population increased by 590 million people, as levels of urbanisation surged from 19 to 56 per cent. The greatest growth happened within three urban agglomerations of cities along the east coast:[1]

- The YRD includes the cities of Shanghai, Nanjing, Hangzhou, Suzhou, Ningbo, Wuxi, Changzhou and Nantong. It has an economy roughly the size of the gross domestic product of Germany or Japan and a population of around 200 million (Map 12).
- The GBA, also called the Pearl River Delta (PRD), includes the cities of Guangzhou, Shenzhen, Hong Kong, Macau, Dongguan, Foshan and Zhuhai. Its population is around 80 million people, and the economy is the size of the gross domestic product of France or the United Kingdom (Map 13).
- The NCR, also called Jing-Jin-Ji,[2] includes the megacities of Beijing and Tianjin and intermediate cities in Hebei province, including Shijiazhuang, Tangshan and Baoding. It has an economy the size of Mexico's, and a population of around 112 million (Map 14).[3]

As John Harrison and Hao Gu (2021) emphasised, we are dealing with megaregions in the case of China, creating a degree of distinctiveness. The mass-scale urbanisation was catalysed by the post-Maoist reforms. Most important was the industrial take-off. With initial liberalisation, industry emerged *in situ* within networks of villages and small towns (the so-called township and village enterprises – TVEs) as a form of rural industrialisation, but patterns changed as market mechanisms were introduced in the large cities from the late 1980s, including, for example, the introduction of a system of urban land leasing. Industry increasingly concentrated in urban-industrial zones where special incentives applied (special economic zones, industrial parks and others). Initially, the focus was on export-oriented industry using low-wage labour, but industry upgraded and China's economy became increasingly innovation-led. As this happened, the core cities focussed on high-tech industry and tertiary activities, with lower-end industry decentralised into the peripheries of urban networks or beyond, into lower-wage countries in South-East Asia (Wu 2016).

The demand for labour in the cities and wider urban agglomerations brought an army of rural migrants into the cities. Historically, there were strict controls on movement from rural to urban areas, with the *hukou* (place-based household registration) the main regulation mechanism. To facilitate labour absorption, the *hukou* was modified but never fully dismantled as China's national elite retained a legacy of fear with regard to large city growth.

While urban populations grew dramatically, the increase in the urban footprint was even greater: 'while the [urban] population increased more than fourfold, the urban footprint increased almost sixfold, in a process of expansion that is referred to as *tandabing* (meaning a pancake)' (Harrison and Yang 2020, 93). The reasons for expansion include the commodification of land and housing through a system of urban land leasing; the development of rental accommodation by village collectives; a system of municipal finances that incentivises extensive land leasing by urban authorities; heavy investment in road, rail and other connecting infrastructure; the changing lifestyle demands and preferences of the urban middle class; and the shift towards more locationally flexible tertiary activities (Harrison and Yang 2020).

This horizontal urban expansion cutting across municipal and provincial boundaries created a major management challenge for a governmental system oriented for centuries (even millennia) along a vertical hierarchy. The historical response to development spilling over a city boundary into a rural county was for the city to annex the county in a process known as 'cities governing counties' (Zhang et al. 2016, 100). This did lead, over time, to fewer but larger and better capacitated urban municipalities, but it did not resolve the challenge of coordination across the boundaries of mega-sized agglomerations where urban areas had coalesced. During the early phases of the reform era, in fact, intense competition for economic activity and infrastructural investment emerged between city governments within the large agglomerations, making collaboration increasingly complicated and exacerbating environmental and social problems (Wu 2016). It was within this context that a discourse emerged around coordination within the large-scale urban regions.

City-region discourse and practice

The idea of city clusters in the 11th Five Year Plan (FYP) (2006 to 2010) captured international attention, with the conclusion quickly drawn that China was promoting mega-scale urban growth (NDRC 2006). The reality was more prosaic – the clusters were 'economic circles' where better spatial coordination could support growth (Map 27).

The idea of the economic circle came from Japan and was transferred to China during a thaw in political relations from the late 1970s on.[4] In its initial form, the economic circle implied a sphere of influence around a dominant core, but it evolved to include a requirement for inter-jurisdiction coordination within the circle.

At first, the economic circle served a geopolitical purpose for the Chinese. In 1988, the State Council formally adopted the idea of 'great international circles' (*guoji daxunhuan*) to facilitate the integration of parts of China into wider regional economies. The concept was deployed most successfully in the south, where a great international circle linked the south of China (Guangdong and Fujian provinces) with Hong Kong, Taiwan and other parts of South-East Asia. By defining the relationship as economic, China could avoid the more complex matters relating to political and administrative jurisdictions (Sum 2002). In the north-east, China had the Yellow Sea Economic Circle, but here geopolitics proved to be too complex. Japan had its Sea of Japan Economic Circle and South Korea had its own proposal (Woodside 2007).

While a transnational arrangement never succeeded, China designated the Bohai Sea Rim Economic Circle in 1996, which fell entirely within its boundaries. The Bohai Sea Rim included Beijing, Tianjin and the provinces of Hebei, Shandong and Liaoning, and was the precursor to the Beijing-centred NCR.

The shift in use of the economic circle from referring to a transnational jurisdiction to a city cluster was also informed by Japan. The mega urban region along the east coast of Japan was conceptualised in terms of three main economic circles, namely the Tokyo Circle, Nagoya Circle and Kansai Circle, with the Tokyo Circle also known as the National Capital Economic Circle. Japan's Law of National Capital Regional Development, 1956, had delineated the national capital circle as the area within a 100- to 120-kilometre radius of Tokyo Central Station – roughly a one-hour commuting belt (which became the rule of thumb for China's economic circles). The law required the prefectural municipalities within this radius to collaborate in reducing the core's congestion (Zhang and Deng 2017).

The transfer of the term 'economic circle' from Japan, to refer to urban agglomerations in China, is indicated in a substantial technical literature in the Chinese language (for example, Wei and Zhao 2005; Zhu 2013). In Chinese, the term used for an economic circle at this scale is 经济圈 or *jingjiquan*. However, the term 'economic circle' evolved to take on the more spatially oriented term 'city cluster' (城市群 or *chengshiqun*), although international influences, including Chinese urban planning students studying in Western universities, also introduced the term 'city-region' (城市区域 or *chengshiquyu*).

The etymology, however, must be interpreted with the political aspects of the concept in mind. The reforms after the 1980s had produced contradictions for the ruling elite. Urbanisation concentrated the workforce required for the mass-based export-oriented industry that underpinned the early phases of reform. But this concentration created political anxieties for the ruling elite, as well as management challenges such as China's air pollution crisis (Wallace 2014).

The national elite battled to manage the contradiction. To provide the necessary labour for expanding industry, it progressively liberalised the *hukou* and introduced land leasing within urban areas. But for fear of accelerating urbanisation, the leadership did not abolish the *hukou*, nor did it reform communal landownership in rural areas.

The economic circle/city cluster offered a means to manage the contradiction. If urban growth could be distributed across a circle or cluster, urbanisation could proceed without the unbalanced growth of the core city. President Hu Jintao was concerned with rebalancing development, and within the city cluster – a territory with an expansive reach incorporating settlements of all types and sizes, as well as swathes of rural land – growth could be diverted away from the largest cities while urbanisation continued. The 11th FYP aimed at 'building the socialist new country-side while promoting urbanization vigorously and prudently', a paradox that could potentially be managed within the city cluster (NDRC 2006, chapter two).

For Yi Li and Fulong Wu (2013), the 2000s marked the departure from urban entrepreneurialism and high levels of local competition in the 1980s and 90s. There was a discursive shift towards harmonious society and rebalancing, and the city cluster was a territory where these could occur. However, they observe that 'the regional scale [was] a layer of "soft institution" without building up a substantial level of regional governmental mechanism' (Li and Wu 2013, 139).

The 12th FYP (2010 to 2015) was also prepared under Hu Jintao's leadership and came in the wake of the global economic crisis. It was also a plan that tried to harmonise interests, but a key feature was the need to give scientific rationality to political compromise. It spoke of 'scientifically programming the functional positioning of cities in the urban agglomeration' and used terms such as the 'objective rules of development' and '[scientifically delineated] carrying capacities' (NDRC 2011, chapter 20, sections 1, 2 and 3). The city cluster was one of the so-called objective realities, and for the first time, the plan included the idea of a national capital circle. Harrison and Gu (2021, 83) argued that this appeal to scientific rationality 'belies what remains a deeply politicized vision'.

The 13th FYP (2016 to 2020) reflected the assertiveness and global ambitions of President Xi Jinping (NDRC 2016). With his political authority as a core leader, there was no need to rationalise proposals in scientific terms. The proposal for city clusters was boldly stated without scientific justification. The 13th FYP also acknowledged for the first time that new governance mechanisms would be needed for the coordinated development of the city clusters, although it did not specify what these might be, and through this period, spatial planning remained the central mechanism for national government-led coordination.

The 14th FYP (2021 to 2025) elaborated on 'the path of new urbanization with Chinese characteristics' (NDRC 2021, Part Eight). Once again, however, the premise was to promote urbanisation but to distribute urban growth to small- and medium-sized cities, capping the growth of the megacities. Restrictions on movement into cities of less than three million people were to be abolished altogether, with significantly relaxed restrictions for movement into cities of three to five million. The FYP once again emphasised the role of city clusters and the need to deepen the mechanisms of coordination. Again, however, there was no clarity on what the coordination instruments would be, apart from emphasising the coordinating role of the core city within each cluster and the importance of planning (which was to be further developed through the designation of functional zones). The 14th FYP identified several city clusters but indicated that national priority would be given to three – the YRD, the Guangdong-Hong Kong-Macau GBA and the Beijing-Tianjin-Hebei region (or NCR).

As indicated, the official discourse can be tracked through the idea of the economic circle and the city cluster, with a slow evolution of the mechanisms for coordination within these territories (regional planning being the exception). The struggle to formulate the promised mechanisms relates to the deeply embedded governmental hierarchy which is difficult to adapt to the requirements of horizontal coordination, and the challenges presented by the mega scale of some of the clusters. For Harrison and Gu (2021, 78), the size of the clusters 'raises a fundamental question, namely: can we actually plan megaregional futures?'

Parallel to and interacting with the official discourse is the work of (mainly) Chinese scholars (for accounts of this scholarship, see Wu 2016; Chan et al. 2021). Without detailing the many contributions, we may note the attempt, from the early reform era on, to grapple with the scale of the emerging urban form. Hongjun Yu and Yuemin Ning (1983) drew on Gottman's megalopolis at an early stage, when China's mega agglomerations were still at an incipient stage. Yixing Zhou (1991) noted the vast scale and complexity of these emergent agglomerations and proposed the term 'metropolitan interlocking regions'. To T.G. McGee and Charles Greenberg (1992), the metropolitan interlocking regions of China were an example of Asia's extended metropolitan regions. S. Yao et al. (1992) wrote of urban clusters (*chengshiqun*), but their terminology has also been interpreted as 'urban agglomeration,' a term now widely used in English-translated Chinese scholarship (Chan et al. 2021). Some scholars retain the use of the term 'urban cluster,' even in English translation (Qiao et al. 2015), but others have turned more conventionally to 'metropolitan areas' (*dushiqu*) (Xu et al. 2007) or 'city-regions' (Luo et al. 2010). Anthony Yeh and Zifeng Chen (2020, 636) have taken the discourse to a new level with their concept of 'super megacity-regions' (*chaodadushiqu*).

For Mi Tang et al. (2022), the layering of scales within an urban agglomeration is the discursive and practical challenge. In this respect, there is gradual progress. The concept of the metropolitan interlocking region, for example, supports the idea of a mega agglomeration such as the YRD consisting of a series of overlapping metropolitan areas, city-regions or urban circles. This has informed recent moves to distinguish sub-forms within the mega spatial structures, for planning and governance purposes.

The texture, however, must come from the actual cases and so I move now, in turn, to the three largest city clusters, showing both the common elements in cluster development, such as the directing role of the national state, and the distinctiveness produced through regional histories, cultures and politics. I begin with the YRD, which is widely regarded as the most advanced region in terms of economic linkages and collaborative governance.

The Yangtze River Delta: the most developed of the city clusters (Maps 12 and 23)

The YRD roughly coincides with the Wuyue region of China, which has its own dialects and cultural practices, with a shared history going back to the formation of an independent coastal kingdom in the tenth century CE during China's Five Dynasties and Ten Kingdoms Period.[5] For Ming-bo Li (2005) there are, therefore, historical and cultural resources to draw on in developing collaborative governance within the YRD.

The extent to which a territorial identity has mattered in the evolution of governance in the YRD is difficult to assess as there are practical reasons why governance arrangements may be more advanced here than elsewhere. The YRD is the most mature city cluster in China, with a closely linked network of cities cross-cutting the boundaries of four provincial-status administrations – the City of Shanghai (that has provincial status), and the provinces of Jiangsu, Zhejiang and Anhui. Many studies now confirm the intensity of economic interlinkages in a cluster that has also coalesced spatially (for example, Liu et al. 2020).

In the early reform years, however, competition rather than collaboration dominated. The economic competition was intense, with many municipalities trying to attract the same sort of industries as their neighbours. Wu (2016) indicated that most cities within the YRD competed for petrochemical industries and manufacturers of automobile parts and information technology equipment, rather than developing their specialisms. There was also strong competition for infrastructural investments, including deep-water ports, airports and new highways, with duplication of costly initiatives in the region. Shanghai, for example, built a deep-water port, the largest in the world, while Zhejiang and Jiangsu provinces attempted similar developments. When Shanghai developed the Hongqiao International Airport, it attracted information technology industries away from Jiangsu province, which had worked hard to attract these industries (Wu 2016).

The first attempt to promote regional-scale collaboration was initiated top-down by the central government in 1982. The Shanghai Economic Region was set up, comprising Shanghai and nine other cities across Jiangsu and Zhejiang provinces with the Shanghai Economic Region Planning Office as its administrative agency. Individual cities established their own economic coordination offices to work with this structure in removing local barriers to collaboration. However, within the highly competitive environment of the time, the initiative had little success and was eventually abandoned in 1988, although some local economic coordination offices remained open (Ding and Li 2015).

A further challenge at the time was that Shanghai struggled to play its role as its leading city, with the Zhejiang and Jiangsu provinces eyeing its position. Shanghai had suffered decades of neglect during the Maoist era and was also neglected during the first decade of reform, when the focus was on experimental initiatives such as the Shenzhen Special Economic Zone in the far south of China.

The change came dramatically in the early 1990s when Jiang Zemin, previous mayor and party secretary of Shanghai, became general secretary of the Communist Party of China and then president. Jiang appointed another previous Shanghai mayor, Zhu Rongji, as prime minister. The Shanghai clique was in power nationally, and the city soon benefitted. Central government designated the Pudong New Area and announced the creation of the Shanghai Stock Exchange, which catalysed dramatic urban growth and transformation. Through the 1990s, Shanghai had a close interactive relationship with the central government, gaining significantly (Zhang and Fu 2009).

Now Shanghai was the clear leader in terms of economics and politics, and those that fell in line would benefit. The national leadership referred to Shanghai as the 'head of the dragon' (Li 2009, 1), and Jiangsu and Zhejiang duly cooperated, working with Shanghai in constructing associational arrangements (Zhang and Fu 2009).

In 1992 the directors of the economic coordination offices in 14 cities across the YRD came together to form the Municipal Economic Coordination Forum with Shanghai in the chair, and in 1997 representation was upgraded to mayoral level (Zhang and Fu 2009; Ding and Li 2015). This was the origin of the annual mayors' conference, which has become a feature of coordination across the city-region but, at the time, was an emergent practice with participation from around one-half of the cities in the region, and without formal recognition from central government.

In 2003, the upcoming World Expo in Shanghai prompted more formal arrangements of collaboration. The party secretaries of Shanghai, Jiangsu and Zhejiang signed an agreement of collaboration, recognising the leading role of Shanghai and agreeing to meet on a regular basis.[6]

In 2004, the mayors met for their economic coordination meeting, developing formal criteria for participation and accepting cities in Anhui province into membership, significantly extending the spatial reach of the YRD. By then, participation had expanded to around 30 cities, including all the major municipalities in the region. In the same year, the mayors' meeting set up a permanent office supported by a research centre and expert committees (Na 2014). In terms of protocol, the mayor of Shanghai chairs the annual mayors' meeting, but the three vice-chairs are from the sub-provincial cities of Nanjing, Hangzhou and Ningbo. Before the meeting, municipal officials meet to draft agreements, but at the meeting, an agreement framework is signed by the municipal mayors, which is subsequently developed into a detailed action plan for the year. Each year has its own theme for coordination, with the 2018 meeting, for example, focussing on environmental governance.

The municipalities had signed agreements, which included setting up a joint structure to convene the 2010 World Expo, developing an integrated transportation network, jointly promoting a regional innovation system, collaborating on measures for ecological protection, coordinating tourism efforts, skills development, technology transfer and the development of integrated regional markets. In 2009, the mayors' meeting jointly addressed how to deal with the global financial crisis (Na 2014). Over time, there was a progression from addressing simple matters of regional coordination, such as tourist signage, to increasingly complex issues such as the integration of social protection (including medical insurance), legal institutions, financial institutions, intellectual property rights and industrial upgrading.[7] While this city-region scale of partnership was evolving, various forms of partnership were emerging within smaller clusters of cities in the YRD or bilaterally between cities in response to the pragmatics of governance, such as the need to manage the inter-municipal expansion of metro systems (Luo and Shen 2009; Li and Wu 2018; Yang et al. 2021).

Provinces have played an interfacing role between cities and national government within the evolving process. An annual meeting of provinces precedes the annual meeting of mayors, formally maintaining the hierarchy, but with the anomaly of Shanghai being both a province and a municipality and chairing both meetings.[8] In June 2018, the provinces adopted a three-year action plan for the integration of the region, incorporating the themes adopted by the municipalities and the perspectives of central government as represented in the YRD plan. The action plan was supported by the RMB 100 billion (US$16 billion) YRD Collaborative Advantage Fund, which supports technology-based projects that enhance integration (China Daily 2018).

The position of the YRD within national policy has evolved over time. The 11th FYP (2006 to 2010) identified the YRD as a reform pilot for coordinated regional development. At the time, Premier Wen Jiabao chaired a forum on the economic and social development of the YRD, stating that the integration of the YRD was a national project. In 2008, the National Development and Reform Commission (NDRC) prepared guidelines for the further development of the YRD and in 2010, it released a regional plan it had commenced in 2005 (Li and Wu 2013). Recognising the complexity of managing this megacity cluster as a single entity, the plan represented the YRD as a set of interlocking city-regions, each focussed on a large city playing a distinctive function within the greater agglomeration. For example, Shanghai was to be the global city with advanced services, focussing on finances and marine logistics, while Hangzhou was to concentrate on electronics and cultural industries such as leisure and tourism (Wu 2016; Lu et al. 2020). The plan also outlined mega-scale projects for regional integration, shifting the emphasis away from freeway construction to a high-speed rail network.

As a top-down process, the plan was an attempt to catch up with developments that had been happening within the region and reassert national direction. However, Li and Wu (2013, 145) recognise that this belies far greater complexity and does not necessarily displace regional initiative: 'the making of top-down regional plans only represents the *intention* [my emphasis] of recentralization by the central state. As illustrated from the case of YRD Regional Plan, the process is much more complicated due to the complex politics between central and local government and different divisions of central ministries'.

In the plan-making process, local governments were anxious to ensure that they were included in the plan, and there was intense behind-the-scenes lobbying and bargaining. Officials I spoke to in Shanghai indicated that the preparation of the plan-from-above was welcomed locally as it indicated that the region had the attention of the national government. They also welcomed the clarity provided by the plan and suggested that it provided adequate space for local interpretation. Li and Wu (2013, 145) point out, however, that the use of the plan may be different from what was intended: 'local government is still driven to develop the economy for political promotion and fiscal revenue. It is thus not surprising that the regional plan is manipulated by the local government to lobby for development rather than coordination'.

China's 12th FYP (2011 to 2015) referred to the YRD as one of the three priority city clusters in China. In the 13th FYP (2016 to 2020), however, the reference was to the Yangtze River Economic Belt, which is a territory far greater than the YRD, incorporating the full reach of the Yangtze Valley, including the major urban agglomerations around Wuhan and Chengdu-Chongqing. At first, there was concern that the economic belt would replace the YRD as a national priority. However, at a high-level symposium in 2018, President Xi affirmed the importance of the YRD, indicating Shanghai's role as the gateway into the economic belt. Vice-Premier Hang Zheng was charged with leading the YRD's integration (Shanghai Municipal People's Government 2018).

In 2016, the NDRC released the YRD City Cluster Development Plan, strengthening the proposals in the 2010 plan, and a further update was issued in 2019. These plans framed the development of sub-clusters within the YRD – the Grand Shanghai Metropolitan Economic Circle (centred on Shanghai), the Su-Xi-Chang Urban Agglomeration (in Jiangsu province), Hangzhou Bay Area (in Zhejiang province) and the Wanbei Urban Agglomeration (in Anhui province). Each region developed its action plan for integration (Lu et al. 2020).

For Haiyan Lu et al. (2020), all provinces and cities in the wider region had accepted the YRD as the overarching brand identity and were collaborating in region-wide initiatives, such as the development of the rapid rail network, but there was also enthusiasm for developing sub-brand identities.

The Grand Shanghai Metropolitan Economic Circle, known more mundanely to the planners as the Shanghai Metropolitan Area, took the lead in developing a plan together with eight surrounding cities (hence the region being known as 1+8). The plan was prepared internally to the circle/region with the support of the World Bank and local universities and institutes. However, with a population of around 70 million people, even the Shanghai Metropolitan Area was mega-sized, raising complicated governance questions.[9] The other circle within the YRD that made early progress with joint planning was the Hangzhou Bay Area. The Bay is an area with a strong sense of historical identity, which may underpin contemporary initiatives.

In summary, the YRD is a vast territory, important for national elites but also the object of intense concern for local and regional actors. Top-down planning has intersected with emergent processes within the region, creating a rich hybridity of territorial governance initiatives. It is work-in-progress, and it is difficult to know what may finally institutionalise within the YRD. It may be the first significant modification to China's age-old governmental hierarchy.

However, the apparent success of collaborations within the YRD does have to be qualified, acknowledging the challenges along the way and the uncertainties that remain. Li and Wu (2018, 315), for example, explore 'the struggles and tensions surrounding the development of city-regionalism' using the case of Shanghai and Kunshan, a neighbouring county-level city. Officials I spoke to in Shanghai used Deng's famous aphorism of 'crossing the river by feeling the stones' when talking of a process of gradually accumulating success, with invariable setbacks along the way. They spoke about the limitations of the existing approaches, but their overall view was that it was better to have these mechanisms than not.

The politics of integration: the Greater Bay Area in the far south of China (Maps 13 and 24)

The GBA comprises the PRD in mainland China, which largely coincides with the province of Guangdong, but also the special administrative regions of Hong Kong and Macau.

The PRD was the zone of experimentation in China's early reform era, where deviation from policy was accepted, even encouraged. The experiments, especially the special economic zones, catalysed a burst of regional development, which may have been unprecedented in global history. The reason for the economic success of the region is debated, with Katsuhiro Sasuga (2004, 56) explaining it in terms of its 'distinctive sub-culture, its history as a trading centre, its distance from Beijing, and its proximity to Hong Kong and Macau'. For Xiangming Chen and Tomás de'Medici (2013), the PRD is sufficiently removed from Beijing for local elites to feel at liberty to act with relative freedom and national elites to be comforted that the contagion of possible failure can be contained. However, with the presence of Hong Kong, the region has a special sensitivity for China's national elites, which has increased in recent years. Far from leaving the PRD – now mainly spoken of as the GBA – to its experimental devices, the national government is taking a close look at the region. Rather than a zone of experimentation, the GBA is the matrix within which Hong Kong and Macau will be integrated into the mainland, and it is a process to be carefully managed.

I will begin the story with the designation of two special economic zones in Guangdong in August 1979 – Shenzhen on the border with Hong Kong and Zhuhai on the border with Macau. Zhuhai had limited success as its neighbour, Macau, was a limited growth catalyst, focussed mainly on the entertainment industry. Shenzhen, however, became the 'instant city' (Chen and de'Medici 2013, 125) as its growth synergised with the economic requirements of Hong Kong at the time (Yang 2006). It was a front-shop, back-factory model, with Hong Kong as the front shop and Shenzhen as the back factory (Yang 2006). However, the economic relationship changed over time as Shenzhen upgraded into a control centre, with labour-intensive manufacturing displaced to cities further into the PRD, such as Dongguan.

Governmentally, many innovations eventually adopted nationwide were first tested in Shenzhen and the wider region, including contractual employment, joint ventures, land leasing and even forms of local democratisation (Chen and de'Medici 2013). There was a sense of openness at the time, with the party secretary of Guangdong adopting the slogan 'To the outside, more open; to the inside, looser; to those below, more power' (Zhang 1996, 71). He adeptly used directives from Beijing, ambiguous because of the ongoing struggles between hardliners and reformists, to carve out greater provincial autonomy.

A massive city cluster was in the making. The development was not, however, confined to the big cities such as Guangzhou, Shenzhen and Dongguan. Township and village enterprises had emerged in the early reform era, transforming a network of thousands of rural settlements into a massive web of industrial hubs producing for global markets (Vogel 2013). This created urbanisation from below, as settlements coalesced in a largely unplanned manner into a mega agglomeration. For Ngai-Ling Sum (2002, 153) the emerging agglomeration was 'the interface of an emerging socialist-capitalist and global-regional economy' with 'new time-space coordinates that cut across the global-regional-national-local domains'. A regional economic circle had evolved for China's national leadership, providing the basis for integrating Hong Kong and Macau into China's wider polity and economy (Woodside 2007).

However, for sustained success, this mega agglomeration required some form of coordinated management. The speed and complexity of growth have created problems including weak environmental protection, poor connecting transport infrastructure, duplication of regional infrastructure such as seaports and airports, poor sewage treatment and mass-scale urban sprawl. There were also challenges of economic coordination between Hong Kong and the mainland, which had different regulatory systems.

In the 1980s, mainland China had only embryonic mechanisms for regulating a market economy, so coordination with Hong Kong and Macau co-evolved experimentally. The coordination of financial circuits was a major challenge, for example. Mainland China had tight controls on the movement of capital and a currency with limited convertibility, whereas Hong Kong was a financially sophisticated hub within liberalised global financial markets. Sum (2002) shows how informal practices emerged, enabling traders and investors to navigate these complications, which, over time, were regularised within joint legislation.[10] Some problems were resolved in 2003 with the signing of the Closer Economic Partnership Arrangement between mainland China and the special administrative regions, but adaptations have continued. For example, Shenzhen has established the Qianhai Cooperation Zone, where firms are free to decide whether to operate in terms of Hong Kong or mainland corporate law.

Other forms of spatial coordination took time to evolve, and remain limited. In the 1980s, political battles raged within the Chinese Communist Party over the designation of the special economic zones, and the region's future was not secure (Zhang 1996). Deng's celebrated visit to Shenzhen in 1992 was a pivotal moment, affirming the region's position within national policy. In 1995, the Guangzhou provincial government produced the Pearl River Delta City Cluster Coordination Development Plan, which recognised the region as a multi-core agglomeration, with the four hubs being Shenzhen-Hong Kong, Dongguan, Guangzhou-Foshan and Macau-Zhuhai. However, the plan was produced technocratically by the Guangdong Construction Commission and had little practical effect because of its lack of attention to the institutional base for implementation (Yang and Jin 2011).

The plan was revised in 2004, and this time attention was given to implementation with the establishment of a PRD City Group Plan Management Coordination Office within the provincial government (Yang and Jin 2011). The plan did not incorporate the special administrative regions, as they fell outside the provincial jurisdiction, but it identified major development corridors extending southwards to Hong Kong and Macau. Implementation remained a challenge as the provincial government lacked the powers necessary for coordinated action, and so provincial officials turned to the NDRC (Yang and Li 2013).[11]

At the time, the PRD did not enjoy high priority in national policy. After Deng, the national government turned its focus elsewhere. Under Jiang Zemin (1993 to 2003) the focus was on Shanghai, while Hu Jintao (2003 to 2013) was concerned with rebalancing growth towards the underdeveloped western parts of China (NDRC 2006). The party secretary for Guangdong, Wang Yang, was, however, a previous senior official in the NDRC, and could play his networks to persuade the central government to prepare a regional plan (Yang and Li 2013; Lu et al. 2020).

The NDRC responded in 2008 with the release of the Outline of the Plan for the Reform and Development of the PRD (2008–2020). The outline plan recognised the difficulty of managing the entire agglomeration by dividing the PRD into three cross-municipal metropolitan areas: Shenzhen-Dongguan-Huizhou, Guangzhou-Foshan-Zhaoqing and Zhuhai-Zhongshan-Jiangmen. The plan was produced at an immensely difficult time for the region as the global financial crisis had seriously damaged the export-oriented industry on which the region depended. However, having a nationally produced plan was an important indication to local actors that the region had not been forgotten.

Under Xi Jinping, the PRD has gathered considerable national attention, given Xi's interest in accelerating the integration of Hong Kong into mainland China. Xi has raised the region's profile but has also exercised greater control over local actors. Responding to cues from Beijing, Hong Kong's chief executive, C.Y. Leung, led a high-profile delegation to Guangzhou 'with one thing on his mind: fitting Hong Kong into Beijing's "Greater Bay Area" integration scheme for the Pearl River Delta' (Cheng 2017, para. 1).

Macau has generally supported the collaborative process, aware of its limited leverage, but Hong Kong's involvement has fluctuated (Lu et al. 2020). While economic and social linkages strengthened in the 1980s, there was no active attempt to achieve spatial integration. In 1997, the colonial era ended with the formal handover of Hong Kong to China, but there was, ironically, a distancing from mainland China in the early post-colonial era of Hong Kong. A Hong Kong-Guangdong Joint Cooperation Conference has been convened annually since 1998, but there was little enthusiasm from the Hong Kong side as local officials tried to assert their autonomy from Beijing (Lu et al. 2020).

From about 2001, there was a gradual increase in cooperation from Hong Kong, although the territory remained divided between factions supporting and factions opposing increased integration with the mainland. In 2009, following the release of the NDRC's outline plan, Guangdong, Hong Kong and Macau jointly released the Greater Pearl River Coordinated Development Plan with the goal of joining forces to create a globally competitive, world-class city-region, and this was followed in 2011 by the release of a draft joint action plan for the Bay Area of the Pearl River Delta. However, the joint action plan was sharply criticised within Hong Kong for lack of participation and mainland bias, and a final consensus could not be reached (Yang and Li 2013).

The impetus for integrated planning eventually came from China's central government. The 13th FYP (2016 to 2020) committed to 'open the mainland up more widely to Hong Kong and Macau . . . and advance the development of the Guangdong-Hong Kong-Macau Greater Bay Area' (NDRC 2016, chapter 54, section 2). On 1 July 2017, the NDRC and the governments of Guangdong, Hong Kong and Macau signed the Framework Agreement on Deepening Guangdong-Hong Kong-Macau Cooperation in the Development of the Greater Bay Area in Hong Kong and, in March 2018, Premier Li Keqiang committed to unveiling a joint plan for the GBA. These agreements and pronouncements caused anxiety among some in Hong Kong, with fears that they foretold attempts to accelerate the political integration of the territory into mainland China. Beijing did, in fact, move to strengthen controls over the territory, provoking the pro-democracy protests of 2019/20, which were contained through measures introduced in the so-called Hong Kong National Security Law of 2020. The coordinated development of the region was given even greater priority in the 14th FYP (2021 to 2025), which emphasised the national significance of developing the Guangdong-Hong Kong-Macau GBA in an integrated way.

Other influences were propelling the move towards greater integration, including academics and business leaders. Chris Meulbroek et al. (2022) remind us that the first call for a GBA was made in 1994 by the founding president of the Hong Kong University of Science and Technology. From the business sector, a key figure was Ma Huateng (Pony Ma), the chairperson of Shenzhen-based Tencent Holdings, a company listed on the Hong Kong Stock Exchange. Ma argued that with 'Hong Kong's advanced financial services, combined with Shenzhen's strength in innovation and the PRD's manufacturing power, the region has great potential to become a prosperous metropolitan [area] powered by cutting-edge technologies' (South China Morning Post 2017). He has even called for the eventual merger of Hong Kong and Shenzhen into a single city administration. The business drive was evident in June 2017, with the launch of the Qianhai-Shenzhen-Hong Kong Cooperation Forum, supported by chief executives of major corporations with interests straddling the Hong Kong-Shenzhen border. The forum promoted the term 'Greater Bay Area', drawing on comparisons with the 'world-class city-regions' around Tokyo Bay and the Bay Area of California in the USA.[12]

The processes came together in 2019 with the release of the Outline Development Plan for the Guangdong-Hong Kong-Macau Greater Bay Area, 2022–2035, which announced the intention to 'create a vibrant world-class city cluster' built on the open economies of Hong Kong and Macau, and the 'reformist administration of Guangdong' and its nine major urban municipalities (NDRC 2019). Economically, the focus was on innovation-driven activity, while spatially, the focus was on strengthening the role of the core cities but developing strong axes of integration between them. The GBA was positioned as a gateway into a pan-PRD region and the global Belt and Road Initiative specific initiatives were identified for strengthening spatial integration, including the further development of the Qianhai Cooperation Zone in Shenzhen – a new international city centre at a border crossing between Shenzhen and Hong Kong – and the Nansha demonstration zone for cooperation between Guangdong, Hong Kong and Macau (NDRC 2019).

While there has been a politically driven initiative to strengthen mainland special administrative region linkages, the mechanics of coordination across the city cluster have proceeded fitfully. The 2008 outline plan had acknowledged the impossibility of a coordination mechanism operating successfully across the entire urban cluster and so had divided the region into the three metropolitan areas, hoping that they would provide the basis for meaningful cooperation.[13] For each metropolitan area, there was to be an annual conference of mayors, drawing on an approach that was evolving in the YRD.

Collaboration in the Guangzhou-Foshan-Zhaoqing Metropolitan Area was embedded in strong historical relationships and preceded the outline plan (Lu et al. 2020). A grassroots movement to create a Guangzhou-Foshan city-region had already begun in the 1990s, and by 2003 the idea of a Guangfo Metropolis was officially recognised. After that, many inter-city collaborative forums were set up around issues such as economic cooperation, environmental protection, resource management and urban planning. In 2008, a joint outline plan was produced for Guangfo, and, in 2009, a metropolitan integration agreement was signed (Lu et al. 2020). Practical steps towards cooperation included the full integration of transport systems across the metropolitan area with the development of a joint metro system and the construction of the Guangzhou and Foshan demonstration zone for science and technology innovation.[14]

Beyond Guangzhou-Foshan-Zhaoqing, cooperation is less evident, with inter-city competition remaining the dominant mode (Li et al. 2015). In the Shenzhen-Dongguan-Huizhou Metropolitan Area, there were initial prospects for collaboration along the lines of the front-shop, back-factory model, which had worked in earlier years in the relationship between Hong Kong and Shenzhen. Shenzhen was upgrading to high-tech industry and tertiary activity, while Dongguan and Huizhou were focussing on labour-intensive manufacturing. The 2008 economic crisis was, however, a blow to the metropolitan area, and inter-city competition has since intensified, complicating institutional relationships.[15] Practical considerations did compel some forms of cooperation including, for example, coordinated waste treatment and road construction between Shenzhen and Dongguan (Wu 2016). There were similar challenges for the Zhuhai-Zhongshan-Jiangmen Metropolitan Area, complicated by the lack of an obvious leader among the cities.

On a broader level, there were institutional tensions between Shenzhen, the upstart, and Guangzhou, the long-established provincial capital. From the beginning, Shenzhen's attention was turned towards Hong Kong rather than the province, declaring its willingness to serve as Hong Kong's backyard if this was a path to further development (Chen and de'Medici 2013). With these tensions, neither Shenzhen nor Guangzhou identified strongly with the PRD as a region, with both aiming for an international rather than a regional identity. Shenzhen remained Hong Kong focussed, and Guangzhou collaborated closely with neighbouring Foshan (Lu et al. 2020). However, while Shenzhen has looked toward Hong Kong, this city has not always been a willing partner. In 2004 the cities did eventually sign the Memorandum on Close Cooperation between Hong Kong and Shenzhen, and the first Hong Kong-Shenzhen Cooperation Forum was held in 2006, with many joint initiatives following. Nevertheless, the geopolitical boundary and the many sensitivities surrounding it mean that Hong Kong and Shenzhen are 'not quite a twin city' (Shen 2014, 138).

A recent dynamic is the construction of the mega bridges across the bay. These have changed geospatial relationships, including commuting and residential patterns. They also created intra-GBA tensions. The development of the Hong Kong-Zhuhai-Macau Bridge raised strong objections from Shenzhen, which felt it was being bypassed. This, in turn, led to the construction of the Shenzhen-Zhongshan Bridge, which is seen as a threat by Hong Kong as it will potentially draw traffic away from its harbour and airport.

The GBA remains an immensely complex region across spatial, economic, institutional and political dimensions. Complex but fractious relationship webs have evolved across parts of the GBA, but no significant institutional mechanism of collaboration has yet evolved at the cluster level. At sub-cluster level, although very unevenly, there are innovative mechanisms that may warrant closer attention.

Overall, the city-region is not as well studied as the PRD, but there are indications of growing interest. A recent significant contribution is Meulbroek et al. (2022), who used critical discourse analysis to show how the GBA has been imagined and reimagined as China's new megaregion within the evolving economic and political context. They explored the language in the succession of plans and other documents for the GBA and PRD, revealing a dynamic vision of megaregionalism. However, their work reveals the dynamism of the region in another sense. As they researched the region, the pro-democracy protests were in full swing, and they concluded that the momentum for integration had been disrupted. However, by the time their article was published, Beijing had reasserted its authority, and a top-down integration process was re-established (although complicated by the physical disconnection introduced by the Covid-19 pandemic).

Orchestrating from above: the National Capital Region (Maps 14 and 25)

Capital cities are symbolically and practically central to national government, but they are also vulnerable to the political threat of large concentrations of people. Jeremy Wallace (2014, 3) writes that 'governments have reshaped the geography of their capitals in response'.

In the case of China, the national capital, Beijing, was a medium-sized city internationally when the People's Republic of China was formed in 1949 and has emerged as a global megacity only in the post-Maoist era. Once one of 'the most austere capitals in the world' (Gu et al. 2015, 914), Beijing has evolved into a modern, economically diverse urban agglomeration, far more than a national capital. While there is national pride in the transformation, evident at the time of the 2022 Summer Olympic Games, for example, Beijing's growth has come with challenges, including severe air pollution, road congestion and water shortages (Tang and Meng 2021), and with political worries intensified by the experience of the youth protests of 1989 (Wallace 2014). In this context, the national elite has attempted to reassert Beijing's role as a national capital, diverting the activities that have diluted its function as a capital into the wider region. In its overall concept, this is not very different from the idea underlying India's NCR, but China has the apparent advantage of stronger bureaucratic capability and a political champion at the highest level for the concept (Mabin and Harrison 2022).

China's NCR is also known as the National Capital Circle. The NCR is a political construction as the delineated region does not have strong levels of internal coherence. Beijing-Tianjin is the dual core of the region, and there are logistical and economic ties between these two large cities, although even these are not as strong as physical proximity suggests.[16] Around this bi-polar core is a belt of prefectural-level and smaller cities in Hebei province, with access to other ports and historically weak linkages to Beijing and Tianjin. There is also an enormous socio-economic disparity between Beijing-Tianjin and Hebei, with the Bluebook of Regional Development in China (2006/07) calling Beijing a 'European city surrounded by African countryside' (Cartier 2015).

Nevertheless, researchers have argued for around 40 years that Beijing-Tianjin should be recognised as the core of an *aspirant* city-region, and there was in fact a brief reference to a capital economic circle in Beijing's 1982 Master Plan (Luo 2014). In 1996, Beijing, Tianjin and Hebei were included within the Bohai Sea Rim Economic Circle, but this was a vast territory across various provinces and including large tracts of rural land. In 1999, an influential think tank at Tsinghua University in Beijing began work on a proposal for the integration of Beijing, Tianjin and Hebei, releasing their first report in 2002. In 2003, a senior official in the NDRC's Macro-Economic Research Unit spoke of a 'national capital economic circle', with a territory more contained than the Bohai Sea Rim, with the Langfang Consensus in 2004 representing an NDRC-facilitated agreement on regional collaboration between Beijing, Tianjin and Hebei. From 2005, the NDRC included the concept of the national capital economic circle in its planning (Yu et al. 2015). However, the region still lacked an obvious rationale and a clear driver. After all, Beijing did not need the region to perform its function as a national capital.

This changed with the rise of Xi Jinping through the party hierarchy, with Xi championing the idea of the national capital economic circle and infusing it with political purpose. Xi came to know the region from the outside-in, having served for a period in the 1980s as a party official in Zhengding, a small county in Hebei. Carolyn Cartier (2015) attributes the first meeting of the party leaders of Beijing, Tianjin and Hebei in 2008 to discuss regional collaboration to the elevation of Xi to the Chinese Communist Party Politburo. For Cartier, the mention of the national capital economic circle in the 12th FYP in 2011 had to do with Xi's influence as a national vice-president (Cartier 2015). In November 2012, Xi was elected as general secretary of the Chinese Communist Party and national president, and events moved on quickly from that point.

In September 2013, the State Council approved the first combined strategy for the region, an action plan for pollution control, which was consistent with Xi's concern for ecological security. On 26 February 2014, President Xi hosted a landmark symposium in Beijing on the coordinated development of the region, with a clear directive to create a dignified national capital surrounded by a well-integrated region (Yu et al. 2015). For Xi, Beijing had developed beyond its natural carrying capacity, so non-essential functions of its role as the national capital should be decanted into the region (Tang and Meng 2021). The *Beijing Review* weighed in with its byline, 'It's time for Beijing to lose some economic weight and synergize with neighbouring Tianjin and Hebei Province' (Yaqing 2014, para. 1). A senior professional I spoke to in Beijing explained that in this scheme, 'the capital is anticipated to become more like Washington or Canberra – a city of government departments'.

The initiative was misunderstood in the Western media, which reported rather breathlessly on plans for the world's largest urban agglomeration, missing the point that it was about downsizing Beijing. NBC News, for example, offered the headline, 'Jing-Jin-Ji: China Planning a Megalopolis the Size of New England' (Baculinao 2017). More extravagantly, the UK's *Daily Mail* reported that 'a mega-city is set to appear in China, which would be home to around one-tenth of the country's population. More than 100 million residents would be living within the "megatropolis", which is larger than Britain, or some 137 times the size of London' (You 2017, para. 2).

The regional scheme was given formal status as a national priority in China in March 2016, when the National People's Congress approved the 13th FYP (2016 to 2020). The FYP was explicit in its instruction that Beijing should be relieved of non-essential functions, but the plan provided further guidance. Beijing was to focus on its capital city function but also on a knowledge economy, a green economy and superior, high-tech, cutting-edge industries. Tianjin was to develop as an advanced manufacturing centre and improve its role in financial innovation while Hebei was to take on the functions transferred from the core cities, applying to its production the scientific and technological innovations from Beijing and Tianjin (NDRC 2016, chapter 38, section 2).

Meanwhile, the political leadership in the region had worked quickly to show that they were responding to the directives from above. In March 2014, the party leaders of Beijing, Tianjin and Hebei met to sign a collaboration agreement. This was followed by a Cooperative Development Outline Plan in 2015 and the more detailed Framework Plan for Beijing-Tianjin-Hebei Synergetic Development in 2016 (Anshun 2016).

In 2015, President Xi ordered the relocation of all municipal government functions out of the centre of Beijing to Tongzhou, a sub-centre east of the city. The move, intended for completion by 2018, involved the relocation of around 400 000 people. In November 2016, the NDRC announced plans to build a 1 100 kilometre network of new high-speed rail across the region at a cost of US$34.8 billion, to bring the entire region into a one-hour commute from Beijing or Tianjin by 2030 (Lawrence et al. 2019). The most dramatic move came on 1 April 2017, when President Xi announced the construction of Xiong'an New Area as a new city 120 kilometres south-west of Beijing to relieve Beijing of non-essential functions and to promote the development of Hebei (Zou and Zhao 2018; Tang and Meng 2021). This was hailed by the State Council as the third major construction in reform-era China, following the designation of Shenzhen as a special economic zone under Deng Xiaoping and of the Pudong New Area by Jiang Zemin (Li and Xie 2018). There were sceptics, with one media report, for example, calling Xiong'an 'Xi Jinping's massive urban monument to himself' (Asia Sentinel 2017). However, the national government was determined to proceed, even appointing a former mayor of Shenzhen as governor of Hebei to bring an understanding of development to the process (Zou and Zhao 2018). By the end of 2021, the construction of Xiong'an was well under way, with the major infrastructure and many residential areas in place (Wen and Zhen 2022).

In September 2017, the State Council approved the new Urban Master Plan for Beijing with features including ambitious environmental targets and proposals to cap the city's population at under 23 million people. Consistent with the regional plan, the city plan follows the principle of 'less is more' or 'reducing for development' (*jianliang fazhan*), rather than the traditional principle of 'expanding for development' (*zengliang fazhan*) (Modu Magazine 2018, para. 1).

The downscaling of Beijing also involved a *push*. While the international media was highly critical of a mass-scale campaign in 2017 to demolish 40 million square metres of irregular construction, including restaurants, bars and thousands of small shops (Palmer 2017), the Beijing city government reports in positive tones that

> taking the opportunity to relieve Beijing of functions nonessential to its role as the capital, we conducted special operations to upgrade the city. We have strictly enforced the Catalogue of Prohibited and Restricted New Additional Industries, rejected a total of 18 600 applications for business registration, shut down 1,992 enterprises in general manufacturing, and relocated 594 regional wholesale markets. We have solved tough problems that were long on the agenda, such as illegal constructions, small shops operated from openings illegally cut in the wall, vending on streets and sidewalks, and poor environment of side streets and back lanes, thus making positive changes to the city's appearance. (Jining 2018, section 1, para. 1)

The plan was, of course, imposed from the top by a president in an authoritarian state who wields enormous state and personal authority. However, even in this context, it was necessary to ensure that loyalists were in place down the hierarchy to ensure implementation. There was a reshuffling of provincial party secretaries, governors and mayors across Beijing, Tianjin and Hebei, with senior politicians and bureaucrats removed, typically on corruption charges.[17] Loyalists who are trusted to implement the plan are now in place, and importantly also, the party secretaries of Beijing and Tianjin now sit on the Chinese Communist Party Politburo, allowing for an easy flow of authority from the centre to the region. Implementation also relies on the acquiescence of professionals, including urban planners. Initially, planners, academic and professional, expressed scepticism, but as the determination of the state to implement became apparent, criticism was muted.[18]

Attention was also given to the institutional mechanisms for implementation. A coordination office for the development of the NCR was set up within the offices of the NDRC, which was replicated in the administrations of Beijing, Tianjin and Hebei, and the 11 prefectural-level cities in Hebei. The NDRC set up a fund for the region's development and so could directly incentivise investments that would help implement the plan (Wang and Cheng 2018).

The future of the region is, of course, a matter of informed speculation. It will take an enormous effort to reshape a megacity such as Beijing and create a coherent region from a fragmented territory the size of the United Kingdom. Mabin and Harrison (2022, 41) observe that even President Xi acknowledged that this is 'a one-thousand-year plan'. While term limits have been removed from Xi's presidency, implementation will require political will far beyond his term of office, and whether this will happen is far from certain.

The economics of implementation is complicated. The decentralisation of Beijing's manufacturing industry into the region happened quite organically. With cost pressures in the urban core and increased environmental regulation, decentralisation may have occurred without the addition of the regional scheme. However, with Beijing's economic structure now dominated by government services, advanced producer services, research and development, finances and high tech, further decentralisation is far more difficult. First, it is tough to replicate environments in which high-order tertiary functions thrive. One of my informants explained: 'There is a mismatch between what Beijing and Tianjin can give and what Hebei can take.' Second, the division of economic activity in Beijing into capital city related and non-capital city related is central to the regional scheme. However, professionals and academics I spoke to in Beijing expressed how historically entangled these activities are, and privately reflected on the economic risks of attempting separation.

Conclusion

As the talking pig, China is a case of importance for city-region scholarship. If China is taken as exceptional, then the case is of curiosity value only. However, if China is seen as distinctive but still a case of processes recognisable elsewhere, even if in different forms, then it holds considerable conceptual and practical interest.

Most obviously, its scale attracts attention. The question is whether hugeness creates exception or whether it underlines governance complexities that are present in some way at lesser scales. The Chinese case indicates, at least, that some forms of coordination are possible at different scales and others not. Creating a rapid rail network, addressing environmental externalities such as air pollution, or even negotiating the economic focus of different cities, may be appropriate to the scale of China's megacity cluster. But there are many other forms of collaboration, ranging from coordinating the development of a metro system to jointly constructing a sewer network, that must be done at a smaller scale. How China has gradually sorted out its scales through practical necessity is instructive.

Some scholars have already pointed out that the Chinese case is a corrective to Western literature, which presents city-regionalism as a scalar alternative to the national and the local. The Chinese case is about state-led regionalism, with the central government playing a crucial role in shaping the agenda (Wu 2016; Yeh and Chen 2020). The literature shows that interest in the city cluster reflects national concerns over the effects of megacity development, but the politics around this are less discussed.

The city cluster is first and foremost a political construct that allows the authoritarian state to balance its competing needs for control and legitimacy. The city-region is the space within which collaboration, innovation and local initiative are encouraged and bounded. It is a space that offers certain privileges, accommodating the demands and desires of the rising middle class, but it also receives the controlling attention of the national political leadership, which has acted to ensure the political loyalty of the key actors within each region. Furthermore, the city-region as a territorial construct mediates between the acceptance of the role of urbanisation in driving the development of the national economy and the persisting fear that the national elites have of large cities.

However, in emphasising the politics, it is important to acknowledge the practicalities of governance that the city cluster responds to. China's urban agglomerations require mechanisms to ensure the coordinated development of services and infrastructure. As a strong hierarchy, China has the instruments of vertical coordination, but these must at least be modified to address the requirements of horizontal coordination. Perhaps because of the entrenched hierarchies, the institutionalisation of mechanisms for horizontal alignment has been slow, and it remains unclear how city-cluster governance will evolve.

While recent scholarship has accepted that city-regionalism is state led, it is not a simple process of top-down instruction. For Liuqing Yang et al. (2021, 4) city-regionalism in China is a 'process of combined commands from upper-level government, negotiations between local governments with different "administrative rankings" and changing central city development strategies and visions'. There are also bottom-up, or intra-regional impulses, expressed for example in the YRD, that intersect with top-down direction.

Finally, the Chinese case illustrates regional variation. While the FYPs and the planning approaches of the NDRC bring a degree of uniformity to city-cluster approaches, there is still considerable regional specificity. In the NCR, the hand of the central government is clearly the strongest. In the far south of the country, there has been far more space for experimentation but the political sensitivities around Hong Kong are now directing more national attention to the region. In the YRD there is a compelling case of hybridised bottom-up and top-down initiative and institutional organisation, which may provide a prototype for emerging city-regionalism elsewhere in China. Replicability is, however, a challenge as the YRD's city-regionalism may be embedded to some degree in a particular history. What the Chinese case does do, however, is direct us to think more closely about intranational variation in any context we may be considering.

Notes

1   Figures drawn from the database of the Brookings Institution and United Nations Population Division.
2   Jing 京 for Beijing, Jin 津 for Tianjin and Ji 冀 for Hebei (a historical reference).
3   For a recent and detailed account of the development of China's mega city-regions, see Yeh and Chen (2020).
4   The concept of the economic circles seems to have emerged during the 1930s in the work of Japanese economists who drew on local cultural resources as they engaged with Western theory of economic clusters.
5   In Chinese, the Yangtze is known as the *Chang Jiang* (or long river) and so the YRD is sometimes known as the Chang Jiang River Delta.
6   At the time, Xi Jinping was the party secretary of Zhejiang province.
7   As explained to me by senior officials who participated in the process.
8   The meeting of provinces is colloquially known as the Meeting of the Big Eight, chaired by the party secretary of Shanghai. It also includes the party secretaries of Zhejiang, Jiangsu and Anhui, the mayor of Shanghai, and the governors of Zhejiang, Jiangsu and Anhui.
9   Information provided during workshops arranged by me and the Shanghai Academy of Social Sciences, a policy-oriented academic institution that played a major role in the development of the plan for the Shanghai Metropolitan Area.
10 Examples of these practices include Chinese traders leaving goods consignments to Hong Kong un-invoiced, depositing earnings in Hong Kong banks, converting into international currencies in Hong Kong and investing profits outside of China, or purchasing shell companies in Hong Kong and then investing in mainland China as a 'Hong Kong investor' (see Sum 2002).
11 Around 2004, there was brief interest across the region for a pan-Pearl River Delta cooperation and development scheme, which would include Guangdong, Hong Kong and Macau, but also eight other provinces across southern China. The

initiative faded away, however, when the central government failed to give it support, fearful that it might prefigure some form of federalism (Yeh and Xu 2011).

12 See the Qianhai website: www.szqh.com.cn/What_is_Qianhai/News_Promotion_
Event/201807/t20180706_13543715.htm.

13 As explained to me by officials in the Shenzhen office of the China Academy of
Urban Planning and Design, which provides critical support for joint planning initiatives in the region.

14 As explained to me by officials in the Shenzhen office of the China Academy of
Urban Planning and Design.

15 As explained to me by officials in the Shenzhen office of the China Academy of
Urban Planning and Design.

16 Tianjin is a port city but with Beijing no longer having a significant manufacturing
base, there is little requirement from Beijing to use its facilities (for exports at least).

17 In both Hebei and Tianjin, the party secretaries were placed under investigation
and expelled from the Chinese Communist Party before being handed long jail
sentences on corruption charges, while the party secretary for Beijing was eased out
of office. There have also been similar reshuffles of the mayors of the two provincial-status cities, and of the governor of Hebei.

18 As explained to me in various discussions with academics and professionals in Beijing.

6 City-region governance in South Africa

Introduction

Political culture in South Africa, and more specifically within South Africa's metropolitan heartland, Gauteng, is derived from a fractured history. For Louis Picard and Thomas Mogale (2014, 3), 'to understand governance in South Africa today, one must look at the region's long, mostly tortured history of governance over the past 400 years', but South Africa's segmented political culture is not easy to describe.

The white population was socialised into a racially prescribed democracy but was divided in their political inheritance into two major threads. British settlers who arrived from the early nineteenth century brought the Westminster system of democracy with its liberal trappings and adapted it to a racial hierarchy. It was a *conservative* liberalism willing, at best, to support a very gradual process of de-racialisation. The Afrikaner population, mainly descendants of European settlers from the seventeenth century onwards (especially Dutch, German and French), leaned towards nationalism and racial prescription driven by resentment of British domination and fear of black majority rule, but were also informed by nationalist movements in Europe from the nineteenth century.[1] Over time, there was a crossover in political cultures, and by the 1980s, these historical differences were not strongly evident.

For the black majority, political socialisation happened within a mainly oppositional context, but there was considerable variation.[2] The muted tradition of British liberalism in the Cape produced a liberal strand of oppositional thought, especially within a mission-educated generation, but there was also ongoing communitarianism in parts of the country where forms of traditional leadership persisted, and there was the rise of more radical forms of opposition such as African nationalism and workerism (including Marxism). It was a complex mix, feeding into different modes of opposition with different inclinations towards democratic values, for example.

By the 1980s, the liberation struggle had largely cohered within the exiled African National Congress (ANC), itself a broad church, which was in an alliance with civic movements leading a broad-based internal uprising against the apartheid regime (Levy et al. 2015).[3] It was not a straightforward struggle; Henning Melber (2002, 164) writes of 'the struggles of the national liberation movement in interaction with the international system represented by a variety of competing actors under the polarised conditions of superpower rivalries during the 1970s and 80s'. It was a struggle involving armed resistance, international diplomacy, exile politics and internal civic mobilisation.

In the final event, there was a negotiated settlement between the liberation movement and its adjuncts, and the frayed apartheid regime. The institutions of the new democracy were classically liberal, with the influence of social democracy in the inclusion of socio-economic rights, for example, within the new national Constitution. However, there are degrees of disillusionment with the performance of this democracy, and there are questions over the degree to which the constitutional arrangements are underpinned by a supportive political culture and whether the political settlement reflects the balance between institutional arrangements and the distribution of benefits that Mushtaq Khan (2011) argues is necessary for social stability.

For Melber (2002, 168), the cultures that emerged from the liberation struggle present challenges for the development of a democratic order: 'as part of abolishing anachronistic, degrading systems of rule [this] created new challenges on the difficult path to establishing sound and robust egalitarian structures and institutions'. Political cultures within segments of the population include, inter alia, an attraction to populism, a willingness to use violence for political purposes (around 20 per cent, according to one study), a loyalty to the party of liberation rather than to values or norms, the we–you divide in political discourse, intolerance of alternative views, and an instrumental use of democracy (Melber 2002; Steyn Kotze 2021).

However, these cultures are mixed in with embedded norms of participation, political tolerance and real commitment to democracy. In the metropolitan heartland, historical loyalties have waned faster than elsewhere, with more political competition than elsewhere. There is also a new generation without a direct memory of apartheid and the struggle (the so-called born frees, born after the transition to democracy), which is more unpredictable in its political loyalty.

In South Africa, political cultures are entwined with the nature of the political settlement. The transition in South Africa was an elite bargain, with the outgoing apartheid regime conceding political rights to the black majority but with an economic system, and patterning of landownership, where the power of the white population was kept largely intact (Marais 2001; Levy et al. 2015). There were hopes that political power would bring material benefits to the black majority, and there was indeed an improvement in social protection and the distribution of basic services, but the expectations of substantial material benefit were not realised. In terms of Khan's conception of political settlement, there was an asymmetry between the institutional arrangements of the new democracy and distributional expectations. The black elites were able to 'mobilise through a set of formal and informal arrangements to bring the distribution of benefits back into line with their actual relative power' (Khan 2011, 2). Formal policies of black economic empowerment and informal networks of patronage created wealth for a modestly sized black elite well connected to the ruling political clique. Referring to the informal mechanisms, Karl von Holdt (2019, 3) writes of a 'pervasive informal political-economic system . . . shaped by the intersection of patronage and factionalism, as patronage networks form political factions in order to gain power in the state'.

However, the majority poor did not have sufficient power to challenge the asymmetry, with many experiencing actual declines in material benefit as unemployment reached record levels. This feeds social instability, including periodic violent protest, although it is uncertain whether the excluded majority can mobilise sufficient power to significantly alter the balance between the institutional order and the distribution of benefits.

This historically produced context has important implications for city-region governance. While there may be continued efforts to achieve city-region governance driven by a desire to overcome territorial fragmentation or, at least, create broader territories in which redistribution of resources can occur, the underlying conditions for success are flawed. Firstly, the levels of trust to support inclusive networks of collaborative governance are low, while violence, intolerance and political populism are continued threats to the process of building robust institutions. Secondly, the capacity of the state to carry through institutional reforms has declined markedly as personal rent-seeking and patronage networks within state structures (in South Africa, referred to as state capture) became endemic (Olver 2017; Palmer et al. 2017).

While there are current attempts to restore the integrity and capacity of the state and talk of renewing a frayed social pact, levels of disillusionment in governance processes are high across many segments of society (De Kadt et al. 2021).

The choice of the Gauteng City-Region as a case study

Official documents put South Africa at around 65 per cent urbanised, although the intricate patterning of spatial linkages makes it difficult to distinguish between urban and rural. South Africa's Integrated Urban Development Framework identifies four city-regions: Gauteng, Cape Town, eThekwini (Greater Durban) and Nelson Mandela Bay (Greater Gqeberha, previously Port Elizabeth) accounting for 42 per cent of South Africa's population and about one-half of the economic output (Map 5).

It is in fact only Gauteng (or the Gauteng City-Region [GCR]) that has been consistently labelled as a city-region, and this is the case study I use in this chapter. Nelson

Mandela Bay is a modest-sized urban agglomeration of about 1.3 million people and is not generally labelled a city-region (an exception being Van Huyssteen et al. 2009). Whether or not Cape Town or Durban are part of a city-region is of course entirely a matter of definition. The United Nations World Urbanization Prospects puts the population of Greater Cape Town at 4.6 million, but an extended definition of a city-region may take the population over five million (United Nations 2018). The OECD (Organisation for Economic Co-operation and Development) undertook a territorial review of Cape Town as a city-region, as it did for the GCR (OECD 2008), with Ken Sinclair-Smith (2015, 131) assessing the 'polycentric spatial form of the Cape Town city-region'.

The United Nations puts the Greater Durban (eThekwini) agglomeration at around 3.2 million, but this is a narrow definition, and a city-region including Pietermaritzburg and the densely populated North and South Coasts of KwaZulu-Natal would bring the population to around 4.5 million, with a highly complex spatial form. Jo Beall et al. (2015) produced an influential account of the Durban city-region, using Greater Durban to challenge the dominating discourse on globally competitive city-regions, which marginalises city-regions in Africa. For Beall et al. (2015), the Durban city-region is a space where multiple interests are negotiated daily, including between traditional authorities with hereditary leadership, and a modern bureaucracy with a democratically elected council. It offers a compelling case of city-region governance in action, which relates to many other instances across Africa.

This chapter deals, however, with the GCR, the only urban agglomeration that is uncontested nationally as a city-region and is referred to widely internationally. It combines at least eight of the agglomerations identified in the United Nations data – Johannesburg, Pretoria (Tshwane), Ekurhuleni, Soshanguve, Rustenburg, Vereeniging, West Rand and Witbank (now Emalahleni) – with a population of around 16 million. The GCR is generally taken to be coterminous with the boundary of Gauteng province but two of these agglomerations – Rustenburg and Witbank, with a combined population of about one million – are beyond the provincial boundaries (United Nations 2018) (Maps 15 and 26).

I turn now to the histories that have produced the complexities of the GCR and the governance responses over time.

The emergent city-region under colonial and apartheid rule

Origins

Gold was discovered in 1886 on the Witwatersrand, a low range of hills in the Boer-controlled *Zuid Afrikaansche Republiek* (ZAR [also known as the Transvaal]). The political consequences were immense, leading to the outbreak of the South African War (1899 to 1902), and eventual British victory, which contributed to the rise of Afrikaner nationalism and decades of apartheid rule (1948 to 1994). But gold mining was also a powerful catalyst for modernisation, as David Yudelman (1984, 9) points out: 'the major influence behind the telescoped development of modern South Africa and the leap from a fledgling quasi-state to a surprisingly advanced modern industrial state within the space of eighty years – a process that took centuries in Europe – was the South African gold mining industry'.

This is important background, but the focus here is on the settlement formation around the gold mines and the governance challenges it produced. The Main Reef Group of conglomerates, which stretches in a linear form for about 40 kilometres, was discovered in present-day Johannesburg but soon afterwards, the East and West Rand Gold Reefs were discovered, and an urban formation evolved that stretched out along the gold reefs for about 150 kilometres. At the core was Johannesburg, which developed within decades into a large city, but there was a series of smaller mining settlements in a roughly linear arrangement, which, west to east, included Westonaria, Randfontein, Krugersdorp, Roodepoort, Alberton, Germiston, Boksburg, Brakpan, Benoni, Springs and Nigel. About 60 kilometres north of Johannesburg is Pretoria, then the small capital of the ZAR, and not part of the mining area, but later recognised as a component of the agglomeration (Beavon 2004).

Importantly also, the mass-scale recruitment of cheap labour for the mines, from the Cape Colony in the south to the southern districts of Tanganyika in the north, produced a vast labour empire with much of southern Africa tied to the Witwatersrand through a system of oscillating movement. African labour was housed in single-sex hostels during their contracted periods of work at the mines, periodically returning to families in rural areas (Crush et al. 1991). This produced high levels of interconnectedness between the Witwatersrand and the wider region, especially with the 'labour reserves' of South Africa, which under apartheid rule were the ethnic homelands.

Until 1900, the goldfields fell under the administration of the ZAR, which lacked the resources and political will to provide critical infrastructures for the mines and adjoining settlements, such as water, energy and transport. The mining companies came together in December 1887 to set up the Chamber of Mines, which coordinated the labour recruitment drive but also lobbied the politically hostile government in Pretoria for infrastructure, and provided the infrastructure when the government failed to do so. The Chamber of Mines successfully lobbied the government for an 80-kilometre rail network along the Witwatersrand but had to take its own initiative to secure local water sources and construct small-scale power generation plants.

At the time, local government was rudimentary and fragmented across the mining settlements, mainly taking the form of quasi-formal diggers committees. In 1896, the British secretary of state for the colonies, Joseph Chamberlain, proposed a kind of super-municipality for the Witwatersrand, performing functions including policing, education and mine regulation. Sensing a cynical ploy by the British to gain control over the goldfields, the ZAR rejected the idea out of hand (Maud 1938; Nimocks 1968).

The British army occupied Johannesburg in May 1900, and post-war reconstruction included the creation of the Johannesburg Town Council along the lines of British local government, with town councils also established for the other towns. As an early strategic move, the Johannesburg Town Council expanded the boundaries of the municipality to incorporate large tracts of empty land in anticipation of future growth. Keith Beavon (2004, 75) explained that, as a result, Johannesburg had 'more space to play with than any other municipality in the world'. However, this did not resolve the challenges of providing regional-scale infrastructure.

The most pressing post-war need was to secure an adequate supply of water. The Witwatersrand was on a continental watershed without any major water source, and from 1895, the goldfields experienced severe water shortages. A special commission was set up after the war to investigate the problem, leading to the creation of the Rand Water Board in 1903. The board was appointed by the lieutenant-governor of the Transvaal, with its membership drawn from mining companies and the newly created local councils, and may have been the first structure for inter-municipal associational government on the Witwatersrand (and, possibly, across South Africa). It evolved into a largely technical agency, separated from the municipal sphere. It has survived to the present but is now a water utility reporting to the national government (Tempelhoff 2004).

In the energy sector, the Chamber of Mines facilitated the joint creation of the Victoria Falls and Transvaal Power Company in 1906, so named because there was an ambitious scheme to harness the hydro potential of the Zambezi River. In 1922, the national government set up Eskom as a national-level state-owned enterprise, which purchased the Victoria Falls and Transvaal Power Company in 1948. Energy, like water, had been taken out of the municipal domain.

There was, however, an early, short-lived experiment with an associative or federal form of municipal governance along the Witwatersrand. The bubonic plague of 1904 had brought about some cooperation between municipalities, but the ongoing provision of health facilities across the Witwatersrand remained a major problem, as did the maintenance of Main Reef Road, the major transport arterial connecting the towns of the Witwatersrand. In 1906, the Transvaal Legislative Assembly passed legislation to establish the Witwatersrand Provisional Joint Committee, which would be responsible for these functions. This structure comprised 20 members, with Johannesburg Town Council represented by eight councillors, and other towns having between one and three councillors each, depending on size, with two members appointed from the Chamber of Mines (Maud 1938).

John Maud (1938, 187) explained that 'the committee was fatally handicapped from the outset by the refusal of most of its members to consider questions from any broader point of view than that of the particular community which had appointed them'. There was also the old political divide between Pretoria and the Witwatersrand; the Pretoria Town Council opposed the initiative as it was threatened by a potential union of municipalities on the Witwatersrand (Maud 1938). The committee struggled on for two years, trying to mediate the different interests, before it collapsed in 1908 (Rand Daily Mail 1908). When the Union of South Africa was formed in 1910, health and road maintenance functions were taken over by the Transvaal provincial government.

Randopolis

By 1933, Johannesburg and Pretoria had both achieved city status, and the goldfields were enjoying an unprecedented economic boom following South Africa's departure from the Gold Standard in December 1932. The outlines of a future urban agglomeration were becoming increasingly visible.

The town planning scheme was modelled on the early British Town and Country Planning Acts, which introduced the town planning scheme as the primary instrument for regulating land use. In 1933, the municipalities on the Witwatersrand came together to form the Witwatersrand Joint Town Planning Committee (WJTPC) to prepare a joint town planning scheme and share professional expertise in an inter-municipal arrangement. The WJTPC was inaugurated in February 1933, with the vision of planning a 'Greater Witwatersrand' inspired by international experience, including the New York regional plan, Greater London and the Ruhr Valley in Germany (Mabin 1993, 50).

The WJTPC's task was to appoint a chief planning officer with municipalities contributing pro rata to the salary, and an Australian, Charles Reade, who had experience in the Federated Malay States and Northern Rhodesia, was recruited to the position (Rand Daily Mail 1933a). Before he arrived in Johannesburg, Reade captured the local imagination with his concept of Randopolis and there were excited media headlines such as 'Randopolis Dream' and 'Randopolis of the Future' (Rand Daily Mail 1933a, 1933b).

The dream ended dramatically when Reade shot himself in a hotel room two weeks after arriving in Johannesburg in October 1933 (Rand Daily Mail 1933c). Alan Mabin (1993) explains how the bold vision for Randopolis was then narrowed into the mundane process of preparing individual town planning schemes for separate municipalities. In 1934, there was still some hope that collaborative planning would lead to the eventual unification of municipalities along the Witwatersrand (Rand Daily Mail 1934), but a year later, the media referred with resignation to the creation of Randopolis as a 'prolonged business' (Rand Daily Mail 1935). Colonel P.J. Bowling was appointed as the new chief planning officer for the WJTPC but, instead of embracing the vision of Randopolis, he warned of 'a nightmare . . . of a Greater Johannesburg' (Mabin 2013, 9).

In service of racial segregation

The next impulse towards inter-municipal collaboration was the need to provide seg-regated housing for the African population.

In the decades immediately after the founding of Johannesburg, black mine-workers were housed in hostels controlled by mining companies, but workers in other industries found their own accommodation in the slums developing around the centre of the emergent city. Many of these slums were racially mixed, adding to a growing anxiety about black urbanisation among the white population. In 1923, the national government responded with the Natives (Urban Areas) Act, which gave municipalities a formal mandate to develop housing estates for black Africans. The City of Johannesburg responded in the 1930s by moving residents from slums into new housing estates, such as the so-called Orlando model native township, but the other municipalities along the Witwatersrand lacked the means (or will) to do so. However, under increasing pressure to act, municipalities along the Witwatersrand began exploring the possibilities of joint action.

In the 1940s, matters became more urgent as the boost to manufacturing dur-ing the war drew a growing number of African migrants to the cities. Finances were diverted to the war effort, and very little housing was produced, leading to the rapid growth of shack settlements along the Witwatersrand. The municipal managers for the different municipalities met regularly, and, in their discussions, the idea emerged of jointly constructing regional-scale native locations (later called African townships) (Maud 1938). Ivan Evans (1997, 174) reports that municipal managers 'acquired a keen interest in regional planning' in the 1940s, with the Rand Water Board consid-ered as a model for addressing the housing challenge.

The municipalities met the national Minister of Health and Housing in March 1947 in an engagement that was hailed as a 'historic turning point' for collaboration between municipalities, provinces and central government (Rand Daily Mail 1947a). By August 1947, a Regional Advisory Council for Non-European Housing was launched, which began preparing a joint 'Master Plan for Native Locations' (Rand Daily Mail 1947b). Evans (1997, 174) observes that 'integrated regional planning in the 1940s came to mean the strategic siting of [African] locations to serve more than one municipal area'.

However, South African politics took an unexpected turn in the national elec-tions of May 1948, when the United Party government under General Smuts was defeated by the National Party. The new government, committed to a radical pro-gramme of racial segregation, took up the idea of building regional-scale African townships with great gusto, but it bypassed the municipalities in doing so, many of which remained under the control of the United Party. In 1952, Dr H.F. Verwoerd appointed his confidante F.E. Mentz to chair a committee that would determine the location of African townships on the Witwatersrand. Their proposals had far-reaching impacts on the spatial form of the Witwatersrand, with the construction of mega townships such as Soweto, Katlehong, Tembisa, Katorus, KwaThema and Mamelodi, where the largest concentrations of population in Gauteng now reside (Evans 1997; Mabin 2013). Verwoerd called the work of the committee 'regional planning in action' (Evans 1997, 177), but segregated housing was now clearly a national rather than an inter-municipal affair.

Pretoria-Witwatersrand-Vereeniging

The apartheid government worked hard to centralise control over the planning of African townships, but it allowed South Africa's Natural Resources Development Council (NRDC) – a quasi-autonomous agency set up by the United Party government in the 1940s – to continue its work. In the 1940s, it planned the towns on the newly discovered Free State goldfields, and in the 1950s, it identified the urban agglomeration in the southern Transvaal as a region in dire need of coordinated planning.

The NRDC prepared a planning survey and guide plan for the southern Transvaal, which was strongly influenced by regionalist thinking in North America where the lead author of the plan, T.J.D. Fair, had spent a period of time (Fair 1957). Mabin (2013, 18) offers a positive assessment of the NRDC plan, writing that 'its sophistication, its grasp of change and its proposals, albeit deeply flawed by immersion in the drive for comprehensive segregation, remain impressive today'. The work of the NRDC was, in fact, fundamentally undercut by the recommendations of the Mentz Committee: whereas the NRDC sought to consolidate the emergent form of the urban region, the Mentz Committee proposed townships that significantly expanded the urban footprint. In 1967, the national government consolidated its control over planning with the Physical Planning Act that abolished the NRDC and set up a national Department of Planning, which administered a centrally coordinated system of guide planning.

Nevertheless, the NRDC, and the continuing work of T.J.D. Fair, who later formed a research unit at the University of the Witwatersrand, had an important shaping effect on the evolution of discourse around city-regions. By the 1950s, the southern Transvaal, which incorporated the Johannesburg-centred Witwatersrand, Pretoria and the emerging industrial complex in the Vaal (the towns of Vereeniging and Vanderbijlpark), had consolidated its position as the 'organising economic centre of South Africa' (Bloch 2000, 249). In this context, Fair introduced the idea of a Pretoria-Witwatersrand-Vereeniging (PWV) urban region in the 1957 'Planning Survey of the Southern Transvaal: The Pretoria-Witwatersrand-Vereeniging Area' (Mabin 2013). International contributions affirmed the rise of the Witwatersrand and adjoining areas as a 'conurbation' of the kind previously identified in Great Britain (Cole 1957, 249).

The PWV was a concept in planning, but it gained prominence in the media, and it was connected to a regionalist sentiment evolving within the white business sector and municipal governments. There were common concerns around the possible future decline in gold mining and the potentially harmful effects of the government's new programme of industrial decentralisation, which aimed to divert manufacturing away from the PWV to the ethnic homelands (to slow the influx of black people into the cities). In 1959, business associations in the region came together with municipalities to form the Southern Transvaal Regional Development Association. However, with an increasing number of municipalities along the Witwatersrand falling under National Party control, opinions within the region were divided, and by the mid-1960s, the Southern Transvaal Regional Development Association faded away (Mabin 2013). There were periodic revivals of regionalist sentiment in the business sector, with business associations on the Witwatersrand jointly responding to the White Paper on decentralisation in 1971, and again in the early 1980s, when Prime Minister P.W. Botha announced his Good Hope Plan to reinvigorate the decentralisation drive (Rand Daily Mail 1983). There was also some excitement in 1973 around the likely emergence of the PWV as a mega agglomeration, 'which would include the great and prosperous belt stretching from Sasolburg in the Free State through to the Black labour concentration north of Pretoria' (Rand Daily Mail 1973, 10). However, the 1976 Soweto uprising against the apartheid state and the economic troubles that followed put a dampener on this dream.

The great freeway controversy

The construction of a network of freeways across the PWV was important both in stretching the urban landscape and in provoking a periodic episode of regionalist sentiment (Mabin 2013). The idea of freeway construction won over against proposals for expanding the rail network, including a 1971 proposal for a metropolitan transport system modelled largely on the London underground (Maxwell 1971).

The impact of President Eisenhower's Federal-Aid Highway Act of 1956 on transport planning in South Africa was evident from the 1960s, but there was a muddle locally, as all levels of government (municipal, provincial and national) announced their building programmes and initiated their plans, some quite contradictory. The Transvaal Provincial Administration's proposal for an expansionist road grid across the Witwatersrand was, for example, at odds with proposals in the guide plan for the PWV to consolidate existing patterns (Fair and Muller 1981). The *Rand Daily Mail* led with an article entitled 'Too many fingers in the planning pie', arguing that 'PWV planning is beginning to look like a comic opera – dozens of characters on stage, the plot thickening and the players all interpreting numerous roles' (Nixon 1975, para. 1).

There were official adjustments to achieve better coordination, including the promulgation of the Urban Transport Act of 1978, which provided for the establishment of metropolitan transport advisory boards. Two metropolitan transport advisory boards were demarcated in the PWV – Jomet for the Johannesburg Metropolitan Area and Ormet for the East Rand (now Ekurhuleni) (Mabin 2013). However, Jomet's plans for freeway construction involved disruptions to suburban neighbourhoods, and there was an outburst of white middle-class activism in the late 1970s and early 80s that took on a regional dimension. The Johannesburg Metropolitan Action Group was set up as a civic counterpart to Jomet, and the two organisations skirmished until the mid-1980s when it was clear that economically depressed and conflict-ridden South Africa had no resources for any further freeway construction (see, for example, Sacks 1981).

Neo-apartheid regionalism

By the late 1970s, the regime was in trouble, and the reformers within the system were searching for ways of modifying apartheid to placate rising black opposition without losing white dominance. Among the proposals were regionalist solutions (a proposed special arrangement for KwaZulu-Natal is the best known).

There was also a proposal by the Africa Institute, a think tank closely linked to reformists in the National Party, that the PWV should be the common territory within a Confederation of States that would link white South Africa with the black ethnic homelands. For the Africa Institute, the PWV was so economically and spatially entangled that it was impossible to separate white from black, and so a multiracial accommodation for this region was necessary (Laurence 1977). The proposal was, however, too radical for most of the National Party caucus, and the only concession at that time was to identify an expanded PWV as Region H in P.W. Botha's Good Hope Plan, which allowed for joint high-level regional strategising, including the mapping of a 'long-term idealised megapolitan structure' (Mabin 2013, 34). Paul Hendler (1992) explains how state-directed spatial planning (the so-called guide plans) was used to detail this idealised structure. Instead of diverting the urbanising black population into rural homeland growth points, they would now be accommodated on the edges of the PWV (deconcentration rather than decentralisation).

The Good Hope Plan identified nine alphabetically numbered development regions which crosscut the South Africa–homeland boundaries, each of which had a multiracial regional development advisory committee (RDAC). The RDACs were supported with technical and infrastructural investment by the Development Bank of Southern Africa (DBSA), which was associated with the reformist wing of the apartheid state. For the reformers, the idea was to gradually consolidate these regions into multiracial institutional formations, but time was running short (Muthien and Khosa 1995).

International economic sanctions were biting and there was growing opposition from the black majority, leaving some of the townships across the PWV ungovernable. President P.W. Botha declared a state of emergency across much of the PWV in July 1985, moving the South African Defence Force into the townships. In May 1986, he declared a national state of emergency. Attempts to pacify the black population with various reform measures, including a relaxation of controls on migration into cities and the establishment of black local authorities, had failed.

Botha's embattled regime came under growing pressure from big business and liberal-leaning think tanks, such as the Urban Foundation, to find an institutional mechanism to coordinate across racially defined jurisdictions and so forestall more radical changes. These pressures led to a short-lived experiment with quasi-metropolitan government. Legislation passed in 1985 enabled the creation of regional services councils, funded by business levies, which allowed for joint exercise of powers across the boundaries of racially constituted local authorities. While the fundamental architecture of racially structured administration did not change, the regional services councils were a modification of apartheid (a form of neo-apartheid) allowing for multiracial cooperation in defined functions ('general affairs' as opposed to 'own affairs') (Mandy 1988; Cameron 1993). The task of setting up the regional services councils was complicated, involving negotiations between municipalities. The Witwatersrand was to be split into three regional services councils, but there was robust contestation over the representation of different municipalities. Although regional services councils were to be multiracial structures, power was clearly skewed towards the dominant white municipalities (Mandy 1988; Cameron 1993).

Despite their limitations, the regional services councils were welcomed by some liberal-minded individuals as a step towards the breakdown of racial barriers and towards some form of functioning regional governance (see, for example, Mandy 1988). The regional services councils in the PWV were eventually established in 1988, but this was only two years before the political landscape changed fundamentally with the unbanning of the liberation movement and the release of the iconic struggle leader, Nelson Mandela. In the early 1990s, the regional services councils were quickly superseded by inter-party negotiating forums. In hindsight, they were a failed attempt to shore up a collapsing political system; however, they do offer a possible lesson for future governance arrangements – their funding through regional business levies provided a revenue source independent of national and local government.

Metropolitan and city-region governance, post-apartheid
Metropolitan governance and the provincial city-state

Political transformations nationally opened the way for negotiations at the local and metropolitan scales. On the central Witwatersrand, focussed on the Johannesburg-Soweto complex, there was a near breakdown in the governance of townships, with a long-standing rent and service boycott having emptied the government coffers. In 1990, the Soweto Civic Association signed the Soweto Accord with the Transvaal Provincial Administration and the electricity utility, Eskom, writing off rental arrears and introducing discounted electricity payments. This also initiated a period of intense metropolitan-level negotiations on new governance arrangements.

The Central Witwatersrand Metropolitan Chamber was set up in April 1991 to negotiate an integrated tax base and governance for the central Witwatersrand, as well as new approaches to spatial planning. These local or regional negotiations were brought into a national process in 1993 with the creation of the Local Government Negotiating Forum, which negotiated a framework for the transition to unified, non-racial municipalities (Van Donk and Pieterse 2006; Mabin 2013).

These were complex negotiations, with the National Party arguing for weak metropolitan government and strong primary local authorities in anticipation of maintaining control over some of the local structures. The ANC, however, was confident of electoral majorities at the metropolitan level and insisted on strong metropolitan authorities that would have the authority to redistribute resources from advantaged white areas to poorer black areas. The ANC won out and the Municipal Structures Act of 1998 enabled the creation of strong metropolitan authorities (Cameron 2000). The idea of metropolitan government for South Africa drew heavily on the established international discourse on metropolitan governance, but was also clearly embedded in a response to a history of racial fragmentation, including the call from civic organisations during the late 1980s for a one-city, one-tax base.

Single metropolitan authorities were created in 2000, after a transitional phase from 1995 when metropolitan and local-level authorities co-existed. In Gauteng province (the old PWV), three metropolitan municipalities were established – Johannesburg, Tshwane (or Greater Pretoria) and Ekurhuleni (or the East Rand) – although outside the metropolitan cities, a two-tier system of governance continued (district municipalities and local municipalities). The shift to metropolitan governance was a major achievement of the early post-apartheid government, ending South Africa's long history of fragmented and locally divided local authorities. In the case of Johannesburg, the single-tier metropolitan authority created at the end of 2000 consolidated 15 previous racially structured local authorities. In the case of the East Rand, the creation of the Ekurhuleni Metropolitan Council was even more sweeping as there was no historical core municipality but rather a cluster of over 30 municipalities governing small racially divided cities, towns and townships.

A performance assessment of these metropolitan authorities has still to be written. They allowed for more integrated forms of planning and budgeting across historically divided territories, and there were periods of heightened energy and success with implementation, such as in the lead-up to the 2010 FIFA World Cup. There were also limitations, however. The powers defined for municipalities in the new national Constitution (1996) were quite limited and with a one-size-fits-all approach. Metropolitan municipalities were not given powers in addition to those of district and local municipalities, despite their vastly greater capacities. Metropolitan authorities had to coordinate with provincial and national agencies within South Africa's complex, quasi-federal system to achieve integrated governance, a process that was often fraught with tension. Matters were further complicated after South Africa's 2016 local government elections when the ANC lost control of the Johannesburg and Tshwane metropolitan councils to unstable coalitions led for various periods by the Democratic Alliance (DA).

The arrival of metropolitan governance did not resolve the question of city-region governance. Within the wider urban agglomeration (the inherited PWV), there were now three metropolitan authorities, two district authorities and six local authorities. There was a provision in the Municipal Systems Act of 2000 to set up inter-jurisdictional service authorities, but this was not taken up.

However, emerging from the inter-party negotiations of the early 1990s, a provincial administration was set up for a region closely aligned to the boundaries of the previous PWV/Region H. This was a city-state of sorts, although with significantly fewer powers than those held by the states in Brazil or India, for example. The powers allocated to South Africa's nine provinces emerged from a compromise during the multi-party negotiating process in 1993 when the ANC argued for a strong unitary state, and smaller parties advocated federalism. The most important functions of the provincial government were health and education, although funding was entirely dependent on transfers from the national government. There were, however, other functions, including housing (which provinces resisted transferring to capacitated metropolitan governments), environmental management, provincial transport and agriculture.

The decision to turn the PWV into a province with a premier and an elected provincial council was made on a recommendation to the multi-party negotiating forum by an ad hoc commission on the delimitation/delineation of states/provinces/regions, which met during June and July 1993. The commission was composed of (mainly academic) experts and was given six weeks to decide how South Africa's new provinces would be configured. It recommended the PWV as a province because it formed an economically functional interdependent area. There was, however, debate over boundaries, with some arguing that the national capital, Pretoria, should be included within the Eastern Transvaal (later Mpumalanga) based on linguistic and cultural characteristics, and others arguing that the PWV was too dominant economically, and so its territory should be divided among neighbouring provinces (Muthien and Khosa 1995). The majority, however, held that the 'PWV is a compact, developed and highly integrated urban-industrial complex that should be retained as such' (Negotiating Council of the Multi-Party Negotiating Process 1993, 27).[4]

The new province was called Gauteng, meaning 'place of gold' in the Sotho language, and has been politically dominated by the ANC, although support has waned in recent years and future control is uncertain. Although the ANC controlled both provincial and metropolitan councils until 2016, ambiguity and overlapping constitutional functions led to provincial–metropolitan tensions at times.

South Africa has a formal system of inter-governmental relations that frames the workings of the constitutional doctrine of cooperative governance. The Constitution creates three *spheres* of government – national, provincial and municipal – that have protected powers and are described as 'distinctive, interdependent and interrelated' (RSA 1996, Section 40(1)). The three spheres are enjoined to 'cooperate with one another in mutual trust and good faith' (RSA 1996, Section 41(1)(h)). Inter-governmental relations mechanisms are codified in the Intergovernmental Fiscal Relations Act of 1997, and include various forums such as the Premier's Coordinating Council and sector-related forums called MinMECs (meaning joint committees of national ministers and provincial members of executive committees). However, in practice, it has been far more complex, with a mix of competition, conflict and collaboration, and with informal processes of mutual adjustment, bargaining and ad hoc collaboration as significant as the formal arrangements.

The Gauteng City-Region as discourse and practice
The lead-up and launch
Our concern here is how a world-city discourse meshed with ideas of the city-region within the Gauteng context. The convergence began in the late 1990s within an inter-personal network cutting across government, academia and the consulting sector. There was close familiarity, locally, with the evolving discourse on world cities (see, for example, Beavon 1998; CDE 2002). The discourse informed the approaches of the new metropolitan administrations, including Johannesburg, which adopted as a controversial mantra 'the world-class African city'.

Ideas of the city-region had, in fact, been circulating locally for decades, from the 1930s with Randopolis and from the 1950s with the PWV (see, for example, Fair and Mallows 1959; Fair and Muller 1981). However, with political change, there was a new cast of actors, and it took a few years for the discourse to resurface. By the late 1990s, there was some awareness in official circles that the new institutional formations, including the metropolitan cities, would be insufficient to support coordinated urban development. A previous senior official in the City of Johannesburg recalls how a prominent academic, Mark Swilling, was brought into the city administration to advise on the preparation of its first Integrated Development Plan. Swilling criticised the administration for behaving as though there were a Chinese wall around Johannesburg, and this struck a chord with the officials in the room. Then, in 1999, Ketso Gordhan, the city manager of Johannesburg, and other senior officials attended Allen Scott's conference on global city-regions organised in Los Angeles.[5] The Urban Futures conference held in Johannesburg in July 2000 brought international academics together with city and provincial officials, further strengthening the discursive networks connecting the global and the local (Tomlinson et al. 2003).

The discourse cohered and was translated into policy in different ways. South Africa's first *State of the Cities Report*, published by the South African Cities Network, was an early statement of the resurfaced discourse. It argued that the metropolitan cities of Johannesburg, Ekurhuleni and Tshwane (Pretoria) 'form part of a much larger urban system that now spans much of Gauteng and beyond' and referred to a 'polycentric Gauteng urban region', which it ranked in significance globally between Los Angeles and Lagos (South African Cities Network 2004, 24).

The key political figure in the story was the premier of Gauteng, Mbhazima (Sam) Shilowa, whose key advisors were part of the network referred to and familiar with the evolving discourse. Shilowa was a previous trade union leader who served as premier from 1999 to 2008 and had the ambition to lead a globally competitive city-state. In his first term, he announced the development of the Gauteng Rapid Rail System (Gautrain), which was to connect Johannesburg, Pretoria and O.R. Tambo International Airport, and launched Blue IQ as an agency to drive investment across the province. In 2003, the national presidency released a draft National Spatial Development Perspective, which affirmed Gauteng as the economic core of South Africa, requiring priority attention. With this cue, the premier convened a Gauteng inter-governmental forum in December 2003 to discuss 'the need for the development of a common Gauteng region that is both globally competitive and smart; and the need for improved mechanisms of integration and inter-governmental relations' (as related in Shilowa 2006a, 50).

At the opening of the provincial legislature in 2004, Shilowa advised that plans 'are underway to turn Gauteng into an integrated, globally competitive urban region'. He said that 'we have started working with all the mayors in Gauteng to join in pooling resources to create the most powerful economic bloc on the continent, promoting Gauteng as a home for investment, tourism, and business in general' (Mail & Guardian 2004).

Shilowa had to secure political support for his vision from the ANC and its alliance partners, the Congress of South African Trade Unions and the South African Communist Party. At the ninth provincial conference of the ANC in 2006, he tabled a discussion document, 'Building Gauteng as a Globally Competitive City Region'. The conference was ambivalent – for some, the idea of a globally competitive city-region sat uneasily with post-apartheid political commitment to the developmental state that implied active state intervention to resolve poverty and inequality. After extensive debate, the conference resolved to adopt a shared vision of Gauteng as a 'city-province' but only *noted* the discussion document as a basis for furthering public debate. Alliance partners were even more wary, concerned that the concept lacked a pro-poor interpretation. Nevertheless, Shilowa negotiated the necessary support and launched the idea for the GCR in August 2006. His speech at the occasion was an adept balancing act. He stressed the importance of becoming competitive as a city-region through accelerated economic growth, improved efficiencies and modernised infrastructure, but also insisted that 'the Gauteng city region must avoid the pitfalls of social exclusion and growing inequality that have been associated with other global city regions' (Shilowa 2006b, para. 94). In 2008, facing further criticism, Shilowa was even more explicit in calling for inclusion: 'As we push ahead with our efforts to build Gauteng as a globally competitive city region, we are conscious of the fact that we need to take deliberate steps to ensure that this city region continues to be socially inclusive and indeed benefits the poorest of the poor' (Shilowa 2008, para. 19).

The other challenge in building support for the GCR was the suspicion within local governments that the concept was a ploy by the provincial government to expand its influence over the municipal sphere.[6] Shilowa called on all spheres of government to think beyond their jurisdictions and work towards common visions. He assured municipalities that there was no intention to 'tamper with the constitutional structures of national, provincial and local government' (Shilowa 2006b, para. 95). At the time there was also a recognition that 'the GCR initiative cannot be confined to provincial and local governments' and that 'there is a need to involve social partners and civil society in a social dialogue' (Steytler 2007, 3), but little progress was made in this area.

Unfolding discourse and practice

The discourse on the GCR was soon embedded within the political-bureaucratic realm and in the work of local scholars. Shilowa was followed as premier by Paul Mashatile (2008 to 2009), Nomvula Mokonyane (2009 to 2014), David Makhura (2014 to 2022) and Panyaza Lesufi (2022 to date). Every premier until Makhura had used their annual state of the province addresses to affirm support for the idea of the GCR. Insiders indicate some variation in commitment levels and in the interpretation of what the GCR might mean in practice. However, there was strong discursive continuity, with Makhura, a previous long-standing provincial ANC party secretary before he became premier, playing a leading role in sustaining interest in the concept.

The establishment of the GCRO (Gauteng City-Region Observatory) in 2008 as a partnership between provincial government (later extended to municipal government) and two leading universities played a key role in sustaining the discourse and providing a knowledge infrastructure for policy development within the structures of the GCR. Carla-Leanne Washbourne et al. (2019) refer to the GCRO as an international example of a boundary-spanning institution at the frontier of different worlds, able to translate the knowledge from one world to the other.

In the 2000s, academic scholarship cautiously affirmed the GCR as a global city-region, or at least as an aspirant global city-region (Pillay 2004; Mabin 2007; Rogerson 2009), while international agencies, including the OECD and the Brookings

Institution, supported the idea of the GCR as a city-region of global standing (OECD 2011; Parilla and Trujillo 2015).

There were critical perspectives, however. To Stephen Greenberg (2010), the idea of the GCR as a global city-region follows the paradigm of urban competition and trickle-down economics rather than opening the space for endogenous and participatory responses to the social-spatial inequalities of the province. Jesse Harber and Kate Joseph (2018, 5) called the GCR 'an unsettled idea' with 'an irreducible complexity'. They argued that a city-region is 'not a straightforward site in which to organise governance' (Harber and Joseph 2018, 2), partly because 'governance is a set of functions *each of which has its own territory*' (Harber and Joseph 2018, 17, italics in the original).

Other writers have focussed on the physical evolution of the city-region with, for example, Graeme Götz et al. (2014) referring to 'the thin oil of urbanisation' in their account of the spatial processes that locate Johannesburg within the dynamics of the wider region. Brian Mubiwa and Harold Annegarn (2013) used satellite imagery to provide a fine-grained view of the incremental expansion of the city-region, while André Brand et al. (2017) used spatial data to observe spatial patterns, including corridor-type development over an extended period. Mabin (2013) combined the shifting spatial form of the GCR across time with the planning initiatives and concepts that tried to influence this form. Other writing has, for example, returned to a consideration of the city-region as an economic agglomeration, after a retreat from the earlier urban competitiveness discourse (see the collection of contributions in Cheruiyot 2018), or has engaged the gradually expanding theme of city-regions and environmental sustainability (for example, Bobbins and Fatti 2015; Götz and Schaeffler 2015).

There is recent debate over the meaning and boundaries of the GCR. Since its inception as an idea launched by the provincial premier, the edge of the GCR has been largely represented as the boundary of the province of Gauteng. This is a pragmatic construction representing administrative and political realities, although there has also been an analytical appreciation of the mismatch between the provincial boundaries and the urban footprint, with urban development spilling over into neighbouring provinces and some parts of the province of Gauteng being visibly rural (see Mabin 2013, for example). However, recently, there has been renewed engagement with the boundary complexities of the city-region. Ngaka Mosiane and Graeme Götz (2022), for example, engage with the large settlements on the edges of the GCR, which were produced under apartheid as black residents were relocated from the urban core to the periphery. They argue, however, that these zones of 'displaced urbanisation' have evolved over time into 'vibrant spaces of displaced urbanism': 'We argue that this "displaced urbanism" – the innovative co-existence of formal and informal land uses and activities; innovative acts of self-realisation by local residents trying to survive and pursue their aspirations; and, in turn, dynamic local economies from below – needs to be taken much more seriously on its own terms (Mosiane and Götz 2022, 1).

This challenges simplistic conceptions of core–periphery, and the delineation of the edge, as this displaced urbanism frequently crosses provincial boundaries, with large-scale daily commuter flows across the provincial boundary. The discourse of the GCR is embedded, although analytical contributions have highlighted complexity, but its practice has been fractious. The GCR is weakly institutionalised in governance terms. Over time, there were attempts to develop an understanding of institutional mechanisms for city-region governance and occasional proposals for implementation. There were study tours to city-regions globally, including to São Paulo (Gauteng Province 2005).

Consultants drew on the experience of cities, including London, Tokyo and Addis Ababa, in proposing a phased approach to the establishment of a Gauteng city-state, which would replace the existing provincial and municipal government, but with sub-city structures to address the considerable management challenge of governing such a large area (Akanani et al. 2007). The idea of this super-municipality did not, however, gain traction and the discussion on institutional reform was reduced to a debate on whether to add one or two more metropolitan cities in Gauteng to replace the dual system of district and local municipalities. A 2011 proposal to create a new metropolitan authority to the south of Johannesburg was accepted by the Municipal Demarcations Board but was put on hold due to intense local opposition (Mkhize 2021).

Without new structures for the GCR, formal inter-governmental relations processes continued within the forums set up in the Intergovernmental Relations Framework Act of 2005. In 2016, however, relationships across the provincial and municipal spheres were negatively affected when the ANC lost control of the Johannesburg and Tshwane metropolitan municipalities to DA-led coalitions. The new mayor of Johannesburg, Herman Mashaba, took an especially hard line in relation to the provincial government, and a senior provincial official advised me that 'after August 2016, the idea of the GCR is off the table' and that the inter-governmental relations forums were barely functioning from this time.

The environment has remained difficult, with municipal coalitions unstable and the ANC only narrowly holding onto its control of provincial government in the May 2019 elections. Nevertheless, the idea of the GCR persisted, although with a new slant when Premier David Makhura presented his state of the province address in February 2019, arguing that 'going forward, we must be more aggressive and decisive in pushing a vision of turning the entire province into a single, multi-tier, mega special economic zone' (Makhura 2019a, para. 19). He referred to the declaration of China's island province of Hainan as a special economic zone as his inspiration here. In June 2019, after his narrowly won re-election, Makhura presented a state of the province address under the banner 'Growing Gauteng Together' and referred again to his vision of creating a province-wide special economic zone (Makhura 2019b).

The Covid-19 pandemic struck in early 2020, diverting the provincial government's attention. Nevertheless, the mechanisms for dealing with the pandemic involved inter-governmental relations. Under the cover of a national state of disaster, the South African government took on special powers and created a hierarchical structure for managing the pandemic with a National Coronavirus Command Council directing instructions downwards to provincial command councils and then to district command councils, although with upward loops in terms of reporting and information. Nevertheless, the common cause of fighting the pandemic brought officials from the three spheres of government and civil society agencies together in ways that had not happened before, and there may be legacy traces from the pandemic for city-region governance in the future.

While the GCR was never institutionalised in any comprehensive way, there were attempts at overarching strategy and sector-based initiatives. The weakness in strategy-making included the inter-governmental relations dimension and the lack of instruments for implementation. Provincial government has prepared and revised its provincial spatial development frameworks, indicating its vision for the spatial future of the GCR. However, the Constitutional Court determined in 2010 that the real power for spatial planning and land-use management rested in the hands of municipalities. Provincial and municipal governments have not succeeded in initiating genuinely collaborative spatial planning processes. At times, the spatial visions of provincial and municipal governments have actively collided. In 2015, for example, the Gauteng provincial government proposed developing a series of so-called mega human settlements, most of them beyond the urban edge where land prices were affordable. This proposal conflicted with the plans of the three metropolitan governments to focus new development in the accessible urban core and along transit corridors (Ballard and Rubin 2017). Margot Rubin (2021) describes the complex process of mutual adjustment as officials in the two spheres of government navigate through a sharp discord in the visions of their political principals.

In terms of economic and overarching developmental strategy, the provincial government followed a cautious process of developing the Gauteng 2055 strategy from 2011 through to the provincial elections of March 2014. However, the newly elected Premier Makhura chose not to release this document and instead used bold language to present his vision of 'ten pillars' of intervention 'to transform, modernise and re-industrialise Gauteng' with five sweeping corridors across the province, each with its economic speciality (Makhura 2015, para. 11). The challenges are in embedding a strategy that was not prepared through inter-governmental relations processes and in implementing economic proposals with few instruments at provincial level for influencing economic activity.

There were, however, two sectors where incipient forms of city-region governance were observed. The drought in Cape Town from 2015 to 2019, which brought that city to near disaster, raised concerns around the precariousness of water supply in the GCR. Premier Makhura convened an inter-governmental initiative to address the concerns with technical support from the GCRO (Kelly 2021). It was an institutionally complex initiative, since formal responsibility for water security rests with the national government. As Gauteng entered a period of good rainfall, the issue retreated from public consciousness and the initiative waned.

The other initiative was in relation to the troubled transport sector. The 1996 national Constitution had left responsibilities for transport fragmented across the spheres of government, and transport modes were poorly coordinated. In 2016, the premier endorsed an earlier proposal for a single transport authority to integrate planning and system operations across the GCR. Implementing the proposal proved immensely complicated, however, as the different agencies across the spheres of government jealously guarded their powers.[7] The promulgation of the provincial Transport Authority Act and the launch of the Gauteng Transport Authority (GTA) were delayed on successive occasions as the protracted negotiations continued. Finally, a compromise was reached that allows dual branding of the transport system by the GTA and municipalities and requires the GTA to report simultaneously to the provincial government, municipalities and the Premier's Coordinating Forum. The Act was promulgated in 2019, and the GTA was set up in late 2020 as a hybrid between a politically constituted and a technocratic body, as it is to consist of six representatives of provincial and municipal government and six selected experts (Venter 2018). The GTA has been low key and whether it has the authority and inter-agency buy-in to act effectively in the region remains to be seen.

In summary, the GCR is a well-embedded concept, but its practice, in formal terms at least, has been fractious and partial. However, city-region governance is not dependent on formal structures, and joint problem solving is happening through interpersonal networks, although with the limitations of not having institutional authority.

Post-apartheid efforts towards city-region governance have come largely from provincial rather than national government, but there is a recent attempt from national government to promote integrated governance through the District Development Model (DDM). However, the DDM has nationwide application rather than being specific to city-regions. Launched in 2019 under the mantra 'One District, One Plan, and One Budget' (COGTA 2019), the DDM seeks to achieve inter-governmental coordination through district-level planning (the 'one plan'), and the creation of district hubs with professional staff appointed by national government. Launched with ambition and haste, the DDM has been criticised for inadequate collaborative processes, failure to build on existing initiatives and plans, and the lack of capacity within government for its implementation (GTAC 2022). Further, at the time of writing, the future of the DDM was uncertain due to the outcome of leadership battles within the ruling ANC.

Conclusion

From its early days as a cluttered collection of mining settlements, the (currently termed) GCR has required collaborative responses to providing infrastructures including water, transport, electricity, health services and housing. In a succession of initiatives, the white elite of the Witwatersrand tried to make governance work for its interests in a spatially fragmented mining region. The relationship with the national government was varied, but a common pattern was for local initiatives to be nationalised, with, for example, initial associational arrangements within the region for providing water, energy and segregated housing taken up into national government structures. Although most of these initiatives were about the pragmatics of governance, forms of regionalist sentiment did emerge within the white business and civic community, largely in response to threats from national policy.

In the late apartheid era, reformers within the governing party turned to regionalism as a patch-up solution for disintegrating segregationist policies. This failed, but a negotiated national settlement in the 1990s brought institutions of non-racial democracy to the region. With a history of fragmented administration and a desire to redistribute resources across territory, there was a shift towards consolidated metropolitan and city-state (or rather, city-province) governance. This was a different outcome to Brazil, for example, where the transition to democracy was associated with localist ideology and resistance to metropolitan or regional government.

The turn to metropolitan and provincial governments did not, however, resolve the challenges of governing the complex urban heartland of South Africa, and a discourse of city-region governance emerged in the early 2000s. Driven by the vision of an ambitious provincial premier, the idea of the GCR was embedded in official, academic and, to a lesser extent, popular discourse, and has been sustained through the ongoing work of the GCRO, for example. However, the practice of the GCR remains limited and fractious. The challenges of collaborative governance within the GCR are related to a low trust environment, obstructive political cultures, political divides and run-down capacities within the state. However, even within this context, interpersonal networks connect the agencies of governance, supporting forms of joint problem solving or inter-agency mediation.

The question for future initiatives is whether the agents of governance within the GCR should attempt a bold institutional fix, risking the possibility (even likelihood) of failure, or whether they should move through processes of progressive incrementalism (Marques 2021) – Swilling (2019, 311) calls it a 'radical incrementalism' – to build trust and collaborative relationships *over time* within a very complex space. However, while the GCR may still lack an institutional mechanism for collaborative governance (bringing the three spheres of government together as well as agents of civil society) it does, somewhat unusually, have a city-region-wide administration in the form of the Gauteng provincial government, and this differs from the other cases in the BRICS. In terms of education and health, for example, there is thus a form of city-region governance. Thus, despite its many deficiencies, the GCR does offer an existing model of sub-national governance more or less aligned to the footprint of a large urban agglomeration.

Notes

1   The genetic origin of the 'white Afrikaner' population has been historically controversial, but recent DNA studies indicate that on average the Afrikaner population has a non-European DNA of around 4.7%, mainly from South Asian slaves and the Khoe-San, a local indigenous population.

2   For example, segments of an emerging black professional class – teachers, nurses, police officers and civil servants – neither supported, nor opposed, active opposition.

3   The ANC was an umbrella organisation for a vast range of social groups, ranging from rural peasants and the urban unemployed to black professionals and the business class, with considerable geographic and ethnic diversity.

4   There were, however, some adjustments to the PWV boundary in creating the new province. For example, the industrial town of Sasolburg, which was part of the PWV's Vaal complex, was incorporated into the Free State province rather than Gauteng. Also, some of the homeland edges of the PWV were placed in the neighbouring provinces of Mpumalanga and North West, as a result of strong local sentiment.

5   This connection to California was explained to me by Professor Allen Scott in a side discussion on 12 September 2019 at the World Forum on China Studies held in Shanghai, China.

6   I observed these concerns first-hand while working as an official for the City of Johannesburg (2006 to 2009).

7   These agencies include: the Passenger Rail Agency of South Africa; metropolitan municipalities, which own and contracted bus services, including the Bus Rapid Transit systems; provincial government, which manages the public-private partnership that runs the Gautrain Rapid Rail System; the powerful minibus taxi (paratransit) industry run by unruly cartels officially regulated by the national Department of Transport; and roads agencies in each sphere of government.

7 Concluding and comparative insights

Introduction

In the preface and introductory chapter, I expressed my normative hope that an enriched understanding of city-region governance may gradually help improve the quality of urban governance, and therefore of urban experience. However, over the course of the study my understanding shifted, and I turned towards a non-normative account of 'the continuous struggle to govern large and dynamic agglomerations of urban settlements that cross multiple jurisdictional boundaries'.

While my research began with the hope that there may be best practice out there which could inform thinking within the Gauteng City-Region (GCR), the key message of the book, as it turns out, is that such a search is misplaced. Governance practices are so embedded within historically produced contexts, including aspects such as political culture and political settlement, that the transfer of practice across contexts is likely to fail. Cross-contextual learning is nevertheless important, as thinking of one place through another provides perspective, provokes new insight and stimulates innovation.

Methodologically, I was drawn towards an inductive approach that builds understanding from the language and meaning used in the places I studied, although I could not fully escape the use of prior concepts and terms in the dominating Anglo literature, such as 'city-region' and 'city-region governance'. I was also drawn towards comparative and historical methods, although with an evolving understanding of what these methods require. Rather late in the research process, for example, I realised that my focus on individual narratives had left me without a broader understanding of the significance of each narrative within the wider context. Using frame-switching as an approach, I moved between a broader synopsis of inter-contextual processes (chapter one) and the in-depth study of each case (chapters two to six). My method had hybridised. I also came to appreciate that historical method is not only about the patient assembling of a rich temporal narrative, but also about a constant appraisal of the meaning and significance of the changes. Ideas of 'process tracing' were helpful here, with Analucia Schliemann et al. (1997, 185) writing, for example, of the need to understand the 'complex relations between characteristics of the subject and those of the setting in which one acts'. These are methodological points which may be of value to future researchers. I turn now to some of the substantive findings that emerged through the BRICS comparison.

The BRICS comparison

The BRICS (Brazil, Russia, India, China and South Africa) countries represent five distinctive national contexts, each with internal variation. These contexts are, however, all part of global circulations of material flow, language, meaning and practice. They are loosely linked to each other through a geopolitical arrangement but are mainly related through wider circulations. It is a complex story of particularity and connectedness and of difference and similarity, which I tell using the following headings:

- The dilemmas of collective action
- Contextual underpinnings
- Language, meaning and discourse
- Drivers and politics
- Learning and innovations
- Outcomes and prospects.

The dilemmas of collective action

City-regions are at the nexus of physical and governmental complexity. They are territories of complex spatial structure where power is diffused across multiple actors. The task of organising connectivity is often hugely difficult, with failures impacting negatively on the lives of ordinary people. This general statement applies across all the BRICS countries, although the shape of the complexity differs in detail.

Brazilian scholars are aware of acute dilemmas of collective action in their context (Souza 2003; Ribeiro and Dos Santos Junior 2010; Klink 2017). Their mega-sized metropolitan areas emerged during a period of rapid urbanisation from the 1930s to the 1970s, but with increasing spatial complexity from the 1980s onwards, as economic activity decentralised from the core cities into satellite towns. This happened within the context of growing institutional fragmentation. Although Brazil's metropolitan regions have large core municipalities, generally governing around one-half of the population of each region, governance on the peripheries is extremely fragmented. As a result, Brazil's metropolitan regions have battled to adequately respond to mounting urban mobility challenges, safety, water security, waste management and housing issues, amongst others.

Russia has a different challenge. It has the large core local authorities of Moscow and Saint Petersburg, with high levels of internal governmental coherence. However, there is a major disjunction along the jurisdictional edge, with poor coordination between the city and *oblast* (regional) governments. Under communist rule, coordination happened within party structures, and the urban areas were quite compact, mainly contained within the city boundaries. This changed rapidly with post-communist liberalisation – with both the disintegration of the party and market-led urban sprawl into the *oblast*.

India's dilemma is to govern large and spatially complex metropolitan areas within a context of institutional chaos. India has weak local governments (although sometimes jurisdictionally large) but with a plethora of institutions dealing with different governmental tasks, reporting variously to state governments and national ministries. In this context, India struggles to deal with mounting problems of infrastructural decay, air pollution, water pollution and more such issues.

China has local governments with large territorial jurisdictions and a wide range of functions, although within a strong governmental and political hierarchy. However, the scale and the pace of urbanisation since the beginning of the reform era in the 1970s have produced massive urban configurations with immense governmental and integration challenges. A core dilemma for China is to manage the great urban agglomerations that have sprawled horizontally across jurisdictional boundaries over the past four decades within an overall governmental system that is overwhelmingly oriented along the axis of a vertical hierarchy.

The scale of South Africa's urban challenge is numerically tiny compared with that of China, but South Africa is left with the legacy of its mining and apartheid histories. With the ending of apartheid, single-tier metropolitan authorities were created, but this has not resolved the challenge of collaboration across the wider reach of the GCR and across the spheres of government within South Africa's complex constitutional framing of cooperative governance.

Clearly, all the BRICS countries face the common dilemma of collective action across city-regions, although the details differ significantly, requiring us to take care in translating lessons across contexts. There are also significant differences between the BRICS countries and the contexts that have produced much of the existing literature on city-regions. In the North American context, local authorities are mainly small and fragmented; in this context, special-purpose districts, inter-municipal consortia and local growth coalitions to strengthen regional identity and competitiveness are common practices. However, across BRICS, with some exceptions, such as the edges of Brazil's metropolitan regions (MRs), where inter-municipal consortia have evolved, local governments are jurisdictionally large. There are, however, other challenges of spatial coordination, such as across India's morass of sector-based territorial agencies, between city and *oblast* in Russia and across the spatial scales within China's super-sized urban regions.

The BRICS may also assist us with an impending dilemma of collective action – how to relate governance practices to urban forms that expand far beyond city-regions. This is, of course, a global challenge, but there are contexts in BRICS that may sharpen our attention. India provides a compelling example as Greater Delhi is part of a great swathe of extended urbanisation along the Ganges River Basin from Bangladesh to Pakistan. In this sense, the BRICS countries may offer a bridge into extended urbanisation, a scale of urban governmental analysis that is still largely unexplored.

Contextual underpinnings

A dominant theme in this book is the historical and contextual embeddedness of evolving forms of city-region governance.

In the case of Brazil, the narrative begins with reference to a long history that has produced a complex hybrid of political cultures that bring together formal legalism with informality, clientelism, personalised politics and more. These cultures permeate urban governance, but are regionally differentiated, explaining some of the variation across the country. In Belo Horizonte, for example, the historical need to accommodate modern and clientelist practices has produced a culture of collaborative governance, which has arguably supported more participatory processes of metropolitan governance than in other places. Context is, however, also shaped by recent histories. For Brazil, like other countries in Latin America, the experience of military dictatorship is a potent psychosocial force that has produced an ideological orientation towards localism, which complicated efforts to govern across larger territories. However, Brazil's political culture also includes a strong element of pragmatism, and the localist impulse has adapted over time to support (limited forms of) inter-jurisdictional collaboration.

Contemporary Russia is ill-famed for its personalised authoritarian rule and intimate networks of political power and private gain (the 'oligarchs'). Russia is a federation in name only, and the concern of the national elite with maintaining strong vertical integration is a clear constraint on empowered governance at the scale of the large urban agglomeration. However, scholars have argued that Russians are not innately authority-loving and that subservience to authoritarian leadership may reflect a social contract, which may alter as conditions change. However, practical challenges like severe road congestion have forced even the national elites to demand better practices of horizontal coordination.

India presents the greatest complexity of all the cases in terms of hybridised political culture and intranational variation. It is, as Nehru proffered, an ancient palimpsest that brings multiple vernaculars together with strands of modernity. Relating the underpinning political culture to the evolution of governance, differences in urban governance between cities such as Mumbai, Kolkata, Hyderabad and Delhi indicate the significance of different intranational histories.[1] Across India, though, the prevalence of informality in governance is a prevailing feature. Ananya Roy (2009a, 84) observes that 'informality exists at the very heart of the state and is an integral part of the territorial practices of state power'. Also, across India, with a few exceptions such as Mumbai, local government is very weak compared with state government, with significant implications for the scope of city-region governance.

China is also an enormous country, with intranational variation in political cultures, but it has had a 2 000-year history of hierarchical governance that has produced greater national conformity than is the case in India. There are many debates over political culture in China and the extent to which hierarchical governance is underpinned by Confucian values, for example. Current consensus accepts the role of underlying cultures but also emphasises the fluidity and political use of culture. In China, city-regionalism represents a pragmatic adaptation to historical hierarchy, although the hierarchy remains a constraint on the future development of new governance arrangements. The Chinese case does emphasise the role of national government in orchestrating city-region governance, consistent with the theme of hierarchy, but it also reveals the complexity of the hierarchy's workings in practice, with, for example, the need to accommodate local and regional interests and the prevalence of forms of informality including interpersonal reciprocity.

Political cultures in South Africa are fragmented, reflecting the divided history of the country. The path to a consolidated democracy with robust institutions is complicated by the extreme, persisting socio-economic inequalities, aspects of political culture such as an acceptance of violence, populism and intolerance, and the rise of rent-seeking and patronage within state structures. These factors, together with growing political factionalism and low levels of social trust, may explain the difficulties in translating an established discourse of city-region governance into collaborative practice.

Like any other collective of countries, the BRICS countries may be used to illustrate the contextual embeddedness of city-regional governance. However, the BRICS countries do highlight areas of focus, including the tensions between vertical and horizontal integration and the significance of informal practices. Informality is a complex area, requiring far more study, as it takes multiple forms with different consequences. In some forms, it is a threatening mode of shadow governance where private rent-seeking and arbitrary decision making undermine the transparency of democratic processes. In other forms, however, it enables governance and problem solving in the face of ineffective or dysfunctional formal processes.

Language, meaning and discourse

The BRICS study highlights both distinctiveness and interconnectedness in language, meaning and discourse. The BRICS countries have sufficient weight in governance and scholarship to have produced their own traditions of thought[2] but are also linked to the global circulations of language, meaning and discourse, which are disproportionately influenced by North American and European scholarship.

In Brazil, the dominant term is *região metropolitana* (metropolitan region) and this reflects a strong North American influence around the 1950s and 60s, at a time when Brazil's major urban centres were reaching a critical threshold in terms of size and complexity. Since then, however, Brazil has developed a strong indigenous urban scholarship, and language has adapted to respond to the continued evolution of metropolitan areas, with reference, for example, to *metropolitano expandido* (expanded metropolitan region) and *macrometrópole* (macrometropolis). One of the major knowledge agents in Brazil is the *Observatório das Metrópoles* (Observatory of the Metropolis), which connects around 380 urban researchers across 17 participating research institutions.

During the Soviet period, Russia had a degree of insulation from Western influence and a language evolved, reflecting the concerns of the Communist Party leadership, to produce urban spaces that supported goals of state-led industrialisation. Russia's urban agglomeration (*gorodskaya aglomeratsiya*) is defined very similarly to the city-region in Western scholarship, but there are still significant traces of its Soviet usage. So, for example, Russia's Spatial Development Strategy for the Russian Federation up to 2025 provides extensive lists of manufacturing activities relevant to each designated urban agglomeration. With the ending of Soviet rule, Russia was more directly influenced by Western discourse. The idea of the globally competitive city-region (à la Allen Scott) was taken up by the city leadership in Moscow and Saint Petersburg and has featured strongly in the annual Moscow Urban Forum, for example.

India was part of the British Empire, and many of the new indigenous elite were trained in Great Britain. It is not surprising, therefore, that the language of urban governance and planning in India reflects colonial origins. The idea of spatial decentralisation, so central to the concept of a national capital region (NCR), clearly reflects ideas circulating in the British Empire in the first part of the twentieth century and the decades immediately following World War II. However, whereas these ideas have lost currency in the UK, they have persisted in India to the present, with some current signs of weakening. This persistence explains some of the divergences in the use of the idea of a city-region. In BRICS, a city-region (or its linguistic equivalent) generally means a large, functionally integrated urban formation that cuts across local jurisdictions. However, in India, as in China, the NCR refers to a large territory surrounding the national capital that is not highly urbanised and that can receive population and economic activity from the capital because of its relatively low density. There were, however, other influences. With regard to national planning, the Soviet Union, with its system of five-year plans, was important, but at the urban or metropolitan scale, the West had greater influence. Ideas of metropolitan governance came to India from North America through agencies such as the Ford Foundation, which were influential in planning cities, including Delhi and Kolkata. These ideas adapted to the context of India's federation, where state governments dominate the local sphere.

China's emergence as an urban power is recent and dramatic. In describing urban expansion, there was a strong Western influence, and the term 'city-region', for example, is well known. However, a historical tracing of official terminology reveals the influence of Japan from the late 1970s, with the translation of the idea of an economic circle into the urban cluster, which was taken up in China's national five-year plans from 2006. Western and Japanese inspiration have evolved as China's scholars have grappled with the challenge of scale caused by the development of mega-sized urban clusters. One approach has been to hyperbolise existing terms, such as 'super megacity-regions' (Yeh and Chen 2020, 636). Another approach has been to find a language that describes some of the spatial formations of these clusters, for example, 'metropolitan interlocking regions' (Zhou 1991).

Like India, South Africa was in the British orbit but also open to other influences. The intricate urban network that evolved on the Witwatersrand mining belt attracted early attention in British literature, with Monica Cole (1957) identifying the Witwatersrand as South Africa's Lancashire. The concept of Randopolis in the 1930s was a play on the term metropolis, most used in the USA but brought to South Africa by an Australian planner. The leading figure in the planning of the PWV (a reference to an extended Witwatersrand) from the 1950s had spent a formative period in the USA. More recently, Allen Scott's concept of the globally competitive city-region influenced the emergence of the GCR as a framing idea. However, these international influences were translated into the particularities of the South African context.

The BRICS study shows the intersection of global, national and regional influences on an evolving language. The extent of mutual influences within the BRICS network is unclear, although China may have a growing demonstration effect as revealed, for example, in a recent call by the premier of Gauteng in South Africa to designate his entire province as a special economic zone.

The diversity of the BRICS countries helps draw attention to the importance of differences in language, meaning and discourses. In this sense, the BRICS may have a similar role in the scholarship to Europe, where diversity has supported a series of comparative studies.

Drivers and politics

There are shrill controversies in the literature over the drivers of city-regionalism, but I follow Jean-Paul Addie and Roger Keil (2015) in this book by trying to pay attention to real existing regionalism. In doing so, I attempt to distinguish between the rationality underlying city-regionalism (that is, the underlying motives or interests) and how city-regionalism is rationalised in different contexts.

While various theorists have emphasised one or other driver (or rationality), often informed by the realities of the context they are familiar with, there is growing consensus that there are multiple drivers. These include a drive for economic competitiveness, an interplay of political interests (one layer of government trying to position itself relative to another), agendas including environmentalism, and integrated planning and the pragmatics of governing (for example, the need to coordinate a public transport system). Through the book, I have shown that the last of these has been underplayed in literature in which the respective emphasis on economic competitiveness and political interests has been the key line of debate.

Growth and competitiveness are significant drivers but do not dominate in a way that some North American-centred literature suggests. In contexts such as Moscow, Gauteng, Mumbai and the Yangtze River Delta (YRD), the influence of competitive city-regionalism is clearly present, although often moderated by other drivers. In China, city-regionalism is used to restrain inter-locality competition to strengthen overall competitiveness. For Moscow, city-regionalism was used to project the city onto the world's political and economic stage, with threats of isolation after Russia's 2014 occupation of Crimea. In post-apartheid South Africa, the idea of the globally competitive city-region was formative in the arrival of the GCR but was quickly moderated in a political context where there was discomfort with competitiveness as the overriding agenda.

The underlying politics are often entangled with the pragmatic drivers of city-region governance, with success in delivering services and infrastructures, strengthening the hand of one or other scale of government.

This is clear in the case of Brazil, for example, where political cultures and ideologies are localist in orientation and are not favourable to metropolitan or city-region governance. However, across Brazil's metropolitan regions, major governmental challenges require degrees of collaboration. Brazil's urban citizens protest periodically en masse in response to dysfunctional governments – for example, during the Passe Livre movement in 2019. Politically, elites have been forced to adapt governance systems over time to improve functionality in delivering services such as public transport, water and waste management, and, in doing so, forms of city-region governance have emerged.

There are no strong political drivers for metropolitan governance in Brazil, with the gradual (and erratic) turn to metropolitan governance a reluctant response by different actors within the federation. It took the national legislature a decade or so to write the Statute of the Metropolis into law, and this was followed by a reversal when Brazilian politics took a right-wing turn. State governments are responsible for designating metropolitan areas, and it is a function they clearly wish to protect. However, very few state governments have acted energetically to implement legislative provisions for metropolitan governance, possibly for fear of creating alternative centres of power. An important exception is the state of Minas Gerais for the Belo Horizonte MR, but this reflects local political cultures and alliances. Local governments have generally resisted the creation of metropolitan-scale structures for fear of losing their autonomy. However, the practical governing requirements have brought some local authorities together in collaborative arrangements for service delivery (most famously, but not only, in the ABC sub-region of Greater São Paulo).[3]

Post-Soviet Russia is also marked by a reluctance to establish inter-governmental mechanisms across city-regions. This has to do with differences of interest and territorial jealousies between city and regional (*oblast*) governments. The cities are hesitant to share resources with the regions, while the regions fear dominance by the cities, although practical considerations have required ad hoc forms of collaboration between these authorities. However, there are sectors where more systematic forms of collaboration are required to resolve problems more sustainably, including, very obviously, transport. The lack of coordination in the transport sector had implications for national elites, especially in Moscow, where federal government ministries are located and where road congestion reached extreme levels. This practical concern compelled the federal government to intervene, forcing the city and *oblast* governments of Greater Moscow and Greater Saint Petersburg to collaborate in coordination councils for transport. Federal government is, however, likely to have an ambivalent view of city-regional governance, mindful of the potential threat to the centre of a unified regional government.

In India, metropolitan governance was initially introduced to address an urban crisis (at first, a crisis of sanitation in Kolkata). However, with the weakness of local government within India's federation, metropolitan structures were captured by state governments and have, over time, become an income source through their control over land development processes. With these embedded interests, attempts to empower local government and make metropolitan governance more inclusive have generally failed. With metropolitan agencies failing as mechanisms of collaboration, or even coordination, informal mechanisms have filled the gap. Joint problem solving across institutions within metropolitan regions happens, but informally and erratically. Governance within the NCR, through the mechanism of the National Capital Region Planning Board (NCRPB), reflects a different set of interests. The NCRPB is an instrument that allows the union government to maintain some hold on the planning of the capital city and its environs. A minister of union government chairs the board, and state governments are compelled to follow the dictates of the regional plan. However, state governments have resisted the intrusions of the centre into their planning powers, and this is reflected in the continuing failings of the NCRPB as a planning authority.

In China, there are many pragmatic reasons for improved governance of city-regions (or city clusters). The early turn towards region-wide collaboration came from the national government that was concerned with the effects of intense inter-municipal and inter-provincial economic competition. Environmental management later emerged as a critical rationale for region-wide collaborations, again driven by national government, with the creation of an integrated rapid rail network a practical driver of functional integration across city-regions. It is possible to explain China's turn towards city-cluster governance in terms of the functional requirements of governing large-scale urbanisation. However, there is an underlying politics, which reflects the concerns of the national elite within an authoritarian governmental system to manage difficult policy dilemmas. The idea of redistributing growth across a city cluster is a means, for example, to benefit economically from continued urbanisation while avoiding the political and environmental threats of large concentrations of people and activities in mega cities. Furthermore, cluster governance managed from above is a means to maintain national control and achieve efficiencies through better collaboration among actors within the cluster. Importantly, the National Development and Reform Commission (NDRC) prepares an overall plan for each cluster, providing the framework for local and regional collaborations.

The Chinese case has been identified in recent literature as a corrective to a West-dominated literature, which emphasises local growth coalitions and inter-municipal associations as the drivers of city-region governance. China's narrative highlights national government-led orchestration of city-region governance. However, even in China, top-down governance must accommodate regional and local interests to maintain overall harmony, and approaches to city-region governance are emerging that involve top-down and bottom-up elements. This is most obviously so with the YRD where there is a regional identity, and local initiatives such as the annual conference of mayors are meshing with national government directives.

In post-apartheid South Africa, there is a process of new elite formation, with political power having shifted from white to black elites and attempts to empower these black elites economically. It is a complex process with different segments of the new elite establishing at different, but overlapping, geographic scales. The idea of city-region governance (as in the GCR) was an initial orchestration of provincial government and was received cautiously by local governments, fearing dominance from the provincial scale. However, while the idea of city-region governance was rhetorically embedded, it has not been institutionalised, suggesting a lack of real political drive. City-region governance was, however, layered on the metropolitan governance that was institutionalised after the creation of single-tier metropolitan authorities when apartheid ended. Metropolitan authorities were introduced by the national government following calls from civil society for a territorial redistribution of benefits and regional-level negotiations for integrated governance structures.

Again, the BRICS is a diverse grouping but collectively it does challenge some of the emphases in existing literature on city-region governance. There is clearly more state *dirigisme* in the BRICS countries than in the West. As indicated, prior literature on China has already made the point about national government-led orchestration of city-regionalism (Wu 2016; Yeh and Chen 2020). While less weighty than in China, other contexts in BRICS also illustrate city-region governance as a strategy of national governments – the NCRPB in India, the Russian federal government order for joint transportation councils for Moscow and Saint Petersburg, and Brazil's Statute of the Metropolis. Rather than weakening the national government, city-region governance may be a means for the national government to strengthen its hand politically or help resolve a pressing dilemma for national elites.

The BRICS study also highlights the role of the much neglected sub-national scale (state or provincial governments). This is very clear in the case of India, where state governments largely captured the impulse towards metropolitan government, but is also evident in South Africa where the GCR was an initiative of a provincial government, and in Brazil where state governments are formally responsible for designating MRs. In the case of Russia and China, the leading municipalities have provincial-level status and their interests in city-region governance are as municipalities *and* provinces. However, while city-regionalism may strengthen the position of state or provincial governments, it may create a competing centre of power, and so may be resisted by sub-national elites.

The role of the local sphere of government varies. In Brazil, local governments are empowered and often resist moves towards metropolitan governance, but in India, local governments are weak and have little role. Across BRICS, there is little evidence of local governments playing an initiating role in the establishment of formal structures of metropolitan governance, with more evidence of resistance than support from local governments. However, local government is engaged in other forms of city-region governance, from the annual meeting of mayors in China's YRD to the inter-municipal consortia on the peripheries of Brazil's MRs, to multiple forms of ad hoc or informal collaboration across municipal boundaries in all the BRICS countries.

For Andrew Jonas and Kevin Ward (2007, 172) framing city-regionalism within the interests and processes of inter-scalar governance helps us avoid the 'reification of the city-region as a discrete "actor-scale"'. In other words, city-region governance is not a new layer of government with its interests, although these may evolve, but is an instrument of one or more existing layers of government (and may be resisted by others). The BRICS countries, with their federal and quasi-federal arrangements, provide a rich context to explore city-regionalism within inter-governmental systems.

However, governance is not only a matter for government; the question is how city-regionalism relates to the identities, interests and strategies of non-governmental actors. Here the BRICS study is less clear. Cases such as the YRD in China and Saint Petersburg in Russia suggest that contemporary city-region governance may be supported by historical forms of territorial identities or a memory of previous collaborations, but deeper investigation is required.

There are also only a few indications that civil society or private business is playing a significant role in shaping city-regionalism within BRICS. In India, this may be the case in Greater Mumbai, where the state government has an active coalition with industry. In the Greater Bay Area in China, business that straddles the divide between mainland China and Hong Kong has played a role in calling for stronger regional integration, but other cases are less obvious. Civil society activism may have played an indirect role, as civil society is rarely organised at the scale of a city-region. However, street protests in Brazil and township protests in South Africa have placed increasing pressure on authorities to improve governance, which may have contributed to ideas and practices of city-regional governance.

The absence of a socio-cultural dimension is a flaw in the construction of city-regionalism. Willem Salet et al. (2015, 253) argue this in relation to Europe, but it relates also to BRICS, with a few possible exceptions:

> The symbolic-cultural dimension is often underdeveloped in many of today's strategies of city-regional integration, in two ways: either it is completely absent – and city-regional governance is considered a technocratic exercise therefore lacking basic legitimacy of a feeling of belonging by the inhabitants – or it is strongly driven by an urban, core-centric vision that symbolically recognises the city region on behalf of the hinterland. Only in a few cases have attempts been made that successfully build on existing cultural perceptions.

Patsy Healey (2009, 833) asks, 'Who is doing the "summoning up" of the idea of a city region, for what purposes, and in what institutional arenas, with what legitimacy and accountability?' In the BRICS countries, at least, the answer to the 'who' is often national and state/provincial leadership and, far less frequently, local government, civil society and private business.

However, the answer to the question of who is practically engaged in city-region governance may be different. Whether understood as city-region governance or not, governance actors at all levels are engaged daily in different modes of inter-agency communication and collaboration. They are compelled to do so by the pragmatics of governance, and through repeated interactions, emergent forms of governance may arise that gradually institutionalise. This produces territorially complex forms of city-regionalism, as the challenges actors grapple with have different territorial underpinnings. Dealing with air pollution, for example, may have a very different territorial requirement from addressing water security, dealing with sewer networks, or integrating transport systems to facilitate daily commuting. Andrew Burridge et al. (2017, 239) write of 'polymorphic borders', recognising the multiple relationships between governance and territory.

Learning and innovations

While I have argued against a simple notion of best-practice transfer, emphasising the contextuality of governance processes, there are innovations or adapted mainstream practices that warrant a closer look and may inspire creative thought in other places.

While Brazil, overall, is not a successful international example of city-region governance, there are practices of interest. Unusually, this is a country with a Statute of the Metropolis that could be considered in other contexts where enabling national legislation may be required. Admittedly, implementation has been poor, but this may be because of the current political environment.

Going back to the 1970s, Brazil had an approach to metropolitan governance involving the joint creation of a decision-making structure, an advisory structure, a technical support agency and a development fund. The model was tarnished by its origins in a military technocracy and its manipulation to ensure control from above. However, the recent experience of the Belo Horizonte MR shows the potential for democratising the model by making the decision-making and advisory structures genuinely inclusive, with a strong voice for local government and civil society, and by launching participatory processes that mobilise the attention of civil society. Technical innovations from Belo Horizonte include the idea of 'metropolitan citizens' and the designation of zones of metropolitan interest.

In terms of voluntary collaboration among municipalities, the Inter-Municipal Consortium of the ABC Region has received national and international attention, although there are debates over its replicability as it is rooted in a sub-region with a shared working-class history and identity, and has enjoyed strong political championing during crucial periods of its development. Brazil also offers lessons in building a knowledge infrastructure for metropolitan governance. Some structures, such as Emplasa in the São Paulo MR, have not survived political change, but a networked organisation, the *Observatorio das Metropoles* (Observatory of the Metropolis), offers interesting insights for elsewhere.

Post-Soviet Russia is another context that, at first glance, is unpromising as a context from which to draw stimulus. However, although initiated from above, the joint councils for transportation have proven effective in a way that transport authorities in many other places have not. There are also recent innovations in joint planning from the Saint Petersburg urban agglomeration, including the zone of mutual influence between Saint Petersburg and the Leningrad *Oblast*. In terms of knowledge infrastructure, this agglomeration has planning institutes such as Urbanica and the Centre for Strategic Research for the North West. Beyond the two major urban agglomerations, a federal government programme incentivises collaboration within smaller urban agglomerations.

In India, the formal structures of metropolitan and city-region governance have not achieved what they intended to do. However, this arguably has to do with the distribution of power across the levels of India's federation rather than the initial concept underlying the creation of these structures. India's metropolitan planning committees and NCRPB may be innovative structures in themselves. However, the main learning from India may be about the ingenuity of governance actors in getting around the dysfunctionality of the formal institutional arrangements. In some cases, this involves the deployment of formal mechanisms, such as special-purpose vehicles and joint ventures, with the use of the high courts as a deadlock-breaking mechanism. In most cases, however, dealing with the institutional morass requires the effective navigation of informal networks.

China's innovation is from both the top down and the bottom up. From the top down, it begins with incorporating city clusters into national policy frameworks and then using cluster-wide planning as a central instrument of coordination. China has focussed strongly on infrastructure investment that supports regional integration, including developing a rapid rail network. It has also strategically deployed special funds to incentivise investments strengthening cluster-scale integration and development. From the bottom up are inter-municipal and inter-provincial collaboration initiatives that are most advanced in the YRD. These include the annual meetings of mayors, which are supported by annual agreement frameworks, detailed action plans and cooperation offices within each municipality. Innovative mechanisms have also evolved sub-regionally, including along the boundary of the Shenzhen Special Economic Zone and the Hong Kong Special Administrative Region, for example, the Qianhai Cooperation Zone.

In South Africa, the introduction of single-tier metropolitan governance was a significant innovation, even though disillusionment with the practice of governance has grown in recent years. Beyond the metros, city-region governance is observed more in rhetoric than in practice. The Gauteng provincial government is a form of city-region-wide governance, and the Gauteng City-Region Observatory has shaped a knowledge infrastructure for the GCR.

Collectively, the BRICS countries reinforce a growing understanding of how wide and diverse governance arrangements and processes are at the scale of the city-region. Recent literature has moved away from discussing city-region or metropolitan governance only in terms of formal structures, giving attention to the role of informal relationships and networks and the hybridisation of the formal and the informal. As Healey (2009) has already pointed out, city-region governance does not only mean the institutional fix but also the thickening inter-agency and interpersonal relationships woven over time across territories (Healey 2009). This is indicated in the BRICS more so than in those regions of the world that still dominate the production of knowledge on city-region governance. The BRICS countries also highlight bottom-up emergence as a process of institutional formation, although in a quite complex relationship with the intentions and initiatives of the higher levels of government.

Outcomes and prospects

I can conclude only tentatively here, as the BRICS study did not include an assessment of outcomes, and on prospects, the best I can offer is informed speculation.

Also, the impact of city-region governance is likely to be long term, with city-region governance one of multiple entangled variables influencing urban outcomes. Nevertheless, it is difficult to avoid matters of outcome and prospects as, ultimately, the legitimacy of city-region governance rests in its ability to improve the lives of people living in urban settings in a long-term, sustainable way.

In the case of Brazil, metropolitan governance has had a patchy effect in improving coordination across urban agglomerations, and it would probably be very difficult to show how the limited efforts have translated into a real improvement in people's lives. The practical significance of formal systems of metropolitan governance may rest in its *absence*, with Luiz Ribeiro and Orlando dos Santos Junior (2010) arguing that Brazil's urban problems have to do with the inability of political elites to mobilise at the metropolitan scale. There are, however, exceptions that warrant further exploration, including the Belo Horizonte MR and the ABC sub-region of Greater São Paulo. Can it be shown that the everyday life of urban citizens is better in these places because of their relative success with collaborative governance?

Prospects rest largely in changes within the troubled politics of the country. The Statute of the Metropolis of 2015 was a high point, but the political change that followed was a major setback. Political fortunes in Brazil are fickle and an imminent turnaround is possible, giving new life to a movement in support of metropolitan governance. However, whatever happens at the broader level, the nature of Brazil's federation gives space for innovative practices within individual MRs. Also, the pragmatics of governing will continue to drive problem-based or sector-specific forms of collaboration across MRs.

In Russia, too, the importance of collaborative governance across urban agglomerations may be most obvious in its absence. However, there are indications of positive impacts in specific sectors of collaboration. The joint transport authorities for Moscow and Saint Petersburg, for example, are reported to have achieved significant impacts over a short period of time.[4] There are reports that cooperation in this sector is providing stimulus for cooperation in other sectors, and an incremental improvement in working relations between city and *oblast* is a reasonable prospect. It is early to evaluate the impact of the innovative approaches in the planning of the Saint Petersburg urban agglomeration, but this is a space to watch. The use of the city-region to project Russia's major cities onto a global stage has, of course, been dealt a deathly blow by the conflict in Ukraine.

India is notorious for its institutional chaos, and problems of air pollution, water pollution and the disarrayed transport system can be ascribed partly to failures of integration across urban territories. However, conditions might be significantly worse if governance actors were not applying their initiative and resourcefulness in problem solving, using both formal instruments and informal networks to keep metropolitan regions functioning. In the context of India's contested urban politics and deeply embedded institutional interests (for example, those of state governments that block meaningful participation from local governments), there is no immediate prospect of a more functional system of metropolitan governance emerging. In terms of the NCR, there are similar challenges with respect to embedded interests. However, there are indications of a greater pragmatism in city-region planning, with a shift away from the impossible ideal of decanting Delhi into counter-magnet cities. By focussing on more attainable goals, city-region planning may gradually exercise greater influence.

In China, city-cluster-wide planning and coordination have been linked more obviously than elsewhere to major infrastructural investments, such as integrated rapid rail systems, which are changing the patterns of everyday life. There are indications also that city-cluster-scale governance is improving responses to major issues such as air pollution and water security, although there is slower progress with soft infrastructures, such as the regional alignment of policies for social security. It is far less clear whether the government can achieve its objective of redistributing urban growth across the network of towns and cities within each cluster and what the impact of efforts to do so will be. In the case of the NCR, attempts to limit the size of Beijing are associated with the closure of informal enterprises, the demolition of irregularly constructed buildings and increased restrictions on migrant populations. There is also concern over the economic impacts on the city of relocating major (non-capital city related) enterprises from Beijing into the region (Mabin and Harrison 2022). China's approach to cluster governance is likely to evolve further, with new mechanisms introduced for strengthened coordination. However, with hierarchical arrangements so deeply entrenched, it is unlikely that city cluster governance will do much more than modify the workings of the existing hierarchy with the addition of some mechanisms for better horizontal coordination.

South Africa's major innovation is the introduction of single-tier metropolitan governance. The current disillusionment with South African local governance may obscure the benefits that this reform has brought, including redistribution of the capital budgets of municipalities from areas of relative privilege to areas of disadvantage. Levels of basic servicing have improved significantly through the post-apartheid era, although there are indications of deterioration in the maintenance of infrastructure systems. The introduction of metropolitan governance was possible because of a major rupture in the governance system with the ending of apartheid. However, a further significant reform such as the institutionalisation of city-region governance in the GCR is now much more difficult.

As a final comment: talking back to the literature and returning to the beginning

The BRICS study is an effort to broaden the geography of knowledge. It acknowledges the richness of existing studies but argues that enlarging the repertoire of informants will lead, over time, to shifting orientations in theory and debate. The study affirms many of the existing and emerging themes in the literature but emphasises aspects including historical embeddedness, the diversity of language and meaning, the orchestrating role of national and state/provincial governments, the role of informality, the emergent nature of many governance processes and the role of pragmatic problem solving in constituting city-region governance. There is, however, a normative underpinning to this book – the hope that a better understanding of city-region governance will lead to improved practice.

The BRICS countries, individually and collectively, do not offer an easy solution to city-region governance. City-region governance in each country is constrained, and prospects are mainly limited and uncertain. However, this is characteristic of many parts of the world, and the lesson from BRICS is how actors adapt and improvise over time, notwithstanding the constraints. There are moments when a favourable conjuncture allows for a leap forward – and there were such cases in BRICS – but these moments are rare although, of course, opportunities should not be missed when they do arise. Our main hope rests in incremental improvements in cooperative relationships and practices that may gradually institutionalise over time.

As mentioned in chapter two, a Brazilian colleague told me that, despite all the travails, '[Brazil's cities] manage somehow'. This accords with the comment by Patrick Le Galès and Tommaso Vitale (2013, 8) that 'urban societies are more or less governed', and with this book's argument that city-region governance in some form does happen. However, in most cases, governance can be a lot better, with outcomes that are more effective, fairer and more sustainable than we have now. In most cases, 'a slower and more strategic learning-oriented path' (De Souza Briggs 2008, 198) is more feasible, with a greater chance of success, than an attempt at a grand institutional fix.

However, given the scale of the crisis that confronts us across all scales of governance, including the city-region, we can hardly leave processes to chance. The alternative to a grand design does not have to be drift or stasis. Wolfgang Streeck and Kathleen Thelen (2005) include intentional redirection and influence among the various forms of incremental adjustment to governance processes, while Mark Swilling (2019) goes as far as referring to 'radical incrementalism' (emphasis added).

At this point, I circle back to the beginning of the book, to the preface, where I outline the origins of the work and the concerns of my context. The research started with the hope that a study of the BRICS countries might offer a template for reform in the GCR. I was soon disabused of this hope, and at the end of the study, I have no best practices to offer, although I can point to innovations in the BRICS countries (and more globally). Instead, I have made the abstruse argument that governance arrangements are distinctive to their context and must be understood as part of a situated historical process.

But I am aware of the burden of my responsibility. What do I say to governance actors within the GCR? My suggestion, in broad outline, is to begin by understanding the actual process of city-region governance in the GCR with greater depth and nuance. City-region governance is happening, although clearly inadequately and mainly hidden within bureaucratic processes and informal relationships. Can we, from these emergent processes, identify forms that we could progressively reinforce and elaborate on?

In the GCR, the politics are difficult, and timing is important, so processes cannot be forced. While provincial premiers have played a significant role in sustaining a discourse around city-regionalism through initiating and then championing the idea of the GCR, the direct association between provincial government and city-regionalism is a limitation. The future of the GCR as a governance proposition depends on its assimilation into the mood and interest calculations of governance actors across the scales and, beyond government, in civil society and the private sector. More important than pressurising participants to agree on new institutional arrangements, which may provoke suspicion and resistance in an environment of extreme trust deficit, is to create an *authorising environment* for stronger collaboration between governance actors. An arena to explore common concerns and potential areas of collaboration, even if very modestly to begin with, may be a step in the process of intentional incrementalism where trust and mutuality are established over time.

Whether more formal structures are established and, if so, what forms these eventually take is a matter for the governance actors within the GCR to decide – informed, of course, by experience from elsewhere, including the BRICS countries. For the institutions to take root and be sustained, they require a political settlement of sorts. They need to reflect a balance of interests which, in the GCR, requires, most importantly, attention to the concerns of both provincial and metropolitan governments. We could, however, usefully propose a forum for the GCR, with equitable representation from all spheres of government and other actors of society, to discuss future forms of collaborative governance in the GCR.

However, while institutional arrangements are being sorted out, a lot can be done to build the relationships and systems that will support collaborative governance over the long term. The experience of working together with a common objective during the Covid-19 pandemic is a resource that should be deployed for other urgent tasks, which may include, for example, economic reconstruction, ensuring food security, building new infrastructure, or addressing South Africa's current energy crisis. Also, inter-jurisdictional systems and processes can be founded or strengthened, including, for example, information and communications technology and data flows, the lack of which was a severe drawback during the pandemic. Finally, city-regional governance requires an embeddedness within society for its legitimacy and sustainability and to avoid the technocratic turn that marked a succession of initiatives in the history of the region we refer to now as the GCR. We must bring society into collaborative initiatives and into the debates around the future of city-region governance.

Notes

1 Interestingly, while intranational variation is a feature of India, common colonial histories across the sub-continent have produced some commonalities in urban governance between countries including India, Pakistan and Bangladesh (see chapter one).

2 They also, of course, have different languages in a very literal sense.

3 An unstated intention of these inter-municipal consortia may be to counter the strength of core municipalities within the metropolitan regions, which generally do not participate in the consortia.

4 As reported to me by officials when I visited Moscow in 2017 and 2018.

References

Abers, Rebecca. 1996. 'From Ideas to Practice: The Partido dos Trabalhadores and Participatory Governance in Brazil'. *Latin American Perspectives* 23, no. 4: 35–53. https://doi.org/10.1177/0094582X9602300404

Abers, Rebecca Neaera and Margaret E. Keck. 2006. 'Muddy Waters: The Political Construction of Deliberative River Basin Governance in Brazil'. *International Journal of Urban and Regional Research* 30, no. 3: 601–622. https://doi.org/10.1111/j.1468-2427.2006.00691.x

Addie, Jean-Paul D. and Roger Keil. 2015. 'Real Existing Regionalism: The Region between Talk, Territory and Technology'. *International Journal of Urban and Regional Research* 39, no. 2: 407–417. https://doi.org/10.1111/1468-2427.12179

Akanani, Wendy Ovens and Associates, and the Resolve Group Consortium. 2007. Feasibility Study on a Metropolitan Form of Governance, Report 2: Gauteng Province: Preparation of Broad Options for Consideration. Report prepared for the Gauteng Provincial Government.

Akishin, Maxwell and Alexander Akishin. 2017. 'A 3-Hour Commute: A Close Look at Moscow the Metropolis'. *STELKA MAG*, 17 August 2017. https://strelkamag.com/en/article/moscow-agglomeration

Aligica, Paul D. and Filippo Sabetti. 2014. 'The Ostrom's Research Programme for the Study of Institutions and Governance: Theoretical and Epistemic Foundations'. In *Choice, Rules and Collective Action*, edited by Elinor Ostrom and Vincent Ostrom, 1–22. Colchester, UK: EPCR Press.

Amézquita, Jose L. Niño. 2021. 'Metropolitan Centralism, Governance and Service Delivery in Bogotá'. In *Metropolitan Governance in Latin America*, edited by Alejandra Trejo Nieto and Jose L. Niño Amézquita, 49–70. London: Routledge.

Ansell, Aaron. 2014. *Zero Hunger: Political Culture and Antipoverty Policy in Northeast Brazil*. Chapel Hill: University of North Carolina Press.

Anshun, Wang. 2016. 'Report on the Work of the Government 2016 (Part I)'. Speech delivered at the fourth session of the Fourteenth Beijing Municipal People's Congress, 22 January 2016. http://english.beijing.gov.cn/government/reports/202005/t20200511_1893945.html

Antunes, Cátia. 2003. 'Industrial Revolution and Urbanization: Towns and Factories, 1750–1850'. *Leidschrift: De Maatschappij Op Stoom* 18 (September): 34–49.

Aragão, Thêmis A. 2018. 'Pioneirismo na Gestão Compartilhada: Considerações Sobre a Experiência da Região Metropolitana de Belo Horizonte'. In *Brasil Metropolitano em foco Desafios à Implementação do Estatuto da Metrópole*, edited by Bárbara O. Marguti, Marco A. Costa and César B. Favarão, 197–216. Brazil: Ipea.

Argenbright, Robert, Victoriya R. Bityukova, Pavel L. Kirillov, Alla G. Makhrova and Tatyana G. Nefedova. 2020. 'Directed Suburbanization in a Changing Context: "New Moscow"

Today'. *Eurasian Geography and Economics* 61, no. 3: 211–239. https://doi.org/10.1080/1
5387216.2019.1707700

Arias, Enrique D. 2006. *Drugs and Democracy in Rio de Janeiro: Trafficking, Social Networks, and Public Security.* Chapel Hill, NC: University of North Carolina Press.

Asia Sentinel. 2017. 'Xi Jinping's Massive Urban Monument to Himself'. *Asia Sentinel*, 24 April 2017. https://www.asiasentinel.com/p/xi-jinping-urban-monument

Association of Siberian and Far Eastern Cities. 2018. Council of the Federation. Meeting of the Working Group on Improving the Legal Regulation of the Development of Urban Agglomerations, 13 November. https://www.asdg.ru/news/364362/

Avritzer, Leonardo. 2006. 'New Public Spheres in Brazil: Local Democracy and Deliberative Politics'. *International Journal of Urban and Regional Research* 30, no. 3: 623–637. https://doi.org/10.1111/j.1468-2427.2006.00692.x

Baculinao, Eric. 2017. 'Jing-Jin-Ji: China Planning Megalopolis the Size of New England'. *NBC News*, 26 March 2017. https://www.nbcnews.com/news/world/jing-jin-ji-china-planning-megalopolis-size-new-england-n734736

Baffi, Solène and Clémentine Cottineau. 2020. 'What is Emerging? Understanding Urbanisation Dynamics in BRICS Countries Through a Geographical Approach, the Case of Russia and South Africa'. In *Theories and Models of Urbanization*, edited by Denise Pumain, 209–234. Cham: Springer.

Baiocchi, Gianpaolo. 2003. 'Radicals in Power'. In *Radicals in Power: The Worker's Party and Experiments in Urban Democracy in Brazil*, edited by Gianpaolo Baiocchi, 1–26. London: Zed Books.

Ballard, Richard and Margot Rubin. 2017. 'A "Marshall Plan" for Human Settlements: How Megaprojects Became South Africa's Housing Policy'. *Transformation: Critical Perspectives on Southern Africa* 95, no. 1: 1–31. https://doi.org/10.1353/trn.2017.0020

Banerjee-Guha, Swapna. 2009. 'Neoliberalising the "Urban": New Geographies of Power and Injustice in Indian Cities'. *Economic and Political Weekly* 44, no. 22: 95–107.

Bansal, Pratima, Wendy K. Smith and Eero Vaara. 2018. 'New Ways of Seeing Through Qualitative Research'. *Academy of Management Journal* 61, no. 4: 1189–1195. https://doi.org/10.5465/amj.2018.4004

Barnes, Trevor J. and Eric Sheppard. 1992. 'Is There a Place for the Rational Actor? A Geographical Critique of the Rational Choice Paradigm'. *Economic Geography* 68, no. 1: 1–21.

Barres, Roger. 2021. 'Exploring Metropolitan Governance in the Öresund Region'. Masters thesis, Malmö University. https://www.diva-portal.org/smash/get/diva2:1524054/FULLTEXT02

Barreto, Ilson J. 2012. 'O Surgimento de Novas Regiões Metropolitanas no Brasil: Uma Discussão a Respeito do Caso de Sorocaba (SP)'. *Espaço e Economia. Revista Brasileira de Geografia Econômica* I, no. 1. https://doi.org/10.4000/espacoeconomia.374

Basten, Ludger. 2011. 'Stuttgart: A Metropolitan City-Region in the Making?' *International Planning Studies* 16, no. 3: 273–287. https://doi.org/10.1080/13563475.2011.591146

Batra, Lalit. 2009. *A Review of Urbanisation and Urban Policy in Post-Independent India.* CSLG Working Paper Series no. CSLG/WP/12. Centre for the Study of Law and Governance,

Jawaharlal Nehru University, New Delhi. https://www.jnu.ac.in/sites/default/files/u63/12-A%20Review%20of%20Urban%20%28Lalit%20Batra%29.pdf

Beall, Jo, Susan Parnell and Chris Albertyn. 2015. 'Elite Compacts in Africa: The Role of Area-Based Management in the New Governmentality of the Durban City-Region'. *International Journal of Urban and Regional Research* 39, no. 2: 390–406. https://doi.org/10.1111/1468-2427.12178

Beavon, Keith. 1998. '"Johannesburg": Coming to Grips with Globalization from an Abnormal Base'. In *Globalization and the World of Large Cities*, edited by Fu-chen Lo and Yue-man Yeung, 352–388. Tokyo: UNU Press.

Beavon, Keith S. 2004. *Johannesburg: The Making and Shaping of the City*. Pretoria: Unisa Press.

Beel, David, Martin Jones and Ian Rees Jones. 2018. 'Elite City-Deals for Economic Growth? Problematizing the Complexities of Devolution, City-Region Building, and the (Re)Positioning of Civil Society'. *Space and Polity* 22, no. 3: 307–327. https://doi.org/10.1080/13562576.2018.1532788

Bengtsson, Bo and Hannu Ruonavaara. 2017. 'Comparative Process Tracing: Making Historical Comparison Structured and Focused'. *Philosophy of the Social Sciences* 47, no. 1: 44–66. https://doi.org/10.1177%2F0048393116658549

Benjamin, Solomon. 2008. 'Occupancy Urbanism: Radicalizing Politics and Economy Beyond Policy and Programs'. *International Journal of Urban and Regional Research* 32, no. 3: 719–729. https://doi.org/10.1111/j.1468-2427.2008.00809.x

Bernsand, Niklas and Barbara Törnquist-Plewa. 2018. 'Introduction: Cultural and Political Imaginaries in Putin's Russia'. In *Cultural and Political Imaginaries in Putin's Russia*, edited by Niklas Bernsand and Barbara Törnquist-Plewa, 1–11. Boston: Brill.

Bhattacharya, Mohit. 1965. 'Government in Metropolitan Calcutta'. *Indian Journal of Public Administration* 11, no. 4: 702–720. https://doi.org/10.1177%2F0019556119650405

Bisht, Arvind S. 2011. 'Yamuna Township Realty in Trouble'. *The Times of India*, 24 October 2011. https://timesofindia.indiatimes.com/india/yamuna-township-realty-in-trouble/articleshow/10467580.cms

Bloch, Robin. 2000. 'Subnational Economic Development in Present-Day South Africa: Retrospect and Prospect'. *Urban Forum* 11, no. 2: 227–271.

Blumenfeld, Hans. 1965. 'The Modern Metropolis'. *Scientific American* 213, no. 3: 63–75.

Bobbins, Kerry and Christina C. Fatti. 2015. 'Green Growth Transitions Through a Green Infrastructure Approach at the Local Government Level: Case Study for the Gauteng City-Region'. *Journal of Public Administration* 50, no. 1: 32–49.

Bon, Bérénice. 2016. 'Megaproject, Rules and Relationships with the Law: The Metro Rail in East Delhi'. In *Space, Planning and Everyday Contestation in Delhi*, edited by Surajit Chakravarty and Rohit Negi, 181–197. New Delhi: Springer.

Borchert, Carol Ann. 2000. 'The Territories of the Russian Federation'. *Journal of Government Information* 27, no. 4: 519–521.

Brand, André, Hermanus S. Geyer and Hermanus S. Geyer Jr. 2017. 'Corridor Development in Gauteng, South Africa'. *GeoJournal* 82, no. 2: 311–327.

Brenner, Neil. 1999. 'Globalisation as Reterritorialisation: The Re-scaling of Urban Governance in the European Union'. *Urban Studies* 36, no. 3: 431–451. https://doi.org/10.1080%2F0042098993466

Brenner, Neil. 2002. 'Decoding the Newest "Metropolitan Regionalism" in the USA: A Critical Overview'. *Cities* 19, no. 1: 3–21. https://doi.org/10.1016/S0264-2751(01)00042-7

Brenner, Neil. 2014. *Implosions/Explosions: Towards a Study of Planetary Urbanization*. Berlin: Jovis.

Brenner, Neil. 2018. 'Debating Planetary Urbanization: For an Engaged Pluralism'. *Environment and Planning D: Society and Space* 36, no. 3: 570–590. https://doi.org/10.1177%2F0263775818757510

Brenner, Neil and Christian Schmid. 2013. 'The "Urban Age" in Question'. *International Journal of Urban and Regional Research* 38, no. 3: 731–755. https://doi.org/10.1111/1468-2427.12115

Brenner, Neil and Christian Schmid. 2015. 'Towards a New Epistemology of the Urban?'. *City* 19, no. 2–3: 151–182. https://doi.org/10.1080/13604813.2015.1014712

Brill, Frances. 2022. 'Constructing Comparisons: Reflecting on the Experimental Nature of New Comparative Tactics'. *Urban Studies* 59, no. 8: 1754–1759. https://doi.org/10.1177%2F00420980221089590

Browne, Junius H. 1869. *The Great Metropolis: A Mirror of New York*. Hartford: American Publishing Company.

Bruz, V. Vladimir, Sergey F. Vititnev and Anatoly V. Solodilov. 2019. 'Peculiarities of the Urban Governance Formation in Moscow in the First Years of Soviet Power and its Historical Significance'. *Religación* 4, no. 13: 145–152.

Büdenbender, Mirjam and Daniela Zupen. 2016. 'The Evolution of Neoliberal Urbanism in Moscow: 1992–2015'. *Antipode* 49, no. 2: 294–313. https://doi.org/10.1111/anti.12266

Bunnell, Tim and Alice M. Nah. 2004. 'Counter-Global Cases for Place: Contesting Displacement in Globalising Kuala Lumpur Metropolitan Area'. *Urban Studies* 41, no. 12: 2447–2467. https://doi.org/10.1080%2F00420980412331297627

Burridge, Andrew, Nick Gill, Austin Kocher and Lauren Martin. 2017. 'Polymorphic Borders'. *Territory, Politics, Governance* 5, no. 3: 239–251. https://doi.org/10.1080/21622671.2017.1297253

Caldeira, Teresa P.R. 2001. *City of Walls: Crime, Segregation, and Citizenship in São Paulo*. Berkeley: University of California Press.

Cameron, Robert. 1993. 'Regional Services Councils in South Africa: Past, Present and Future'. *Public Administration* 71, no. 3: 417–439. https://doi.org/10.1111/j.1467-9299.1993.tb00983.x

Cameron, Robert. 2000. 'Megacities in South Africa: A Solution for the New Millennium?'. *Public Administration and Development* 20, no. 2: 155–165. https://doi.org/10.1002/1099-162X(200005)20:2%3C155::AID-PAD120%3E3.0.CO;2-A

Campbell, Adrian. 2016. '"Imperialism" and "Federalism": The Ambiguity of State and City in Russia'. In *Theoretical Foundations and Discussions on the Reformation Process in Local Governments*, edited by Ugur Sadioglu and Kadir Dede, 353–372. Hershey, USA: IGI Global.

Cartier, Carolyn. 2015. 'Fire 火: The City That Ate China: Restructuring and Reviving Beijing'. In *China Story Yearbook 2015 Pollution*, edited by Gloria Davies, Jeremy Goldkorn and Luigi Tomba, 182–201. Canberra, Australia: ANU Press.

CDE (Centre for Development and Enterprise). 2002. 'Johannesburg, Africa's World City: A Challenge to Action'. *CDE*, 18 October 2002. https://www.cde.org.za/johannesburg-africas-world-city-a-challenge-to-action/

Chan, Roger C.K., Xin Mai and Shimou Yao. 2021. 'A Review of Urban Agglomeration and China's Urbanisation Strategy'. In *Mega-City Region Development in China*, edited by Anthony G.O. Yeh, George C.S. Lin and Fiona F. Yang, 22–40. Oxon: Routledge.

Chen, Xiangming and Tomás de'Medici. 2013. 'From a Fishing Village via an Instant City to a Secondary Global City: The "Miracle" and Growth Pains of Shenzhen Special Economic Zone in China'. In *Rethinking Global Urbanism*, edited by Xiangming Chen and Ahmed Kanna, 125–144. London: Routledge.

Cheng, Tony. 2017. 'CY Leung Leads Hong Kong Delegation on Greater Bay Area Tour as Part of Integration Drive'. *South China Morning Post*, 19 April 2017. https://www.scmp.com/news/hong-kong/politics/article/2088769/cy-leung-leads-hong-kong-delegation-greater-bay-area-tour

Cheruiyot, Koech, ed. 2018. *The Changing Space Economy of City Regions: The Gauteng City-Region, South Africa*. Cham: Springer.

China Daily. 2018. 'China Begins 3-yr Plan to Integrate Yangtze Delta Region'. *ChinaDaily.com.cn*, 20 July 2018. https://www.chinadaily.com.cn/a/201807/20/WS5b51a8d2a310796df4df7bdf.html

Chiriyankandath, James. 1996. 'Hindu Nationalism and Regional Political Culture in India: A Study of Kerala'. *Nationalism and Ethnic Politics* 2, no. 1: 44–66. https://doi.org/10.1080/13537119608428458

Choplin, Armelle and Alice Hertzog. 2020. 'The West African Corridor from Abidjan to Lagos: A Megacity-Region Under Construction'. In *Handbook of Megacities and Mega-City Regions*, edited by Danielle Labbé and André Sorenson, 206–222. Cheltenham, UK: Edward Elgar Publishing.

Coakley, John. 2009. 'The Foundations of Statehood'. In *Politics in the Republic of Ireland*, 5th edition, edited by John Coakley and Michael Gallagher, 3–36. London: Routledge.

COGTA (Department of Cooperative Governance and Traditional Affairs). 2019. 'Concept Note: District Development Model to Improve the Coherence and Impact of Government Service Delivery and Development'. Electronic copy in the possession of the author.

Cole, Monica M. 1957. 'The Witwatersrand Conurbation: A Watershed Mining and Industrial Region'. *Transactions and Papers (Institute of British Geographers)* 23: 249–265. https://doi.org/10.2307/621166

Collin, Jean-Pierre and Mariona Tomàs. 2004. 'Metropolitan Governance in Canada or the Persistence of Institutional Reforms'. *Urban Public Economics Review* 2: 13–39.

Colton, Timothy J. 1995. *Moscow: Governing the Socialist Metropolis*. London: The Belknap Press of Harvard University Press.

Corbridge, Stuart and John Harriss. 2000. *Reinventing India: Liberalization, Hindu Nationalism and Popular Democracy*. Cambridge: Polity Press.

Corbridge, Stuart, Glyn Williams, Manoj Srivistava and René Veron. 2005. *Seeing the State: Governance and Governmentality in India.* Cambridge: Cambridge University Press.

Costa, Heloisa, João Tonucci and Jupira Mendonca. 2014. 'Metropolitan Planning Revisited: Evolution Since the Pioneer Experience of Plambel, Belo Horizonte, Brazil'. In *International Planning History Society Proceedings* 16, no. 1: 153–166.

Costa, Marco A., Cesar B. Favarão, Sara R. Tavares and Cid Blanco Júnior. 2018. 'Do Processo de Metropolização Institucional à Implementação do Estatuto da Metrópole: Dois Balanços, Suas Expectativas e Incertezas'. In *Brasil Metropolitano em Foco: Desafios à Implementação do Estatuto da Metrópole,* edited by Bárbara O. Marguti, Marco A. Costa and César B. Favarão, 19–54. Brazil: Ipea.

Cox, Kevin R. and Emil Evenhuis. 2020. 'Theorising in Urban and Regional Studies: Negotiating Generalisation and Particularity'. *Cambridge Journal of Regions, Economy and Society* 13, no. 3: 425–442. https://doi.org/10.1093/cjres/rsaa036

Croese, Sylvia. 2018. 'Global Urban Policymaking in Africa: A View from Angola Through the Redevelopment of the Bay of Luanda'. *International Journal of Urban and Regional Research* 42, no. 2: 198–209. https://doi.org/10.1111/1468-2427.12591

Crush, Jonathan, Alan Jeeves and David Yudelman. 1991. *South Africa's Labor Empire: A History of Black Migrancy to the Gold Mines.* Boulder, CO: Westview Press.

Dash, Padma L. 2010. 'Ancient Nisa: Centre of Synergy Along the Silk Route'. *The Journal of Central Asian Studies* XIX: 17–24.

Davis, Michael C. 1998. 'Constitutionalism and Political Culture: The Debate over Human Rights and Asian Values'. *Harvard Human Rights Journal* 11: 109–148.

Davoudi, Simin and Elizabeth Brooks. 2021. 'City-Regional Imaginaries and Politics of Rescaling'. *Regional Studies* 55, no. 1: 52–62. https://doi.org/10.1080/00343404.2020.1762856

DDA (Delhi Development Authority). 1962. *Master Plan for 1962.* https://dda.gov.in/master-plan-1962

De Boeck, Filip. 2020. 'Urban Expansion, the Politics of Land, and Occupation as Infrastructure in Kinshasa'. *Land Use Policy* 93: 103880. https://doi.org/10.1016/j.landusepol.2019.02.039

De Boeck, Filip and Marie-Françoise Plissart. 2014. *Kinshasa: Tales of the Invisible City.* Belgium: Leuven University Press.

De Kadt, Julia, Christian Hamann, Sthembiso Mhkize and Alexandra Parker. 2021. *Quality of Life Survey 6 (2020/21),* a report of the Gauteng City-Region Observatory. https://cdn.gcro.ac.za/media/documents/2021.09.09_QoL_6_2020-21_overview_report_v7.pdf

De Lima Caldas, Eduardo and Ivaldo Moreira. 2013. 'Políticas de Desenvolvimento Territorial e Intermunicipalidade no Brasil: Complementaridades e Tensões'. *Sustentabilidade em Debate* 4, no. 2: 41–61.

De Souza Briggs, Xavier. 2008. *Democracy as Problem Solving: Civic Capacity in Communities across the Globe.* Cambridge, MA: The MIT Press.

Del Fabbro, Matteo. 2020. 'Representing the Milan Metropolitan Region from a Public Policy Perspective'. *Area* 52, no. 1: 126–135.

Demazière, Christophe and Olivier Sykes. 2021. 'Acting for Cities and Towns? The Perpetual Reinvention of Categories and Tools of National Urban Policies in France'. In *A Modern*

Guide to National Urban Policies in Europe, edited by Karsten Zimmermann and Valeria Fedeli, 34–57. Cheltenham, UK: Edward Elgar Publishing.

Dickinson, Robert E. 1947. *City Region and Regionalism: A Geographical Contribution to Human Ecology*. London: Trubner.

Dickinson, Robert E. 1964. *City and Region: A Geographical Interpretation*. London: Routledge & Kegan Paul.

Ding, Xuedong and Jun Li. 2015. *Incentives for Innovation in China: Building an Innovative Economy*. London: Routledge.

Diniz, Clélio C. 1994. 'Polygonized Development in Brazil: Neither Decentralization nor Continued Polarization'. *International Journal of Urban and Regional Research* 18, no. 2: 293–314. https://doi.org/10.1111/j.1468-2427.1994.tb00267.x

Dogra, Chander S. 2013. 'Undermining Urban Planning'. *The Hindu*, 22 November 2013. https://www.thehindu.com/opinion/op-ed/undermining-urban-planning/article 5376474.ece?homepage=true

Doxiadis, Constantinos A. 1962. 'Ecumenopolis: Toward a Universal City'. *Ekistics* 13, no. 75: 3–18.

Doxiadis, Constantinos A. 1975. 'Metropolis and Megalopolis'. *Ekistics* 39, no. 233: 213–216.

Durose, Catherine and Vivien Lowndes. 2021. 'Why are Designs for Urban Governance so Often Incomplete? A Conceptual Framework for Explaining and Harnessing Institutional Incompleteness'. *Politics and Space C: Policy and Space* 39, no. 8: 1773–1790. https://doi.org/10.1177/2399654421990673

Dutt, A.K. and S.C. Chakraborty. 1963. 'Reality of Calcutta Conurbation'. *National Geographical Journal of India* 9, no. 3&4: 161–174.

Eisenhardt, Kathleen M., Melissa Graebner and Scott Sonenshein. 2016. 'Grand Challenges and Inductive Methods: Rigor without Rigor Mortis'. *Academy of Management Journal* 59, no. 4: 1113–1123. https://doi.org/10.5465/amj.2016.4004

Ekdi, Fatma Pelin and Mahyar Arefi. 2019. 'An Interstitial Reading of Istanbul'. *ICONARP International Journal of Architecture and Planning* 7: 182–211. https://doi.org/10.15320/ICONARP.2019.85

Elmes, J. 1828. *Metropolitan Improvements; or London in the Nineteenth Century*. London: Jones and Co.

Etzold, Benjamin and Markus Keck. 2009. 'Politics of Space in the Megacity Dhaka: Negotiation of Rules in Contested Urban Arenas'. *UGEC Viewpoints* 2: 13–15.

Europa. 2016. *The Territories of the Russian Federation, 2016*, 17th edition. London and New York: Routledge

Evans, Ivan. 1997. *Bureaucracy and Race: Native Administration in South Africa*. Berkeley: University of California Press.

Fair, Thomas J.D. 1957. 'Regions for Planning in South Africa'. *South African Geographical Journal* 39, no. 1: 26–50. https://doi.org/10.1080/03736245.1957.10559326

Fair, Thomas J.D. and Edward W.N. Mallows. 1959. 'The Southern Transvaal: An Emerging Metropolitan Complex in Africa'. *The Town Planning Review* 30, no. 2: 138–152.

Fair, Thomas J.D. and John Muller. 1981. 'The Johannesburg Metropolitan Area'. In *Urban Problems and Planning in the Developed World*, edited by Michael Pacione, 157–188. New York: Routledge.

Faludi, Andreas. 2015. 'The "Blue Banana" Revisited'. *European Journal of Spatial Development* 13, no. 1. https://doi.org/10.5281/zenodo.5141230

Fawcett, Charles B. 1922. 'British Conurbations in 1921'. *The Sociological Review* 14, no. 2: 111–122. https://doi.org/10.1111/j.1467-954X.1922.tb02860.x

Feiock, Richard C. 2009. 'Metropolitan Governance and Institutional Collective Action'. *Urban Affairs Review* 44, no. 3: 356–377. https://doi.org/10.1177/1078087408324000

Feiock, Richard C. 2013. 'The Institutional Collective Action Framework'. *Policy Studies Journal* 41, no. 3: 397–425. https://doi.org/10.1111/psj.12023

Feldmann, Magnus and Honorate Mazepus. 2018. 'State-Society Relations and the Sources of Support for the Putin Regime: Bridging Political Culture and Social Contract Theory'. *East European Politics* 34, no. 1: 57–76. https://doi.org/10.1080/21599165.2017.1414697

Fernandes, Antonio S.A. 2013. 'Metropolitan Governance and Institutional Change in Brazil: The Autonomous Localism and Metropolitan Local Finance'. Paper presented at the First International Conference of Public Policy (1st ICPP), Sciences Po Grenoble, France, 26–28 June 2013.

Fernandes, Leela. 2004. 'The Politics of Forgetting: Class Politics, State Power and the Restructuring of Urban Space in India'. *Urban Studies* 41, no. 12: 2415–2430. https://doi.org/10.1080%2F00420980412331297609

Filtzer, Donald. 2006. 'Standard of Living Versus Quality of Life: Struggling with the Urban Environment in Russia During the Early Years of Post-War Reconstruction'. In *Late Stalinist Russia: Society Between Reconstruction and Reinvention*, edited by Juliane Fürst, 81–102. Abingdon, Oxon: Routledge.

Fink, Alexander. 2012. 'The Hanseatic League and the Concept of Functional Overlapping Competing Jurisdictions'. *Kyklos* 65, no. 2: 194–217. https://doi.org/10.1111/j.1467-6435.2012.00534.x

Firman, Tommy. 2014. 'Inter-Local-Government Partnership for Urban Management in Decentralizing Indonesia: From Below or Above? Kartamantul (Greater Yogyakarta) and Jabodetabek (Greater Jakarta) Compared'. *Space and Polity* 18, no. 3: 215–232. https://doi.org/10.1080/13562576.2014.959252

Florida, Richard, Tim Gulden and Charlotta Mellander. 2008. *The Rise of the Mega-Region*. CESIS Electronic Working Paper Series no. 129. Royal Institute of Technology, Stockholm. https://static.sys.kth.se/itm/wp/cesis/cesiswp129.pdf

Fox, William T.R. and Annette Baker Fox. 1940. 'Municipal Government and Special-Purpose Authorities'. *The ANNALS of the American Academy of Political and Social Science* 207, no. 1: 176–184. https://doi.org/10.1177%2F000271624020700123

Freeman, Richard. 2007. 'Epistemological Bricolage: How Practitioners Make Sense of Learning'. *Administration and Society* 39, no. 4: 476–496. https://doi.org/10.1177%2F0095399707301857

Freeman, Thomas W. 1959. *The Conurbations of Great Britain*. Manchester: Manchester University Press.

Friedmann, John R. 1956. 'The Concept of a Planning Region'. *Land Economics* 32, no. 1: 1–13.

Friedmann, John. 1964. 'Regional Development in Post-industrial Society'. *Journal of the American Institute of Planners* 30, no. 2: 84–90. https://doi.org/10.1080/01944366408978101

Friedmann, John. 2020. 'Thinking About Mega-Conurbations and Planning'. In *Handbook of Megacities and Megacity Regions*, edited by Danielle Labbé and André Sorenson, 21–32. Cheltenham, UK: Edward Elgar Publishing.

Friedmann, John and André Sorensen. 2019. 'City Unbound: Emerging Mega-Conurbations in Asia'. *International Planning Studies* 24, no. 1: 1–12. https://doi.org/10.1080/13563475.2019.1555314

Friedmann, John and Goetz Wolff. 1982. 'World City Formation: An Agenda for Research and Action'. *International Journal of Urban and Regional Research* 6, no. 3: 309–344. https://doi.org/10.1111/j.1468-2427.1982.tb00384.x

Fuchs, Ralph. 1936. 'Regional Agencies for Metropolitan Areas'. *Washington University Law Quarterly* 22, no. 1: 64–78.

Gallois, Lucien. 1923. 'The Origin and Growth of Paris'. *Geographical Review* 13, no. 3: 345–367. https://doi.org/10.2307/208275

Gastrow, Claudia. 2020. 'Urban States: The Presidency and Planning in Luanda, Angola'. *International Journal of Urban and Regional Research* 44, no. 2: 366–383. https://doi.org/10.1111/1468-2427.12854

Gauteng Province. 2005. 'Study Tour Report: Lessons for the Global City-Region Strategy'. Gauteng delegation to Sao Paulo, 15–22 January 2005. Unpublished document loaned to the author.

Geddes, Patrick. 1915. *Cities in Evolution: An Introduction to the Town-Planning Movement and the Study of Cities*. London: Williams and Norgate.

Gehman, Joel, Vern L. Glaser, Kathleen M. Eisenhardt, Denny Gioia, Ann Langley and Kevin G. Corley. 2018. 'Finding Theory–Method Fit: A Comparison of Three Qualitative Approaches to Theory Building'. *Journal of Management Inquiry* 27, no. 3: 284–300. https://doi.org/10.1177%2F1056492617706029

Gel'man, Vladimir. 2015. *Authoritarian Russia: Analyzing Post-Soviet Regime Changes*. Pittsburgh, PA: University of Pittsburgh Press.

Gel'man, Vladimir and Sergei Ryzhenkov. 2011. Local Regimes, Sub-national Governance and the "Power Vertical" in Contemporary Russia'. *Europe-Asia Studies* 63, no. 3: 449–465. https://doi.org/10.1080/09668136.2011.557538

Geography. n.d. 'City Agglomerations of Russia' (translated). Accessed 12 August 2022. https://geographyofrussia.com/gorodskie-aglomeracii-rossii/

Ghosh, Swamabh and Ayan Meer. 2021. 'Extended Urbanisation and the Agrarian Question: Convergences, Divergences and Openings'. *Urban Studies* 58, no. 6: 1097–1119. https://doi.org/10.1177%2F0042098020943758

Glover, Will. 2021. 'The Other Agrarian Urbanisation: Urbanism in the Village'. *Urbanisation* 6, no. 1: 35–48. https://doi.org/10.1177%2F24557471211016591

Godo, Yoshihisa. 2020. 'Thriving Tokyo and Declining Osaka: The Role of the Local Governance System'. In *Metropolitan Circles Development and the Future of Urbanization*, edited by Wei Shan and Lijun Yang, 19–33. Singapore: World Scientific Publishing.

Goldsmith, Michael. 2004. 'The Experience of Metropolitan Government in England'. In *Metropolitan Governance in the 21st Century*, edited by Hubert Heinelt and Daniel Kübler, 93–111. London: Routledge.

Golubchikov, Oleg. 2004. 'Urban Planning in Russia: Towards the Market'. *European Planning Studies* 12, no. 2: 229–247. https://doi.org/10.1080/0965431042000183950

Golubchikov, Oleg. 2010. 'World-City-Entrepreneurialism: Globalist Imaginaries, Neoliberal Geographies, and the Production of New St Petersburg'. *Environment and Planning A: Economy and Space* 42, no. 3: 626–643. https://doi.org/10.1068%2Fa39367

Golubchikov, Oleg and Nicholas A. Phelps. 2011. 'The Political Economy of Place at the Post-socialist Urban Periphery: Governing Growth on the Edge of Moscow'. *Transactions of the Institute of British Geographers* 36, no. 3: 425–440. https://doi.org/10.1111/j.1475-5661.2011.00427.x

Gomme, G.L. 1914. *London*. London: JB Lippincott Company.

Gordon, Douglas, ed. 2019. *Nordic-Baltic Space Transnational Development Perspective*. Urban Environmental Publications 2019/09. City of Helsinki: Urban Environment Division. https://www.hel.fi/static/liitteet/kaupunkiymparisto/julkaisut/julkaisut/julkaisu-09-19.pdf

Gottman, Jean. 1957. 'Megalopolis or the Urbanization of the Northeastern Seaboard'. *Economic Geography* 33, no. 3: 189–200.

Gottman, Jean. 1961. *Megalopolis. The Urbanized Eastern Seaboard of the United States*. New York: Twentieth Century Fund.

Gottman, Jean. 1981. 'Managing Megalopolis in Europe: Review'. *The Geographical Journal* 147, no. 1: 85–87. https://doi.org/10.2307/633413

Götz, Graeme and Alexis Schaeffler. 2015. 'Conundrums in Implementing a Green Economy in the Gauteng City-Region'. *Current Opinion in Environmental Sustainability* 13: 79–87.

Götz, Graeme, Chris Wray and Brian Mubiya. 2014. 'The "Thin Oil of Urbanisation"? Spatial Change in Johannesburg and the Gauteng City-Region'. In *Changing Space, Changing City: Johannesburg After Apartheid*, edited by Philip Harrison, Graeme Götz, Alison Todes and Chris Wray, 42–62. Johannesburg: Wits University Press.

Government of Brazil. 2018. *Statute of the Metropolis Federal Law No. 13,089*. http://www.planalto.gov.br/ccivil_03/_ato2015-2018/2015/lei/l13089.htm

Government of India. 1992. 'The Constitution (74th Amendment) Act, 1992. Part IXA, P243(c)'. https://legislative.gov.in/constitution-seventy-fourth-amendment-act-1992

Government of India. 2017. 'Aravallis to be Delineated in the Entire NCB'. *Press Information Bureau*, 4 December 2017. http://pib.nic.in/newsite/PrintRelease.aspx?relid=174084

Government of the Russian Federation. 2011a. 'Decree of the Government of the Russian Federation of February 15, 2011 N 82 on the Coordinating Council for the Development of the Transport System of Moscow and the Moscow Region' (translated). https://base.garant.ru/6748326/

Government of the Russian Federation. 2011b. 'The Decree of the Government of the Russian Federation of April 4, 2011, No. 241'. https://spbtrd.ru/en/coordinating-council/

Government of the Russian Federation. 2019. 'Spatial Development Strategy for the Russian Federation for the Period up to 2025'. *Government Gazette* 13 February, no. 207-p. http://static.government.ru/media/files/UVAlqUtT08o60RktoOXl22JjAe7irNxc.pdf

Government of Saint Petersburg. 2005. 'Law of St. Petersburg "On the General Plan of St. Petersburg" of December 22, 2005 N 728-99'. https://peterburg-pravo.ru/zakon/2005-12-22-n-728-99/

Granqvist, Kalsa, Alois Humer and Raine Mäntysalo. 2021. 'Tensions in City-Regional Spatial Planning: The Challenge of Interpreting Layered Institutional Rules'. *Regional Studies* 55, no. 5: 844–856. https://doi.org/10.1080/00343404.2019.1707791

Grant, James. 1837. *The Great Metropolis*. London: Saunders and Otley.

Greenberg, Stephen. 2010. 'The Gauteng City-Region: Private and Public Power in the Shaping of the City'. *Politikon* 37, no. 1: 107–127. http://dx.doi.org/10.1080/02589346.2010.492152

GTAC (Government Technical Advisory Centre), National Treasury. 2022. 'Institutional Arrangements and Capacity in the Presidency re District Development Model (DDM)'. https://www.gtac.gov.za/wp-content/uploads/2022/03/DDM-GTAC-weekly-webinar.pdf

Gu, Chaolin, Yehua D. Wei and Ian G. Cook. 2015. 'Planning Beijing: Socialist City, Transitional City, and Global City'. *Urban Geography* 36, no. 6: 905–926. https://doi.org/10.1080/02723638.2015.1067409

Gualini, Enrico and Carola Fricke. 2019. 'Who Governs Berlin's Metropolitan Region? The Strategic-Relational Construction of Metropolitan Scale in Berlin–Brandenburg's Economic Development Policies'. *Environment and Planning C: Politics and Space* 37, no. 1: 59–80. https://doi.org/10.1177%2F2399654418776549

Gupta, Akhil. 2012. *Red Tape: Bureaucracy, Structural Violence, and Poverty in India*. Durham, NC: Duke University Press.

Guzman, Luis A., Daniel Oviedo and Juan Pablo Bocarejo. 2017. 'City Profile: The Bogotá Metropolitan Area That Never Was'. *Cities* 60: 202–215. https://doi.org/10.1016/j.cities.2016.09.004

Hagler, Yoav. 2009. 'Defining US Megaregions'. *America 2050*: 1–8.

Hagopian, Frances. 1996. *Traditional Politics and Regime Change in Brazil*. Cambridge: Cambridge University Press.

Hahn, Gordon M. 2002. *Russia's Revolution from Above, 1985–2000: Reform, Transition and Revolution in the Fall of the Soviet Communist Regime*. New York: Routledge.

Hahn, Jeffrey W. 1988. *Soviet Grassroots: Citizen Participation in Local Soviet Government*. London: Tauris & Co.

Hall, Peter. 1966. *The World Cities*. London: Weidenfeld and Nicolson.

Harber, Jesse and Kate Joseph. 2018. *Institutionalising the Gauteng City Region*. Governing the Gauteng City-Region Provocations Series, no. 03. Gauteng City-Region Observatory, Johannesburg. http://www.gcro.ac.za/media/reports/Provocation_Institutionalisting_the_GCR.pdf

Harrison, John. 2010. 'Networks of Connectivity, Territorial Fragmentation, Uneven Development: The New Politics of City-Regionalism'. *Political Geography* 29, no. 1: 17–27. https://doi.org/10.1016/j.polgeo.2009.12.002

Harrison, John. 2017. 'Constructing Alternative Paths to City-Region Policy and Governance'. In *Territorial Policy and Governance: Alternative Paths*, edited by Iain Deas and Stephen Hincks, 53–70. Abingdon, Oxon: Routledge.

Harrison, John and Hao Gu. 2021. 'Planning Megaregional Futures: Spatial Imaginaries and Megaregion Formation in China'. *Regional Studies* 55, no. 1: 77–89. https://doi.org/10.1080/00343404.2019.1679362

Harrison, John and Jesse Heley. 2015. 'Governing Beyond the Metropolis: Placing the Rural in City-Region Development'. *Urban Studies* 52, no. 6: 1113–1133. https://doi.org/10.1177%2F0042098014532853

Harrison, Philip and Yan Yang. 2020. 'Drivers of Density Change: The Case of Beijing, China'. In *Densifying the City? Global Cases and Johannesburg*, edited by Margot Rubin, Alison Todes, Philip Harrison and Alexandra Appelbaum, 93–102. Cheltenham, UK: Edward Elgar Publishing.

Harriss-White, Barbara. 1997. *Informal Economic Order: Shadow States, Private Status States, States of Last Resort and Spinning States: A Speculative Discussion Based on S. Asian Case Material*. QEH Working Paper Series 6. Queen Elizabeth House, Oxford.

Haveman, Heather A., Hayagreeva Rao and Srikanth Paruchuri. 2007. 'The Winds of Change: The Progressive Movement and the Bureaucratization of Thrift'. *American Sociological Review* 72, no. 1: 117–142. https://doi.org/10.1177%2F000312240707200106

He, Baogang and Mark E. Warren. 2011. 'Authoritarian Deliberation: The Deliberative Turn in Chinese Political Development'. *Perspectives on Politics* 9, no. 2: 269–289. https://doi.org/10.1017/S1537592711000892

Healey, Patsy. 2005. 'Network Complexity and the Imaginative Power of Strategic Spatial Planning'. In *The Network Society: A New Context for Planning*, edited by Louis Albrechts and Seymour J. Mandelbaum, 146–160. London: Routledge.

Healey, Patsy. 2009. 'City Regions and Place Development'. *Regional Studies* 43, no. 6: 831–843. https://doi.org/10.1080/00343400701861336

Heller, Patrick. 2012. 'Democracy, Participatory Politics and Development: Some Comparative Lessons from Brazil, India and South Africa'. *Polity* 44, no. 4: 643–665. https://doi.org/10.1057/pol.2012.19

Heller, Patrick and Partha Mukhopadhyay. 2016. 'Delhi'. Centre for Policy Research. http://www.urbaneconomics.ru/sites/default/files/3._india_patrick_heller_partha_mukhopadhyay.pdf

Hendler, Paul. 1992. 'Living in Apartheid's Shadow: Residential Planning for Africans in the PWV Region 1970–1990'. *Urban Forum* 3, no. 2: 39–80.

Hermelin, Brita and Bo Persson. 2021. 'Regional Governance in Second-Tier City-Regions in Sweden: A Multi-scalar Approach to Institutional Change'. *Regional Studies* 55, no. 8: 1365–1375. https://doi.org/10.1080/00343404.2021.1896693

Hodson, Mike, Andrew McMeekin, Julie Froud and Michael Moran. 2020. 'State-Rescaling and Re-designing the Material City-Region: Tensions of Disruption and Continuity in Articulating the Future of Greater Manchester'. *Urban Studies* 57, no. 1: 198–217. https://doi.org/10.1177%2F0042098018820181

Hofmeyr, Isabel and Michelle Williams. 2011. *South Africa and India: Shaping the Global South*. Johannesburg: Wits University Press.

Holloway, James. 2012. 'New Moscow: Plans Afoot to Double the Size of Russia's Capital'. *New Atlas*, 14 September 2012. https://newatlas.com/new-moscow/24139/

Huang, Tsung-yi M. 2006. 'The Cosmopolitan Imaginary and Flexible Identities of Global City-Regions: Articulating New Cultural Identities in Taipei and Shanghai'. *Inter-Asia Cultural Studies* 7, no. 3: 472–491. https://doi.org/10.1080/14649370600849330

Huchzermeyer, Marie. 2004. *Unlawful Occupation: Informal Settlements and Urban Policy in South Africa and Brazil*. Trenton, NJ: Africa World Press.

Hunn, David. 2019. 'Better Together Pulls St. Louis City-County Merger Proposal'. *Saint Louis-Post Dispatch*, 7 May 2019. https://www.stltoday.com/news/local/govt-and-politics/better-together-pulls-st-louis-city-county-merger-proposal/article_c71a51d2-998b-5e95-9926-ad3707671690.html

Huynh, Du. 2020. *Making Megacities in Asia: Comparing National Economic Development Trajectories*. Singapore: Springer.

Hwang, Uijeong and Myungje Woo. 2020. 'Analysis of Inter-relationships between Urban Decline and Urban Sprawl in City-Regions of South Korea'. *Sustainability* 12, no. 4: 1656. https://doi.org/10.3390/su12041656

Inglehart, Ronald. 1988. 'The Renaissance of Political Culture'. *The American Political Science Review* 82, no. 4: 1203–1230. https://doi.org/10.2307/1961756

International Statistical Institute. 1911. *Journal of the Royal Statistical Society* 75, no. 1: 51–63. https://doi.org/10.2307/2340337

IPEA (Institute for Applied Economic Research). 2019. *Politica Metropolitana: Governança, Instrumentos e Planejamento Metropolitanos: II Seminário*. Brazil: Ipea. http://repositorio.ipea.gov.br/bitstream/11058/9126/1/Pol%C3%ADtica%20metropolitana_governança_%20instrumentos%20e%20planejamento.pdf

Ito, Tatsuo and Catherine Nagashima. 1980. 'Tokaido – Megalopolis of Japan'. *GeoJournal* 4, no. 3: 231–246.

Jackson, James H. Jr. 1977. *Migration and Urbanization in the Ruhr Valley, 1821–1914*. Boston, MA: Humanities Press.

Jacuniak-Suda, Marta, Cormac Walsh and Jörg Knieling. 2015. 'Governance Arrangements in the Hamburg Metropolitan Region: Between Hard and Soft Institutional Spaces'. In *Soft Spaces in Europe: Re-negotiating Governance, Boundaries and Borders*, edited by Phil Allmendinger, Graham Haughton, Jörg Knieling and Frank Othengrafen, 67–98. Abingdon, Oxon: Routledge.

Jain, Pankaj. 2021. 'Sad Day for Indian Democracy: Delhi CM Kejriwal on Passage of NCT Bill in Rajya Sabha'. *India Today*, 24 March 2021. https://www.indiatoday.in/india/story/delhi-cm-kejriwal-reacts-to-passage-nct-bill-rajya-sabha-1783262-2021-03-24

Jensen, Donald N. 2000. 'The Boss: How Yuri Luzhkov Runs Moscow'. *Demokratizatsiya* 8: 83–122.

Jining, Chen. 2018. 'Report on the Work of the Government 2018 (Part I)'. Speech delivered at the first session of the Fifteenth Beijing Municipal People's Congress, 24 January 2018. http://english.beijing.gov.cn/government/reports/202005/t20200511_1893828.html

Jodkha, Surinder S. 2002. 'Nation and Village: Images of Rural India in Gandhi, Nehru and Ambedkar'. *Economic and Political Weekly* 37, no. 32: 3343–3353.

John, Jonathan D. and James Putzel. 2009. 'Political Settlements Issues Paper', Governance
and Social Development Resource Centre Report. International Development
Department, University of Birmingham. http://epapers.bham.ac.uk/645/1/EIRS7.pdf

Johnson, Katherine M. 2006. 'Sovereigns and Subjects: A Geopolitical History of
Metropolitan Reform in the USA'. *Environment and Planning A: Economy and Space* 38, no.
1: 149–168. https://doi.org/10.1068%2Fa37263

Jonas, Andrew E.G. and Kevin Ward. 2007. 'Introduction to a Debate on City-Regions:
New Geographies of Governance, Democracy and Social Reproduction'. *International
Journal of Urban and Regional Research* 31, no. 1: 167–178. https://doi.org/10.1111/
j.1468-2427.2007.00711.x

Jonson, Lena. 2018. 'Introduction'. In *Russia: Art Resistance and the Conservative-Authoritarian
Zeitgeist*, edited by Lena Jonson and Andrei Erofeev, 1–24. London: Routledge.

Kanai, J. Miguel and Seth Schindler. 2022. 'Infrastructure-Led Development and the Peri-
urban Question: Furthering Crossover Comparisons'. *Urban Studies* 59, no. 8: 1597–1617.
https://doi.org/10.1177%2F00420980211064158

Kasraian, Dena, Kees Maat and Bert van Wee. 2016. 'Development of Rail Infrastructure
and its Impact on Urbanization in the Randstad, the Netherlands'. *Journal of Transport and
Land Use* 9, no. 1: 151–170.

Keil, Roger. 2017. *Suburban Planet: Making the World Urban from the Outside In*. Hoboken,
NJ: John Wiley & Sons.

Keil, Roger. 2018. 'Extended Urbanisation, "Disjunct Fragments" and Global Suburbanisms'.
Environment and Planning D: Society and Space 36, no. 3: 494–511. https://doi.
org/10.1177/0263775817749594

Keil, Roger, and Jean-Paul D. Addie. 2015. '"It's Not Going to be Suburban, it's Going
to be All Urban": Assembling Post-suburbia in the Toronto and Chicago Regions'.
International Journal of Urban and Regional Research 39, no. 5: 892–911. https://doi.
org/10.1111/1468-2427.12303

Kelly, Kirsten. 2021. 'Is Gauteng Water Secure or is Day Zero Looming?' *Water&Sanitation
Africa* 16, no. 2: 20–24.

Kelsall, Tim. 2018. 'Towards a Universal Political Settlement Concept: A Response to
Mushtaq Khan'. *African Affairs* 117, no. 469: 656–669. https://doi.org/10.1093/afraf/
ady018

Kennedy, Loraine. 2009. 'New Patterns of Participation Shaping Urban Governance'. In
Governing India's Metropolises: Case Studies of Four Cities, edited by Joël Ruet and Stéphanie
T. Lama-Rewal, 55–80. London: Routledge.

Kennedy, Loraine. 2014. *The Politics of Economic Restructuring in India: Economic Governance
and State Spatial Rescaling*. London: Routledge.

Kennedy, Loraine. 2020. 'Actors and Shifting Scales of Urban Governance in India'. In
Handbook of Megacities and Megacity Regions, edited by Danielle Labbé and André
Sorenson, 101–118. Cheltenham, UK: Edward Elgar Publishing.

Khan, Mushtaq M. 2011. 'The Political Settlement and its Evolution in Bangladesh'. https://
eprints.soas.ac.uk/12845/1/The_Political_Settlement_and_its_Evolution_in_
Bangladesh.pdf

Khilnani, Sunil. 2003. *The Idea of India*, 2003 edition. New Delhi: Penguin Books India.

Khudolei, Konstantin and Dmitry Lanko. 2009. 'Saint-Petersburg in the Baltic Sea Region'. *Baltic Region* 1: 54–64.

Kinossian, Nadir. 2016. 'State-Led Metropolisation in Russia'. *Urban Research & Practice* 10, no. 4: 466–476. https://doi.org/10.1080/17535069.2016.1275619

Klink, Jeroen. 2013. 'Development Regimes, Scales and State Spatial Restructuring: Change and Continuity in the Production of Urban Space in Metropolitan Rio de Janeiro, Brazil'. *International Journal of Urban and Regional Research* 37, no. 4: 1168–1187. https://doi.org/10.1111/j.1468-2427.2012.01201.x

Klink, Jeroen. 2014. 'The Hollowing out of Brazilian Metropolitan Governance as we Know it: Restructuring and Rescaling the Developmental State in Metropolitan Space'. *Antipode* 46, no. 3: 629–649. https://doi.org/10.1111/anti.12064

Klink, Jeroen. 2017. 'Recent Trajectory and Perspectives in Greater Sao Paulo'. In *Steering the Metropolis: Metropolitan Urban Governance for Sustainable Urban Development*, edited by David Gómez-Alvarez, Robin Rajack, Eduardo López-Moreno and Gabriel Lanfranchi, 323–331. Washington, D.C.: Inter-American Development Bank.

Krueger, Rob, David Gibbs and Constance Carr. 2018. 'Examining Regional Competitiveness and the Pressures of Rapid Growth: An Interpretive Institutionalist Account of Policy Responses in Three City Regions'. *Environment and Planning C: Politics and Space* 36, no. 6: 965–986. https://doi.org/10.1177/2399654418767661

Kübler, Daniel. 2017. 'Citizenship in the Fragmented Metropolis: An Individual-Level Analysis from Switzerland'. *Journal of Urban Affairs* 40, no. 1: 63–81. https://doi.org/10.1111/juaf.12276

Kunzmann, Klaus K. 1996. 'Euro-Megalopolis or Themepark Europe? Scenarios for European Spatial Development'. *International Planning Studies* 1, no. 2: 143–163. https://doi.org/10.1080/13563479608721649

Labbé, Danielle and André Sorensen, eds. 2020. *Handbook of Megacities and Megacity Regions*. Cheltenham, UK: Edward Elgar Publishing.

Lackowska, Marta and Donald F. Norris. 2017. 'Metropolitan Governance (or Not!) in Poland and the United States'. *Miscellanea Geographica* 21, no. 3: 114–123.

Lalehpour, Manijeh. 2016. 'Recognition of Management Structure and Spatial Planning in Tehran Metropolitan Area'. *Journal of Urban Management* 5, no. 1: 3–15. https://doi.org/10.1016/j.jum.2016.05.001

Lambregts, Bart, Leonie Janssen-Jansen and Nadav Haran. 2008. 'Effective Governance for Competitive Regions in Europe: The Difficult Case of the Randstad'. *GeoJournal* 72, no. 1: 45–57. http://dx.doi.org/10.1007/s10708-008-9164-6

Lampton, David M. 1992. 'A Plum for a Peach: Bargaining, Interest, and Bureaucratic Politics in China'. In *Bureaucracy, Politics, and Decision Making in Post-Mao China*, edited by Kenneth G. Lieberthal and David M. Lampton, 33–58. Berkeley, CA: University of California Press.

Lanfranchi, Gabriel. 2021. 'The Challenging Evolution of Integrated Governance in Metropolitan Buenos Aires'. In *Metropolitan Governance in Latin America*, edited by Alejandra T. Nieto and Jose L. Niño Amézquita, 121–144. London: Routledge.

Lang, Robert and Paul K. Knox. 2009. 'The New Metropolis: Rethinking Megalopolis'. *Regional Studies* 43, no. 6: 789–802. https://doi.org/10.1080/00343400701654251

Lappo, G.M. and V. Ya. Lyubovnyi. 2011. 'Largest Urban Agglomerations in Russia at the Beginning of the 21st Century: Status, Problems, and Approaches to Solving Them'. *Regional Research of Russia* 1, no. 2: 34–43.

Larkey, Levi B. and Bradley C. Love. 2003. 'CAB: Connectionist Analogy Builder'. *Cognitive Science* 27, no. 5: 781–794. https://doi.org/10.1207/s15516709cog2705_5

Laurence, Patrick. 1977. 'A Stake in South Africa's Heartland'. *Rand Daily Mail*, 24 March 1977.

Lawrence, Martha, Richard Bullock and Ziming Liu. 2019. *China's High-Speed Rail Development*. Washington: The World Bank. https://documents1.worldbank.org/curated/en/933411559841476316/pdf/Chinas-High-Speed-Rail-Development.pdf

Leaf, Michael. 2020. 'City Limits: Bounding and Unbounding in Conceptualizing the Megacity'. In *Handbook of Megacities and Megacity Regions*, edited by Danielle Labbé and André Sorenson, 33–46. Cheltenham, UK: Edward Elgar Publishing.

Lee, Ching K. and Yonghong Zhang. 2014. 'The Power of Instability: Unraveling the Microfoundations of Bargained Authoritarianism in China'. *American Journal of Sociology* 118, no. 6: 1475–1508.

Le Galès, Patrick and Tommaso Vitale. 2013. 'Governing the Large Metropolis: A Research Agenda'. *Cahiers de recherche du Programme Cities are Back in Town*, no. 2013-8. https://hal-sciencespo.archives-ouvertes.fr/hal-01070523/document

Leibovitz, Joseph. 2003. 'Institutional Barriers to Associative City-Region Governance: The Politics of Institution-Building and Economic Governance in Canada's Technology Triangle'. *Urban Studies* 40, no. 13: 2613–2642. https://doi.org/10.1080%2F0042098032000146812

Lepawsky, Albert. 1936. 'Redefining the Metropolitan Area'. *National Municipal Review* 7: 417–422.

Levy, Brian, Allan Hirsch and Ingrid Woolard. 2015. *Governance and Inequality: Benchmarking and Interpreting South Africa's Evolving Political Settlement*. ESID Working Paper no. 51. ESID, School of Environment and Development, University of Manchester. https://www.effective-states.org/wp-content/uploads/working_papers/final-pdfs/esid_wp_51_levy_hirsch_woolard.pdf

Lewis, Paul. 2012. 'Emergent Properties in the Work of Friedrich Hayek'. *Journal of Economic Behavior & Organization* 82, no. 2–3: 368–378. https://doi.org/10.1016/j.jebo.2011.04.009

Li, Cheng. 2009. 'Reclaiming the "Head of the Dragon": Shanghai as China's Center for International Finance and Shipping'. *China Leadership Monitor* 28: 1–16.

Li, Cheng and Gary Xie. 2018. 'A Brave New World: Xi's Xiong'an'. *Brookings Opinions*, 20 April 2018. https://www.brookings.edu/opinions/a-brave-new-world-xis-xiongan/

Li, Jie, Xingjian Liu, Jianzheng Liu and Weifeng Li. 2016. 'City Profile: Taipei'. *Cities* 55: 1–8. https://doi.org/10.1016/j.cities.2016.03.007

Li, Ming-bo. 2005. 'The Past and Now of the Cultural Identity in the Yangtze Delta'. *Journal of East China University of Science and Technology (Social Science Edition)* 1. http://en.cnki.com.cn/Article_en/CJFDTotal-HDLS200501017.htm [translated]

Li, Yi and Fulong Wu. 2013. 'The Emergence of Centrally Initiated Regional Plan in China: A Case Study of Yangtze River Delta Regional Plan'. *Habitat International* 39: 137–147. https://doi.org/10.1016/j.habitatint.2012.11.002

Li, Yi and Fulong Wu. 2018. 'Understanding City-Regionalism in China: Regional Cooperation in the Yangtze River Delta'. *Regional Studies* 52, no. 3: 313–324. https://doi.org/10.1080/00343404.2017.1307953

Li, Yi, Fulong Wu and Iain Hay. 2015. 'City-Region Integration Policies and Their Incongruous Outcomes: The Case of Shantou-Chaozhou-Jieyang City-Region in East Guangdong Province, China'. *Habitat International* 46: 214–222. https://doi.org/10.1016/j.habitatint.2014.12.006

Li, Yingcheng and Nicholas Phelps. 2018. 'Megalopolis Unbound: Knowledge Collaboration and Functional Polycentricity Within and Beyond the Yangtze River Delta Region in China, 2014'. *Urban Studies* 55, no. 2: 443–460. https://doi.org/10.1177%2F0042098016656971

Lidström, Anders and Linze Schaap. 2018. 'The Citizen in City-Regions: Patterns and Variations'. *Journal of Urban Affairs* 40, no. 1: 1–12. https://doi.org/10.1080/07352166.2017.1355668

Lim, Hye K. and Jaan-Henrik Kain. 2016. 'Compact Cities are Complex, Intense and Diverse But: Can we Design Such Emergent Urban Properties?' *Urban Planning* 1, no. 1: 95–113. https://doi.org/10.17645/up.v1i1.535

Lima, Ricardo and Raul Neto. 2018. 'Secession of Municipalities and Economies of Scale: Evidences from Brazil'. *Journal of Regional Science* 58, no. 1: 159–180. https://doi.org/10.1111/jors.12348

Limonov, Leonid. 2013. 'St. Petersburg Metropolitan Region: Problems of Planning Coordination and Spatial Development'. Paper presented at the 53rd Congress of the European Regional Science Association, Palermo, Italy, 27–31 August 2013.

Liu, Weidong. 2015. 'Governance, Politics and Culture'. In *The Geographical Transformation of China*, edited by Michael Dunford and Weidong Liu, 22–59. Abingdon, Oxon: Routledge.

Liu, Yaolin, Xianghui Zhang, Xingyu Pan, Xiuxin Ma and Mingyang Tang. 2020. 'The Spatial Integration and Coordinated Industrial Development of Urban Agglomerations in the Yangtze River Economic Belt, China'. *Cities* 104: 102801. https://doi.org/10.1016/j.cities.2020.102801

Lobo, Carlos, Ralfo Matos, Leandro Cardoso, Lidia Comini and Guilherme Pinto. 2015. 'Expanded Commuting in the Metropolitan Region of Belo Horizonte: Evidence for Reverse Commuting'. *Revista Brasileira de Estudos de População* 32, no. 2: 219–233.

Lopes, Lucas. 1952. 'Planejamento de Zonas Metropolitanas'. *Colaboração*, June 1952. https://revista.enap.gov.br/index.php/RSP/article/view/6340/3615

Loureiro, Vicente and Vera França e Leite. 2018. 'Por uma Região Metropolitana Eficiente, Equilibrada e Sustentável – Contribuição da Câmara Metropolitana de Integração Governamental do Rio de Janeiro'. In *Brasil Metropolitano em foco Desafios à Implementação do Estatuto da Metrópole*, edited by Bárbara O. Marguti, Marco A. Costa and César B. Favarão, 241–265. Brazil: Ipea.

Lu, Haiyan, Martin de Jong, Yun Song and Miaoxi Zhao. 2020. 'The Multi-level Governance of Formulating Regional Brand Identities: Evidence from Three Mega City Regions in China'. *Cities* 100: 102668. https://doi.org/10.1016/j.cities.2020.102668

Luo, Xiaolong and Jianfa Shen. 2009. 'A Study on Inter-city Cooperation in the Yangtze River Delta Region, China'. *Habitat International* 33, no. 1: 52–62. https://doi.org/10.1016/j.habitatint.2008.04.002

Luo, Xiaolong, Jianfa Shen and Wen Chen. 2010. 'Urban Networks and Governance in City-Region Planning: State-Led Region Building in Nanjing City-Region, China'. *Geografiska Annaler: Series B, Human Geography* 92, no. 4: 311–326. https://doi.org/10.1111/j.1468-0467.2010.00355.x

Luo, Yuanjun. 2014. 'Build a Capital Economic Circle for Coordinated Development'. *China Today*, 24 June 2014. http://www.chinatoday.com.cn/english/economy/2014-06/24/content_625781.htm

Mabin, Alan. 1993. 'The Witwatersrand Joint Town Planning Committee 1933–1945: Of Rigour and Mortis'. *Planning History: Bulletin of the International Planning History Society* 15, no. 2: 49–54.

Mabin, Alan. 2007. 'Johannesburg: (South) Africa's Aspirant Global City'. In *The Making of Global City-Regions: Johannesburg, Mumbai/Bombay, São Paulo, and Shanghai*, edited by Klaus Segbers, 32–63. Baltimore, MD: Johns Hopkins University Press.

Mabin, Alan. 2013. *The Map of Gauteng: Evolution of a City-Region in Concept and Plan*. GCRO Occasional Paper no. 5. Gauteng City-Region Observatory, Johannesburg. https://cdn.gcro.ac.za/media/documents/gcro_occasional_paper_5_-_mabin_map_of_gauteng_july_2013_final.pdf

Mabin, Alan. 2021. 'Sprawl Politics: Comparing the City Regions of Paris (France) and Gauteng (South Africa)'. *disP – The Planning Journal* 57, no. 3: 119–137. https://doi.org/10.1080/02513625.2021.2026680

Mabin, Alan and Philip Harrison. 2022. 'Contemporary Planning and Emergent Futures: A Comparative Study of Five Capital City-Regions on Four Continents'. *Progress in Planning* 169, 100664. https://doi.org/10.1016/j.progress.2022.100664

Maglio, Ivan. 2019. 'In Defence of EMPLASA: São Paulo Loses its Urban Planning Body'. *Folha de S. Paulo*, 3 June 2019. https://www1-folha-uol-com-br.translate.goog/opiniao/2019/06/em-defesa-da-emplasa.shtml?_x_tr_sl=pt&_x_tr_tl=en&_x_tr_hl=en&_x_tr_pto=sc [translation]

Mail & Guardian. 2004. 'Shoulder to the Wheel for Shilowa'. *Mail & Guardian*, 7 June 2004. https://mg.co.za/article/2004-06-07-shoulder-to-the-wheel-for-shilowa/

Makhura, David. 2015. 'The Ten Pillars which Form our Core Mandate'. State of the Province address, 23 February 2015. https://www.politicsweb.co.za/news-and-analysis/sopa-the-ten-pillars-which-form-our-core-mandate

Makhura, David. 2019a. 'Re-igniting the Spirit of Resilience and Excellence in Gauteng'. State of the Province address, 18 February 2019. https://www.gov.za/sites/default/files/gcis_documents/GP_SoPA.pdf

Makhura, David. 2019b. 'State of the Province Address'. Filmed 30 June 2019. Office of the Premier Video. https://www.gauteng.gov.za/Videos/VideoDetails/%7B732D858B-8011-4924-8C5E-1E6ECC454703%7D

Manasan, Rosario G. and Ruben G. Mercado. 1999. *Governance and Urban Development: Case Study of Metro Manila*. PIDS Discussion Paper Series no. 1999-03, Philippine Institute for Development Studies. https://www.econstor.eu/bitstream/10419/187389/1/pidsdps9903.pdf

Mandy, Nigel. 1988. 'A Metropolitan Identity: RSCs and the Rand'. *Indicator South Africa* 5, no. 3: 13–18.

Marais, Hein. 2001. *South Africa: Limits to Change: The Political Economy of Transition*. London: Zed Books.

Maram, Sheldon. 1990. 'Juscelino Kubitschek and the Politics of Exuberance, 1956–1961'. *Luso-Brazilian Review* 27, no. 1: 31–45.

Marques, Eduardo C.L. 2016. 'São Paulo Histories, Institutions and Legacies'. In *São Paulo in the Twenty-First Century: Spaces, Heterogeneities, Inequalities*, edited by Eduardo C.L. Marques, 31–56. New York: Routledge.

Marques, Eduardo C.L. 2021. *The Politics of Incremental Progressivism: Governments, Governances and Urban Policy Changes in São Paulo*. Hoboken, NJ: John Wiley & Sons.

Martin, Ron and James Simmie. 2008. 'Path Dependence and Local Innovation Systems in City-Regions'. *Innovation* 10, no. 2–3: 183–196. https://doi.org/10.5172/impp.453.10.2-3.183

Martin, Ron and Peter Sunley. 2007. 'Complexity Thinking and Evolutionary Economic Geography'. *Journal of Economic Geography* 7, no. 5: 573–601. https://doi.org/10.1093/jeg/lbm019

Maud, John P.R. 1938. *City Government: The Johannesburg Experiment*. Oxford: Clarendon Press.

Maxwell, Gordon. 1971. 'Study of a Proposed Rapid Rail System for Johannesburg'. London Transport Executive. Research Archives, University of the Witwatersrand, Johannesburg.

McArthur, Jenny. 2017. 'Auckland: Rescaled Governance and Post-suburban Politics'. *Cities* 64: 79–87. https://doi.org/10.1016/j.cities.2017.01.010

McFarlane, Colin. 2010. 'The Comparative City: Knowledge, Learning, Urbanism'. *International Journal of Urban and Regional Research* 34, no. 4: 725–742. https://doi.org/10.1111/j.1468-2427.2010.00917.x

McGee, T.G. and Charles Greenberg. 1992. 'The Emergence of Extended Metropolitan Regions in ASEAN: Towards the Year 2000'. *ASEAN Economic Bulletin* 9, no. 1: 22–44.

McGuirk, Pauline. 2007. 'The Political Construction of the City-Region: Notes from Sydney'. *International Journal of Urban and Regional Research* 31, no. 1: 171–187. https://doi.org/10.1111/j.1468-2427.2007.00712.x

McKenzie, Kermit E. 1982. 'Zemstvo Organization and Role Within the Administrative Structure'. In *The Zemstvo in Russia: An Experiment in Local Self-Government*, edited by Terence Emmons and Wayne S. Vucinich, 31–78. New York: Cambridge University Press.

Meara, Paul. 2006. 'Emergent Properties of Multilingual Lexicons'. *Applied Linguistics* 27, no. 4: 620–644. https://doi.org/10.1093/applin/aml030

Mehra, Diya. 2013. 'Planning Delhi ca. 1936–1959'. *South Asia, Journal of South Asian Studies* 36, no 3: 354–374. https://doi.org/10.1080/00856401.2013.829793

Melber, Henning. 2002. 'From Liberation Movements to Governments: On Political Culture in Southern Africa'. *African Sociological Review* 6, no. 1: 161–172.

Merrifield, Andy. 2013. 'The Urban Question Under Planetary Urbanization'. *International Journal of Urban and Regional Research* 37, no. 3: 909–922. https://doi.org/10.1111/j.1468-2427.2012.01189.x

Meulbroek, Chris, Jamie Peck and Jun Zhang. 2022. 'Bayspeak: Narrating China's Greater Bay Area'. *Journal of Contemporary Asia* (online). https://doi.org/10.1080/00472336.2021.1998579

Meuriot, Paul. 1914. 'Du Critérium Adopté Pour la Définition de la Population Urbaine'. *Journal de la Société Française Statistique de Paris* 55: 418–430.

Michelutti, Lucia. 2007. 'The Vernacularization of Democracy: Political Participation and Popular Politics in North India'. *Journal of the Royal Anthropological Institute* 13, no. 3: 639–656. https://doi.org/10.1111/j.1467-9655.2007.00448.x

Ministry of Health, Government of India. 1956. *Interim General Plan for Greater Delhi*. Accessed 23 June 2022. http://ncrpb.nic.in/pdf_files/Interim%20General%20Plan%20for%20Greater%20Delhi.PDF

Mintzberg, Henry and James A. Waters. 1985. 'Of Strategies, Deliberate and Emergent'. *Strategic Management Journal* 6, no. 3: 257–272. https://doi.org/10.1002/smj.4250060306

Mishra, Alok K.N. 2018. 'PM Modi Neither Talks to Me nor Looks at Me Nor Allows Me to Talk'. *The Times of India*, 17 June 2018. https://timesofindia.indiatimes.com/city/delhi/pm-modi-neither-talks-to-me-nor-looks-at-me-nor-allows-me-to-talk/articleshow/64618278.cms

Mkhize, Thembani. 2021. *Rescaling Municipal Governance Amidst Political Competition in Gauteng: Sedibeng's Proposed Re-demarcation*. GCRO Occasional Paper no. 18. Gauteng City-Region Observatory, Johannesburg. https://cdn.gcro.ac.za/media/documents/Occassional_Paper.pdf

Modu Magazine. 2018. 'Promoting "Less is More": Beijing's New Master Plan'. *Modu Magazine*, 4 May 2018. www.modumag.com/articles/promoting-less-is-more-beijings-new-urban-master-plan/

Montero, Sergio and Gianpaolo Baiocchi. 2021. 'A Posteriori Comparisons, Repeated Instances and Urban Policy Mobilities: What "Best Practices" Leave Behind'. *Urban Studies* 59, no. 8: 1536–1555. https://doi.org/10.1177%2F00420980211041460

Moon, M. Jae. 2017. 'Government-Driven Sharing Economy: Lessons from the Sharing City Initiative of the Seoul Metropolitan Government'. *Journal of Developing Societies* 33, no. 2: 223–243. https://doi.org/10.1177%2F0169796X17710076

Mosiane, Ngaka and Graeme Götz. 2022. *Displaced Urbanisation or Displaced Urbanism? Rethinking Development in the Peripheries of the GCR*. Governing the Gauteng City-Region Provocations Series, no. 08. Johannesburg: Gauteng City-Region Observatory. DOI: 10.36634/SVRW2580

Mtengwa, Emmanuel. 2021. 'Tanzania: President Magufuli Officially Dissolves Dar es Salaam City Council'. *The Citizen*, 25 February 2021. https://allafrica.com/stories/202102250209.html

Mubiwa, Brian and Harold Annegarn. 2013. *Historical Spatial Change in the Gauteng City Region*. GCRO Occasional Paper no. 4. Gauteng City-Region Observatory, Johannesburg. https://cdn.gcro.ac.za/media/documents/mubiwe_occasional_paper_new.pdf

Mukharji, G. 1962. 'Metropolitan Planning in India'. *Ekistics* 13, no. 78: 251–256.

Mumford, Louis. 1946. *City Development: Studies in Disintegration and Renewal*. London: Secker & Warburg.

Musah, Mohammed. 2022. 'Towards Organising Sustainable Urbanism: The Accra City-Region (ACR) Within Africa's West Coast Urban Corridor'. Masters diss., University of the Witwatersrand, Johannesburg.

Musinova, N. 2019. 'Development of Urban Agglomerations as One of the Strategic Directions of the Spatial Development of Russia'. *University Bulletin* 2: 46–51. https://doi.org/10.26425/1816-4277-2019-2-46-51

Muthien, Yvonne and Meshack Khosa. 1995. 'The Kingdom, the Volkstaat and the New South Africa: Drawing South Africa's New Regional Boundaries'. *Journal of Southern African Studies* 21, no. 2: 303–322.

Myers, Garth. 2015. 'A World-Class City-Region? Envisioning the Nairobi of 2030'. *American Behavioral Scientist* 59, no. 3: 328–346. https://doi.org/10.1177%2F0002764214550308

Na, Ziya. 2014. 'The City Network and the Regional Evolution in Yangtze River Delta, China'. Doctoral diss., Politecnico di Milano. https://www.politesi.polimi.it/bitstream/10589/89770/3/2014_03_PhD_Na.pdf

Nardi, Bonnie A. 1996. 'Studying Context: A Comparison of Activity Theory, Situated Action Models, and Distributed Cognition'. In *Context and Consciousness: Activity Theory and Human-Computer Interaction*, edited by Bonnie Nardi, 69–102. Cambridge, MA: The MIT Press.

Nath, V. 1988. 'Regional Planning for Large Metropolitan Cities: A Case Study of the National Capital Region'. *Economic and Political Weekly* 23, no. 5: 201–214.

Nath, V. 2007. 'Urbanization, Urban Development and Metropolitan Cities'. In *Regional Development and Planning in India: Selected Essays by V. Nath*, edited by S.K. Aggarwal. New Delhi: Concept Publishing.

NCR Tribune. 2002. 'NCR Board Gets Stick for Failing to Cap Population'. *NCR Tribune*, 23 June 2002. https://www.tribuneindia.com/2002/20020624/ncr1.htm#5

NCRPB (National Capital Region Planning Board). 1995. Agenda Items for the 36th Meeting of the Planning Committee of the NCRPB, 31 May 1995, New Delhi. http://ncrpb.nic.in/pdf_files/A&M%20of%20PC%20Meetings/1995.05.31_36th%20PCM_A&M.pdf

NCRPB. 2000. 'Agenda and Minutes of the 25th Meeting of the NCRPB, 12 July 2000, New Delhi'. https://ncrpb.nic.in/pdf_files/Board%20Meeting%20Agenda%20&%20Minutes/25th%20Board%20Meeting%20Agenda%20&%20Minutes.pdf

NCRPB. 2004. 'Agenda and Minutes of the 27th Meeting of the NCRPB, 28 October 2004, New Delhi'. https://ncrpb.nic.in/pdf_files/Board%20Meeting%20Agenda%20&%20Minutes/27th%20Board%20Meeting%20Agenda%20&%20Minutes.pdf

NCRPB. 2005. 'Regional Plan – 2021: National Capital Region'. https://ncrpb.nic.in/region-alplanchapters.html

NCRPB. 2014. 'Agenda and Minutes of the 34th Meeting of the NCRPB, 6 January 2014, New Delhi'. https://ncrpb.nic.in/pdf_files/Board%20Meeting%20Agenda%20&%20Minutes/34th%20Board%20Meeting%20Agenda%20&%20Minutes.pdf

NCRPB. 2015. 'Agenda Notes and Minutes of the 36th Meeting of the NCRPB, 9 June 2015, New Delhi'. https://ncrpb.nic.in/pdf_files/Board%20Meeting%20Agenda%20&%20Minutes/36th%20Board%20Meeting%20Agenda%20&%20Minutes.pdf

NCRPB. 2016. 'Agenda and Minutes of a Special Meeting of the NCRPB, 20 December 2016, New Delhi'. https://ncrpb.nic.in/pdf_files/Board%20Meeting%20Agenda%20&%20Minutes/Spl.%20B.M%2020.12.16%20Agenda%20&%20Minutes.pdf

NCRPB. 2021a. 'Draft Regional Plan – 2041: National Capital Region'. http://awas.up.nic.in/LoginAwas/pdf/gov/NCRPB%20Draft%20Regional%20Plan-2041_pwbuxw.pdf

NCRPB. 2021b. 'Agenda Notes and Minutes of the 41st Meeting of the NCRPB, 31 August 2021'. http://ncrpb.nic.in/pdf_files/41BM.pdf

NDRC (National Development and Reform Commission). 2006. 'Guidelines of the Eleventh Five-Year Plan for National Economic and Social Development'. https://policy.asiapacificenergy.org/sites/default/files/11th%20Five-Year%20Plan%20%282006-2010%29%20for%20National%20Economic%20and%20Social%20Development%20%28EN%29.pdf

NDRC. 2011. 'China's Twelfth Five-Year Plan, 2011–2015'. https://cbi.typepad.com/china_direct/2011/05/chinas-twelfth-five-new-plan-the-full-english-version.html

NDRC. 2016. 'The 13th Five-Year Plan for Economic and Social Development of the People's Republic of China, 2016–2020'. https://en.ndrc.gov.cn/policies/202105/P020210527785800103339.pdf

NDRC. 2019. 'Outline Development Plan for the Guangdong-Hong Kong-Macao Greater Bay Area' (translation by the Government of Hong Kong). https://www.bayarea.gov.hk/filemanager/en/share/pdf/Outline_Development_Plan.pdf

NDRC. 2021. 'Outline of the People's Republic of China 14th Five-Year Plan for National Economic and Social Development, 2021–2025, and Long-Range Objectives for 2035'. https://cset.georgetown.edu/wp-content/uploads/t0284_14th_Five_Year_Plan_EN.pdf

Negotiating Council of the Multi-Party Negotiating Process. 1993. 'Report of the Commission on the Demarcation/Delimitation of States/Provinces/Regions'. https://wiredspace-extra.wits.ac.za/items/91693c13-51c6-48d8-aa68-9468a389f438

Nelles, Jen and Frédéric Durand. 2014. 'Political Rescaling and Metropolitan Governance in Cross-Border Regions: Comparing the Cross-Border Metropolitan Areas of Lille and Luxembourg'. *European Urban and Regional Studies* 21, no. 1: 104–122. https://doi.org/10.1177%2F0969776411431103

Neuman, Michael. 2007. 'Multi-scalar Large Institutional Networks in Regional Planning'. *Planning Theory & Practice* 8, no. 3: 319–344. https://doi.org/10.1080/14649350701514645

Newman, Peter and Andy Thornley. 2013. 'Case Study Window – Global Cities: Governance Cultures and Urban Policy in New York, Paris, Tokyo and Beijing'. In *The Ashgate Research Companion to Planning and Culture*, edited by Greg Young and Deborah Stevenson, 69–84. London: Routledge.

Nguyen, Thanh Bao, D. Ary A. Samsura, Erwin van der Krabben and Anh-Duc Le. 2016. 'Saigon-Ho Chi Minh City'. *Cities* 50: 16–27. https://doi.org/10.1016/j.cities.2015.08.007

Nijman, Jan. 2007. 'Introduction: Comparative Urbanism'. *Urban Geography* 28, no. 1: 1–6. https://doi.org/10.2747/0272-3638.28.1.1

Nimocks, Walter. 1968. *Milner's Young Men: The "Kindergarten" in Edwardian Imperial Affairs.* London: Duke University Press.

Nixon, Peter. 1975. 'Too Many Fingers in the Planning Pie'. *Rand Daily Mail*, 3 September 1975, para. 1.

Observatory of the Metropolis. 2017. *The Rio de Janeiro-São Paulo Megarregion: Metropolitanization of Space and Global Integration* (translation). Observatory of the Metropolis, news section, 28 September 2017. http://observatoriodasmetropoles. net.br/wp/megarregiao-rio-de-janeiro-sao-paulo-metropolizacao-do-espaco-e-integra-cao-global/

OECD (Organisation for Economic Co-operation and Development). 2008. *OECD Territorial Reviews: Cape Town, South Africa 2008.* Paris: OECD Publishing. https://doi.org/10.1787/9789264049642-en

OECD. 2011. *OECD Territorial Reviews: The Gauteng City-Region, South Africa 2011.* Paris: OECD Publishing. https://doi.org/10.1787/9789264122840-en

OECD. 2015. *Governing the City: Policy Highlights.* Paris: OECD Publishing. https://www.oecd.org/regional/regional-policy/Governing-the-City-Policy-Highlights%20.pdf

Office of the Registrar General, India. 2018. 'Census of India 2021, Circular 3: Formation of Urban Agglomerations for the 2021 Census, 11 December 2018'. https://censuskarnataka.gov.in/rgicirculars2021/Circular%203.pdf

Olukesusi, Femi and Samuel D. Wapwera. 2017. 'Political Stability, Metropolitan Governance, and Transformation in Lagos'. In *Steering the Metropolis: Metropolitan Governance for Sustainable Urban Development,* edited by David Gómez-Álvarez, Robin M. Rajack, Eduardo López-Moreno and Gabriel Lanfranchi, 260–268. Washington: Inter-American Development Bank.

Olver, Crispian. 2017. *How to Steal a City: The Battle for Nelson Mandela Bay.* Cape Town: Jonathan Ball Publishers.

O'Neill, Jim. 2001. *Building Better Global Economic BRICs.* Goldman Sachs Global Economic Paper no. 66. Goldman Sachs Economic Research Group, New York. https://www.goldmansachs.com/insights/archive/archive-pdfs/build-better-brics.pdf

Ostrom, Elinor. 1990. *Governing the Commons: The Evolution of Institutions for Collective Action.* Cambridge: Cambridge University Press.

Ostrom, Elinor. 2009. 'Analyzing Collective Action'. Paper presented at the International Association of Agricultural Economists, Beijing, China, 16–22 August 2009.

Palmer, Ian, Nishendra Moodley and Susan Parnell. 2017. *Building a Capable State: Service Delivery in Post-apartheid South Africa.* London: Zed Books.

Palmer, James. 2017. 'How to Destroy the Heart of a Chinese City'. *Foreign Policy*, 31 May 2017. https://foreignpolicy.com/2017/05/31/how-to-destroy-the-heart-of-a-chinese-city-beijing/

Parilla, Joseph and Jesus Leal Trujillo. 2015. *South Africa's Global Gateway: Profiling the Gauteng City-Region's International Competitiveness and Connections*. Washington: Global Cities Initiative. https://www.brookings.edu/wp-content/uploads/2016/07/GCI_Johannesburg_Nov16REVfinal_LowRes-1.pdf

Patti, Daniela. 2017. 'Metropolitan Governance in the Peri-urban Landscape: The Tower of Babel? The Case of the Vienna-Bratislava Metropolitan Region'. *Planning Practice & Research* 32, no. 1: 29–39.

Peck, Jamie. 2015. 'Cities Beyond Compare?' *Regional Studies* 49, no. 1: 160–182. DOI: 10.1080/00343404.2014.980801

Perloff, Harvey S. 1968. 'Key Features of Regional Planning'. *Journal of the American Institute of Planners* 34, no. 3: 153–159. https://doi.org/10.1080/01944366808977798

Pertsev, Andrey. 2022. 'Snow, Trash, and "Influential People": St. Petersburg Governor Alexander Beglov is Under More Pressure Than Ever Before. Is His Departure Imminent?' Translated by Ellish Hart. *Meduza*, 12 February 2022. https://meduza.io/en/feature/2022/02/12/snow-trash-and-influential-people

Picard, Louis A. and Thomas Mogale. 2014. *The Limits of Democratic Governance in South Africa*. Boulder, CO: Lynne Renier Publishers.

Pillay, Udesh. 2004. 'Are Globally Competitive "City Regions" Developing in South Africa? Formulaic Aspirations or New Imaginations?' *Urban Forum* 15, no. 4: 340–364. http://dx.doi.org/10.1007%2Fs12132-004-0013-5

Pines, Yurl. 2012. *The Everlasting Empire: The Political Culture of Ancient China and its Imperial Legacy*. Princeton, NJ: Princeton University Press.

Pipes, Richard. 2004. 'Flight from Freedom: What Russians Think and Want'. *Foreign Affairs* 83, no. 3: 9–15. https://doi.org/10.2307/20033971

Potter, Robert B. and Ashok Kumar. 2004. *A Profile of NOIDA: A New Town in the National Capital Region of India*. Geographical Paper no. 174. University of Reading. https://www.reading.ac.uk/web/files/geographyandenvironmentalscience/GP174.pdf

PwC (PricewaterhouseCoopers). 2017. 'The Effect of Scale: First Global Ranking of Metropolitan Area'. Report prepared for the City of Moscow [translated]. https://mosurbanforum.com/upload/iblock/f1d/f1da10359fea7ce364b6056aea-c62e8a.pdf

Qiao, Xiaoyang, Yanchun Meng and Xiangyu Zhu. 2015. 'Research on the Hierarchical Structure of the Metropolitan System and Economic Development of the Provincial Capital Urban Circle in Shandong'. *Chinese Journal of Population Resources and Environment* 13, no. 1: 78–86. https://doi.org/10.1080/10042857.2014.998873

Rae, Alasdair and Garrett Nelson. 2020. On the Road Again: Geography and the Characteristics of American Commuter Megaregions. In *Handbook of Megacities and Megacity Regions*, edited by Danielle Labbé and André Sorenson, 188–205. Cheltenham, UK: Edward Elgar Publishing.

Rajamani, Lavanya. 2007. 'Public Interest Environmental Litigation in India: Exploring Issues of Access, Participation, Equity, Effectiveness and Sustainability'. *Journal of Environmental Law* 19, no. 3: 293–321. https://doi.org/10.1093/jel/eqm020

Rajput, Vinod. 2013. 'Law Buried Under Urbanisation'. *Hindustan Times*, 23 July 2013. https://www.hindustantimes.com/noida/law-buried-under-urbanisation/story-68NwhaPaJDTqVcLA9DDNlK.html

Rand Daily Mail. 1908. 'The Joint Committee: Last Meeting: Work Reviewed'. *Rand Daily Mail*, 13 June 1908.

Rand Daily Mail. 1933a. 'Planning a Greater Reef: Mr. C. Reade's Big Job?: "Randopolis of the Future"'. *Rand Daily Mail*, 28 July 1933.

Rand Daily Mail. 1933b. 'Randopolis Dream: £12 000 to Plan New City: Town Planner Arrives'. *Rand Daily Mail*, 18 October 1933.

Rand Daily Mail. 1933c. 'Town Planning Expert Found Shot: Depressed by Malaria?: Empty Envelopes Found in Room'. *Rand Daily Mail*, 30 October 1933.

Rand Daily Mail. 1934. 'Randopolis'. *Rand Daily Mail*, 9 August 1934.

Rand Daily Mail. 1935. 'Town Planning Harvest for Lawyers: Difficulties Ahead'. *Rand Daily Mail*, 23 January 1935.

Rand Daily Mail. 1947a. 'Regional Non-European Housing Body Agreed to in Principle'. *Rand Daily Mail*, 29 March 1947.

Rand Daily Mail. 1947b. 'Master Plan Will Set out Housing for Non-Europeans'. *Rand Daily Mail*, 27 August 1947.

Rand Daily Mail. 1973. 'The Master Plan is Taking Shape'. *Rand Daily Mail*, 28 July 1973, p. 10.

Rand Daily Mail. 1983. 'Industry Upset over Preference for Homelands'. *Rand Daily Mail*, 1 June 1983, p. 11.

Rautray, Samanwaya. 2018. 'In Big Win for Arvind Kejriwal, Supreme Court Rules Against LG in Delhi'. *The Economic Times*, 5 July 2018. https://economictimes.indiatimes.com/news/politics-and-nation/lt-governor-cannot-act-as-an-obstructionist-chief-justice-of-india/articleshow/64851415.cms

Reed, Thomas H., ed. 1929. 'Notes on Rural Local Government'. *The American Political Science Review* 23: 121–138.

Ren, Julie. 2022. 'A More Global Urban Studies, Besides Empirical Variation'. *Urban Studies* 59, no. 8: 1741–1748. https://doi.org/10.1177%2F00420980221085113

Ren, Xuefei. 2020. *Governing the Urban in China and India: Land Grabs, Slum Clearance, and the War on Air Pollution*. Princeton, NJ: Princeton University Press.

Ren, Xuefei and Liza Weinstein. 2013. 'Urban Governance, Mega-Projects and Scalar Transformations in China and India'. In *Locating Right to the City in the Global South*, edited by Tony R. Samara, Shenjing He and Guo Chen, 107–126. Abingdon, Oxon: Routledge.

Resnick, Danielle. 2021. 'The Politics of Urban Governance in Sub-Saharan Africa'. *Regional & Federal Studies* 31, no. 1: 139–161. https://doi.org/10.1080/13597566.2020.1774371

Ribeiro, Luiz C. de Q. and Ana L.N. de P. Britto. 2018. 'Local Democracy and Metropolitan Governance: The Case of Rio de Janeiro'. In *Urban Transformations in Rio de Janeiro: Development, Segregation, and Governance*, edited by Luiz C. de Q. Ribeiro, 257–271. Cham: Springer.

Ribeiro, Luiz C. de Q. and Orlando A. dos Santos Junior. 2010. 'Large Cities and the Brazilian Social Question: Reflections About the "State of Exception" in Brazilian Metropolises'. In *Inclusion, Collaboration and Urban Governance: Challenges in Metropolitan Regions of Brazil and Canada*, edited by Terry McGee and Erika de Castro, 51–69. Vancouver: University of British Columbia.

Robert, Jacques. 1976. 'Prospective Study on Physical Planning and the Environment in the Megalopolis in Formation in North-West Europe'. *Urban Ecology* 1, no. 4: 331–411. https://doi.org/10.1016/0304-4009(76)90013-9

Robinson, Jennifer. 2011. 'Cities in a World of Cities: The Comparative Gesture'. *International Journal of Urban and Regional Research* 35, no. 1: 1–23. https://doi.org/10.1111/j.1468-2427.2010.00982.x

Robinson, Jennifer. 2016a. 'Thinking Cities Through Elsewhere: Comparative Tactics for a More Global Urban Studies'. *Progress in Human Geography* 40, no. 1: 3–29. https://doi.org/10.1177%2F0309132515598025

Robinson, Jennifer. 2016b. 'Comparative Urbanism: New Geographies and Cultures of Theorizing the Urban'. *International Journal of Urban and Regional Research* 40, no. 1: 187–199. https://doi.org/10.1111/1468-2427.12273

Robinson, Jennifer. 2022. 'Introduction: Generating Concepts of "the Urban" Through Comparative Practice'. *Urban Studies* 59, no. 8: 1521–1535. https://doi.org/10.1177%2F00420980221092561

Robinson, Jennifer and Ananya Roy. 2016. 'Debate on Global Urbanisms and the Nature of Urban Theory'. *International Journal of Urban and Regional Research* 40, no. 1: 181–186. https://doi.org/10.1111/1468-2427.12272

Robinson, Jennifer, Fulong Wu, Phil Harrison, Zheng Wang, Alison Todes, Romain Dittgen and Katia Attuyer. 2022. 'Beyond Variegation: The Territorialisation of States, Communities and Developers in Large-Scale Developments in Johannesburg, Shanghai and London'. *Urban Studies* 59, no. 8: 1715–1740. https://doi.org/10.1177%2F00420980211064159

Rodger, Richard. 2012. 'The Significance of the Metropolis'. In *Thick Space: Approaches to Metropolitanism*, edited by Dorothee Brantz, Sasha Disko and Georg Wagner-Kyora, 85–104. Bielefeld: Transcript Verlag.

Rodríguez-Pose, Andrés. 2008. 'The Rise of the "City-Region" Concept and its Development Policy Implications'. *European Planning Studies* 16, no. 8: 1025–1046. https://doi.org/10.1080/09654310802315567

Rodríguez-Pose, Andrés, John Tomaney and Jeroen Klink. 2001. 'Local Empowerment Through Economic Restructuring in Brazil: The Case of the Greater ABC Region'. *Geoforum* 32, no. 4: 459–469. https://doi.org/10.1016/S0016-7185(01)00011-2

Rogerson, Christian M. 2009. 'The Turn to "New Regionalism": South African Reflections'. *Urban Forum* 20, no. 2: 111–140.

Rojas, Francisca M. 2017. 'Advancing Metropolitan Governance in Buenos Aires'. In *Steering the Metropolis: Metropolitan Governance for Sustainable Urban Development*, edited by David Gómez-Alvarez, Robin Rajack, Eduardo López-Moreno and Gabriel Lanfranchi, 280–289. Washington, D.C.: Inter-American Development Bank.

Rolnik, Raquel. 2011. 'Democracy on the Edge: Limits and Possibilities in the Implementation of an Urban Reform Agenda in Brazil'. *International Journal of Urban and Regional Research* 35, no. 2: 239–255. https://doi.org/10.1111/j.1468-2427.2010.01036.x

Rosenau, James N. 2007. 'Governing the Ungovernable: The Challenge of a Global Disaggregation of Authority'. *Regulation and Governance* 1, no. 1: 88–97. https://doi.org/10.1111/j.1748-5991.2007.00001.x

Rosenn, Keith S. 1984. 'Brazil's Legal Culture: The Jeito Revisited'. *Florida International Law Journal* 1, no. 1: 1–43.

Roy, Ananya. 2009a. 'Why India Cannot Plan its Cities: Informality, Insurgence and the Idiom of Urbanization'. *Planning Theory* 8, no. 1: 76–87. https://doi.org/10.1177%2F1473095208099299

Roy, Ananya. 2009b. 'Strangely Familiar: Planning and the Worlds of Insurgence and Informality'. *Planning Theory* 8, no. 1: 7–11. https://doi.org/10.1177%2F1473095208099294

Roy, Ananya. 2011. 'The Blockade of the World-Class City: Dialectical Images of Indian Urbanism'. In *Worldling Cities: Asian Experiments and the Art of Being Global*, edited by Ananya Roy and Aihwa Ong, 259–278. Chichester: Blackwell.

RSA (Republic of South Africa). 1996. *Constitution of the Republic of South Africa, 1996* (Act 108 of 1996). https://www.gov.za/documents/constitution-republic-south-africa-1996

Rubin, Margot. 2013. 'Exclusion and Exceptionalism: The Site of the Courts in Urban Governance'. *Géocarrefour* 88, no. 3: 207–216. https://doi.org/10.4000/geocarrefour.9179

Rubin, Margot. 2021. 'Local Government as the Stage for Resistance: Strategies and Tactics of Opposing Mega Projects in Gauteng'. In *Refractions of the National, the Popular and the Global in African Cities*, edited by Simon Bekker, Sylvia Croese and Edgar Pieterse, 71–84. Somerset West: African Minds.

Rustiadi, Ernan, Didit Okta Pribadi, Andrea Emma Pravitasari, Galuh Syahbana Indraprahasta and Laode Syamsul Iman. 2015. 'Jabodetabek Megacity: From City Development Toward Urban Complex Management System'. In *Urban Development Challenges, Risks and Resilience in Asian Mega Cities*, edited by Ram Babu Singh, 421–445. Tokyo: Springer.

Sachdeva, S. 2004. 'Yet Another Plan Which Didn't Take Off'. *The Times of India*, 24 January 2004. https://timesofindia.indiatimes.com/city/delhi/yet-another-plan-which-didnt-take-off/articleshow/443443.cms

Sacks, Anne. 1981. 'PWV Stirs Troubled Water in Boksburg'. *Rand Daily Mail*, 24 June 1981.

Salet, Willem, Andy Thornley and Anton Kreukels. 2003. 'Practices of Metropolitan Governance in Europe: Experiences and Lessons'. In *Metropolitan Governance and Spatial Planning: Comparative Case Studies of European City-Regions*, edited by Willem Salet, Andy Thornley and Anton Kreukels, 377–390. Abingdon, Oxon: Taylor & Francis.

Salet, Willem, Rick Vermeulen, Federico Savini and Sebastian Dembski. 2015. 'Planning for the New European Metropolis: Functions, Politics, and Symbols/Metropolitan Regions: Functional Relations Between the Core and the Periphery/Business Investment Decisions and Spatial Planning Policy/Metropolitan Challenges, Political Responsibilities/Spatial Imaginaries, Urban Dynamics and Political Community/Capacity-Building in the City Region: Creating Common Spaces/Which Challenges for Today's European Metropolitan Spaces?' *Planning Theory and Practice* 16, no. 2: 251–275. http://dx.doi.org/10.1080/14649357.2015.1021574

Salvati, Luca, Adele Sateriano and Sofia Bajocco. 2013. 'To Grow or to Sprawl? Land Cover Relationships in a Mediterranean City Region and Implications for Land Use Management'. *Cities* 30: 113–121. https://doi.org/10.1016/j.cities.2012.01.007

Santos, Angela and Pedro Vasques. 2016. 'Estatuto da Metrópole e Gestão de Aglomerados Urbanos no Brasil'. *Revista del CESLA. International Latin American Studies Review* 19: 125–152.

Sassen, Saskia. 1991. *The Global City: New York, London, Tokyo*. Princeton: Princeton University Press.

Sassen, Saskia. 2001. 'Global Cities and Global City-Regions: A Comparison'. In *Global City-Regions: Trends, Theory, Policy*, edited by Allen J. Scott, 78–95. Oxford: Oxford University Press.

Sasuga, Katsuhiro. 2004. *Microregionalism and Governance in East Asia*. Abingdon, Oxon: Routledge.

Sawyer, R. Keith. 2007. 'Simulating Complexity'. In *The SAGE Handbook of Social Science Methodology*, edited by William Outhwaite and Stephen P. Turner, 316–332. London: Sage.

Sayin, Özgür, Michael Hoyler and John Harrison. 2022. 'Doing Comparative Urbanism Differently: Conjunctural Cities and the Stress-Testing of Urban Theory'. *Urban Studies* 59, no. 2: 263–280. https://doi.org/10.1177/0042098020957499

Schenk, Karl-Ernst. 2006. 'Complexity of Economic Structures and Emergent Properties'. *Journal of Evolutionary Economics* 16: 231–253.

Schenkel, Walter and Larissa Plüss. 2021. 'Spatial Planning and Metropolitan Governance in Switzerland: A Condensed Overview'. *disP-The Planning Review* 57, no. 4: 4–11. https://doi.org/10.1080/02513625.2021.2060571

Schindler, Seth. 2014a. 'Producing and Contesting the Formal/Informal Divide: Regulating Street Hawking in Delhi, India'. *Urban Studies* 51, no. 12: 2596–2612. https://doi.org/10.1177%2F0042098013510566

Schindler, Seth. 2014b. 'A New Delhi Every Day: Multiplicities of Governance Regimes in a Transforming Metropolis'. *Urban Geography* 35, no. 3: 402–419. https://doi.org/10.1080/02723638.2014.881019

Schliemann, Analucia D., David W. Carraher and Stephen J. Ceci. 1997. 'Everyday Cognition'. In *Handbook of Cross-Cultural Psychology: Volume 2 Basic Processes and Human Development*, edited by John W. Berry, Ype H. Poortinga, Janak Pandey, Pierre R. Dasen, T.S. Saraswathi, Marshall H. Segall and Cigdem Kâgitçibaşi, 177–216. Boston, MA: Allyn & Bacon.

Schmid, Christian. 2018. 'Journeys Through Planetary Urbanization: Decentering Perspectives on the Urban'. *Environment and Planning D: Society and Space* 36, no. 3: 591–610. https://doi.org/10.1177%2F0263775818765476

Schmid, Christian, Ozan Karaman, Naomi C. Hanakata, Pascal Kallenberger, Anne Kockelkom, Lindsay Sawyer, Monika Streule and Kit P. Wong. 2018. 'Towards a New Vocabulary of Urbanisation Processes: A Comparative Approach'. *Urban Studies* 55, no. 1: 19–52. https://doi.org/10.1177%2F0042098017739750

Schmidt, R. 1928. 'Country Planning in the Ruhr District'. *Journal of the Town Planning Institute* 14: 47–56.

Scott, Allen J., ed. 2001. *Global City-Regions: Trends, Theory, Policy*. Oxford: Oxford University Press.

Scott, Allen. J. 2019. 'City-Regions Reconsidered'. *Environment and Planning A: Economy and Space* 51, no. 3: 554–580. https://doi.org/10.1177%2F0308518X19831591

Scruggs, Gregory. 2019. 'Ministry of Cities RIP: The Sad Story of Brazil's Great Urban Experiment'. *The Guardian*, 18 July 2019. https://www.theguardian.com/cities/2019/jul/18/ministry-of-cities-rip-the-sad-story-of-brazils-great-urban-experiment, para. 1

Segbers, Klaus. 2007. 'Introduction: Global Politics and the Making of Global City-Regions'. In *The Making of Global City Regions: Johannesburg, Mumbai/Bombay, São Paulo, and Shanghai*, edited by Klaus Segbers, 1–31. Baltimore, MD: Johns Hopkins University Press.

Selcher, Wayne A. 1989. 'A New Start Toward a More Decentralized Federalism in Brazil?' *Pubius* 19, no. 3: 167–183. https://doi.org/10.1093/oxfordjournals.pubjof.a037799

Selcher, Wayne A. 1998. 'The Politics of Decentralized Federalism, National Diversification, and Regionalism in Brazil'. *Journal of Interamerican Studies and World Affairs* 40, no. 4: 25–50. https://doi.org/10.2307/166453

Shanghai Municipal People's Government. 2018. '2018 High-Level Symposium on Integrated Development of the Yangtze River Delta Region Held in Shanghai'. Information Office of Shanghai Municipality, 4 June 2018. http://en.shio.gov.cn/government-news/municipal/3824.shtml

Shannon, Margaret. 2002. 'Understanding Collaboration as Deliberative Communication, Organisational Form and Emergent Institution'. *National Forest Programmes in a European Context. EFI Proceedings* 44: 7–25.

Sharma, Jyotirmaya. 2003. *Hindutva: Exploring the Idea of Hindu Nationalism*. New Delhi: Penguin Books.

Sharma, Ravi T. 2012. 'NCR Planning Board Approves Greater Noida Masterplan'. *The Economic Times*, 25 August 2012. https://economictimes.indiatimes.com/news/economy/infrastructure/ncr-planning-board-approves-greater-noida-masterplan/articleshow/15638544.cms?from=mdr

Shatkin, Gavin. 2020. 'Rethinking Megacity-Region Development: The Land-Infrastructure-Finance Nexus as Political Project'. In *Handbook of Megacities and Mega-City Regions*, edited by Danielle Labbé and André Sorenson, 345–359. Cheltenham, UK: Edward Elgar Publishing.

Shen, Jianfa. 2014. 'Not Quite a Twin City: Cross-Boundary Integration in Hong Kong and Shenzhen'. *Habitat International* 42: 138–146. https://doi.org/10.1016/j.habitatint.2013.12.003

Shestopal, Elena and Elena Yakovleva. 2016. 'Regional Leaders: Governors'. In *New Trends in Russian Political Mentality: Putin 3.0*, edited by Elena Shestopal, 345–366. Langham, MD: Lexington Books.

Shilowa, Mbhazima. 2006a. 'Developing Gauteng as a Global Competitive City Region'. *Creating a Caring Society, Umrabulo* no. 27: 50–55. https://www.ortamboschool.org.za/wp-content/uploads/2022/05/Umrabulo-Journal-27.pdf

Shilowa, Mbhazima. 2006b. 'Launch of Strategy to Build Gauteng as a Globally Competitive City Region'. Speech delivered at the launch of the Strategy to Build Gauteng as a

Globally Competitive Region, Johannesburg, 29 August 2006. https://www.gov.
za/m-shilowa-launch-strategy-build-gauteng-globally-competitive-city-region

Shilowa, Mbhazima. 2008. 'Gauteng Provincial Legislature Prov Budget Vote 2008/09'.
Speech delivered in the Gauteng Provincial Legislature, 30 June 2008. http://m.
polity.org.za/article/sa-shilowa-gauteng-provincial-legislature-prov-budget-v
ote-200809-30062008-2008-06-30

Shukla, Srijan. 2021. *The Rise of the Xi Gang: Factional Politics in the Chinese Communist Party*.
ORF Occasional Paper no. 300. Observer Research Foundation, New Delhi. https://www.
orfonline.org/research/the-rise-of-the-xi-gang/

Simmie, James. 2012. 'Learning City Regions: Theory and Practice in Private and Public
Sector Spatial Planning'. *Planning Practice and Research* 27, no. 4: 423–439. https://doi.org
/10.1080/02697459.2012.686223

Sims, David. 2017. 'Greater Cairo: Dominating National Authorities and Fragmenting
Responsibilities'. In *Steering the Metropolis: Metropolitan Urban Governance for Sustainable
Urban Development*, edited by David Gómez-Alvarez, Robin Rajack, Eduardo López-
Moreno and Gabriel Lanfranchi, 241–250. Washington, D.C.: Inter-American
Development Bank.

Sinclair-Smith, Ken. 2015. 'Polycentric Development in the Cape Town City-Region:
Empirical Assessment and Consideration of Spatial Policy Implications'. *Development
Southern Africa* 32, no. 2: 131–150. https://doi.org/10.1080/0376835X.2014.984378

Singh, Amar. 1989. 'Urban Accretion Versus Urbanization: A Case Study of the National
Capital Region of India'. In *Spectrum of Modern Geography: Essays in Memory of
Professor Mohammed Anas*, edited by Sheel C. Nuna, 181–192. New Delhi: Concept
Publishing.

Singh, K.P. 2015. *Whatever the Odds: The Incredible Story Behind DLF*. New York: Harper
Collins.

Sinha, Neha. 2017. 'Saving the Aravallis from Gurgaon'. *The Hindu*, 29 October 2017. https://
www.thehindu.com/sci-tech/energy-and-environment/saving-the-aravallis-from-
gurgaon/article19932597.ece

Sivaramakrishnan, K.C. 2013. 'Revisiting the 74th Constitutional Amendment for Better
Metropolitan Governance'. *Economic and Political Weekly* 48, no. 13: 86–94.

Sivaramakrishnan, K.C. 2014. *Governance of Megacities: Fractured Thinking, Fragmented Setup*.
New Delhi: Oxford University Press.

Skidmore, Thomas E. 1988. *The Politics of Military Rule in Brazil, 1964–1985*. Oxford: Oxford
University Press.

Smith, H.W. 1931. *Bombay: The Metropolis of the East*. Bombay: Bennett, Coleman & Co.

Sorensen, André. 2018. 'Multiscalar Governance and Institutional Change: Critical Junctures
in European Spatial Planning'. *Planning Perspectives* 33, no. 4: 615–632. https://doi.org/
10.1080/02665433.2018.1512894

Sorensen, André. 2020. 'Urbanization and Developmental Pathways: Critical Junctures
of Urban Transition'. In *Handbook of Megacities and Mega-City Regions*, edited
by Danielle Labbé and André Sorenson, 47–64. Cheltenham, UK: Edward Elgar
Publishing.

Sorensen, André and Danielle Labbé. 2020. 'Megacities, Megacity-Regions, and the Endgame of Urbanization'. In *Handbook of Megacities and Mega-City Regions*, edited by Danielle Labbé and André Sorenson, 1–20. Cheltenham, UK: Edward Elgar Publishing.

South African Cities Network. 2004. *State of the Cities Report 2004*. https://www.sacities. net/state-of-cities-reports-2004/

South China Morning Post. 2017. 'Pony Ma: Creating a "Bay Area" for Tech Firms in Guangdong, Hong Kong and Macau Needs Beijing's Support'. *South China Morning Post*, 3 March 2017. https://www.scmp.com/news/hong-kong/article/2075929/ pony-ma-creating-bay-area-tech-firms-guangdong-hong-kong-and-macau

Souza, Celina. 2003. 'Regiões Metropolitanas: Condicionantes do Regime Politico'. *Lua Nova* 59: 137–158.

Spaans, Marjolein and Wil Zonneveld. 2016. 'Informal Governance Arrangements in the Southern Randstad: Understanding the Dynamics in a Polycentric Region'. *Tijdschrift Voor Economische en Sociale Geografie* 107, no. 1: 115–125. https://doi.org/10.1111/tesg. 12174

Spelt, Jac. 1963. 'The Development of the Toronto Conurbation'. *Buffalo Law Review* 13, no. 3: 557–573.

Spink, Peter K. 2005. 'The Inter-municipal Consortia in Brazil: An Institutional Introduction'. Paper presented at X Congreso Internacional del CLAD Sobre la Reforma del Estado y de la Administración Pública, Santiago, Chile, 18–21 October 2005.

Stern, Donnel B. 2015. *Relational Freedom: Emergent Properties of the Interpersonal Field*. East Sussex: Routledge.

Steyn Kotze, Joleen. 2021. 'Political Culture in South Africa'. In *South African Politics: An Introduction*, 2nd edition, edited by Nicole de Jager, Joleen Steyn and David Welsh, 296–328. Cape Town: Oxford University Press. http://www.hsrc.ac.za/en/research-data/ ktree-doc/24473

Steytler, Nico. 2007. 'Gauteng: Building a Globally Competitive City-Region'. *Local Government Bulletin* 9, no. 2. https://dullahomarinstitute.org.za/multilevel-govt/ local-government-bulletin/volume-9-issue-2-april-may-2007/vol-9-no-2-global-city- regions-international-perspectives.pdf

Stiglich, Matteo and María Luisa Vásquez. 2021. 'Governance Structures and the Unequal Provision of Services in Metropolitan Lima'. In *Metropolitan Governance in Latin America*, edited by Alejandra Trejo Nieto and Jose L. Niño Amézquita, 71–94. London: Routledge.

Streeck, Wolfgang and Kathleen Thelen. 2005. 'Introduction: Institutional Change in Advanced Political Economies'. In *Beyond Continuity: Institutional Change in Advanced Political Economies*, edited by Wolfgang Streeck and Kathleen Thelen, 1–39. Oxford: Oxford University Press.

Sum, Ngai-Ling. 2002. 'Re-articulation of Spatial Scales and Temporal Horizons of a Cross-Border Mode of Growth: The (Re-)making of "Greater China"'. In *Globalization, Regionalization and Cross-Border Regions: Scales, Discourses and Governance*, edited by Markus Perkmann and Ngai-Ling Sum, 151–175. Basingstoke, UK: Palgrave MacMillan.

Swilling, Mark. 2019. *The Age of Sustainability: Just Transitions in a Complex World*. London: Routledge.

Swyngedouw, Erik. 2009. 'The Antinomies of the Postpolitical City: In Search of a Democratic Politics of Environmental Production'. *International Journal of Urban and Regional Research* 33, no. 3: 601–620. https://doi.org/10.1111/j.1468-2427.2009.00859.x

Taipei City Government. 2022. 'Taipei and New Taipei Expanding the Collaboration in the Post-Pandemic Era'. Research, Development and Evaluation Commission of Taipei City Government. https://english.rdec.gov.taipei/News_Content. aspx?n=50819E2E63622F17&sms=DFFA119D1FD5602C&s=DC7B4DE0BBEFFF9B

Tang, Mi, Ziaolong Luo and Wanyun Ying. 2022. 'Multi-level Governance in the Uneven Integration of the City Regions: Evidence of the Shanghai City Region, China'. *Habitat International* 121: 102518. https://doi.org/10.1016/j.habitatint.2022.102518

Tang, Yan and Xiangyi Meng. 2021. 'From Concentration to Decentralization: The Spatial Development of Beijing and the Beijing–Tianjin–Hebei Capital Region'. In *Chinese Urban Planning and Construction: From Historical Wisdom to Modern Miracles*, edited by Lanchun Bian, Yan Tang and Zhenjiang Shen, 89–112. Cham: Springer.

Tavares, Antonio F. and Richard C. Feiock. 2018. 'Applying an Institutional Collective Action Framework to Investigate Intermunicipal Cooperation in Europe'. *Perspectives on Public Management and Governance* 1, no. 4: 299–316. https://doi.org/10.1093/ppmgov/gvx014

Tempelhoff, Johann W.N. 2004. 'Rand Water and the Transition to a Multiracial Democratic South Africa 1989–94'. *Kleio* 36, no. 1: 79–106.

Teo, Shaun S.K. 2022. 'Shared Projects and Symbiotic Collaborations: Shenzhen and London in Comparative Conversation'. *Urban Studies* 59, no. 8: 1694–1714. https://doi.org/10.1177/00420980211048675

The Economic Times. 2018. 'Fight Between AAP-LG Intensifies; Delhi CM Arvind Kejriwal, His Cabinet Colleagues March to LG House'. *The Economic Times*, 14 May 2018. https://economictimes.indiatimes.com/news/politics-and-nation/fight-between-aap-lg-intensifies-delhi-cm-arvind-kejriwal-his-cab-colleagues-march-to-lg-house/articleshow/64159291.cms

The Hindu. 2018. 'Narendra Modi Opens Eastern Peripheral Expressway'. *The Hindu*, 27 May 2018. https://www.thehindu.com/news/national/narendra-modi-inaugurates-first-phase-of-delhi-meerut-expressway/article24005047.ece

The Times of India. 2016. 'Army Takes Control of Munak Canal in Haryana'. *The Times of India*, 22 February 2016. https://timesofindia.indiatimes.com/city/delhi/army-takes-control-of-munak-canal-in-haryana/articleshow/51086361.cms

The Times of India. 2018. 'Delhi HC Tells Haryana to Stick to 2014 Water Agreement'. *The Times of India*, 14 March 2018. https://timesofindia.indiatimes.com/city/delhi/hc-tells-haryana-to-stick-to-2014-water-agreement/articleshow/63291469.cms

Tolkki, Helena and Arto Haveri. 2020. 'The Dynamics Between State Control and Metropolitan Governance Capacity'. *Administrative Sciences* 10, no. 2: 26. https://doi.org/10.3390/admsci10020026

Tomàs, Mariona. 2012. 'Exploring the Metropolitan Trap: The Case of Montreal'. *International Journal of Urban and Regional Research* 36, no. 3: 554–567. https://doi.org/10.1111/j.1468-2427.2011.01066.x

Tomlinson, Richard. 2017. 'An Argument for Metropolitan Government in Australia'. *Cities* 63: 149–153. https://doi.org/10.1016/j.cities.2016.10.013

Tomlinson, Richard, Robert Beauregard, Lindsay Bremner and Xolela Mangcu, eds. 2003. *Emerging Johannesburg: Perspectives on the Postapartheid City*. London: Routledge.

Tosics, Iván. 2007. 'City-Regions in Europe: The Potentials and the Realities'. *Town Planning Review* 78, no. 6: 775–795.

Townroe, Peter M. and David Keen. 1984. 'Polarization Reversal in the State of São Paulo, Brazil'. *Regional Studies* 18, no. 1: 45–54. https://doi.org/10.1080/09595238400185041

Trejo Nieto, Alejandra. 2021a. 'A Framework for Contextualising Metropolitan Governance in Latin America'. In *Metropolitan Governance in Latin America*, edited by Alejandra T. Nieto and Jose L. Niño Amézquita, 23–46. London: Routledge.

Trejo Nieto, Alejandra. 2021b. 'Fragmented Governance, Service Provision and Inequality in Mexico City Metropolitan Area'. In *Metropolitan Governance in Latin America*, edited by Alejandra T. Nieto and Jose L. Niño Amézquita, 95–120. London: Routledge.

Trejo Nieto, Alejandra and Jose L Niño Amézquita, eds. 2021. *Metropolitan Governance in Latin America*. London: Routledge.

Turok, Ivan. 2014. 'The Urbanization–Development Nexus in the BRICS'. In *The Routledge Handbook on Cities of the Global South*, edited by Susan Parnell and Sophie Oldfield, 122–138. New York: Routledge.

United Nations. 2018. '2018 Revision of World Urbanization Prospects'. https://population.un.org/wup/

Urushima, Andrea Flores. 2015. 'Territorial Prospective Visions for Japan's High Growth: The Role of Local Urban Development'. *Nature and Culture* 10, no. 1: 12–36. https://doi.org/10.3167/nc.2015.100102

Vaitans, Andrei, Victor Volkov and Sergey Mityagin. 2020. 'The General Plan of St. Petersburg 2005–2025: Prerequisites, Ideas, Implementation'. *E3S Web of Conferences* 164: 05008. https://doi.org/10.1051/e3sconf/202016405008

Van Assche, Kristof, Raoul Beunen, Stefan Verweij, Joshua Evans and Monica Gruezmacher. 2021. 'Policy Learning and Adaptation in Governance; a Co-evolutionary Perspective'. *Administration & Society (online)*. https://doi.org/10.1177%2F00953997211059165

Van Donk, Mirjam and Edgar Pieterse. 2006. 'Reflections on the Design of a Post-apartheid System of (Urban) Local Government'. In *Democracy and Delivery: Urban Policy in South Africa*, edited by Udesh Pillay, Richard Tomlinson and Jacques du Toit, 107–134. Cape Town: HSRC Press.

Van Hamme, Gilles, Julien Descamps, Moritz Lennert, Pablo M. Lockhart and Université Libre de Bruxelles. 2021. *The Role and Future Perspectives of Cohesion Policy in the Planning of Metropolitan Areas and Cities*. Luxembourg: ESPON. www.espon.eu/sites/default/files/attachments/12%20ESPON%20METRO_CS%20Brussels%20Metropolitan%20Area.pdf

Van Huyssteen, Elsona, Mark Oranje, Shirley Robinson and Eric Makoni. 2009. 'South Africa's City Regions: A Call for Contemplation... and Action'. *Urban Forum* 20: 175–194.

Van Meeteren, Michiel, David Bassens and Ben Derudder. 2016. 'Doing Global Urban Studies: On the Need for Engaged Pluralism, Frame Switching, and Methodological Cross-Fertilization'. *Dialogues in Human Geography* 6, no. 3: 296–301. https://doi.org/10.1177/2043820616676653

Van Treek, Esteban Valenzuela, Claudia Toledo and Osvaldo Henríquez. 2021. 'Metropolitan Santiago: The Challenge of Moving from Dispersion and Inequality to Effective Intergovernmental Governance'. In *Metropolitan Governance in Latin America*, edited by Alejandra T. Nieto and Jose L. Niño Amézquita, 145–163. London: Routledge.

Venter, Irma. 2018. 'Gauteng Transport Authority Set for Rollout in Q1 2019'. *Engineering News*, 11 July 2018. https://www.engineeringnews.co.za/print-version/gauteng-transport-authority-set-for-rollout-in-q1-2019-2018-07-11

Vicente, Agustín. 2013. 'Where to Look for Emergent Properties'. *International Studies in the Philosophy of Science* 27, no. 2: 137–156. https://doi.org/10.1080/02698595.2013.813256

Vogel, Ezra F. 2013. *Deng Xiaoping and the Transformation of China*. Cambridge, MA: Harvard University Press.

Von Holdt, Karl. 2019. *The Political Economy of Corruption: Elite Formation, Factions and Violence*. Working Paper no. 10. Society, Work and Politics Institute, University of the Witwatersrand, Johannesburg. https://www.swop.org.za/post/2019/02/18/working-paper-10-the-political-economy-of-corruption-open-access

Waite, David. 2021. 'Agglomeration is in the Eye of the Beholder: The Changing Governance of Polycentrism'. *Territory, Politics, Governance (online)*. https://doi.org/10.1080/2162267 1.2021.1886978

Wallace, Jeremy L. 2014. *Cities and Stability: Urbanization, Redistribution and Regime Survival in China*. Oxford: Oxford University Press.

Wampler, Brian. 2007. *Participatory Budgeting in Brazil: Contestation, Cooperation and Accountability*. Pennsylvania: Pennsylvania State University Press.

Wang, Yanfei and Yang Cheng. 2018. 'Beijing-Tianjin-Hebei Cluster to see Organized Development'. *The State Council of the PRC*, 28 February 2018. http://english.gov.cn/news/top_news/2018/02/28/content_281476061200846.htm

Ward, Kevin. 2008. 'Toward a Comparative (Re)turn in Urban Studies? Some Reflections'. *Urban Geography* 29, no. 5: 405–410. https://doi.org/10.2747/0272-3638.29.5.405

Ward, Kevin. 2010. 'Towards a Relational Comparative Approach to the Study of Cities'. *Progress in Human Geography* 34, no. 4: 471–487. https://doi.org/10.1177 %2F0309132509350239

Ward, Kevin and Andrew E.G. Jonas. 2004. 'Competitive City-Regionalism as a Politics of Space: A Critical Reinterpretation of the New Regionalism'. *Environment and Planning A: Economy and Space* 36, no. 12: 2119–2139. https://doi.org/10.1068%2Fa36223

Washbourne, Carla-Leanne, Christina Culwick, Michele Acuto, Jason J. Blackstock and Robin Moore. 2019. 'Mobilising Knowledge for Urban Governance: The Case of the Gauteng City-Region Observatory'. *Urban Research & Practice* 14, no. 1: 27–49. https://doi.org/10.1080/17535069.2019.1651899

Watson, Vanessa. 2021. 'The Return of the City-Region in the New Urban Agenda: Is this Relevant in the Global South?' *Regional Studies* 55, no. 1: 19–28. https://doi.org/10.1080 /00343404.2019.1664734

Weber, Ryan, Ilpo Tammi, Timothy Anderson and Shinan Wang. 2016. *A Spatial Analysis of City-Regions: Urban Form and Service Accessibility*. Nordregio Working Paper 2016:2.

Nordic Centre for Spatial Development, Stockholm. https://www.diva-portal.org/smash/get/diva2:933727/FULLTEXT01.pdf

Webster, Douglas and Chuthatip Maneepong. 2009. 'Bangkok'. *City* 13, no. 1: 80–86. https://doi.org/10.1080/13604810902726236

Wei, W. and G. Zhao. 2005. 'Research on the Patterns of Japanese Metropolitans Circles: A Literature Review' [translated title]. *Contemporary Economy in Japan* 140: 40–45.

Weinstein, Liza. 2014. '"One-Man Handled": Fragmented Power and Political Entrepreneurship in Globalizing Mumbai'. *International Journal of Urban and Regional Research* 38, no. 1: 14–35. https://doi.org/10.1111/1468-2427.12040

Wen, Hongyan and Li Zhen. 2022. 'Xiong'an New Area a Mirror of Future China'. *People's Daily Online*, 2 April 2022. http://en.people.cn/n3/2022/0402/c90000-10079267.html

Williams, Daryle. 2001. *Culture Wars in Brazil: The First Vargas Regime 1930–1945*. Durham, NC: Duke University Press.

Williams, Michelle. 2017. 'Practising Democratic Communism: The Kerala Experience'. *Socialist Register* 54: 27–33.

Wolfe, Joel. 1994. '"Father of the Poor" or "Mother of the Rich"? Getúlio Vargas, Industrial Workers, and Constructions of Class, Gender, and Populism in Sao Paulo, 1930–1954'. *Radical History Review* 1994, no. 58: 80–111. https://doi.org/10.1215/01636545-1994-58-80

Wood, Astrid. 2022. 'Tracing as Comparative Method'. *Urban Studies* 59, no. 8: 1749–1753. https://doi.org/10.1177%2F00420980221086124

Woodside, Alexander. 2007. 'The Centre and the Borderlands in Chinese Political Theory'. In *The Chinese State at the Borders*, edited by Diana Lary, 11–28. Vancouver: UBC Press.

World Bank. 2015. 'Metropolitan Governance in Brazil: Inputs for an Agenda and a Strategy, May 2015'. https://openknowledge.worldbank.org/bitstream/handle/10986/22052/Final0report.pdf?sequence=1&isAllowed=y

Wu, Fulong. 2016. 'China's Emergent City-Region Governance: A New Form of State Spatial Selectivity Through State-Orchestrated Rescaling'. *International Journal of Urban and Regional Research* 40, no. 6: 1134–1151. https://doi.org/10.1111/1468-2427.12437

Wu, Fulong, Jiang Xu and Anthony Gar-On Yeh. 2006. *Urban Development in Post-reform China: State, Market, and Space*. London: Routledge.

Xu, Chi, Maosong Liu, Cheng Zhang, Shuging An, Wen Yu and Jing M. Chen. 2007. 'The Spatiotemporal Dynamics of Rapid Urban Growth in the Nanjing Metropolitan Region of China'. *Landscape Ecology* 22, no. 6: 925–937.

Xu, Jiang and Anthony Yeh. 2011. 'Governance and Planning of Mega-City Regions: Diverse Processes and Reconstituted State Spaces'. In *Governance and Planning of Mega City-Regions: An International Comparative Perspective*, edited by Jiang Xu and Anthony Yeh, 17–42. London: Routledge.

Yang, Baojun and Dongxiao Jin. 2011. 'Regionally Coordinated Planning and Development in the Pearl River Delta'. In *China's Pan-Pearl River Delta: Regional Cooperation and Development*, edited by Anthony G.O. Yeh and Jiang Xu, 81–102. Hong Kong: Hong Kong University Press.

Yang, Chun. 2006. 'Cross-Boundary Integration of the Pearl River Delta and Hong Kong: An Emerging Global City-Region in China'. In *Globalization and the Chinese City*, edited by Fulong Wu, 125–146. Abingdon, Oxon: Routledge.

Yang, Chun and Si-ming Li. 2013. 'Transformation of Cross-Boundary Governance in the Greater Pearl River Delta, China: Contested Geopolitics and Emerging Conflicts'. *Habitat International* 40: 25–44. https://doi.org/10.1016/j.habitatint.2013.02.001

Yang, Liuqing, Wen Chen, Fulong Wu, Yi Li and Wei Sun. 2021. 'State-Guided City Regionalism: The Development of Metro Transit in the City Region of Nanjing'. *Territory, Politics, Governance (online)*. https://doi.org/10.1080/21622671.2021.1913217

Yao, S., R. Chan and Y. Zhu. 1992. *Zhongguo de Chengshiqun [China's Urban Clusters]*. Hefei: Chinese Science and Technology University Press.

Yaqing, Deng. 2014. 'A Trio Bands Together'. *Beijing Review*, 18 May 2014. http://www. bjreview.com.cn/print/txt/2014-04/28/content_615585_3.htm

Yeh, Anthony Gar-On and Zifeng Chen. 2020. 'From Cities to Super Mega City Regions in China in a New Wave of Urbanisation and Economic Transition: Issues and Challenges'. *Urban Studies* 57, no. 3: 636–654. https://doi.org/10.1177%2F0042098019879566

Yeh, Anthony G.O. and Jiang Xu, eds. 2011. *China's Pan-Pearl River Delta: Regional Cooperation and Development*. Hong Kong: Hong Kong University Press.

Yeh, Anthony Gar-On, Fiona F. Yang and Jiejing Wang. 2015. 'Producer Service Linkages and City Connectivity in the Mega-City Region of China: A Case Study of the Pearl River Delta'. *Urban Studies* 52, no. 13: 2458–2482. https://doi.org/10.1177%2F0042098014544762

Yongnian, Zheng. 2009. *The Chinese Communist Party as Organizational Emperor: Culture, Reproduction and Transformation*. Abingdon, Oxon: Routledge.

You, Tracy. 2017. 'China Builds a Mega-City Larger Than Britain with over 100 Million People'. *MailOnline*, 8 March 2017. https://www.dailymail.co.uk/news/article-4356676/China-builds-mega-city-larger-Great-Britain.html

Young, Oran R. 2010. *Institutional Dynamics: Emergent Patterns in International Environmental Governance*. Cambridge, MA: The MIT Press.

Youngman, Elmer H. 1939. 'An Introduction: New York: Metropolis of the Western Hemisphere'. *The Bankers Magazine* 138, no. 1: 19.

Yu, Hongjun and Yuemin Ning. 1983. *Introduction to Urban Geography*. Anhui: Anhui Science and Technology Press.

Yu, Ronghua, Bo Jin and Liu Yang. 2015. 'Beijing-Tianjin-Hebei Integration Offers New Engines of Economic Growth'. *Chinese Social Sciences Today*, 21 May 2015. http://www.csstoday.com/Item/2101.aspx

Yudelman, David. 1984. *The Emergence of Modern South Africa: State, Capital, and the Incorporation of Organized Labor on the South African Gold Fields, 1902–1939*. Cape Town: David Philip.

Zérah, Marie-Hélène. 2020. 'The Incomplete and Paradoxical "Neoliberal Turn" in Mumbai'. In *Handbook of Megacities and Mega-City Regions*, edited by Danielle Labbé and André Sorenson, 119–133. Cheltenham, UK: Edward Elgar Publishing.

Zhang, Jun and Yong Fu. 2009. 'Shanghai and Yangtze River Delta: A Revolving Relationship'. In *Regional Economic Development in China*, edited by Saw Swee-Hock and John Wong, 123–154. Singapore: ISEAS Publishing.

Zhang, Li, Richard LeGates and Min Zhao. 2016. *Understanding China's Urbanization: The Great Demographic, Spatial, Economic and Social Transformation.* Cheltenham, UK: Edward Elgar Publishing.

Zhang, Qian and Xiangzheng Deng. 2017. *Urban Development in Asia: Pathways, Opportunities and Challenges.* Singapore: Springer.

Zhang, Shanruo N. 2015. *Confucianism in Contemporary Chinese Politics: An Actionable Account of Authoritarian Political Culture.* Langham, MD: Lexington Books.

Zhang, Wei-Wei. 1996. *Ideology and Economic Reform Under Deng Xiaoping 1978–1993*, 1st edition. London: Kegan Paul International.

Zhao, Miaoxi, Ben Derudder and Junhao Huang. 2017. 'Examining the Transition Processes in the Pearl River Delta Polycentric Mega-City Region Through the Lens of Corporate Networks'. *Cities* 60, no. A: 147–155. https://doi.org/10.1016/j.cities.2016.08.015

Zhao, Yimin. 2020. '*Jiehebu* or Suburb? Towards a Translational Turn in Urban Studies'. *Cambridge Journal of Regions, Economy and Society* 13, no. 3: 527–542. https://doi.org/10.1093/cjres/rsaa032

Zhou, Yixing. 1991. 'The Metropolitan Interlocking Region in China: A Preliminary Hypothesis'. In *The Extended Metropolis: Settlements Transition in Asia*, edited by Norton Ginsburg, Bruce Koppel and T.G. McGee, 89–112. Honolulu: University of Hawaii Press.

Zhu, Erqian. 2013. 'On the Adjustment of Industrial Structure and the Development of Metropolitan Economic Circles: A Comparative Analysis Based on the U.S., Japan and China'. *Journal of Xiangtan University (Philosophy and Social Sciences) [translated title]* 2: 65–68.

Zimmermann, Karsten. 2017. 'Re-scaling of Metropolitan Governance in Germany'. *Raumforsch Raumordn* 75, no. 3: 253–263. https://doi.org/10.1007/s13147-017-0480-5

Zimmermann, Karsten and Patricia Feiertag. 2018. 'Return of the Metro-Model? Governance and Planning in Metropolitan Regions under Change. An International Comparison of France, Italy and Germany'. *Papers: Regió Metropolitana de Barcelona: Territori, Estratègies, Planejament* 61: 16–26.

Zou, Yonghua and Wanxia Zhao. 2018. 'Making a New Area in Xiong'an: Incentives and Challenges of China's "Millennium Plan"'. *Geoforum* 88, 45–48. https://doi.org/10.1016/j.geoforum.2017.11.007

Index

BRICS (Brazil, Russia, India, China, South
  Africa) countries 3, 6–7, 11, 94, 117
    challenges to existing literature on city-
      regions by 178–180, 184–185
    diversity of 12–13, 16n7, 74, 171, 175, 178,
      182
    geopolitical links between 170
    on scholarly language and terminology
      across 3–4, 173–175, 184
    spatial coordination challenges across 172

C

Calcutta 21, 24, 95, 99 *see also* Kolkata
California 19, 26, 134, 167n5
Canada 64
  Metro Vancouver 37–38
  Ottawa 37, 101
  see also Greater Toronto
Cape Town xxii*map*, 147–148, 164
Cardoso, Fernando 51–52, 56
Catholic Church 49, 52
centralised urban governance 38–39, 41,
  44–45
  bureaucratic 42, 52–53, 55
  under military autocracy 50–51
Centre for Strategic Research for the
  North-West, Russia 88, 181
Chengdu-Chongqing 20, 129
Chennai xx*map*, 21, 96–97, 99
Chile 51
  Santiago Metropolitan Region 41
China
  accelerated economic reform in 94
  metropolitan regions of xxi*map*
  urban footprint of 122
  see also Greater Bay Area, China; National
    Capital Region, China
China's political culture
  Confucian 118
  entrenched vertical hierarchies within
    118–122, 125, 130, 139, 141, 173
  of Han Dynasty 119
  Maoist era 19, 118–120, 126
  pro-democracy protests 118, 133, 136
  regional variations in 140, 173
  role of party factions in 120, 133
city cluster
  concept of 3, 26, 117–118, 122–123, 141
  governance of 125–126, 177–178, 182, 184
  as mechanism to coordinate urban growth
    119, 123–126, 128, 134, 136, 141–142

see also economic circle; Guangdong-Hong
  Kong-Macau GBA city cluster; Pearl
  River Delta: City Cluster Coordination
  Development Plan; Yangtze River Delta:
  city cluster
City of Moscow *see* Moscow
city-region governance 2–3
  and concept of 'radical incrementalism' 166,
    185
  contextual embeddedness of 2, 13, 49, 170,
    172, 185
  fragmentation of 28, 31, 33, 38, 40, 43, 56,
    59, 66, 147, 149, 165–166, 171
  hierarchical approaches to 8, 28–29, 31,
    43–45, 173
  historical approach studies of 7–8, 13, 169, 185
  politicised nature of 31
  urbanisation as challenge to 14–15, 17, 28,
    171, 178
city-region governance in China
  challenge of horizontal coordination to 117,
    122, 124–125, 141, 171
  environmental management 118, 178
  Five Year Plans (FYP) for 94, 122, 124–125,
    128–129, 133–134, 137–138, 142, 175
  impact of vertical hierarchy on 119–122,
    128, 130, 139, 141, 173
  infrastructure investment and coordination
    19, 122, 139, 182, 184
  and management of environment and
    infrastructure requirements 118
  state-orchestrated rescaling of 118
  see also National Development and Reform
    Commission
city-regionalism 32
  absence of socio-cultural dimension in 180
  drivers of 175–176, 178
  environmental 26, 37
  inter-scalar 179
  politicised nature of 31, 130, 176
  state-led 14, 141–142, 173, 178
  as 'territorialisation of politics' 26, 32, 180
  see also megaregionalism; USA: new
    regionalism of
city-regions
  competitive logic of 2, 22, 26, 31–32, 36, 63,
    87, 113, 133, 148, 160–162, 174–176
  and dilemma of collective action 1–2, 28,
    49, 170–172
  discursive dimensions of 12, 17–18, 21–23,
    31, 46–47, 122

as geographic imaginary 4, 7
'interstitial spaces' between 14–15, 27
materiality of 12, 17–18, 22, 27–28, 46–47
meaning and usage of term 3–4, 22–26, 77, 169, 174–175
political-administrative dimensions of 21–22, 27, 40–41, 47
relational complexity of 1, 113
self-built 22
as 'talking pigs' 1, 15n1, 117, 140
see also mega-city regions; urban agglomerations
civil society participation in urban governance 28, 30
in Australia 38
in Brazil 51–53, 56, 58–59, 61, 63–65, 176
in India 95, 179–180
in South Africa 180, 186
clientelism
in Brazil 50–53, 55, 59, 172
in India 94, 114
climate change 22, 35
collaborative interactions 6
building of trust through 2
impact of institutional fragmentation on 56
inter-municipal 31–36, 38–40, 49, 58–60, 177, 179, 182–183, 187n3
see also informal interpersonal networks: collaborative interactions within; PDUI, Brazil
Colton, Timothy
on evolvement of Moscow Capital Region 72, 75–76, 79
Communist Party of Brazil 52
Communist Party of China
battles over designated economic zones within 132
bureaucratic hierarchy of 120, 171
factionalism within 120, 133
Communist Party of India 95
Communist Party of the Soviet Union (CPSU) 72, 76–77
dissolution of 78–79
Leningrad Regional Committee 76
as mechanism of territorial integration 75, 78
comparison 3–4, 6, 9, 134, 170
traditional approaches 10
see also new comparative urbanism
Constitution of India 92, 103, 105

Constitution of South Africa 146, 157, 159, 161, 165
Constitutional Court 164
framing of cooperative governance 171
Copenhagen 29, 35, 88
corruption
in Brazil 52–53
in China 140, 143n17
in India 114
in Russia 80
Covid-19 pandemic 41, 53, 68, 136, 164, 186
Crimea 73
2014 Russian occupation of 86, 176
Cymbalista, Renato
on metropolitan coordination 60, 69

D

da Costa Paes, Eduardo 55, 68
da Silva, Lula 52, 60–61, 68
right-wing curb on initiatives of 69
Dar es Salaam, Tanzania 20, 45–46
De Oliveira, Kubitschek 50
Delhi xxmap, 3, 54, 92, 95, 175
Delhi Development Authority (DDA) 100–103, 106, 109, 115n5
Master Plan 99
parallel governance systems in 41, 101
population of 96
see also National Capital Region, India
Delhi Metropolitan Area (DMA) 107, 109–110, 113
conflicts in water sector 101, 105–108
coordination of transport in 109
Delhi's satellite cities xxxviiimap
Gurgaon 97, 106–107, 110–111
Noida/Greater Noida 106–107, 110–111
democracy 44, 92, 173
local 30, 41, 65, 93
racially subscribed 145
sustainable 71
transitions to 41–42, 49, 51, 55, 69, 74, 94, 146–147, 166
troubled development of 71–72, 106
Democratic Alliance (DA) 158, 163
democratisation 38, 41, 45, 131, 181
Deng Xiaoping 119–120, 130, 132, 139
Dhaka 21, 41
Dongguan xxx&map, xlimap, 121, 131–132 135
Durban see eThekwini

local governance 5–7
  centralised 38, 43, 99
  decentralised 29, 38–39, 93
  norms of cooperation in 31
London 11, 18–19, 24, 26, 86, 138, 163
  underground, 154
  see also Greater London
Luanda, Angola 20, 45
Luzkhov, Yury 89n2
  patrimonial regime of 79–80

M

Macau xxx*map*, xli&*map*, 121, 125, 130–134, 136, 142
Maharashtra 95, 99, 104, 113
Makhura, David 161, 163–165
Malmö, Sweden 4, 8, 29, 35
Manchester, UK, 7, 18, 30–31
Manila, Philippines 14, 21, 42
  Metro Manila Commission/Authority 43
Mao Zedong 118–119 *see also* China's political culture: Maoist era
Marinho, Luiz 61–62
McFarlane, Colin
  on new comparative urbanism 9–11
Medvedev, Dmitry 83, 85–86
mega-city regions *see* megaregionalism
megalopolis 25, 39, 117
  Jean Gottman's use of term 25, 47n2, 125
megaregionalism 21–22, 25–26, 62–63, 113, 121, 123, 125, 128, 136, 138
metropolis 3, 24 *see also* Greater Paris Metropolis; Randopolis, concept of
metropolitan and city-region governance in India 91, 98, 174–175
  and 73rd and 74th Constitutional amendments 93, 96, 104, 107
  decentralisation drive 93, 96–97, 99, 110, 112–113, 174
  establishment of metropolitan development authorities (MDAs) 99–100, 104
  link between infrastructural development and 97, 107
  significance of intranational histories to 172–173, 187n1
  special economic zones as challenge to 97–98, 105
  see also Government of the NCT of Delhi; informality of governance: in India
metropolitan governance in Brazil 39–40
  decentralised federalism of 56, 66, 69

under democratic government 58–59
  federal legislation around 62–63, 65, 69
  under military rule 40, 49–51, 57–58, 60, 64, 181
  and rise of inter-municipal collaboration 60–62, 64–65, 69, 176–177, 183
  in transport sector 52, 59–63
  see also civil society participation in urban governance: in Brazil; *Estatuto da Cidade*; *Estatuto da Metrópole* of 2015
metropolitan governance in Russia 78
  centralised versus decentralised approach to 74, 80
  fitful evolution of 71–72, 75, 83–84
  horizontal integration/collaboration as challenge to 71, 75, 81–82, 89, 177, 183
  impact of joint transport authorities on 84–87, 127, 135, 177, 179, 181, 183
  impact of vacillating spatial policy on 83–84, 86
  incentivisation approach 84, 89
  and lost opportunities of transition 78–79
Mexico 121
Mexico City Metropolitan Area 20, 40
Middle East 44–45
migrant labour system, South Africa *see under* gold mining industry, South Africa
migrants
  rural-urban 20, 50, 54, 57, 107, 121, 152, 171
Minas Gerais xxv&*map*, 50, 55, 60, 64–66, 69, 176
Modi, Nahendra 94, 106, 112
Moscow xix*map*, 78, 176
  administrative divisions of xxxvi*map*, 73
  amalgamation proposals for 78–79
  centralised mechanisms of coordination in 80, 85
  Duma 79, 81
  1989 General Plan 76
  strong local autonomy of 73, 80–81
  urban footprint of xxvi*map*, 74
  weak intersectoral coordination in 85
  see also Moscow *Oblast*; New Moscow
Moscow City Council 75
Moscow *Oblast* xxxvi&*map*, 74–75
  environmental issues within 76, 82
Moscow *Oblast* interface with Moscow City
  entwining of national and local politics 81
  horizontal integration/coordination as challenge to 81–82, 85–87, 171, 183
  impact of large-scale development on 82, 171

Fundrem planning agency 58–59
lack of political continuity in 55
lack of coordination in governance of 63–64
legislation on governance of 67–68
municipal boundaries of xxxivmap, 57
regional level conflicts within 67
re-territorialisation of 54
rightwards turn within 68–69
urban footprint of xxivmap, 54
see also Guanabara Bay
Robinson, Jennifer
on value of comparison 10–11, 13
Rousseff, Dilma 52, 65–66
Roy, Ananya
on informality in India 94–95, 173
Russia *see* Russian Federation
Russian Federation
coordination challenges within 34
metropolitan regions of xixmap, 3, 73
post-Soviet economic crisis in 72
threats of international isolation of 86–87, 176
Russian Federation's political culture
centralism of 71
differences between Saint Petersberg and
Moscow 74, 76, 80–81, 89
historical shaping of 71–72, 75
see also political settlement in Russia

S

Saint Petersburg xixmap, 19, 71, 78
as critical transport hub 76
decentralised collaborative governance
structure of 80
municipal boundaries of xxxviimap, 73
urban footprint of xxviimap, 74
see also Leningrad *Oblast*
Saint Petersburg-Leningrad interface 74, 79,
82, 87–89, 171, 181, 183
acceptance of regional integration 87–88
Fifth General Plan 87–88
growing competition for resources and
investments 82–83, 87, 177
taxation system as obstacle to collaboration
83
Salvador da Bahia 54, 57, 62
Santos xxiiimap
São Jose dos Campos xxiiimap
São Paulo metropolitan region xviiimap, 3, 49,
113
complex spatial formation of xxiiimap,
54–55

Emplasa planning agency 58–59, 63, 66–68,
181
governance and planning legislation
62–63
municipal boundaries of xxxiiimap, 56–57
Observatório das Metrópoles 63, 174, 181
political settlement within 50, 55
rightward turn within 68–69
transport sector in 59
see also ABC sub-region of São Paulo
Scandinavia 29
Osloregionen 35
Scott, Allen
on city-regions 21–22, 26, 159, 167n5,
174–175
service delivery 7
participatory processes for 37, 60, 177
Shanghai xl&map, xxix&map, xi&map, 11, 54,
113, 118–119, 126
development of Pudong New Area in 119,
127, 139
Economic Region 126
explosive growth of 19–20
as gateway to Yangtze River Economic Belt
129
Metropolitan Area 129–130
Shenzhen xxx&map, 11, 20, 118, 131, 134
Special Economic Zone 119, 126, 139,
182
see also Qianhai Cooperation Zone
Shenzhen-Dongguan-Huizhou Metropolitan
Area 135
Shilowa, Mbhazima (Sam) 160–161
Sivaramakrishnan, K.C.
assessment of MDAs by 100, 104
Sobyanin, Sergey 81, 85–86
Sorensen, André
on local governance 5, 8, 14, 17
on mega city regions 22
South Africa
divided political culture of 145–146, 166,
169, 173
metropolitan regions of xxiimap
patronage networks and rent-seeking in 147,
173
transition to democracy in 94, 166
South African War 149–150
South-East Asia 29, 41
urbanisation in 21
South Korea 123
Seoul 39, 43, 86

www.ingramcontent.com/pod-product-compliance
Lightning Source LLC
Chambersburg PA
CBHW040934030426
42337CB00006B/54